READING CLASSICAL LATIN

The Second Year

Second Edition

Robert J. Ball
University of Hawaii

The McGraw-Hill Companies, Inc.
Primis Custom Publishing

*New York   St. Louis   San Francisco   Auckland   Bogotá
Caracas   Lisbon   London   Madrid   Mexico   Milan   Montreal
New Delhi   Paris   San Juan   Singapore   Sydney   Tokyo   Toronto*

McGraw·Hill

A Division of The McGraw·Hill Companies

READING CLASSICAL LATIN
The Second Year

McGraw-Hill's Primis Custom Publishing consists of products that are produced from camera-ready copy. Peer review, class testing, and accuracy are primarily the responsibility of the author(s).

2 3 4 5 6 7 8 9 0 QSR QSR 9 0 9

ISBN 0-07-006070-3

Editor: Lorna Adams
Cover Design: Mary Good
Printer/Binder: Quebecor Printing Dubuque, Inc

CONTENTS

For J. D. Ellsworth

NEC MINUS GRAECE QUAM LATINE DOCTUS

PREFACE to Second Edition

This edition contains numerous revisions and corrections of errors (some discovered by students) worked on continuously since the publication of the first edition by Coronado Press in 1990. The text has been completely reformatted, and many improvements have been introduced, affording the students additional practice with much of the grammatical material learned.

For the methodology used in this text, see the Preface to my first-year text, *Reading Classical Latin: A Reasonable Approach,* 2nd edition (New York, McGraw-Hill, 1997), as well as the series of articles co-authored with J. D. Ellsworth, also of the University of Hawaii:

> "Teaching Classical Languages: A Reasonable Approach," *Classical World* 83 (1989) 1–12.

> "Against Teaching Composition in Classical Languages," *Classical Journal* 85 (1989) 54–62.

> "Pabulum-Pushers and Weak-Willed Students: Elitism and Teaching Classical Languages," *Modern Language Journal* 73 (1989) 465–68.

> "Flushing Out the Dinosaurs: Against Teaching Composition II," *Classical Journal* 88 (1992) 55–65.

> "The Emperor's New Clothes: Hyperreality and the Study of Latin," *Modern Language Journal* 80 (1996) 77–84.

References in this text to the first-year text have been re-keyed to the second edition cited above, which the students need to consult continuously while preparing their second-year lessons. Throughout the second-year text, the students are directed to the appropriate place in the first-year text, especially the Appendices, for the purpose of review and additional instruction.

Honolulu, Hawaii
June 1998

R.J.B.

PREFACE to First Edition

The aim of this textbook is to present a viable second-year course in classical Latin for the general college student who can devote a reasonable amount of time to pursuing this goal. It is a sequel to the author's *Reading Classical Latin: A Reasonable Approach;* the methodology used is based on the methodology developed by J. D. Ellsworth for teaching classical Greek.

Most intermediate Latin courses are actually designed not for the general student but for the exceptional student, that is, the potential Latin major as well as the future Classics professor. In the most intimidating version of these courses, the student is asked to translate a Latin author directly from an Oxford Classical Text, with the 'help' of some scholarly commentary. Most intermediate Latin textbooks (the annotated readers and anthologies) provide no review of first-year grammar and virtually no instruction in the new grammar used in the readings. These textbooks usually include sizable (yet dry and tedious) selections from Caesar and Cicero, who have long outlived their role as the war-horses of the lower-level Latin curriculum.

*   *   *

Reading Classical Latin: The Second Year—like its predecessor—has as its central aim to enable the general student to read and understand classical Latin texts in the original language. In order to help fulfill this goal, the textbook reviews all the grammar learned during the first-year sequence and furnishes instruction in additional grammar not previously studied. In the first twelve lessons, the students review the models (paradigms) learned during the first year (the models are continuously referred to in the Appendices of the first-year textbook). In these and later lessons, the students also study supplementary grammar, especially the imperative mood, the future tenses, and irregular verbs (accompanied by simple exercises).

Second-year textbooks generally do not contain lesson vocabularies, on the assumption that by the second year the students can use a dictionary and memorize words at their own discretion. Yet this practice forces them to engage in the wasteful drudgery of wading through more pages than necessary to find an entry, which often lacks the meaning that fits the context. In this textbook, the lesson vocabularies are retained, listing each word the first time it occurs in the readings and including all the meanings for that word found throughout the readings. The students are also required to memorize high-frequency vocabulary (marked with an asterisk), including previously learned vocabulary items having new forms or new meanings.

Since most students probably will not study Latin beyond the second year, this textbook provides them with a survey of great authors rather than a limited exposure to one or two of them. In this regard, the students are exposed to six writers—three prose selections and three poetry selections—all clear, lively, and powerful pieces, most of them having a narrative context. The prose selections are taken from *Apollonius of Tyre* (sections of this late Latin novel), Pliny (his letters on the eruption of Vesuvius), and Livy (his stories of Coriolanus and Lucretia). The poetry selections are taken from Catullus (poems in several different meters), Ovid (his Apollo/Daphne and Pyramus/Thisbe), and Vergil (his fall of Troy and Dido's love for Aeneas).

The prose selections are presented in an order enabling the students to proceed in gradual, successive stages, from moderately simple passages to stylistically more challenging passages. (The more challenging passages involve a more complex word order—something to be expected at this point, to which the students will now need to devote increasingly greater attention.) The poetry selections are presented on the same principle, with brief introductions to the meters employed (hendecasyllables, choliambics, elegiac couplets, and dactylic hexameters). Here, however, the individual teacher must decide, in accordance with the situation in his/her classroom, how strictly to enforce scansion—if at all—at this intermediate level of learning.

At the end of each reading, the students are provided with a concise commentary, in the 'Notes and Queries' section of the lesson—a technique carried over from the first-year textbook. This section of the lesson again serves several important functions, among them, to review inflections and constructions as they occur in the readings, at appropriately spaced intervals. It also fulfills its traditional function (as with all such commentaries) of explaining and interpreting the more difficult sentences and constructions that appear in the reading selections. It furnishes students with information essential for reading and understanding the classical text, short of indulging in useless elitist memorabilia (Greek models, Latin parallels, etc.)

At the end of every twelve lessons, after the completion of the readings on an individual Latin author, there appears (for the more serious students) a section entitled 'Classical Tradition.' In this section, the students are presented with a stimulating passage written by a great English writer, a passage inspired by something that they have just studied in the original Latin. Shakespeare, Edward Bulwer-Lytton, Alfred Tennyson, and Christopher Marlowe—the authors quoted in this regard—exemplify writers inspired by Latin writers down through the ages. By bringing something of the classical tradition to their students, the teacher can reinforce in their minds the importance of the classical texts and their influence on modern literature.

*   *   *

xiii

The textbook has been planned for classes meeting one hour a day, three days a week; Lessons 1–36 are to be done during the first semester, Lessons 37–72, during the second semester. Lessons 1–36 contain the three prose selections listed above; Lessons 37–72 contain the three poetry selections also listed above (formal grammatical instruction is completed by Lesson 36). Although the textbook can be used by classes meeting more or less often, each lesson presumes one hour of classwork (or one class period) and approximately two hours of homework. However, as experience has shown, some students may need to spend more than two hours preparing a lesson and should be instructed from the beginning to develop sound study habits.

It is hoped that this textbook will help make the study of Latin a positive and more enjoyable learning experience for those students continuing with the second year of the classical language. It is also hoped that this textbook, in conjunction with its predecessor, will help teachers achieve higher enrollments in classical languages, as they have at the University of Hawaii.

Honolulu, Hawaii   Robert J. Ball
June 1990

ABBREVIATIONS

abl. = ablative
acc. = accusative
act. = active
adj. = adjective
adv. = adverb
App. = Appendix
ARA = *Reading Classical Latin: A Reasonable Approach,* 2nd ed.
compar. = comparative
conj. = conjunction
dat. = dative
decl. = declension
fem. = feminine
fut. = future
fut. perf. = future perfect
gen. = genitive
imperf. = imperfect

ind. = indicative
indecl. = indeclinable
inf. = infinitive
masc. = masculine
neut. = neuter
nom. = nominative
part. = participle
pass. = passive
perf. = perfect
pers. = person
plup. = pluperfect
plur. = plural
prep. = preposition
pres. = present
sing. = singular
subj. = subjunctive
superl. = superlative

LESSON 1

REVIEW: FIRST DECLENSION NOUNS. AP. TYRE. AP. TYRE: ARCHISTRATES' DAUGHTER ASKS ABOUT APOLLONIUS.

§A   **Review.** Lessons 1–12 of this textbook contain a review of the models learned in *Reading Classical Latin: A Reasonable Approach,* referred to hereafter as *ARA* (see *ARA,* App. A, for the models).

Review (1) **terra,** the model for first declension nouns (*ARA,* App. A, p. 374). Review also first declension Greek names, presented in *ARA,* Lesson 4, Section A, for which the noun **terra** serves as the model.

§B   **Exercise.** The words used here consist primarily of vocabulary that you learned in *ARA.* All words, whether learned in *ARA* or occurring here for the first time, are listed in the Cumulative Vocabulary.

I. How do you know if a noun has **terra** as its model?

II. Write out the declensions of **silva** and **Aenéas** (**Aenéas** in sing. only). What Greek endings does the declension of **Aenéas** retain?

III. Identify the case and number of the following nouns and translate:

     (1) **puellae**   (4) **sagittis**

     (2) **feminas**   (5) **Iarban**

     (3) **lacrima**   (6) **Daphnes**

§C   **Apollonius of Tyre.** *Apollonius of Tyre,* an anonymous novel written during the fifth or sixth century A.D., deals with the travels and travails of the hero named Apollonius. Lessons 1–12 contain two sections of this novel: the first, on Apollonius's reception at a royal banquet; the second, on his daughter's encounter with a brothel-keeper.

§D **Vocabulary.** This section contains words that appear in the reading selection presented in the lesson, with words to be memorized marked (as in *ARA*) with an asterisk. However, it does not include words marked for memorization in the lesson vocabularies of *ARA*, except when such words appear with new forms or new meanings.

adultus, adulta, adultum ... *mature, grown-up*

***amícus, amíca, amícum** ... *friendly, loving;* (masc. sing. as substantive) *friend*

Apollonius, Apollonii, m. ... *Apollonius,* king of Tyre

***aut** ... *or;* **aut . . , aut . . ,** *either . . , or . .*

cena, cenae, f. ... *dinner*

decet, decére, decuit ... (impersonal verb) **decet** = *it is fitting,* **decére** = *to be fitting,* **decuit** = *it was fitting*

discumbo, discumbere, discubui ... *to recline* at a table

doleo, dolére, dolui ... *to grieve*

flebilis, flebile ... *tearful, weeping*

forsitan ... *perhaps*

fulgeo, fulgére, fulsi ... *to flash, to gleam, to shine*

gratus, grata, gratum ... *pleasing; grateful, thankful;* **grate:** *willingly, obligingly*

gymnasium, gymnasii, n. ... *gymnasium*

honorátus, honoráta, honorátum ... *honored, respected*

hortor, hortári, hortátus sum ... *to urge, to exhort*

igitur ... *then, therefore*

invíto, invitáre, invitávi, invitátus ... *to invite; to entertain*

***iuvenis, iuvene** ... *young;* (masc. sing. as substantive) *young man*

***mihi** or **mi** ... (dat. sing. of **ego**) *to/for me*

naufrágus, naufrága, naufrágum ... *shipwrecked*

nescio, nescíre, nescívi or **nescii** ... *to not know, not to know;* **nescio quis, nescio quid:** (masc./fem.) *someone or other, suitable for someone or other,* (neut.) *something or other, for some unexplained reason*

*scio, scire, scivi or **scii** ... *to know, to understand*

nosco, noscere, novi, notus ... (perf. may have pres. meaning) *to know; to get to know, to investigate*

osculor, osculári, osculátus sum ... *to kiss*

*osculum, osculi, n. ... (plur. may have sing. meaning) *kiss; mouth, lips*

pervenio, perveníre, pervéni ... *to come* to, *to arrive* at; *to come through, to pass through*

propter ... *because of, on account of* (+ acc.)

retrorsum ... *back, backwards, back again*

sapiens, sapientis ... *wise, intelligent*

sermo, sermónis, m. ... *talk, speech; rumor, gossip*

servitium, servitii, n. ... *slavery; duty, service*

subitus, subita, subitum ... *sudden;* **subito:** *suddenly*

*te ... (acc. or abl. sing. of **tu**) *you* or *by/with you*

verecundus, verecunda, verecundum ... *modest, restrained*

vultus, vultus, m. ... (plur. may have sing. meaning) *head, face; appearance*

§E   **Reading.**

Archistrates' Daughter Asks about Apollonius.

Lessons 1–6 contain the section of *Apollonius of Tyre* set in Cyrene (a city in northern Africa), where the hero called Apollonius meets the daughter of King Archistrates. Having been shipwrecked in this foreign land, Apollonius is welcomed and entertained in the palace of Archistrates, where he arouses the curiosity of the king's daughter.

Et dum hortarétur iuvenem, subito introívit filia regis speciósa atque auro fulgens, iam adulta virgo. Dedit osculum patri, post haec discumbentibus omnibus amícis. Quae dum oscularétur, pervénit ad naufrágum. Retrorsum rediit ad patrem et ait:

5   "Bone rex et pater optime, quis est nescio hic iuvenis, qui contra te in honoráto loco discumbit et nescio quid flebili vultu dolet?" Cui rex ait: "Hic iuvenis naufrágus est et in gymnasio mihi servitium gratissime fecit. Propter quod ad cenam illum invitávi. Quis autem sit aut unde, nescio. Sed si vis, interroga

10   illum! Decet enim te, filia sapientissima, omnia nosse. Et forsitan, dum cognoveris, misereberis illi." Hortante igitur patre, verecundissimo sermóne interrogátur a puella Apollonius.

§F   **Notes and Queries.** This section includes translations of forms not yet learned, which are no longer given in the interlinear (as in *ARA*) but in the notes, until they are formally presented in subsequent lessons.

(1) **dum:** In *Apollonius of Tyre,* this conjunction may be regarded as the equivalent of **cum.**—**hortarétur:** Imperfect subjunctive third person singular of the deponent verb **hortor** (see *ARA,* Lesson 59, Section A), with the subject here being Archistrates. In the subjunctive, deponent verbs are normally conjugated like regular verbs, with their subjunctive forms corresponding to those of regular verbs in the passive voice.—**iuvenem:** Refers to Apollonius, unhappy about his being shipwrecked.—**introívit:** Translate *entered.*—**filia:** Case and number? Function of this case?—**speciósa:** Case, number, and gender? What noun does this adjective modify?

(2) **fulgens:** Tense, voice, and mood? (See *ARA,* Lesson 51, Section A.)—**Dedit:** Of what verb is this a form? How does its third principal part differ from those of most first conjugation verbs?

(2–3) **post haec:** In *Apollonius of Tyre,* this prepositional phrase occurs frequently and may be regarded as the equivalent of **post hoc.**

(3) **amícis:** This noun functions in the same way as **patri** does in relation to the verb **Dedit.**—**Quae:** How do you translate the relative pronoun when it appears at the beginning of the sentence? (See *ARA,* Lesson 28, Section G, note to line 2.)

(4) **naufrágum:** What use of the adjective? (See *ARA,* Lesson 20, Section D.)—**rediit:** Translate *she returned.*

(5) **Bone:** Translate *good.*—**optime:** Translate *excellent* or *exceptional.*—**nescio hic:** Here the equivalent of **hic.**

(6) **te:** The accusative singular of the personal pronoun **tu.** (See *ARA,* App. C, p. 408, for the declension of this pronoun.)

(7) **mihi:** The dative singular of the personal pronoun **ego.** (See *ARA,* App. C, p. 408, for the declension of this pronoun.)

(8) **servitium . . . fecit:** Here Archistrates refers to how Apollonius impressed him in the gymnasium with his skill at playing catch-ball and with his ability to provide him with a massage and a tub-bath.—**gratissime:** The superlative degree of adverbs has the same form as the superlative degree of adjectives in the genitive singular, with the ending **-i** changed to **-e** (see *ARA,* App. D, p. 420).—**cenam:** Case and number? Why is this case used here?

(9) **sit:** Translate *he is.*—**vis:** Translate *you wish.*—**interroga:** Translate *ask* or *question.*

(10) **Decet:** An example of an impersonal verb, one having no personal subject and found almost exclusively in the third person singular.—**te . . . nosse:** What construction? (See *ARA,* Lesson 47, Section A.) What is the uncontracted form of **nosse?** (See *ARA,* Lesson 37, Section F, note to line 5.)—**sapientissima:** Degree of adjective? (See *ARA,* Lesson 47, Section E, note to line 11, and *ARA,* App. D, p. 418, for a more detailed explanation.)

(11) **cognoveris:** Translate *you find out.*—**misereberis:** Translate *you will have pity.*

(11–12) **Hortante . . . patre:** What construction? (See *ARA,* Lesson 53, Section A.)

(12) **interrogátur:** What use of the present tense? (See *ARA,* Lesson 20, Section H, note to line 9.)—**puella:** Case and number? Why is this case used here?

LESSON 2

REVIEW: PRESENT ACTIVE INDICATIVE. AP. TYRE: ARCHISTRATES' DAUGHTER QUESTIONS APOLLONIUS DIRECTLY.

§A   **Review.** Review (2) **amo,** (3) **moneo,** (4) **traho,** and (5) **audio**—the models for the present active indicative (*ARA,* App. A, p. 374). Review also **amans** and **amátus,** the models for the present active and perfect passive participle (*ARA,* Lesson 51, Section A / Lesson 52, Section A).

§B   **Exercise.**

I. How do you know if a verb is conjugated like **amo,** or **moneo,** or **traho,** or **audio?**

II. Write out the conjugations of **gusto, ardeo, mitto,** and **dormio,** in the present active indicative and infinitive.

III. Identify the tense, voice, mood, person, and number of the following verbs and translate:

      (1) **vocas**   (4) **venio**

      (2) **habent**   (5) **frangitis**

      (3) **credit**   (6) **facimus**

§C   **Vocabulary.**

accédo, accedere, accessi ... *to approach, to come near*

adulescens, adulescentis, m. ... *young man*

agnosco, agnoscere, agnóvi, agnitus ... *to find out, to get to know*

*ago, agere, egi, actus ... *to do, to drive; to act, to perform; to discuss, to consider; to give* thanks, *to live* life, *to hunt* animals

apertus, aperta, apertum ... *open, clear;* **aperte:** *openly, clearly*

*casus, casus, m. ... (plur. may have sing. meaning) *fall, falling; fate, fortune; peril, dilemma, predicament*

dolor, dolóris, m. ... (plur. may have sing. meaning) *pain, distress*

dulcis, dulce ... *sweet; delightful*

effundo, effundere, effúdi, effúsus ... *to pour out; to shed* tears

ergo ... *therefore*

expóno, exponere, exposui, expositus ... *to put out, to display; to explain, to set forth*

finio, finíre, finívi or **finii, finítus** ... *to end, to finish; to stop speaking, to draw to a close*

fleo, flere, flevi ... *to cry, to weep; to cry for, to weep for*

gemitus, gemitus, m. ... a *sigh, a* groan; *a* sighing, a *groaning*

generositas, generositátis, f. ... *manner, noble bearing*

indulgentia, indulgentiae, f. ... *kindness, indulgence*

iustus, iusta, iustum ... *just, proper*

liberalitas, liberalitátis, f. ... *kindness, generosity*

licet ... (conj.) *although*

locupléto, locupletáre, locupletávi, locupletátus ... *to enrich, to make wealthy*

maeror, maeróris, m. ... *grief, sorrow*

*meus, mea, meum ... (possessive adj. related to **ego**) *my*

molestus, molesta, molestum ... *annoying, troublesome*

*nata, natae, f. ... *daughter*

nobilitas, nobilitátis, f. ... *high birth, nobility of birth*

*noster, nostra, nostrum ... (possessive adj. related to **nos**) *our*

pecco, peccáre, peccávi ... *to sin, to do wrong, to make a mistake*

perdo, perdere, perdidi, perditus ... *to lose, to ruin, to destroy; to use without purpose, to waste* one's *time on;* **perditus, perdita, perditum:** *lost, ruined, destroyed;* **perdite:** *desperately, without restraint*

permitto, permittere, permísi, permissus ... *to allow, to permit*

quasi ... *as if, just as; as it were, so to speak*

quia ... *that; since, because*

renovo, renováre, renovávi, renovátus ... *to renew, to revive*

respicio, respicere, respexi ... *to look back, to look around; to look at, to take notice of, to turn* one's *thoughts to*

taciturnitas, taciturnitátis, f. ... *silence*

thesaurus, thesauri, m. ... *treasure*

*tibi ... (dat. sing. of **tu**) *to/for you*

tristis, triste ... *bitter; sad, gloomy*

*tuus, tua, tuum ... (possessive adj. related to **tu**) *your*

universus, universa, universum ... *all, whole, entire*

veritas, veritátis, f. ... *truth*

vetus, veteris ... *old, ancient*

§D   Reading.

Archistrates' Daughter Questions Apollonius Directly.

Et accédens ad eum ait: "Licet taciturnitas tua sit tristior,

generositas autem tuam nobilitátem ostendit. Sed si tibi

molestum non est, indica mihi nomen et casus tuos!"

Apollonius ait: "Si nomen quaeris, Apollonius sum vocátus; si

5   de thesauro quaeris, in mari perdidi." Puella ait: "Apertius

indica mihi ut intellegam!" Apollonius vero universos casus suos exposuit et finíto sermóne lacrimas effundere coepit. Quem ut vidit rex flentem, respiciens filiam suam ait: "Nata dulcis, peccasti, quod dum eius nomen et casus adulescentis

10 agnosceres, veteres ei renovasti dolóres. Ergo, dulcis et sapiens filia, ex quo agnovisti veritátem, iustum est ut ei liberalitátem tuam quasi regína ostendas." Puella vero respiciens Apollonium ait: "Iam noster es, iuvenis, depóne maerórem! Et quia permittit indulgentia patris mei, locupletábo te." Apollonius vero

15 cum gemitu egit gratias.

§E Notes and Queries.

(1) **accédens:** Tense, voice, and mood? Subject of the verbal action?—**sit:** Translate *is*.—**tristior:** Degree of adjective? (See *ARA*, Lesson 45, Section F, note to line 13, and *ARA*, App. D, p. 418, for a more detailed explanation.)

(2) **ostendit:** Tense, voice, mood, person, and number?—**tibi:** The dative singular of the personal pronoun **tu**. (See *ARA*, App. C, p. 408, for the declension of this pronoun.)

(3) **indica:** Translate *reveal* or *disclose*.

(4) **sum vocátus:** An example of the perfect passive used as present passive to denote a state resulting from a completed act (here translate *I am called*), and an example of the perfect passive in which the form of **sum** precedes the participial element (see *ARA*, Lesson 62, Section F, note to lines 16–17).

(5) **Apertius:** Degree of adverb? (See *ARA*, Lesson 47, Section E, note to line 8, and *ARA*, App D, p. 420, for a more detailed explanation.)

(6) **ut intellegam:** What construction? (See *ARA*, Lesson 63, Section D.)

(7) **finíto sermóne:** What construction?—**lacrimas:** Case and number? Function of this case?

(8) **ut vidit:** What meaning of **ut**? Why this meaning here? (See *ARA,* Lesson 64, Section F, note to line 16.)—**flentem:** Tense, voice, and mood? Subject of the verbal action?

(9) **peccasti:** This form is contracted for **peccavisti,** from which the **vi** has dropped out.—**dum:** See above, Lesson 1, note to line 1.—**eius:** What noun does this adjective modify? (Keep in mind that an adjective need not be adjacent to the noun that it modifies.)

(10) **renovasti:** What is the uncontracted form?

(11) **quo:** Here the relative has its antecedent (actually its 'postcedent') in the pronoun **ei** later in the same sentence (see *ARA,* Lesson 50, Section E, note to line 11).

(11–12) **ut . . . ostendas:** A substantive clause of result (see *ARA,* App. K, p. 473, Result Clauses).

(13) **noster:** After this adjective supply *guest* or *friend.*—**es:** Of what verb is this a form? (See *ARA,* Lesson 55, Section A.)—**depóne:** Translate *put aside.*

(14) **locupletábo:** The future active indicative of a first conjugation verb (see *ARA,* Lesson 22, Section A).

LESSON 3

REVIEW: SECOND DECLENSION NOUNS. AP. TYRE: ARCHISTRATES' DAUGHTER PERFORMS FOR APOLLONIUS.

§A **Review.** Review (6) **annus,** the model for second declension masculine and feminine nouns, and (7) **donum,** the model for second declension neuter nouns (*ARA,* App. A, p. 375). Review also second declension Greek names for all genders (*ARA,* Lesson 14, Section D, and *ARA,* Lesson 16, Section D), for which **annus** and **donum** serve as the models.

§B **Exercise.**

I. How do you know if a noun has **annus** as its model? How do you know if a noun has **donum** as its model?

II. Write out the declensions of **oculus** and **regnum.** What Greek endings does the declension of **Delos** retain?

III. Identify the case and number of the following nouns and translate:

(1) **filios**   (4) **templi**

(2) **studia**   (5) **servis**

(3) **puerum**   (6) **Tenedos**

§C **Vocabulary.**

*ante ... *before* (+ acc.); *previously* (as adv.)

Archistrátes, Archistrátis, m. ... *Archistrates,* king of Cyrene

ars, artis, f. (gen. plur. **artium**) ... *art, craft, skill*

bonitas, bonitátis, f. ... *goodness, kindness*

chorda, chordae, f. ... *string* of a lyre

convíva, convívae, c. ... *guest*

convivium, convivii, n. ... (plur. may have sing. meaning) *feast, banquet*

denique ... *finally; in short, to sum up*

disco, discere, didici ... *to learn; to master, to acquire skill in*

dulcédo, dulcedinis, f. ... *sweetness*

foedus, foeda, foedum ... *foul; horrible, shameful*

gaudeo, gaudére, gavísus sum ... (semi-deponent verb) *to rejoice; to delight* in (+ abl.)

incido, incidere, incidi ... *to occur, to happen; to fall* or *stumble* in, on, into (followed by dat. or prep. + acc.); *to come up in conversation, to present itself in conversation*

*__iste, ista, istud__ (gen. sing. **istíus, istíus, istíus**) ... *that man, that woman, that thing* (as a pronoun); *that, that of yours, such as you offer* (as an adjective)

laudo, laudáre, laudávi, laudátus ... *to praise*

locuples, locuplétis ... *rich; richly endowed*

lyra, lyrae, f. ... *lyre*

*__melior, melius__ ... (compar. of **bonus;** see *ARA*, App. D, p. 419) *better*

melos, meleos, n. (Greek word with gen. sing. **meleos** and acc. sing. **melos**) ... *song, tune*

miror, mirári, mirátus sum ... *to wonder, to be amazed;* (gerundive) **mirandus, miranda, mirandum:** *amazing, astonishing*

*__misceo, miscére, miscui, mixtus__ ... *to mix, to mingle; to stir up, to throw into confusion; to mix* or *mingle* something (acc.) with something (dat. or abl.)

musicus, musica, musicum ... *musical*

nimius, nimia, nimium ... *too much; excessive, very great;* **nimium:** (adv.) *too much; excessively, exceedingly*

*plus, pluris ... (compar. of **multus;** see *ARA,* App. D, p. 419) *more, several*

quare ... (relative adv.) *why, wherefore, for which reason;* (interrogative adv.) *why? wherefore? for which reason?*

salvus, salva, salvum ... *safe, well;* **salve:** *safe, well*

sonus, soni, m. ... *sound*

taceo, tacére, tacui ... *to be silent*

*tu ... (second person sing. pronoun) *you*

validus, valida, validum ... *strong, powerful;* **valide** or **valde:** *greatly, very much, exceedingly*

vitupero, vituperáre, vituperávi, vituperátus ... *to criticize, to find fault with*

*vox, vocis, f. ... *voice; word, sound; saying, expression; sentence, utterance*

§D   Reading.

Archistrates' Daughter Performs for Apollonius.

Rex vero, videns tantam bonitátem filiae suae, valde gavísus est,

et ait ad eam: "Nata dulcis, salvum habeas. Iube tibi afferre

lyram, et aufer iuveni lacrimas, et exhilara ad convivium!"

Puella vero iussit sibi afferri lyram. At ubi accépit, cum nimia

5   dulcedine vocis chordárum sonos, melos cum voce miscébat.

Omnes convívae coepérunt mirári dicentes: "Non potest esse

melius, non esse dulcius plus isto quod audivimus." Inter quos

solus tacébat Apollonius. Ad quem rex ait: "Apollóni, foedam

rem facis. Omnes filiam meam in arte musica laudant. Quare

10   tu solus tacendo vituperas?" Apollonius ait: "Domine rex, si

permittis, dicam quod sentio. Filia enim tua in artem musicam incidit, sed non didicit. Denique iube mihi dari lyram, et statim scies quod ante nesciébas." Rex Archistrátes dixit: "Apollóni, ut intellego, in omnibus es locuples."

§E **Notes and Queries.**

(1) **videns:** Tense, voice, and mood? Subject of the verbal action?—**filiae:** Case and number? Function of this case?—**gavísus est:** An example of a semi-deponent verb, with the present system conjugated in the active voice and the perfect system conjugated in the passive voice.

(2) **salvum habeas:** Translate *may you be well* or *may you have good health.*—**Iube:** Translate *Order.*—**afferre:** Either understand some unspecified person (perhaps a servant) as the subject of the active infinitive **afferre** *(to bring)* or understand this active infinitive as the equivalent of the passive infinitive **afferri** *(to be brought)* occurring in line 4.

(3) **aufer:** Translate *take away.*—**iuveni:** The dative is translated by *from* when it is used with verbs of separation (see *ARA,* Lesson 34, Section F, note to line 12, on the dative of separation).—**exhilara:** Translate *cheer (him) up.*

(5) **miscébat:** Here this verb is used with two direct objects. What is the first direct object and what is the second direct object?

(6) **coepérunt:** Translate *began.*—**mirári:** Why are the principal parts of this verb given in the passive?—**dicentes:** Tense, voice, and mood? Subject of the verbal action?—**potest:** Translate *it is able.*

(7) **dulcius plus:** The comparative adjective **plus** is redundant, since the adjective **dulcius** is already comparative.—**isto:** The ablative is translated by *than* when it is used with a comparative adjective (see *ARA,* App. E, p. 425, Ablative of Comparison).—**audivimus:** An example of the present perfect (in contrast to the aoristic perfect), used to express the action of the verb as completed in present time (see *ARA,* Lesson 31, Section A). Now that you are reading stories more sophisticated than those of Hyginus, you should expect to see (and be able to distinguish between) these two uses of the perfect tense.—**quos:** How do you translate the relative pronoun when it appears at the beginning of the sentence?

(8) **solus:** Modifies what noun?—**Apollóni:** Translate *Apollonius*.

(9) **facis:** Tense, voice, mood, person, and number?—**laudant:** Tense, voice, mood, person, and number?

(10) **tu:** The second person singular pronoun. (See *ARA,* App. C, p. 408, for the declension of this pronoun.)—**tacendo:** What verbal form? Case and number? (See *ARA,* Lesson 57, Section C.)—**vituperas:** Tense, voice, mood, person, and number?—**Domine:** Translate *Lord*.

(11) **dicam:** Translate *I will say*.

(13) **scies:** Translate *you will know*.

(13–14) **ut intellego:** What meaning of **ut?** Why this meaning here?

LESSON 4

**REVIEW: FIRST AND SECOND DECLENSION ADJECTIVES.
IMPERFECT ACTIVE INDICATIVE. AP. TYRE: APOLLONIUS
PERFORMS FOR ARCHISTRATES' DAUGHTER.**

§A **Review.** Review (8) **ferus,** the model for first and second declension adjectives (*ARA,* App. A, p. 375), and (9) **amábam,** the model for the imperfect active indicative (*ARA,* App. A, p. 376).

§B **Exercise.**

I. How do you know if an adjective has **ferus** as its model? What verb elements (stem, infix, endings) does **amábam** contain? What kind of past action (continued or completed) does **amábam** express?

II. Identify the case, number, and gender of the following adjectives:

(1) **multo**   (4) **irátis**

(2) **primas**   (5) **candidae**

(3) **aurea**   (6) **pulchrum**

III. Identify the tense, voice, mood, person, and number of the following verbs and translate:

(1) **rogábat**   (4) **sentiébas**

(2) **iubebátis**   (5) **rapiébant**

(3) **vincimus**   (6) **scribébam**

§C **Vocabulary.**

accommodo, accommodáre, accommodávi, accommodátus ... *to fit, to put on*

actio, actiónis, f. ... *deed, action*

admirabilis, admirabile ... *wonderful, remarkable;* **admirabiliter:** *wonderfully, remarkably*

*animus, animi, m. ... (plur. may have sing. meaning) *mind, heart; spirit, courage*

Apollo, Apollinis, m. ... *Apollo*

arripio, arripere, arripui, arreptus ... *to seize, to grab hold of*

clamo, clamáre, clamávi ... *to call, to shout*

comicus, comica, comicum ... *comic*

complaceo, complacére, complacui ... *to please greatly* (+ dat.); *(impersonal use) to seem very pleasing*

coróna, corónae, f. ... *crown, wreath*

coróno, coronáre, coronávi, coronátus ... *to crown, to wreathe*

cumulo, cumuláre, cumulávi, cumulátus ... *to heap, to pile up;* (in pass.) *to be gifted in, to be endowed with* (+ gen.)

depóno, deponere, deposui, depositus ... *to put down, to put aside; to slake* or *quench* one's thirst

existimo, existimáre, existimávi, existimátus ... *to judge, to think*

exprimo, exprimere, expressi, expressus ... *to press out; to convey, to express; to bear a resemblance to*

habitus, habitus, m. ... *manner, posture; costume, clothing*

*ignis, ignis, m. (abl. sing. **igne** or **igni,** gen. plur. **ignium**) ... *fire, flame; lightning, thunderbolt*

inaudítus, inaudíta, inaudítum ... *unheard; unheard of, remarkable*

induo, induere, indui, indútus ... *to put on; to clothe, to dress*

ingredior, ingredi, ingressus sum ... *to enter; to step on, to walk on* (+ abl.); *to begin, to begin to deal with*

laus, laudis, f. ... *praise; award, prize; honor, renown*

mirabilis, mirabile ... *wonderful, remarkable*

modulor, modulári, modulátus sum ... *to attune, to modulate; to play* or *sing to the accompaniment of* an instrument (+ abl.)

nihilominus ... *nevertheless, none the less*

numquam ... *never*

*opto, optáre, optávi, optátus ... *to desire; to wish, to pray; to wish for, to pray for*

paulum, pauli, n. ... *little, little bit;* **paulum:** (adv.) *a little bit, for a little while;* **paulo ante:** *a little while ago, a little while earlier*

plectrum, plectri, n. ... *plectrum*

saevus, saeva, saevum ... *cruel, fierce, savage*

saltus, saltus, m. ... *jump, leap, bound*

*sic ... *so, thus, in such a way*

silentium, silentii, n. ... *silence*

status, status, m. ... *state, stance; costume, clothing*

*studium, studii, n. ... *zeal, eagerness; study, skill, pursuit; artistic* or *literary skill; artistic* or *literary pursuit*

*tamen ... *yet, however, nevertheless*

testor, testári, testátus sum ... *to assert* or *declare solemnly*

tragicus, tragica, tragicum ... *tragic*

triclinium, triclinii, n. ... *dining-room*

*unus, una, unum ... (see *ARA*, App. C, p. 416, for the declension of this numeral) *one, only, alone;* **una:** (adv.) *along, together, at the same time*

vulnus, vulneris, n. ... *wound, injury;* (as the prospective source of a wound) *weapon*

Apollonius Performs for Archistrates' Daughter.

Et induit statum, et coróna caput coronávit, et accipiens lyram
introívit triclinium. Et ita fecit ut discumbentes non Apollonium
sed Apollinem existimárent. Atque ita, facto silentio, 'arripuit
plectrum, animumque accommodat arti.' Miscétur vox cantu

5   moduláta chordis. Discumbentes una cum rege in laude
clamáre coepérunt et dicere: "Non potest melius, non potest
dulcius." Post haec, depónens lyram, ingreditur in comico
habitu, et mirabili manu et saltu inaudítas actiónes expressit;
post haec induit tragicum. Et nihilominus admirabiliter

10   complacuit ita ut omnes amíci regis et hoc se numquam
audisse testarentur nec vidisse. Inter haec, filia regis ut vidit
iuvenem omnium artium studiorumque esse cumulátum,
vulneris saevo capitur igne. Incidit in amórem. Et finíto
convivio sic ait puella ad patrem suum: "Permiseras mihi paulo

15   ante, ut si quid voluissem (de tuo tamen) Apollonio darem, rex
et pater optime." Cui dixit: "Et permísi et permitto et opto."

§E	Notes and Queries.

(1) **statum:** That is, the costume of a musician—the first of three cos-
tumes worn by Apollonius during his performance.—**coróna:** That
is, a wreath of leaves or flowers.

(2) **introívit:** Translate *he entered*.—**discumbentes:** Here the present
participle is used as a substantive referring to the dinner guests.
Supply an appropriate pronoun to indicate the subject of the verbal
action, in this instance, *those* reclining or *the ones* reclining.

(2–3) **ut . . . existimárent:** What construction? (See *ARA*, Lesson 67, Section D.). The verb **existimárent** itself introduces an indirect statement, in which the accusative **eum** and the infinitive **esse** should be supplied from the context.

(3) **Apollinem:** That is, Apollo in his aspect as god of music.—**facto silentio:** What construction?

(3–4) **arripuit plectrum, animumque accommodat arti:** A line of poetry quoted from some unidentifiable poet, written in dactylic hexameter—the meter traditionally used in Greek and Latin epic poetry.

(5) **moduláta:** The perfect passive participle of a deponent verb (see *ARA*, Lesson 59, Section A).—**una:** The adverb or the adjective?

(6) **coepérunt:** Translate *began*.—**Non potest:** Translate *it is not able*. What word should be supplied after this phrase? (See above, Lesson 3, Section D, lines 6–7.)

(8) **habitu:** What meaning best fits this context? (See above, note to line 1, on **statum**.)—**manu et saltu:** Translate *with gestures and movements*. What is the literal meaning of these words?

(9) **tragicum:** What noun should be supplied after this adjective?

(10) **et hoc:** The equivalent of **etiam hoc**.

(10–11) **se . . . audisse . . . vidisse:** What construction? What is the uncontracted form of **audisse?**

(11) **testarentur:** Why are the principal parts of this verb given in the passive?—**ut vidit:** See above, Lesson 2, Section E, note to line 8.

(12) **esse cumulátum:** See *ARA*, Lesson 60, Section D, note to line 2.

(13) **saevo:** Modifies what noun grammatically? Modifies what noun according to sense? (Translate the words involved according to sense.)—**igne:** Explained by the words **Incidit in amórem**.

(15) **ut . . . darem:** What construction? (See *ARA*, Lesson 71, Section A.)—**si quid voluissem:** Translate *whatever I wished*.—**tuo:** After this adjective supply *property* or *possessions*.

(16) **optime:** Translate *excellent* or *exceptional*.—**Cui:** How do you translate the relative pronoun when it appears at the beginning of the sentence?

LESSON 5

REVIEW: PRONOUNS. NEW: VOCATIVE CASE. AP. TYRE: APOLLONIUS RECEIVES GENEROUS GIFTS AND GUEST-QUARTERS.

§A **Review.** Review (10) **is,** the model for pronouns (*ARA,* App. C, p. 409). Review also the pronouns modeled on **is** (*ARA,* App. C, pp. 410–12) and the reflexive pronoun **sui** (*ARA,* Lesson 29, Section C).

§B **Exercise.**

I. How do you know if a pronoun has **is** as its model?

II. Identify the case, number, and gender of the following pronouns, then translate:

  (1) **eam et eos**   (4) **isti mali viri**

  (2) **sine his telis**   (5) **ipsa non luget**

  (3) **illa quae dormit** (6) **eídem se amant**

§C **New: Vocative Case.** Latin has forms for a sixth case called the vocative, used for direct address (**O pater,** *O father*). The vocative may be preceded by the interjection **O** and is set off from the rest of the sentence by commas. Its forms are generally the same as those of the nominative, except for second declension nouns and adjectives.

Nominative	Vocative
annus	**anne**
ferus	**fere**
filius	**fili**

Second declension nouns and adjectives with nominative singular in -us have their vocative singular in -e; those with nominative singular in -ius have their vocative in -i. First, second, and third declension Greek names have a special vocative singular—a subject considered in *ARA*, App. F, pp. 427–28, in the extended treatment of this case.

§D **Exercise.** Identify the case, number, and gender of the following nouns, then translate:

(1) **dea ipsa canit**   (4) **"o dea, audiébam"**

(2) **"Brute, quid facis?"**   (5) **ita Brutus fugit**

(3) **at Livius negábat**   (6) **"Livi, non timémus"**

§E **Vocabulary.**

abscédo, abscedere, abscessi ... *to depart, to go away*

amatrix, amatrícis, f. ... (applied to a woman) *lover*

bene ... *well, kindly; at peace, contentedly*

*****bonus, bona, bonum** ... *good; presentable, respectable;* (neut. plur. as substantive) *goods, property*

consolátor, consolatóris, m. ... *consoler, comforter*

copiósus, copiósa, copiósum ... *rich, opulent*

denego, denegáre, denegávi, denegátus ... *to deny*

*****dignus, digna, dignum** ... *worthy, deserving; worthy of, deserving of* (+ gen. or abl.); *fitting, suitable, appropriate;* **digne:** *worthily, as is fitting, in a suitable manner*

discédo, discedere, discessi ... *to depart, to go away*

*****domina, dominae, f.** ... *lady* or *mistress* of a household

ducenti, ducentae, ducenta ... *two hundred*

famulus, famuli, m. ... *slave, attendant*

hodie ... *today*

hospitális, hospitále ... *hospitable, used for a guest;* (neut. plur. as substantive) *guest-accommodations*

intueor, intuéri, intuitus sum ... *to watch, to gaze at, to look at*

*****laudo, laudáre, laudávi, laudátus** ... *to praise*

levo, leváre, levávi, levátus ... *to lift up;* (used with the reflexive **se,** which is not translated in this idiom) *to arise, to get up*

magister, magistri, m. ... *master, teacher*

mansio, mansiónis, f. ... *lodging, dwelling*

*****miser, misera, miserum** ... *sad, poor, wretched*

misericors, misericordis ... *having pity* or *compassion* for (+ gen.)

nobis ... (dat. or abl. plur. of **ego**) *to/for us* or *by/with us*

optimus, optima, optimum ... (superl. of **bonus;** see *ARA,* App. D, p. 419) *best; excellent, exceptional*

perago, peragere, perégi, peractus ... *to drive through; to finish, to complete*

placeo, placére, placui ... *to please* (+ dat.); (impersonal use) *to seem good* (+ dat. sometimes) [e.g., **placet ei** = *it seems good to him*]

pondus, ponderis, n. ... *weight; pound*

praesens, praesentis ... *present, in person; pressing, immediate; favorable, well-disposed;* **in praesenti:** *instantly, immediately*

praesto, praestáre, praestiti, praestátus ... *to stand out, to be superior to; to furnish, to present, to provide*

promitto, promittere, promísi, promissus ... *to promise; to promise someone* (dat.) *something* (acc.); *to promise someone that* (+ indirect statement)

quiesco, quiescere, quiévi ... *to rest, to sleep; to remain still* or *steady*

*****quoque** ... (placed after the word it emphasizes) *also*

requiesco, requiescere, requiévi ... *to rest, to repose*

talentum, talenti, n. ... *talent* (= unit of weight)

*torqueo, torquére, torsi, tortus ... *to turn, to twist; to torment, to torture; to hurl, to throw, to fling*

ultro ... *of* one's *own accord, on* one's *own initiative*

zaeta, zaetae, f. ... *room, apartment*

§F   Reading.

Apollonius Receives Generous Gifts and Guest-Quarters.

Permisso sibi a patre, quod ipsa ultro praestáre volébat, intuens
Apollonium ait: "Apollóni magister, accipe indulgentia patris
mei ducenta talenta auri, argenti pondera XL, servos XX, et
vestem copiosissimam." Et intuens Apollonii famulos, quos

5   donaverat, dixit: "Afferte quaequae promísi, et praesentibus
omnibus exponíte in triclinio!" Laudant omnes liberalitátem
puellae. Peractoque convivio, levavérunt se universi; vale
dicentes regi et regínae, discessérunt. Ipse quoque Apollonius
ait: "Bone rex, miserórum misericors, et tu, regína amatrix

10   studiórum, valéte!" Et haec dicens, respiciens famulos, quos
illi puella donaverat, ait: "Tollíte, famuli, hoc quod mihi regína
donávit—aurum, argentum, et vestem; et eámus hospitalia
quaerentes." Puella vero timens ne (amátum non videns)
torquerétur, respexit patrem suum et ait: "Bone rex, pater

15   optime, placet tibi ut hodie Apollonius a nobis locupletátus
abscédat, et quod illi dedisti, a malis hominibus ei rapiátur?"
Cui rex ait: "Bene dicis, domina; iube ergo ei dari unam
zaetam, ubi digne quiescat!" Accepta igitur mansióne,

Apollonius bene acceptus requiévit, agens deo gratias, qui ei non

20 denegávit regem consolatórem.

§G **Notes and Queries.**

(1) **quod ipsa . . . volébat:** This clause is subject of the verbal action of **permisso** (i.e., *what she herself was wishing . . . having been allowed . . .*).—**intuens:** Tense, voice, and mood? Subject of the verbal action?

(2) **Apollóni:** Case and number?—**accipe:** Translate *receive.*

(3) **XL . . . XX:** The Roman numerals **X** = 10 and **L** = 50. When **X** precedes **L,** it is subtracted from **L;** when **X** follows **L,** it is added to **L.**

(5) **Afferte:** Translate *Bring.*—**quaequae:** Acc. plur. neut. of **quisquis.**

(6) **exponíte:** Translate *display.* What should be supplied as the direct object of this verb?

(7) **Peractoque convivio:** What construction?—**vale:** Translate *farewell.*—**levavérunt se:** See the entry for **levo** in the lesson vocabulary.

(8) **regínae:** Refers to Archistrates' daughter (see above, Lesson 2, Section D, line 12).—**Ipse:** Case, number, and gender?

(9) **miserórum:** What use of the adjective?

(10) **valéte:** Translate *farewell.*—**haec:** Case, number, and gender?

(11) **illi:** Case, number, and gender?—**Tollíte:** Translate *Take.*

(12) **eámus:** Translate *let us go.*

(13) **timens:** See *ARA,* Lesson 14, Section I, note to line 9.—**amátum:** Translate *her beloved.* What is the literal meaning?

(15) **locupletátus:** Tense, voice, and mood? Subject of the verbal action?

(16) **quod:** Here the relative means *what,* in the sense of *that which.*—**ei:** What kind of dative?

(17) **iube:** Translate *order.*—**dari:** Tense, voice, and mood?

(19) **deo:** Refers to some god whom the author does not identify.

(20) **regem consolatórem:** See *ARA,* Lesson 3, Section J, note to line 1.

LESSON 6

REVIEW: PERFECT AND PLUPERFECT ACTIVE INDICATIVE. NEW: IMPERATIVE MOOD. AP. TYRE: ARCHISTRATES' DAUGHTER FALLS IN LOVE WITH APOLLONIUS.

§A   **Review.** Review (11) **amávi,** the model for the perfect active indicative (*ARA,* App. A, p. 376), and (12) **amaveram,** the model for the pluperfect active indicative (*ARA,* App. A, p. 376).

§B   **Exercise.**

I. What verb elements does **amávi** contain? What kind of past action does **amávi** express? What verb elements does **amaveram** contain? What kind of past action does **amaveram** express?

II. Identify the tense, voice, mood, person, and number of the following verbs, then translate:

(1)	**nuntiávi**	(4)	**ducébas**
(2)	**moverant**	(5)	**strinxerat**
(3)	**operuimus**	(6)	**interfecistis**

§C   **New: Imperative Mood.** The imperative is used for direct commands (**credite,** *believe*) and prohibitions (**ne credite,** *don't believe*). It is found in the present tense (second person only) and in the future tense (second and third persons). Be able to recognize the present active imperative of **amo, moneo, traho, audio,** and **capio** (listed below):

Sing.	**ama**	(you <u>sing</u>.) *love*		
Plur.	**amáte**	(you <u>plur</u>.) *love*		

Sing.	**mone**	**trahe**	**audi**	**cape**
Plur.	**monéte**	**trahite**	**audíte**	**capite**

In the singular, the present active imperative normally has the same form as the present stem; in the plural, it consists of the present stem and the imperative ending -te. The imperative also occurs in the present passive, future active, and future passive—a subject considered in *ARA*, App. I, pp. 447–49, in the extended treatment of this mood.

§D   **Exercise.** Identify the tense, voice, mood, person, and number of the following verbs, then translate:

(1) "filia, pete deam!"   (4) filiae non sedent

(2) socii se violábant   (5) "socii, ne lugéte!"

(3) "O Plini, naviga!"   (6) iam Plinius lavábat

§E   **Vocabulary.**

adhibeo, adhibére, adhibui, adhibitus ... *to hold out to; to summon, to call upon*

aegritúdo, aegritudinis, f. ... *illness, sickness*

brevis, breve ... *brief, short*

concupisco, concupiscere, concupívi, concupítus ... *to conceive a desire; to desire greatly* or *ardently*

consuetúdo, consuetudinis, f. ... *habit, custom*

cubiculum, cubiculi, n. ... *bedroom*

cura, curae, f. ... *care; anxiety, concern; heartache, lovesickness*

doceo, docére, docui, doctus ... *to teach, to instruct*

*ego ... (first person sing. pronoun) I

excito, excitáre, excitávi, excitátus ... *to cause to move; to excite, to stir up; to arouse, to awaken; to heighten, to intensify*

felicitas, felicitátis, f. ... *happiness; enjoyable exercise, delightful practice*

fluxus, fluxa, fluxum ... *flowing; weak, sick*

gaudium, gaudii, n. ... *joy, delight, gladness*

hesternus, hesterna, hesternum ... *yesterday's, of yesterday*

iaceo, iacére, iacui ... *to lie; to recline* at a table; *to lie down, to lie sick, to lie dead* or *dying*

iamdúdum ... *now for a long time*

imbecillis, imbecille ... *weak, sick*

incurro, incurrere, incurri ... *to run* or *come* into; *to acquire, to contract*

infirmitas, infirmitátis, f. ... *weakness, sickness*

interpóno, interponere, interposui, interpositus ... *to place* someone or something *between;* (in pass.) *to pass, to elapse, to intervene*

irrumpo, irrumpere, irrúpi, irruptus ... *to break in* or *into, to burst in* or *into*

*****rumpo, rumpere, rupi, ruptus** ... *to break* in, into, or open, *to burst* in, into, or open

iuro, iuráre, iurávi, iurátus ... *to swear*

mane ... (adv.) *in the morning, early in the morning;* **primo mane:** *at the crack of dawn*

*****me** ... (acc. or abl. sing. of **ego**) *me* or *by/with me*

medicus, medici, m. ... *doctor, physician*

*****membrum, membri,** n. ... *limb* of the body

omníno ... *altogether; at all, in any degree*

pareo, parére, parui ... *to obey* (+ dat.)

*****per** ... *through* (root meaning); *through, because of, by means of* (+ acc.); *along, among, in the midst of* (+ acc.); *for, during, during the course of* (+ acc.); *by, by the power of, in the name of* (+ acc.)

percipio, percipere, percépi, perceptus ... *to lay hold of; to learn, to take lessons in*

plenus, plena, plenum ... *full, full* of (+ gen. or abl.)

prosterno, prosternere, prostrávi, prostrátus ... *to cast down, to stretch out*

quies, quiétis, f. ... *rest, peace, sleep*

*****quisquis, quaequae, quicquid** or **quidquid** ... (indefinite relative pronoun; only **quisquis** and **quicquid/quidquid** are regularly used) *whoever, whatever*

ratio, ratiónis, f. ... *reason, method, manner*

saucius, saucia, saucium ... *wounded; smitten* or *afflicted* with

sicut or **sicuti** ... *as, just as*

singuli, singulae, singula ... (plur. adj. with sing. meaning) *single, separate, individual*

sollicitus, sollicita, sollicitum ... *anxious, concerned*

somnus, somni, m. ... (plur. may have sing. meaning) *sleep*

spatium, spatii, n. ... *space, period, interval*

subitaneus, subitanea, subitaneum ... *sudden*

tango, tangere, tetigi, tactus ... *to touch; to examine, to explore*

tempto, temptáre, temptávi, temptátus ... *to try, to test*

thorus, thori, m. ... *bed*

tolero, toleráre, tolerávi, tolerátus ... *to endure, to sustain*

ullus, ulla, ullum (gen. sing. **ullíus, ullíus, ullíus**) ... *any;* (as substantive) *anyone, anything*

valetúdo, valetudinis, f. ... *health; illness, sickness*

vena, venae, f. ... *vein, artery;* (sometimes in plur.) *pulse*

verbum, verbi, n. ... (plur. may have sing. meaning) *word; talk, mere talk*

vigilo, vigiláre, vigilávi, vigilátus ... *to be awake, to stay awake*

*****vultus, vultus,** m. ... (plur. may have sing. meaning) *head, face; appearance*

Archistrates' Daughter Falls in Love with Apollonius.

Sed 'regína' sui 'iamdúdum saucia cura' Apollóni 'figit in

pectore vultus verbaque,' cantusque memor 'credit genus esse

deórum.' Nec somnum oculis 'nec membris dat cura quiétem.'

Vigilans primo mane irrumpit cubiculum patris. Pater videns

5   filiam ait: "Filia dulcis, quid est quod tam mane praeter

consuetudinem vigilasti?" Puella ait: "Hesterna studia me

excitavérunt. Peto itaque, pater, ut me tradas hospiti nostro

Apollonio studiórum percipiendórum gratia." Rex vero gaudio

plenus iussit ad se iuvenem vocári. Cui sic ait: "Apollóni,

10 studiórum tuórum felicitátem filia mea a te discere concupívit.

Peto itaque ut desiderio natae meae parueris, et iuro tibi per

regni mei vires: quidquid tibi irátum abstulit mare, ego in terris

restituam." Apollonius hoc audíto docet puellam, sicuti et ipse

didicerat. Interposito brevi temporis spatio, cum non posset

15 puella ulla ratióne vulnus amóris toleráre, in multa infirmitáte

membra prostrávit fluxa, et coepit iacére imbecillis in thoro.

Rex ut vidit filiam suam subitaneam valetudinem incurrisse,

sollicitus adhibet medicos, qui temptantes venas tangunt

singulas corporis partes, nec omníno inveniunt aegritudinis

20 causas.

(1–3) '**regína . . . quiétem**': The phrases within the single quotation marks are adapted from Vergil's *Aeneid*, a Roman epic in which Dido, Queen of Carthage, falls in love with the Trojan hero Aeneas.

(1) **saucia cura:** These words are used in two different cases. Case and number of **saucia?** Case and number of **cura?**—**sui . . . Apollóni:** Although genitive, this phrase is best translated as dative.

(2) **cantusque:** To what song does this refer? (See above, Lesson 4, Section D, especially lines 1–5.)—**credit:** What construction does this verb introduce? What element of this construction is understood in this sentence? (See *ARA*, Lesson 55, Section G, note to lines 4–5.)

(5) **quid est quod:** Translate *why is it that . . .*

(6) **vigilasti:** What is the uncontracted form of this verb?

(7) **ut . . . tradas:** What construction?—**me:** The accusative singular of the personal pronoun **ego.** (See *ARA*, App. C, p. 408, for the declension of this pronoun.)

(8) **studiórum percipiendórum gratia:** Translate *for the purpose of learning his artistic skills.* (The ablative **gratia** is used with the genitive of the word or phrase that precedes it [see *ARA*, Lesson 68, Section F, note to line 9], in this instance the genitive of the gerundive construction **studiórum percipiendórum** [see *ARA*, App. K, p. 471].)

(9) **iussit:** Tense, voice, mood, person, and number?

(11) **parueris:** Here the perfect subjunctive is used instead of the present subjunctive, implying that Archistrates conceives of his command as fulfilled with his utterance.

(12) **vires:** Of what noun is this a form? (See *ARA*, Lesson 50, Section E, note to line 3.)—**tibi:** What kind of dative?—**abstulit:** Translate *took away.*—**ego:** The first person singular pronoun. (See *ARA*, App. C, p. 408, for the declension of this pronoun.)

(13) **restituam:** Translate *will restore.*—**hoc audíto:** What construction?

(14) **didicerat:** Tense, voice, mood, person, and number?—**Interposito . . . spatio:** What construction?—**posset:** Translate *was able.*

(17) **filiam . . . incurrisse:** What construction?

LESSON 7

REVIEW: THIRD DECLENSION NOUNS. AP. TYRE: APOLLONIUS'S DAUGHTER IS SOLD AT A PUBLIC AUCTION.

§A **Review.** Review (13) **pater,** the model for third declension masculine and feminine nouns, and (14) **caput,** the model for third declension neuter nouns (*ARA*, App. A, p. 377). Review also third declension Greek names (*ARA*, Lesson 38, Section A) and i-stem nouns (*ARA*, Lesson 40, Section A), for which **pater** and **caput** serve as the models.

§B **Exercise.**

I. How do you know if a noun has **pater** as its model? How do you know if a noun has **caput** as its model?

II. Write out the declensions of **miles** and **pectus.** What Greek endings does the declension of **Minos** retain?

III. Identify the case and number of the following nouns and translate:

    (1) **arbori**   (4) **tempore**

    (2) **corpora**   (5) **hostium**

    (3) **matres**   (6) **Pythóna**

§C **Vocabulary.**

*amplus, ampla, amplum ... *large; a lot, much;* **amplius** (neut. compar.) *more, any more, for more* than

Athenagora, Athenagorae, m. ... *Athenagora,* prince of Mytilene

*civitas, civitátis, f. (gen. plur. **civitátum** or **civitatium**) ... *state; city, town*

decem (indecl.) ... *ten*

*****emo, emere, emi, emptus** ... *to buy, to purchase*

forum, fori, n. ... *forum* (= public square or market place)

infaustus, infausta, infaustum ... *unlucky; hateful, sinister*

intro, intráre, intrávi, intrátus ... *to enter, to go in*

*****leno, lenónis,** m. ... *procurer, brothel-keeper*

mancipium, mancipii, n. ... *property; slave, chattel*

Mytiléna, Mytilénae, f. ... the city *Mytilene*

nobilis, nobile ... *noble, well-born*

nodus, nodi, m. ... *knot, bond*

pretium, pretii, n. ... *price*

*****princeps, principis,** m. ... *first man; chief, prince;* (of the ruler of the Roman Empire) *emperor*

*****prior, prius** ... (compar. adj.: see *ARA,* App. D, p. 419) *first, former, earlier;* **prius:** (adv.) *first, in advance, beforehand*

propóno, proponere, proposui, propositus ... *to put out, to display; to hold out, to propose*

prostibulum, prostibuli, n. ... *brothel, house of prostitution*

sestertium, sestertii, n. ... *sesterce* (= unit of money)

supra ... (adv.) *more, in addition*

Tharsia, Tharsiae, f. ... *Tharsia,* daughter of Apollonius

venális, venále ... *on sale, for sale*

venditor, venditóris, m. ... *seller, vendor*

vilis, vile ... *cheap*

*****virginitas, virginitátis,** f. ... *virginity*

Reading.

Apollonius's Daughter Is Sold at a Public Auction.

Lessons 7–12 contain the section of *Apollonius of Tyre* set in Mytilene (a city on the island of Lesbos), where Apollonius's daughter Tharsia has been taken against her will. Having been kidnapped by pirates, Tharsia (only fourteen years old at this point in the story) is put up for sale with slaves at a public auction, to be sold to the highest bidder.

Igitur qui Tharsiam rapuérunt, advenérunt in civitátem

Mytilénam. Deponiturque inter cetera mancipia, et venális in

foro proponitur. Audiens autem hoc, leno vir infaustissimus nec

virum nec mulierem voluit emere nisi Tharsiam puellam, et

5   coepit contendere ut eam emeret. Sed Athenagora nomine,

princeps eiusdem civitátis, intellegens nobilem et sapientem et

pulcherrimam virginem ad venalia positam, obtulit decem

sestertia auri. Sed leno XX dare voluit. Athenagora obtulit

XXX, leno XL, Athenagora L, leno LX, Athenagora LXX, leno

10   LXXX, Athenagora LXXXX, leno in praesenti dat C sestertia

auri et dicit: "Si quis amplius dederit, X dabo supra."

Athenagora ait: "Ego si cum hoc lenóne contendere voluero ut

unam emam, plurium venditor sum. Sed permittam eum

emere, et cum ille eam in prostibulo posuerit, intrábo prior ad

15   eam, et eripiam nodum virginitátis eius vili pretio, et erit mihi

ac si eam emerim."

§E   **Notes and Queries.**

(1) **qui:** What should be supplied as the antecedent?—**civitátem:** Case and number? Why is this case used here?

(2) **Mytilénam:** The chief city of Lesbos (the largest of the Greek is-lands off the coast of Turkey), which became a favorite holiday resort with the Romans.—**Deponiturque:** The equivalent of **Et deponitur.** What is the subject of this verb?

(3) **foro:** Refers to the public square in the center of a city or town, which in classical antiquity normally served as a location where peo-ple assembled for political, economic, and social functions, among them, the buying and selling of goods and wares, including slaves.—**infaustissimus:** Degree of adjective?

(4) **voluit:** Translate *wished.*

(5) **ut . . . emeret:** Here the subjunctive clause is used as the object of **contendere.**—**Athenagora nomine:** With this phrase supply *a certain man* or *a certain person.*

(6) **eiusdem:** Of what pronoun is this a form?—**intellegens:** Tense, voice, and mood? Subject of the verbal action? What construction does this word introduce? What are the elements of this construction in this sentence?

(7) **venalia:** Translate *things for sale.* What use of the adjective?—**positam:** The equivalent of **positam esse.**—**obtulit:** Translate *offered.*

(8–11) **XX . . . X:** See above, Lesson 5, Section G, note to line 3. (By pil-ing up the numbers in such rapid succession, the author presents his readers with a glimpse at the kind of auction that took place in his own day and that may be compared with the kind that still takes place today, with the merchandise always sold to the highest bidder.)

(10) **dat:** Tense, voice, mood, person, and number?

(11) **dederit:** The future perfect indicative of a first conjugation verb (see *ARA,* Lesson 35, Section A).—**dabo:** Tense, voice, mood, person, and number? (See above, Lesson 2, Section E, note to line 14.)

(12) **lenóne:** Case and number? Why is this case used here?—**voluero:** Translate *wish.*

(13) **unam:** What noun should be supplied after this adjective?—**plu-rium venditor sum:** Translate *I will have to sell more.* What is the lit-eral meaning of these words? (Here Athenagora implies that if he tries to outbid the brothel-keeper in order to buy Tharsia, he will have to sell several other slaves in order to make up the financial losses thus incurred.)—**permittam:** Translate *I will allow.*

(14) **posuerit, intrábo:** See above, note to line 11.

(15) **eripiam:** Translate *I will loosen.*—**pretio:** The ablative may be used to designate the price for which something is bought or sold.—**erit:** Translate *it will be.*

(16) **ac si . . . emerim:** Here **ac si** (the equivalent of the conjunction **tamquam**) is used with the perfect active subjunctive **emerim** to indicate an unreal circumstance, providing the ground on which the action of the main clause is based. (Here Athenagora implies that he will get off far more cheaply by simply depriving Tharsia of her virginity in the brothel than he would have had he decided to outbid the brothel-keeper and actually purchase the woman.)

LESSON 8

REVIEW: THIRD DECLENSION ADJECTIVES. PRESENT AND IMPERFECT PASSIVE INDICATIVE. AP. TYRE: APOLLONIUS'S DAUGHTER IS TAKEN TO THE BROTHEL-KEEPER.

§A   **Review.** Review (15) **omnis,** the model for third declension adjectives (*ARA,* App. A, p. 377), (16) **amor,** the model for the present passive indicative (*ARA,* App. A, p. 378), and (17) **amábar,** the model for the imperfect passive indicative (*ARA,* App. A, p. 378).

§B   **Exercise.**

I. How do you know if an adjective has **omnis** as its model? What verb elements does **amor** contain? What verb elements does **amábar** contain?

II. Identify the case, number, and gender of the following adjectives:

(1) **talia**		(4) **fortes**	
(2) **tanto**		(5) **facilium**	
(3) **gravi**		(6) **liberálem**	

III. Identify the tense, voice, mood, person, and number of the following verbs and translate:

(1) **lugétur**		(4) **putábas**	
(2) **occidébar**		(5) **liberantur**	
(3) **tingimur**		(6) **tollebamini**	

§C   **Vocabulary.**

addíco, addicere, addixi, addictus ... *to give over; to sell, to assign*

adóro, adoráre, adorávi, adorátus ... *to beg, to entreat; to worship, to pay homage to*

*oro, oráre, orávi, orátus ... *to beg, to entreat, to implore; to pray to* someone (acc.) for something (acc.)

allevo, alleváre, allevávi, allevátus ... *to lift up;* (used with the reflexive **se,** which is not translated in this idiom) *to arise, to get up*

avárus, avára, avárum ... *greedy*

cella, cellae, f. ... *room, chamber*

contremesco, contremescere, contremui ... *to tremble, to tremble with fear*

corpusculum, corpusculi, n. ... *small body*

diligens, diligentis ... *careful;* **diligenter:** *carefully*

dimidius, dimidia, dimidium ... *half*

*dominus, domini, m. ... *lord* or *master* of a household

gemma, gemmae, f. ... *jewel*

ignóro, ignoráre, ignorávi, ignorátus ... *to not know, to not recognize*

introdúco, introducere, introduxi, introductus ... *to lead in, to bring in*

Lampsacénus, Lampsacéna, Lampsacénum ... *of Lampsacus* or *from Lampsacus*

libra, librae, f. ... *pound* (= unit of weight)

mei ... (gen. sing. of **ego**) *of me*

misereor, miseréri, miseritus or **misertus sum** ... *to have pity, to show compassion; to have pity for, to show compassion for* (+ gen. or dat.)

numen, numinis, n. ... (plur. may have sing. meaning) *majesty, divinity, divine power*

numquid ... (interrogative adverb introducing a question that expects a negative answer) *surely it cannot be that . . .* or *it is not possible, is it, that . . .*

orno, ornáre, ornávi, ornátus ... *to furnish, to decorate*

*__populus, populi,__ m. ... *people;* (in plur.) *peoples, nations*

prex, precis, f. ... *prayer, entreaty*

Priápus, Priápi, m. ... *Priapus*

*__quis, quid__ (gen. sing. **cuius, cuius**) ... (interrogative pronoun) *who? which? what?;* **quid:** (interrogative adverb) *why?*

recondo, recondere, recóndidi, reconditus ... *to put away; to set, to cover; to close* the eyes *again*

salutatorium, salutatorii, n. ... *reception-room*

succurro, succurrere, succurri ... *to run under; to help save* or *preserve* (+ dat.); *to come to* or *occur in* one's *mind*

titulus, tituli, m. ... *sign, placard*

tortor, tortóris, m. ... *tormentor, torturer*

*__turpis, turpe__ ... *foul, horrible, shameful*

*__valeo, valére, valui__ ... *to be well; to have strength* or *influence;* **vale:** (imperative sing.) *goodbye! farewell!*

*__villicus, villici,__ m. ... *overseer, supervisor*

§D   Reading.

Apollonius's Daughter Is Taken to the Brothel-Keeper.

Quid plura? Addicitur virgo lenóni, a quo introducitur in

salutatorio, ubi habébat Priápum aureum gemmis et auro

reconditum, et ait ad eam: "Adóra numen praesentissimum

meum!" Puella ait: "Numquid Lampsacénus es?" Leno ait:

5   "Ignóras, misera, quia in domum avári lenónis incurristi?"

Puella vero, ut haec audívit, toto corpore contremuit et

prosternens se pedibus eius dixit: "Miserére mei, domine, succurre virginitáti meae! Et rogo te, ne velis hoc corpusculum sub tam turpi prostibulo constituere." Cui leno ait: "Alleva te,

10   misera! Tu autem nescis quia apud lenónem et tortórem nec preces nec lacrimae valent." Et vocávit ad se villicum puellárum et ait ad eum: "Cella ornétur diligenter; in qua scribátur titulus: QUI THARSIAM VIRGINEM VIOLARE VOLUERIT, DIMIDIAM AURI LIBRAM DABIT; POSTEA

15   VERO SINGULOS AUREOS POPULO PATEFIT." Fecit villicus quod iusserat ei dominus suus leno.

§E   **Notes and Queries.**

(1) **Quid:** The interrogative adverb, after which the word *say* should be supplied.—**Addicitur:** Tense, voice, mood, person, and number?

(2) **salutatorio:** Located in the house of the brothel-keeper, not in the actual brothel.—**habébat:** What is the subject of this verb? Tense, voice, mood, person, and number?—**Priápum:** Refers to a statue of Priapus, an ancient god of fertility, frequently depicted with a huge phallus, and famous (or infamous) for his clumsy and unsuccessful attempts to ravish two goddesses in the moonlight (Lotis, during a festival of Bacchus, and Vesta, during a celebration of Cybele).

(3) **reconditum:** Tense, voice, and mood? Subject of the verbal action?—**Adóra:** Tense, voice, mood, person, and number?

(4) **Lampsacénus:** Lampsacus was a Greek city on the Hellespont (the present-day Dardanelles), famous for its uninhibited cult of Priapus.

(5) **misera:** What use of the adjective? (See above, Lesson 5, Section G, note to line 9, for the same use of this adjective in another case.)—**incurristi:** An example of the present perfect (in contrast to the aoristic perfect), used to express the action of the verb as completed in present time (see above, Lesson 3, Section E, note to line 7).

(6) **contremuit:** Tense, voice, mood, person, and number?

(7) **prosternens:** Tense, voice, and mood? Subject of the verbal action?—**pedibus:** The equivalent of **ad pedes.**—**Miserére:** The present imperative second person singular of a deponent verb ends in **-re.**—**mei:** This form of the pronoun loses its genitive meaning when it follows the imperative **Miserére.**—**domine:** Case and number? Function of this case?

(8) **velis:** Translate *you wish.*—**corpusculum:** What kind of noun as shown by the suffix? (See *ARA,* Lesson 15, Section D.)

(9) **sub:** Here the preposition may be translated as *under the power of* or *under the control of.*—**turpi:** Modifies what noun? Case, number, and gender?—**te:** The second person reflexive pronoun, identical in form to the second person singular pronoun (see *ARA,* App. C, p. 408, for the declension of the reflexive).

(12–13) **ornétur . . . scribátur:** What use of the subjunctive? (See *ARA,* Lesson 62, Section A.)

(13) **QUI:** Here the relative may be translated as *he who* or *whoever.*

(14) **VOLUERIT:** Translate *wishes.*—**DABIT:** See above, Lesson 7, Section E, note to line 11.—**DIMIDIAM AURI LIBRAM:** A high price for the first customer because of the great value placed on virginity.

(15) **AUREOS:** Here the adjective is used as a substantive meaning *gold coins* and is found in the accusative instead of the ablative to designate price (compare above, Lesson 7, Section E, note to line 15).—**PATEFIT:** Translate *she is available.*

(16) **iusserat:** Tense, voice, mood, person, and number? (Here the verb takes its direct object in the dative rather than the accusative.)

LESSON 9

REVIEW: FOURTH DECLENSION NOUNS. PERFECT AND
PLUPERFECT PASSIVE INDICATIVE. AP. TYRE:
APOLLONIUS'S DAUGHTER IS VISITED BY PRINCE
ATHENAGORA.

§A   **Review.** Review (18) **manus,** the model for fourth declension nouns (*ARA,* App. A, p. 378), (19) **amátus sum,** the model for the perfect passive indicative (*ARA,* App. A, p. 379), and (20) **amátus eram,** the model for the pluperfect passive indicative (*ARA,* App. A, p. 379).

§B   **Exercise.**

I. How do you know if a noun has **manus** as its model? What forms of **amo** and **sum** does **amátus sum** consist of? What forms of **amo** and **sum** does **amátus eram** consist of?

II. Identify the case and number of the following nouns and translate:

(1) **casus**		(4) **cornua**	
(2) **vultum**		(5) **domibus**	
(3) **cantuum**		(6) **exercitui**	

III. Identify the tense, voice, mood, person, and number of the following verbs and translate:

(1) **missum est**		(4) **serváta sum**	
(2) **mutátus eras**		(5) **cognovistis**	
(3) **positae erámus**		(6) **intellecti erant**	

§C   Vocabulary.

antecédo, antecedere, antecessi ... *to go before; to precede, to lead the way*

confundo, confundere, confúdi, confúsus ... *to pour together; to confuse, to disturb, to embarrass*

considero, consideráre, considerávi, considerátus ... *to examine, to consider*

contineo, continére, continui, contentus ... *to hold together; to control, to restrain*

deprecor, deprecári, deprecátus sum ... *to entreat, to implore*

*duco, ducere, duxi, ductus ... *to lead; to lead into marriage; to induce, to influence; to think, to regard, to consider; to acquire, to develop, to receive*

*ecce ... (interjection) *see! look! behold!*

erigo, erigere, erexi, erectus ... *to lift up; to open* one's eyes; (with the reflexive **se,** which is not translated in this idiom) *to arise, to get up*

expostulo, expostuláre, expostulávi, expostulátus ... *to demand*

fortúna, fortúnae, f. ... *fortune;* (as proper noun) **Fortúna:** *Fortune*

impudícus, impudíca, impudícum ... *brazen, shameless; impure, unchaste, unfaithful*

infelicitas, infelicitátis, f. ... *unhappiness; deplorable condition, unfortunate situation*

iuventus, iuventútis, f. ... *youth,* the *youth*

*libído, libidinis, f. ... (plur. may have sing. meaning) *pleasure; lust, passion*

lupánar, lupanáris, n. ... *brothel, house of prostitution*

*maximus, maxima, maximum ... (superl. of **magnus;** see *ARA*, App. D, p. 419) *greatest, very great; very brave, very heroic;* **maxime:** *very greatly, most of all*

metuo, metuere, metui ... *to fear, to be afraid of*

obstipesco, obstipescere, obstipui ... *to be dazed, to be astonished, to be dumbfounded*

origo, originis, f. ... *origin, source*

*****pietas, pietátis,** f. ... *piety; duty, devotion; respect, sympathy*

procido, procidere, procidi ... *to fall down, to fall forward*

profundo, profundere, profúdi, profúsus ... *to pour forth; to shed tears*

*****quam** ... (conj.) *as;* (after compar. word) *than, rather than*

quousque ... *until*

*****similis, simile** ... *similar, similar* to (+ dat.); **similiter:** *similarly, in a similar manner*

stemma, stemmátis, n. ... (plur. may have sing. meaning) *descent, lineage, pedigree*

symphoniacus, symphoniaca, symphoniacum ... *singing* or *playing in a band;* (masc. as substantive) *singer, musician*

tertius, tertia, tertium ... *third*

turba, turbae, f. ... *tumult; crowd, crowd of people*

vehemens, vehementis ... *violent, vehement;* **vehementer:** *exceedingly, tremendously*

vel ... *or; even, at least;* **vel . . , vel . . ,** *either . . , or . .*

velo, veláre, velávi, velátus ... *to cover, to clothe*

§D   Reading.

Apollonius's Daughter Is Visited by Prince Athenagora.

Tertia die, antecedente turba, cum symphoniacis ducitur ad

lupánar. Sed Athenagora princeps affuit prior, et veláto capite

ingreditur ad lupánar. Sed dum fuisset ingressus, sedit. Et

advénit Tharsia et procidit ad pedes eius et ait: "Miserére mei!

5 Per iuventútem tuam, te deprecor, ne velis me violáre sub tam

turpi titulo. Contine impudícam libidinem, et audi casus

infelicitátis meae, vel originem stemmátum considera!" Cui

cum universos casus suos exposuisset, princeps confúsus est, et

pietáte ductus, vehementer obstipuit et ait ad eam: "Erige te!

10 Scimus fortúnae casus; homines sumus. Habeo et ego filiam

virginem, ex qua similem possum casum metuere." Haec

dicens, protulit XL aureos et dedit in manu virginis et dicit ei:

"Domina Tharsia, ecce habes plus quam virginitas tua

expostulat. Advenientibus age similiter quousque liberaberis!"

15 Puella vero profúsis lacrimis ait: "Ago pietáti tuae maximas

gratias."

§E   Notes and Queries.

(1) **Tertia die:** That is, two days after Tharsia was sold to the brothel-keeper. What kind of ablative is **die?** (See *ARA*, Lesson 49, Section H, note to line 2).—**antecedente turba:** What construction?—**sympho-niacis:** What use of the adjective?—**ducitur:** What is the subject of this verb? Tense, voice, mood, person, and number?

(2) **affuit:** Translate *arrived.*

(3) **dum:** See above, Lesson 1, Section F, note to line 1.—**fuisset in-gressus:** Translate *he had entered.*

(4) **Miserére mei:** See above, Lesson 8, Section E, note to line 7.

(5) **Per iuventútem tuam:** One normally entreats a person by something precious to that person, as here, where Tharsia entreats Athenagora by his youth.—**velis:** Translate *you wish.*

(6) **Contine:** Tense, voice, mood, person, and number?

(7) **vel:** Here the equivalent of **et.—stemmátum:** That is, **stemmátum meórum.**

(8) **cum . . . exposuisset:** What construction? Explain the use of the mood (see *ARA,* Lesson 69, Section D).—**confúsus est:** Tense, voice, mood, person, number?

(9) **ductus:** Tense, voice, and mood? Subject of the verbal action?—**obstipuit:** Tense, voice, mood, person, and number?—**te:** See above, Lesson 8, Section E, note to line 9.

(10) **Scimus . . . sumus:** Here the first person plural is used instead of the first person singular, since Athenagora is speaking not only for himself but for the other customers entering the brothel.

(10–11) **filiam virginem:** Although Athenagora is depicted as being unmarried at this point in time, this single reference makes clear that he had been married sometime earlier.

(11) **possum:** Translate *I am able.*

(12) **dicens:** Tense, voice, and mood? Subject of the verbal action?—**protulit:** Translate *he held out.*—**XL aureos:** See above, Lesson 5, Section G, note to line 3, and Lesson 8, Section E, note to line 15.

(13) **Domina:** Case and number? Function of this case?

(14) **Advenientibus:** Here the present participle (in the dative) is used as a substantive referring to the other customers. Supply an appropriate pronoun to indicate the subject of the verbal action (see above, Lesson 4, Section E, note to line 2).—**quousque liberaberis:** At this point Athenagora implies that by telling her story to her customers, Tharsia may be able to save enough money to buy her freedom from the brothel-keeper. (Although **liberaberis** is best translated as *you are freed,* it actually means *you will be freed,* since it is the future passive indicative of a first conjugation verb.)

(15) **profúsis lacrimis:** What construction?

LESSON 10

REVIEW: FIFTH DECLENSION NOUNS. PRESENT ACTIVE SUBJUNCTIVE. AP. TYRE: APOLLONIUS'S DAUGHTER IS VISITED BY ATHENAGORA'S COLLEAGUE.

§A   **Review.** Review (21) **res,** the model for fifth declension nouns (*ARA,* App. A, p. 379). Review also (22) **amem,** (23) **moneam,** (24) **traham,** and (25) **audiam**—the models for the present active subjunctive (*ARA,* App. A, p. 380).

§B   **Exercise.**

I. How do you know if a noun has **res** as its model? How do you know for each conjugation if a verb is in the present active subjunctive?

II. Identify the case and number of the following nouns and translate:

(1) **diem**	(4) **fidei**
(2) **ventis**	(5) **vultus**
(3) **patriae**	(6) **coniuges**

III. Identify the tense, voice, mood, person, and number of the following verbs:

(1) **narres**	(4) **violátis**
(2) **petámus**	(5) **torqueat**
(3) **relinquam**	(6) **inveniant**

§C   **Vocabulary.**

averto, avertere, averti, aversus ... *to turn away; to turn away* someone (acc.) *from* something (abl.)

*verto, vertere, verti, versus ... *to turn; to change, to reverse; to turn over* or *around* or *upside-down*

*claudo, claudere, clausi, clausus ... *to shut, to close, to block*

colléga, collégae, m. ... *colleague, associate*

deni, denae, dena ... (plur. adj. with plur. meaning) *ten each, ten together*

dives, divitis ... *rich, wealthy*

*exitus, exitus, m. ... (plur. may have sing. meaning) *exit, way out; fate, death, outcome*

*foris, foris, f. (gen. plur. **forium**) ... *door;* **foras** or **foris:** (adv.) *outside, out of doors*

indico, indicáre, indicávi, indicátus ... *to show, to reveal, to disclose*

insidior, insidiári, insidiátus sum ... *to lie in wait, to wait and watch*

integer, integra, integrum ... *whole, intact, untouched*

*modo ... *just, only; just now, recently;* **modo . . , modo . . ,** *now . . , now . . ;* **non modo . . , sed (etiam) . . ,** *not only . . , but (also) . .*

mos, moris, m. ... *way, custom, manner*

nos ... (nom. or acc. plur. of **ego**) *we* or *us*

novicius, novicia, novicium ... *new, newly purchased;* (fem. sing. as substantive) *new girl*

ostium, ostii, n. ... *door*

ploro, ploráre, plorávi ... *to weep; to lament*

*quantus, quanta, quantum ... *how great, how much, of what size;* **quanto . . , tanto . . ,** *by how much . . , by so much . .*

quater (indecl.) ... *four times*

solitus, solita, solitum ... *usual, normal, customary*

*sto, stare, steti ... *to stand*

subiaceo, subiacére, subiacui ... *to lie below* or *at the foot of; to lie exposed to, to be subject to* (+ dat.)

subsequor, subsequi, subsecútus sum ... *to follow closely, to follow secretly*

usque ... *all the way, continuously*

§D   Reading.

Apollonius's Daughter Is Visited by Athenagora's Colleague.

Quo exeunte, colléga suus affuit et ait: "Athenagora, quomodo tecum novicia?" Athenagora ait: "Non potest melius; usque ad lacrimas!" Et haec dicens, eum subsecútus est. Quo introeunte, insidiabátur exitus rerum vidére. Ingresso itaque illo,

5   Athenagora foris stabat. Solito more puella claudit ostium. Cui iuvenis ait: "Si salva sis, indica mihi, quantum dedit ad te iuvenis, qui ad te modo introívit?" Puella ait: "Quater denos mihi aureos dedit." Iuvenis ait: "Malum illi sit! Quid magnum illi fuisset, homini tam diviti, si libram auri tibi daret

10   integram? Ut ergo scias me esse meliórem, tolle libram auri integram!" Athenagora vero de foris stans dicébat: "Quantum plus dabis, plus plorábis!" Puella autem prostrávit se ad eius pedes et similiter casus suos exposuit. Confúdit hominem et avertit a libidine. Et ait iuvenis ad eam: "Alleva te, domina! Et

15   nos homines sumus, casibus subiacentes." Puella ait: "Ago pietáti tuae maximas gratias."

(1) **Quo exeunte:** An ablative absolute meaning *as he was going out.*—**affuit:** Translate *was there.*

(1–2) **quomodo . . . novicia:** Sometimes the verb *to be* (when used as a main verb) does not appear in the sentence, as here, where the form **erat** does not appear and should be supplied from the overall context.

(2) **tecum:** What two elements does this word consist of?—**Non potest:** See above, Lesson 4, Section E, note to line 6.

(2–3) **usque ad lacrimas:** Although Tharsia actually shed the tears in question out of gratitude for Athenagora's kindness and compassion (see above, Lesson 9, Section D, lines 15–16), Athenagora here misleads his companion through this elliptical expression, by implying that he himself shed tears of joy as the result of the sexual encounter.

(3) **subsecútus est:** Tense, voice, mood, person, and number? Why are the principal parts given in the passive?—**Quo introeunte:** An ablative absolute meaning *as he was going in.*

(4) **insidiabátur:** Tense, voice, mood, person, and number?—**vidére:** In *Apollonius of Tyre,* purpose may be expressed by the infinitive, although it is normally expressed by **ut** (or **ne**) and the subjunctive.—**Ingresso . . . illo:** What construction?

(6) **Si salve sis:** Although the Latin idiom is *if you would be well,* how would you express it in normal English? (See above, Lesson 3, Section E, note to line 2, for the comparable Latin idiom **salvum habeas.**)—**indica:** Tense, voice, mood, person, and number?—**ad te:** Here the equivalent of **tibi.**

(6–7) **iuvenis . . . iuvenis:** To whom does the first **iuvenis** refer? To whom does the second **iuvenis** refer?

(7) **introívit:** Translate *went in.*

(7–8) **Quater denos . . . aureos:** Here **Quater** and **denos** combine to form a single numeral that goes with **aureos.** (See above, Lesson 8, Section E, note to line 15, on the use of the adjective **aureos.**)

(8) **Malum illi sit:** Although the Latin idiom is *let it be bad for him,* how would you express it in normal English?

(9) **fuisset:** Translate *would it have been.*—**si . . . daret:** A conditional clause in which the imperfect subjunctive should be translated according to sense.

(10) **Ut . . . scias:** What construction? Tense, voice, mood, person, and number of **scias?** What construction does **scias** itself introduce? What are the elements of this construction in this sentence?—**tolle:** Tense, voice, mood, person, and number?

(11) **de foris:** The equivalent of the adverbial form included in the vocabulary entry for **foris.**

(11–12) **Quantum . . . plorábis:** Here Athenagora continues to mislead his companion through a double-entendre, by implying that he will weep with joy as the result of the sexual exerience (something that his companion understands), while also implying that he will lament over losing a great deal of money without receiving sexual gratification (something that his companion will understand later).

(14) **avertit:** What is the subject of this verb? What should be supplied as the direct object?—**te:** See above, Lesson 8, Section E, note to line 9.

(15) **nos . . . sumus:** See above, Lesson 9, Section E, note to line 10.— **subiacentes:** Tense, voice, and mood? Subject of the verbal action?

LESSON 11

REVIEW: IMPERFECT, PERFECT, AND PLUPERFECT ACTIVE SUBJUNCTIVE. AP. TYRE: APOLLONIUS'S DAUGHTER REPORTS TO THE BROTHEL-KEEPER.

§A   **Review.** Review (26) **amárem,** (27) **amaverim,** and (28) **amavissem**—the models for the imperfect, perfect, and pluperfect active subjunctive respectively (*ARA,* App. A, p. 380).

§B   **Exercise.**

I. What verb elements does **amárem** contain? What verb elements does **amaverim** contain? What verb elements does **amavissem** contain?

II. Identify the tense, voice, mood, person, and number of the following verbs:

    (1) **aestimáres**　　　　(4) **tradidissem**

    (2) **navigavisset**　　　　(5) **vivebámus**

    (3) **descenderint**　　　　(6) **regnaveritis**

III. Translate the following sentences into English; then identify the subjunctive construction in each sentence:

    (1) **Athenagora collégae dixit: "Ducat te usque ad lacrimas."**

    (2) **Athenagora apud ostium stabat ut exitus rerum vidéret.**

    (3) **Tharsia ita plorábat ut hominem a libidine vero averteret.**

§C   **Vocabulary.**

adiúro, adiuráre, adiurávi, adiurátus ... *to swear to, to pledge to*

*alter, altera, alterum (gen. sing. **alteríus, alteríus, alteríus**) *the other, another; the second, the next (best);* **alter . . , alter . . ,** *the one . . , the other . .*

aspectus, aspectus, m. ... *look, sight; watching-place, vantage-point*

colligo, colligere, collégi, collectus ... *to pick up, to gather together; to infer, to deduce, to conclude*

cotidie ... *daily, every day*

custodio, custodíre, custodívi, custodítus ... *to guard; to keep, to save*

eo ... (adv.) *there, to that place, for that reason*

*ergo ... *therefore*

*eripio, eripere, eripui, ereptus ... *to snatch from* (+ dat.); *to untie* or *loosen* a knot; *to rescue* someone (acc.) *from* something (dat.); *to take away* something (acc.) *from* someone (dat.)

*exspecto, exspectáre, exspectávi, exspectátus ... *to await, to wait for; to wait in expectation; to delay, to waste time*

hilaris, hilare ... *cheerful*

invicem ... *in turn, each in turn*

*latus, lata, latum ... *wide, broad;* **late:** *widely, over a large area*

occultus, occulta, occultum ... *hidden, secret;* **in occulto:** *in hiding, in a secret place*

*pecunia, pecuniae, f. ... (plur. may have sing. meaning) *money*

prodo, prodere, prodidi, proditus ... *to put forth, to bring forth; to betray* someone (acc.) *to* someone (dat.)

propíno, propináre, propinávi, propinátus ... *to drink* a toast; *to pass along, to make a present of*

*quicumque, quaecumque, quodcumque ... (indefinite relative pronoun; formed from **qui, quae, quod** and the suffix **-cumque**) *whoever, whatever*

rideo, ridére, risi, risus ... *to laugh, to laugh at*

§D   **Reading.**

Apollonius's Daughter Reports to the Brothel-Keeper.

Et exiens foris invénit Athenagoram ridentem et ait: "Magnus
homo es! Non habuisti cui lacrimas tuas propináres?" Et
adiurantes se invicem ne alicui proderent, aliórum coepérunt
exspectáre exitum. Quid plura? Illis exspectantibus per
5   occultum aspectum, omnes quicumque iníbant, dantes singulos
aureos, plorantes abscedébant. Facto autem huius rei fine,
obtulit puella pecuniam lenóni dicens: "Ecce pretium virginitátis
meae!" Et ait ad eam leno: "Quantum melius est hilarem te
esse et non lugentem! Sic ergo age ut cotidie mihi latióres
10   pecunias adferas." Item ait ad eum altera die: "Ecce pretium
virginitátis meae, quod similiter precibus et lacrimis collégi, et
custodio virginitátem meam." Hoc audíto, irátus est leno eo,
quod virginitátem suam serváret, et vocat ad se villicum
puellárum et ait ad eum: "Sic te tam neglegentem esse video ut
15   nescias Tharsiam virginem esse. Si enim virgo tantum adfert,
quantum mulier? Duc eam ad te, et tu eripe nodum virginitátis
eius!"

§E   **Notes and Queries.**

(1) **exiens:** Translate *going out.*—**ridentem:** Tense, voice, and mood?
Subject of the verbal action?

(1–2) **Magnus homo es:** A remark uttered somewhat sarcastically,
since Athenagora's colleague really means just the opposite.

(2) **cui:** Supply *anyone else* or *any other person* as the antecedent.—**lacrimas . . . propináres:** Tense, voice, mood, person, and number of **propináres?** (The verb shows an unreal supposition on the part of the speaker and should be translated according to the overall sense.) Here Athenagora's colleague lets on by means of a double-entendre that he knows that Athenagora tricked him, by implying that Athenagora presented him with his own (misleading) version of the tears as tears of joy, while also implying that Athenagora passed along the tears as tears of sorrow over losing a great deal of money.

(3) **proderent:** What should be supplied as the direct object of this verb?—**alicui:** Here translate the indefinite pronoun as *anyone else* or *any other person.*—**coepérunt:** Translate *they began.*

(4) **Quid:** See above, Lesson 8, Section E, note to line 1.—**Illis exspectantibus:** What construction?

(5) **iníbant:** Translate *went in.*

(6) **aureos:** See above, Lesson 8, Section E, note to line 15.—**plorantes abscedébant:** Here, as they leave her room—one man after another—Tharsia's customers are depicted not as weeping with joy but as lamenting (as Athenagora and his colleague may also have lamented) not simply over losing their money but upon hearing about Tharsia's predicament—her imprisonment by the brothel-keeper.—**Facto . . . fine:** What construction? Of what verb is **Facto** a form? Tense, voice, and mood of **Facto?**

(7) **obtulit:** Translate *presented.*

(8) **melius est:** What construction do these words introduce? What are the elements of this construction in this sentence?

(9) **latióres:** Degree of comparison? Here **latióres** may simply mean *more* or *larger sums of.*

(10) **adferas:** Translate *you bring.* (Assume that this verb is in the subjunctive.)—**die:** What kind of ablative?

(12) **eo:** The adverb or the pronoun?

(13) **quod . . . serváret:** The subjunctive is found in clauses introduced by **quod, quia, quoniam** *(because)* when the reason is not that of the writer (see *ARA,* App. K, p. 474, Causal Clauses).

(14) **te . . . esse:** What construction?

(14–15) **ut nescias:** What construction?

(15) **adfert:** Translate *brings*. This verb (or a form of it) should be used first in the clause with **virgo,** then in the clause with **mulier.**

(15–16) **virgo . . . mulier:** That is, the brothel-keeper thinks that by depriving Tharsia of her virginity, he will be able to raise her value—for whatever reason—not specified in the text but subject to interpretation. Perhaps he believes that if she remains a virgin, only a few men will visit her to pay the higher price, and that if she becomes a woman, many more men will visit her to pay the cheaper price. In any case, the brothel-keeper is depicted as a shrewd businessman, who may believe (with respect to Tharsia) that he can make up in volume what he may lose by advertising her at the cheaper price.—**tantum . . . quantum:** Here translate *so much . . . how much.*

(16) **Duc:** The present active imperative second person singular of the verb **duco**—an example of a verb lacking the present active imperative ending in the singular.—**eripe:** Tense, voice, mood, person, and number?

LESSON 12

REVIEW: PASSIVE SUBJUNCTIVE. AP. TYRE: APOLLONIUS'S DAUGHTER ENTREATS THE BROTHEL-KEEPER'S OVERSEER. CLASSICAL TRADITION: SHAKESPEARE'S PERICLES, PRINCE OF TYRE.

§A   **Review.** Review (29) **amer,** (30) **amárer,** (31) **amátus sim,** and (32) **amátus essem**—the models for the present, imperfect, perfect, and pluperfect passive subjunctive respectively (*ARA,* App. A, p. 381).

§B   **Exercise.**

I. What verb elements does **amer** contain? What verb elements does **amárer** contain? What forms of **amo** and **sum** does **amátus sim** consist of? What forms of **amo** and **sum** does **amátus essem** consist of?

II. Identify the tense, voice, mood, person, and number of the following verbs:

    (1)   **accipiámur**   (4)   **cognoscerer**

    (2)   **ostentae sitis**   (5)   **reddita essent**

    (3)   **nominátus esses**   (6)   **simulátum erat**

III. Translate the following sentences into English; then identify the subjunctive construction in each sentence:

    (1)   **Cum homines ridentes intrárent, plorantes abscedébant.**

    (2)   **Leno puellam rogávit quis tantam pecuniam ei dedisset.**

    (3)   **Leno villicum rogávit ut nodum virginitátis eius eriperet.**

§C   **Vocabulary.**

acclamatio, acclamatiónis, f. ... *shout, shout of approval*

*adhuc ... *still*

amplio, ampliáre, ampliávi, ampliátus ... *to enlarge, to increase*

*ars, artis, f. (gen. plur. **artium**) ... *art, craft, skill*

commendo, commendáre, commendávi, commendátus ... *to commit, to entrust*

crastinus, crastina, crastinum ... *of tomorrow*

*dein or **deinde** ... *then, next; afterwards, henceforth*

erudio, erudíre, erudívi or **erudii, erudítus** ... *to educate, to instruct;* **erudítus, erudíta, erudítum:** *educated; learned, scholarly*

excrebresco, excrebrescere, excrebui ... *to grow thick; to spring forth*

facundia, facundiae, f. ... *eloquence*

frequens, frequentis ... *crowded, frequented; in a crowd, in large numbers; densely* or *thickly populated;* **frequenter:** *often, frequently*

illído, illidere, illísi, illísus ... *to drive into; to strike, to beat on* (+ dat.)

*liberális, liberále ... *kind, generous; (referring to studies, education, etc.) artistic, liberal, humane;* **liberaliter:** *kindly, generously*

*lyra, lyrae, f. ... *lyre*

memoro, memoráre, memorávi, memorátus ... *to speak, to mention, to call to mind;* **memorátus, memoráta, memorátum:** *famous for, celebrated for* (+ gen.)

modulátus, moduláta, modulátum ... *rhythmical, modulated;* **modulanter:** *rhythmically, melodiously*

nimis ... *too much; excessively, exceedingly*

pello, pellere, pepuli, pulsus ... *to drive; to strike, to beat upon*

perfectus, perfecta, perfectum ... *perfect, complete, flawless;* **perfecte:** *perfectly, completely, flawlessly*

permaneo, permanére, permansi ... *to stay, to remain*

*maneo, manére, mansi ... *to stay, to remain; to await, to be in store for*

praebeo, praebére, praebui, praebitus ... *to offer, to furnish, to provide*

quamdiu ... *as long as, for how long*

scamnum, scamni, n. ... *bench, stool*

spectaculum, spectaculi, n. ... (plur. may have sing. meaning) *show, sight, spectacle*

subvenio, subveníre, subvéni ... *to come under; to come to the aid* of, *to bring help* or *relief* to (+ dat.)

unicus, unica, unicum ... *only, sole; unique, special*

*****universus, universa, universum** ... *all, whole, entire*

§D   **Reading.**

Apollonius's Daughter Entreats the Brothel-Keeper's Overseer.

Statim eam villicus duxit in suum cubiculum et ait ad eam:

"Verum mihi dic, Tharsia, adhuc virgo es?" Tharsia puella ait:

"Quamdiu vult deus, virgo sum." Villicus ait: "Unde ergo his

duóbus diébus tantam pecuniam obtulisti?" Puella dixit:

5   "Lacrimis meis, expónens ad omnes universos casus meos; et

illi dolentes miserti sunt virginitáti meae." Et prostrávit se ad

pedes eius et ait: "Miserére mei, domine, subvéni captívae regis

filiae!" Cumque ei universos casus suos exposuisset, motus

misericordia ait ad eam: "Nimis avárus est iste leno; nescio si

10   tu possis virgo permanére." Puella respondit: "Habeo auxilium

studiórum liberalium; perfecte erudíta sum; similiter et lyrae

†pulsum modulanter illídor†. Iube crastina die in frequenti loco

poni scamna, et facundia sermónis mei spectaculum praebeo;

deinde plectro modulábor et hac arte ampliábo pecunias cotidie."

15 Quod cum fecisset villicus, tanta populi acclamatio tantusque

amor civitátis circa eam excrebuit, ut et viri et feminae cotidie

ei multa conferrent. Athenagora autem princeps memorátam

Tharsiam integrae virginitátis et generositátis ita iam

custodiébat ac si unicam suam filiam, ita ut villico multa

20 donáret et commendáret eam.

§E   Notes and Queries.

(2) **dic:** The present active imperative second person singular of the verb **dico** (see above, Lesson 11, Section E, note to line 16).

(3) **vult:** Translate *wishes.*—**deus:** See above, Lesson 5, Section G, note to line 19.

(4) **diébus:** What kind of ablative?—**tantam:** Adjust the meaning to fit the phrase **tantam pecuniam.**—**obtulisti:** Translate *did you obtain.*

(5) **expónens:** Tense, voice, and mood? Subject of the verbal action?

(6) **miserti sunt:** Tense, voice, mood, person, and number? Why are the principal parts given in the passive?

(7) **Miserére mei:** See above, Lesson 8, Section E, note to line 7.—**subvéni:** Tense, voice, mood, person, and number?

(8) **Cumque . . . exposuisset:** See above, Lesson 9, Section E, note to line 8.—**motus:** Tense, voice, and mood? Subject of the verbal action?

(10) **possis:** Translate *are able.*

(11) **erudíta sum:** Tense, voice, mood, person, and number?

(12) †**pulsum modulanter illídor**†: A corruption in the text (see *ARA,* Lesson 17, Section I, note to lines 1–2), since one cannot tell how the words in question function in relation to the rest of the sentence. Whatever the author wrote, he here presented Tharsia as testifying to her musical aptitude and very likely uttering the statement *I play the lyre with a rhythmical beat.*—**crastina die:** Although the Latin idiom is *on tomorrow's day,* how would you express it in normal English?

(13) **poni:** Tense, voice, and mood?—**praebeo:** Here the present active indicative refers to the future, where it has the meaning *I will provide* (compare the English expression *I am going to the market*).

(14) **modulábor:** The future indicative of a first conjugation deponent verb.—**ampliábo:** Tense, voice, mood, person, and number? (See above, Lesson 2, Section E, note to line 14).

(15) **cum fecisset:** What construction? Explain the use of the mood.

(16) **excrebuit:** Here the third person singular is used, since the two subjects taken together are understood as a single concept, in this case, general approval.

(17) **conferrent:** Translate *brought.*—**memorátam:** What noun does this adjective modify and what genitives does it also introduce? (Here translate this adjective after the noun it modifies and before the genitives it introduces.)

(18–19) **ita . . . ita:** The first **ita** goes with the idiom **ac si** (see above, Lesson 7, Section E, note to line 16). What construction does the second **ita** introduce in the words **ut . . . donáret . . . commendáret?**

§F **Classical Tradition.** This section, found at the end of every twelve lessons, considers the influence of the Latin author just completed on some famous writer of modern literature. The passages selected are intended to show students—especially those interested in English literature—how such a writer modeled his work on a classical source.

In general, the Greek and Roman classics exerted a strong influence on authors of later periods, who regarded these ancient literary texts as genuine sources of inspiration. The Roman classics in particular were quoted and adapted extensively for as long as Latin functioned as the international language of communication in western Europe.

Apollonius of Tyre became one of the most popular Latin works read during the Middle Ages and Renaissance, for which numerous Latin versions existed in various forms. This fascinating story was translated into many languages, and eventually into virtually every modern European language (including French, Spanish, and Italian).

Adaptations of this story strongly influenced Shakespeare's *Pericles, Prince of Tyre,* a play whose plot (for the most part) corresponds to the story line of the classical novel. In the following passage, a dialogue—which you should be able to recognize—takes place between Marina and Lysimachus (Shakespeare's Tharsia and Athenagora).

MARINA

If you were born to honor, show it now;
If put upon you, make the judgment good
That thought you worthy of it.

LYSIMACHUS

How's this? How's this? Some more; be sage.

MARINA   For me,

That am a maid, though most ungentle fortune
Have placed me in this sty, where, since I came,
Diseases have been sold dearer than physic—
That the gods
Would set me free from this unhallowed place,
Though they did change me to the meanest bird
That flies i' th' purer air!

LYSIMACHUS   I did not think

Thou couldst have spoke so well; ne'er dreamt thou couldst.
Had I brought hither a corrupted mind,
Thy speech had altered it. Hold, here's gold for thee:
Persever in that clear way thou goest,
And the gods strengthen thee!

MARINA   The good gods preserve you!

LYSIMACHUS

For me, be you thoughten
That I came with no ill intent; for to me
The very doors and windows savor vilely.
Fare thee well. Thou art a piece of virtue, and
I doubt not but thy training hath been noble.
Hold, here's more gold for thee.
A curse upon him, die he like a thief,
That robs thee of thy goodness! If thou dost
Hear from me, it shall be for thy good.

LESSON 13

FIRST AND SECOND CONJUGATIONS: FUTURE ACTIVE INDICATIVE. PLINY. PLINY: PLINY THE ELDER OBSERVES A LARGE VOLCANIC CLOUD.

§A   **First and Second Conjugations: Future Active Indicative.** You will now study the future tense, where **amo** will serve as the model for the future active indicative of first and second conjugation verbs.

Ind. Sing.	amábo	monébo
⇓	amábis	monébis
	amábit	monébit
Ind. Plur.	amabimus	monebimus
⇓	amabitis	monebitis
	amábunt	monébunt

The future active indicative of **amo** and **moneo** *(I will love/I will warn)* consists of the present stem **ama-** or **mone-**, the future indicative infix **-bi-** or **-bu-**, and the present active endings (**i** is lost before **o**).

§B   **Exercise.** Identify the tense, voice, mood, person, and number of the following verbs and translate (**ceno, cenáre, cenávi** ... *to dine;* **teneo, tenére, tenui, tentus** ... *to hold*):

(1) **cenábis**   (4) **tenebitis**

(2) **tenébunt**   (5) **cenábo**

(3) **cenábat**   (6) **tenebimus**

§C   **Pliny.** Pliny (c. 61 A.D.–c. 112 A.D.) became famous for his *Letters,* two of which he addressed to the Roman historian Tacitus about the eruption of Mt. Vesuvius in 79 A.D. Lessons 13–24 contain the narrative sections of these letters, in which Pliny describes the eruption, and how it buried the cities of Pompeii, Herculaneum, and Stabiae.

§D   **Vocabulary.**

appareo, apparére, apparui ... *to appear; to become clear* or *evident*

ascendo, ascendere, ascendi ... *to climb, to ascend; to climb* or *ascend to a place; to go on board* a ship, *to embark* on a journey

cinis, cineris, c. ... *ashes*

classis, classis, f. (gen. plur. classium) ... *fleet, naval force*

conspicio, conspicere, conspexi, conspectus ... *to look at, to watch*

destituo, destituere, destitui, destitútus ... *to set down; to desert, to forsake; to leave unsupported*

diffundo, diffundere, diffúdi, diffúsus ... *to spread, to spread out*

eveho, evehere, evexi, evectus ... *to carry out, to carry up*

fere ... *almost, approximately; generally, for the most part*

frigidus, frigida, frigidum ... *cold;* (fem. sing. as substantive) *cold water*

*****gusto, gustáre, gustávi, gustátus** ... *to taste; to eat, to have lunch*

hora, horae, f. ... *hour*

imperium, imperii, n. ... (plur. may have sing. meaning) *order, command; power, authority; empire, dominion*

incertus, incerta, incertum ... *unsure, uncertain*

interdum ... *at times, sometimes*

inusitátus, inusitáta, inusitátum ... *strange, unusual*

Kalendae, Kalendárum, f, (abbreviated **Kal.**) ... the *Calends*

latitúdo, latitudinis, f. ... *width, breadth;* **in latitudinem:** *horizontally*

maculósus, maculósa, maculósum ... *spotted, blotched*

*magis ... (compar. of **magnopere;** see *ARA,* App. D, p. 421) *more, rather;* **magis . . , quam . . ,** *more . . , than . .*

magnitúdo, magnitudinis, f. ... *size, magnitude*

miraculum, miraculi, n. ... *wonder, marvel*

Misénum, Miséni, n. ... the town *Misenum*

mox ... *then, soon, presently*

nonus, nona, nonum ... *ninth*

nubes, nubis, f. (gen. plur. **nubium**) ... *cloud*

pinus, pini, f. ... *pine*

*posco, poscere, poposci ... *to demand*

procul ... *from afar, from a distance*

prout ... *as if, just as if*

ramus, rami, m. ... *branch*

recens, recentis ... *fresh, recent*

*rego, regere, rexi, rectus ... *to rule; to command, to be in charge of;* **rectus, recta, rectum:** *direct; straight, straight ahead*

senesco, senescere, senui ... *to grow old; to subside, to die down*

September, Septembris, Septembre ... *of September*

septimus, septima, septimum ... *seventh*

similitúdo, similitudinis, f. ... *likeness, appearance*

*sol, solis, m. ... *sun*

solea, soleae, f. ... *sandal*

sordidus, sordida, sordidum ... *dark, dirty; base, shabby*

spiritus, spiritus, m. ... *breath, breathing; blast, blast of air*

*studeo, studére, studui ... *to be eager, to be zealous; to study, to apply* oneself *to* one's *books*

truncus, trunci, m. ... *trunk* of a tree; *body* of a man

utor, uti, usus sum ... *to use* (+ abl.)

vanesco, vanescere ... *to disperse; to break up, to spread out*

*-ve ... (attached to the word it connects) *or* (e.g., **filius filiave,** *son or daughter*); **-ve . . , -ve . . ,** *either . . , or . .*

velut ... *as if, just as; as it were, so to speak*

Vesuvius, Vesuvii, m. ... the volcano *Vesuvius*

§E   **Reading.**

Pliny the Elder Observes a Large Volcanic Cloud.

Lessons 13–17 contain the narrative portions of the first of Pliny's two letters addressed to the Roman historian Tacitus concerning the eruption of Mt. Vesuvius in 79 A.D. In it Pliny ('Pliny the Younger') describes how his uncle ('Pliny the Elder'), admiral of the Roman fleet at Misenum, sailed toward the eruption in order to investigate it.

Erat Miséni, classemque imperio praesens regébat. Nonum Kal.

Septembres, hora fere septima, mater mea indicat ei apparére

nubem inusitáta et magnitudine et specie. Usus ille sole, mox

frigida; gustaverat iacens, studebatque; poscit soleas, ascendit

5   locum, ex quo maxime miraculum illud conspici poterat.

Nubes (incertum procul intuentibus ex quo monte; Vesuvium

fuisse postea cognitum est) oriebátur, cuius similitudinem et

formam non alia magis arbor quam pinus expresserit. Nam

longissimo velut trunco eláta in altum, quibusdam ramis

10   diffundebátur, credo quia recenti spiritu evecta, dein senescente

eo destitúta, aut etiam pondere suo victa, in latitudinem

vanescébat, candida interdum, interdum sordida et maculósa,

prout terram cineremve sustulerat.

§F   Notes and Queries.

(1) **Erat:** The subject is Pliny the Elder.—**Miséni:** The locative case, here meaning *at Misenum* (see *ARA,* App. E, p. 426, note 1).

(1–2) **Nonum Kal. Septembres:** Translate *on the ninth (day before) the Calends of September.* What specific date (month/day) is indicated by this phrase? (The Calends designated the first day of the month and was included in the count backward to the previous month.)

(2) **hora . . . septima:** Approximately what time? (The first hour began at sunrise.)—**indicat:** What construction does this verb introduce? What are the elements of this construction in this sentence?

(3–4) **Usus:** The equivalent of **Usus est.**—**Usus . . . sole:** Translate *took a sunbath.* What is the literal meaning?—**Usus . . . frigida:** Translate *washed with cold water.* What is the literal meaning?

(5) **conspici:** Tense, voice, and mood?—**poterat:** Translate *was able.*

(6) **Nubes:** Separated from **oriebátur** by the extended parenthesis.—**intuentibus:** Here the present participle (in the dative) is used as a substantive referring to other onlookers (see above, Lesson 9, Section E, note to line 14).—**quo:** What noun does this adjective modify?

(7) **fuisse:** Translate *to have been.*—**cuius:** What is the antecedent?

(7–8) **cuius . . . expresserit:** The subjunctive is found in relative clauses that express a characteristic of an indefinite antecedent (see *ARA,* App. K, p. 474, Clauses of Characteristic), as here, where the relative **cuius** means *whose (= the kind whose),* and the subjunctive **expresserit** should be translated according to sense.

(8) **pinus:** Refers to the Mediterranean pine, whose trunk culminates in a crown of branches bearing a resemblance to a volcanic cloud.

(9) **eláta:** Translate *having risen.*—**in altum:** Translate *to a high place.* What use of the adjective **altum?**—**quibusdam:** Of what pronoun is this a form? (See *ARA,* Lesson 50, Section E, note to line 10.)

(10–11) **evecta . . . destitúta . . . victa:** Tense, voice, and mood? Subject of the verbal action?—**senescente eo:** What construction?

LESSON 14

THIRD AND FOURTH CONJUGATIONS: FUTURE ACTIVE INDICATIVE. PLINY: PLINY THE ELDER LEAVES MISENUM ON A RESCUE MISSION.

§A **Third and Fourth Conjugations: Future Active Indicative.** As you can see from the following chart, **traho** will serve as the model for the future active indicative of third and fourth conjugation verbs.

Ind. Sing.		traham	audiam	capiam
⇓		trahes	audies	capies
		trahet	audiet	capiet
Ind. Plur.		trahémus	audiémus	capiémus
⇓		trahétis	audiétis	capiétis
		trahent	audient	capient

The future active indicative of **traho, audio,** and **capio** consists of a variation of the present stem (**traha-/trahe-, audia-/audie-, capia-/capie-**) and the present active endings (future infix not found here).

§B **Exercise.** Identify the tense, voice, mood, person, and number of the following verbs and translate (**tango, tangere, tetigi, tactus** ... *to touch;* **finio, finíre, finívi, finítus** ... *to finish*):

    (1) **tangent**   (4) **finiet**

    (2) **finiam**   (5) **tangis**

    (3) **tangétis**   (6) **finiémus**

§C Vocabulary.

amoenitas, amoenitátis, f. ... *pleasantness; pleasant area* or *stretch*

apto, aptáre, aptávi, aptátus ... *to fit; to make ready, to put in position*

codicilli, codicillórum, m. ... (plur. noun with sing. meaning) *letter, petition*

copia, copiae, f. ... *plenty, abundance; force of men, supply of men;* **copiam facere:** *to give* someone (dat.) *the chance* or *opportunity*

cursus, cursus, m. ... (plur. may have sing. meaning) *a running; voyage, journey;* **cursu:** (of animals) *at a run, at a gallop*

dedúco, deducere, deduxi, deductus ... *to lead down; to launch* a ship; *to escort, to conduct*

deprehendo, deprehendere, deprehendi, deprehensus ... *to grasp; to observe, to examine*

dicto, dictáre, dictávi, dictátus ... *to recite, to dictate*

discrímen, discriminis, n. ... *dividing line; critical point, dangerous situation*

*domus, domus, f. ... (see *ARA*, App. C, p. 400, for the declension of this noun) *house, home*

egredior, egredi, egressus sum ... *to go out; to get beyond*

enoto, enotáre, enotávi, enotátus ... *to note down, to write down*

exterreo, exterrére, exterrui, exterritus ... *to scare, to terrify, to frighten*

forte ... *by chance, as it happened*

*fuga, fugae, f. ... *flight, escape*

gubernaculum, gubernaculi, n. ... (plur. may have sing. meaning) *oar; helm*

illuc ... *that way, to that place*

immineo, imminére ... *to overhang, to project over; to threaten, to be imminent; to press closely* on, *to follow closely* on (+ dat.)

incoho, incohāre, incohāvi, incohātus ... *to begin, to start*

Liburnica, Liburnicae, f. ... *Liburnian galley*

***malus, mala, malum** ... *bad, evil; harmful, poisonous;* (neut. sing. as substantive) *bad thing, evil thing;* **male:** *badly, unfavorably*

***metus, metus,** m. ... *fear*

motus, motus, m. ... (plur. may have sing. meaning) *motion, movement; outbreak, uprising*

***nam** or **namque** ... (conj. introducing an explanation) *for*

ora, orae, f. ... *coast, shore*

propero, properāre, properāvi, properātus ... *to hurry, to hasten*

propius ... (compar. of **prope;** see *ARA,* App. D, p. 421) *nearer, more closely*

quadrirēmis, quadrirēmis, f. ... *quadrireme*

Rectina, Rectinae, f. ... *Rectina,* wife of Tascius

studiōsus, studiōsa, studiōsum ... *eager, zealous; studious, scholarly*

Tascius, Tascii or **Tasci,** m. ... *Tascius,* husband of Rectina

***teneo, tenēre, tenui, tentus** ... *to hold, to possess; to keep, to retain; to clasp, to grasp; to live in, to dwell in; to hold to, to continue on; to hold sway, to be in control*

***video, vidēre, vidi, visus** ... *to see;* (in passive) *to be seen; to seem, to appear;* (impersonal use) *to seem, to appear* (+ dat. sometimes) [e.g., **visum est ei** = *it seemed to him* or *it appeared to him*]

villa, villae, f. ... *villa, estate*

§D   **Reading.**

Pliny the Elder Leaves Misenum on a Rescue Mission.

Magnum propiusque noscendum ut eruditissimo viro visum.

Iubet Liburnicam aptāri; mihi, si venīre una vellem, facit

copiam. Respondi studére me malle; et forte ipse, quod

scriberem, dederat. Egrediebátur domo; accipit codicillos

5   Rectinae Tasci, imminenti periculo exterritae (nam villa eius

subiacébat, nec ulla nisi navibus fuga); ut se tanto discrimini

eriperet, orábat. Vertit ille consilium, et quod studióso animo

incohaverat, obit maximo. Dedúcit quadrirémes; ascendit ipse

non Rectinae modo, sed multis (erat enim frequens amoenitas

10   orae) latúrus auxilium. Properat illuc, unde alii fugiunt,

rectumque cursum, recta gubernacula in periculum tenet, adeo

solútus metu, ut omnes illíus mali motus, omnes figúras (ut

deprehenderat oculis) dictáret enotaretque.

§E   **Notes and Queries.**

(1) **magnum . . . noscendum:** These two words refer to the eruption—
the first, an adjective used as a substantive, the second, the gerundive (see *ARA*, Lesson 55, Section C), here meaning *(something) worthy of being investigated.*—**ut eruditissimo viro:** This phrase depends
on **visum** (the equivalent of **visum est**) and needs to be expanded in
Latin in order to become more intelligible. Translate as if the Latin
consisted of the words **ei ut eruditissimo viro** (i.e., *to him as [someone
being] . . .* or *to him as [it would to someone being] . . .*).

(2) **Liburnicam:** The light, fast-sailing warship of the Roman fleet.—
aptári: Tense, voice, and mood?—**vellem:** Translate *I wished.*

(3) **Respondi studére me malle:** Instead of using these words (where
me malle means *I preferred*), Pliny could have written the sentence
Respondi: "Studébo et scribam." If he had chosen to do so, what form
of the verbs **studeo** and **scribo** (tense, voice, mood, person, and number) would he have used and how would you translate these verbs?

(3–4) **quod scriberem:** The subjunctive is found in relative clauses
that express a characteristic of an indefinite antecedent (see above,
Lesson 13, Section F, note to lines 7–8), as here, where the relative
quod means *something which (= the kind of thing which),* and the
subjunctive **scriberem** should be translated according to sense.

(4) **domo:** The equivalent of **e domo.** (The noun **domus** may have second declension endings [see *ARA,* App. C, p. 400, for the declension of this noun].)

(5) **Rectinae Tasci:** Between these words supply *wife.* (See *ARA,* Lesson 64, Section F, note to line 1, for a similar instance of two names appearing in the genitive connected by an understood idea.) Here Pliny may be referring to the lyric poet Caesius Bassus—if one accepts **Tasci** as a corruption of **Caesi** or **Bassi**—a poet who (according to one ancient source) perished in his villa during the eruption.— **imminenti:** See *ARA,* App. C, p. 405, note 13.—**exterritae:** Tense, voice, and mood? Subject of the verbal action?

(6) **subiacébat:** After this verb supply the understood direct object to show where the villa in question was apparently located.—**ulla . . . fuga:** Sometimes the verb *to be* (when used as a main verb) does not appear in the sentence (see above, Lesson 10, Section E, note to lines 1–2).—**se:** To whom does this pronoun refer? (See *ARA,* Lesson 29, Section G, note to line 3.)—**discrimini:** What kind of dative?

(7) **orábat:** What construction does this verb introduce?—**quod:** See above, Lesson 5, Section G, note to line 16.

(8) **obit:** Translate *he completes* or *completed,* depending on whether or not you treat this verb as a historical present.—**maximo:** What noun should be supplied after this adjective?—**quadrirémes:** The large, standard battleships of the Roman fleet.

(9) **multis:** That is, other people who were also exposed to the danger, as explained by the words **erat enim frequens amoenitas orae.**

(10) **latúrus:** Translate *intending to bring.*

(11) **rectumque . . . recta:** Here the participle of **rego** is used as an adjective, with appropriate meanings listed under **rego** in the vocabulary entry for this verb.

(12) **solútus metu:** Although the Latin idiom is *loosened from fear,* how would you express it in normal English?—**omnes . . . omnes:** What noun does the first **omnes** modify? What noun does the second **omnes** modify?—**illíus mali:** Translate *of that dreadful spectacle* or *of that terrifying phenomenon.* What use of the adjective **malus?** Literal meaning of this use of the adjective?

(12–13) **ut . . . dictáret enotaretque:** What construction? (Pliny the Elder would normally have a slave present in order to help him record all his observations.)—**ut deprehenderat:** What meaning of **ut?** Why this meaning here?

LESSON 15

FUTURE PERFECT ACTIVE INDICATIVE. PLINY: PLINY THE ELDER ALTERS HIS COURSE AND REACHES A FRIEND.

§A **Future Perfect Active Indicative.** You will now study the future perfect tense, expressing action completed in the future, where **amo** will serve as the model for the future perfect active indicative of all verbs.

amavero	monuero	traxero	audivero	cepero
amaveris	monueris	traxeris	audiveris	ceperis
amaverit	monuerit	traxerit	audiverit	ceperit
amaverimus	monuerimus	traxerimus	audiverimus	ceperimus
amaveritis	monueritis	traxeritis	audiveritis	ceperitis
amaverint	monuerint	traxerint	audiverint	ceperint

The future perfect active indicative (*I will have loved, I will have warned,* etc.) consists of the perfect stem, the future perfect indicative infix **-eri-,** and the present active endings (**i** is again lost before **o**).

§B **Exercise.** Identify the tense, voice, mood, person, and number of the following verbs and translate (**augeo, augére, auxi, auctus** ... *to increase;* **fingo, fingere, finxi, fictus** ... *to form*):

(1) **auxeris**

(2) **finxerint**

(3) **auxeram**

(4) **finxerit**

(5) **auxeritis**

(6) **finxerimus**

§C   **Vocabulary.**

accubo, accubáre ... *to recline* at a table

aequus, aequa, aequum ... *equal; just, right;* **aeque:** *equally; justly, rightly;* **ex aequo:** *equally, on equal terms*

ambúro, amburere, ambussi, ambustus ... *to burn up, to scorch*

*****an** ... (in direct question) *or;* (in indirect question) *whether, if;* (in double indirect question, appearing once but translated twice) *whether . . , or . .*

appropinquo, appropinquáre, appropinquávi ... *to approach*

*****avunculus, avunculi,** m. ... *uncle*

balineum, balinei, n. ... *bath, bathroom*

calidus, calida, calidum ... *hot*

ceno, cenáre, cenávi ... *to eat, to dine*

*****certus, certa, certum** ... *sure, certain; unerring, sure of aim; resolved* on, *determined* on (+ gen.); **certe:** *surely, certainly*

circumágo, circumagere, circumégi, circumactus ... *to bend around, to curve around*

complector, complecti, complexus sum ... *to clasp, to embrace*

consólor, consolári, consolátus sum ... *to console, to comfort*

conspicuus, conspicua, conspicuum ... *visible, in full view*

contrarius, contraria, contrarium ... *opposite, unfavorable*

cresco, crescere, crevi, cretus ... *to spring* from; *to grow, to increase*

cunctor, cunctári, cunctátus sum ... *to delay, to linger, to hesitate*

curvo, curváre, curvávi, curvátus ... *to form* or *extend in a curve*

densus, densa, densum ... *thick, thick of; crowding, thronging*

dirimo, dirimere, dirémi, diremptus ... *to separate*

flecto, flectere, flexi, flexus ... *to bend; to turn* back, *to change* one's course; *to influence* or *prevail upon* one's mind

gubernátor, gubernatóris, m. ... *helmsman*

infundo, infundere, infundi, infúsus ... *to pour in* or *into* (+ dat.)

*****inquit** ... *he, she, it says* or *said*

inveho, invehere, invexi, invectus ... *to carry in;* (in passive) *to sail, to sail to* (+ acc.); *to run over, to drive over* (+ dat.)

iuvo, iuváre, iuvi, iutus ... *to help, to assist*

*****lavo, laváre, lavi, lautus** or **lotus** ... *to wash, to bathe; to clean, to brush*

lenio, leníre, lenívi, lenítus ... *to calm, to appease, to alleviate*

litus, litoris, n. ... *beach, shore*

*****magnus, magna, magnum** ... *great; brave, heroic*

niger, nigra, nigrum ... *black*

nondum ... *not yet*

obsto, obstáre, obstiti ... *to block the way; to stand in the way* of (+ dat.)

Pomponiánus, Pomponiáni, m. ... *Pomponianus,* friend of Pliny

proximus, proxima, proximum ... (superl. related to **prope:** see *ARA,* App. D, p. 419) *nearest, very near;* **ex proximo:** *close at hand*

pumex, pumicis, m. ... *pumice-stone*

*****quamquam** ... *although*

quo ... (adv.) *where, to which place* (= *there, to that place*)

resído, residere, resédi ... *to sit down; to subside, to die down*

retro ... *back, backwards, back again*

ruína, ruínae, f. ... a *falling down; ruin, collapse, destruction*

sarcina, sarcinae, f. ... *bundle;* (in plur.) *belongings, possessions*

secundus, secunda, secundum ... *second; following, favorable*

securitas, securitátis, f. ... *unconcern; composure, complacence*

sensim ... *slowly, gradually*

sinus, sinus, m. ... *curve; embrace; bay, gulf*

Stabiae, Stabiárum, f. ... (plur. noun with sing. meaning) *Stabiae*

timor, timóris, m. ... *fear*

trepido, trepidáre, trepidávi ... *to be anxious, to be agitated*

vadum, vadi, n. ... *ford, shoal* (= shallow part of the water)

§D   Reading.

Pliny the Elder Alters His Course and Reaches a Friend.

Iam navibus cinis inciderat, quo propius accederent, calidior et
densior; iam pumices etiam, nigrique et ambusti et fracti igne
lapides; iam vadum subitum, ruinaque montis litora obstantia.
Cunctátus paulum an retro flecteret, mox gubernatóri ut ita
5   faceret monenti "Fortes" inquit, "Fortúna iuvat; Pomponiánum
pete!" Stabiis erat, diremptus sinu medio (nam sensim
circumactis curvatisque litoribus mare infunditur); ibi,
quamquam nondum periculo appropinquante (conspicuo tamen
et, cum cresceret, proximo), sarcinas contulerat in naves,
10   certus fugae si contrarius ventus resedisset. Quo tunc
avunculus meus secundissimo invectus, complectitur
trepidantem, consolátur, hortátur; utque timórem eius sua
securitáte leníret, deferri in balineum iubet; lotus accubat, cenat,
aut hilaris aut (quod aeque magnum) similis hilari.

(1) **quo . . . accederent:** An indefinite relative clause introduced by **quo** (i.e., *by whatever direction . . .*), in which the subjunctive should be translated according to sense.—**calidior:** Degree of adjective?

(3) **ruinaque:** The noun **ruína** is either nominative, with another **-que** to be supplied after **litora,** or ablative to designate cause (i.e., *because of the collapse . . .*), explaining the phrase **litora obstantia.**

(4) **Cunctátus:** Tense, voice, and mood? Subject of the verbal action?—**an . . . flecteret:** What construction? (See *ARA*, App. K, p. 473.)

(4–5) **mox gubernatóri ut ita faceret monenti . . . inquit:** These words need to be rearranged in Latin in order to become more intelligible. Translate as if the Latin followed the order **mox inquit gubernatóri monenti ut ita faceret . . .** Indirect object of **inquit?** Tense, voice, and mood of **monenti?** Subject of the verbal action of **monenti?** What construction does **monenti** introduce? What advice does this construction contain? (Assume that **ut ita faceret = ut retro flecteret.**)

(6) **pete:** Here the verb **peto** has the meaning *to go to* or *to head for.*—**Stabiis:** The locative case, here meaning *at Stabiae* (see *ARA*, App. E, p. 426, note 1).—**erat:** The subject is Pomponianus.—**diremptus sinu medio:** That is, Pomponianus (at Stabiae) was separated from Pliny the Elder (at Herculaneum) by the bay described in lines 6–7.

(8) **periculo appropinquante:** What construction?

(9) **contulerat:** Translate *he had brought.*

(10) **si . . . resedisset:** A conditional clause in which the subjunctive should be translated according to sense.—**Quo:** The adverb or the pronoun? What meaning seems best at the beginning of the sentence?

(11) **secundissimo:** Degree of adjective? This adjective refers to the wind, which favored Pliny by allowing him to reach Pomponianus.

(12) **trepidantem:** What use of the participle? (Since the participle is singular, supply *him* or *the one* as subject of the verbal action.)

(12–13) **utque . . . leníret:** What construction?

(13) **deferri:** Translate *to be carried.*—**iubet:** That is, **iubet se.**

(14) **quod . . . magnum:** See above, Lesson 5, Section G, note to line 16, on the meaning of the relative, and Lesson 10, Section E, note to lines 1–2, on the omission of the verb.—**similis hilari:** Translate *pretending to be cheerful.* What is the literal meaning of these words?

LESSON 16

SEQUENCE OF TENSES: PRIMARY SEQUENCE. PLINY: PLINY THE ELDER TRIES TO SLEEP AMID A WORSENING SITUATION.

§A **Sequence of Tenses: Primary Sequence.** When the subjunctive is used dependently in a subordinate clause, the choice of tense usually conforms to a rule called sequence of tenses. In primary sequence, as shown in the chart below, the tenses of the indicative expressing present or future time are followed by the present or perfect subjunctive.

	Indicative	**Subjunctive**
Primary	Present	Present
⇓	Future	Perfect
	Future Perfect	

In primary sequence, the present subjunctive denotes action happening at the same time as or after that of the main verb; the perfect subjunctive, action happening before it. In translating the subjunctive in a subordinate clause, try to do so in a way that shows the time of the action denoted by the subjunctive in relation to that of the main verb.

§B **Exercise.** Translate the following sentences with primary sequence into English; then indicate the tense of the subjunctive used and the kind of action it denotes in relation to the main verb:

(1) **Plinius gubernatórem rogat ut ad Pomponiánum naviget.**

(2) **Plinius Pomponiánum rogat an nigram nubem viderit.**

(3) **Plinius cum Pomponiáno gustábit ut timórem eius leniat.**

§C   **Vocabulary.**

agrestis, agrestis, m. (gen. plur. **agrestium**) ... *rustic, peasant*

amplitúdo, amplitudinis, f. ... *size, greatness*

anima, animae, f. ... *life, soul; breath, breathing*

area, areae, f. ... *space; court, courtyard*

claritas, claritátis, f. ... *clearness, brightness*

collatio, collatiónis, f. ... *comparison*

commúnis, commúne ... *common to, shared by* (+ dat.); **in commúne:** *together, with one another*

consulto, consultáre, consultávi, consultátus ... *to consult, to discuss*

creber, crebra, crebrum ... *frequent, repeated*

desero, deserere, deserui, desertus ... *to desert, to abandon*

diaeta, diaetae, f. ... *room, apartment*

dictito, dictitáre, dictitávi, dictitátus ... *to keep saying*

dium, dii, or **divum, divi,** n. ... *open sky, open air*

eligo, eligere, elégi, electus ... *to choose; to lead* someone *to choose*

emoveo, emovére, emóvi, emótus ... *to move out; to dislodge from*

exedo, exedere, exédi, exésus ... *to eat up; to make porous*

formído, formidinis, f. ... *fear, alarm; dreadful* or *frightful thing*

fulgor, fulgóris, m. ... *brightness; lightning, flash of lightning*

huc ... *this way, to this place*

incendium, incendii, n. ... *fire, flame*

*****levis, leve** ... *light, gentle;* **leviter:** *lightly, gently*

*****limen, liminis,** n. ... (plur. may have sing. meaning) *doorway, entrance, threshold*

meátus, meátus, m. ... *way, path, passage*

mora, morae, f. ... *delay*

*__**nego, negáre, negávi, negátus**__ ... *to deny, to say no; to deny* that, *to say* that . . . *not; to block, to prevent, to prohibit*

nuto, nutáre, nutávi ... *to nod; to rock, to sway*

obversor, obversári, obversátus sum ... *to go to and fro; to walk before* or *in front of* (+ dat.)

oppleo, opplére, opplévi, opplétus ... *to fill up, to fill completely*

pervigilo, pervigiláre, pervigilávi, pervigilátus ... *to stay awake all night*

procédo, procedere, processi ... *to go forth, to come out; to advance, to increase in extent*

quidem ... *indeed, certainly*

*__**reddo, reddere, reddidi, redditus**__ ... *to give back; to return, to deliver;* (used with the reflexive **se,** which is not translated in this idiom) *to return* or *go back* to someone (dat.)

*__**relinquo, relinquere, reliqui, relictus**__ ... *to leave, to leave behind*

reluceo, relucére, reluxi ... *to shine out, to blaze forth*

remedium, remedii, n. ... *remedy; drug, antidote*

rursus or **rursum** ... *again, back again; on the other hand*

sedes, sedis, f. (gen. plur. **sedium**) ... (plur. may have sing. meaning) *seat, place; base, foundation*

solitúdo, solitudinis, f. ... *solitude; solitary* or *desolate area(s)*

sono, sonáre, sonui ... *to sound, to shout; to rattle, to clatter;* **sonans, sonantis:** *loud, noisy*

subsisto, subsistere, substiti ... *to stand firm; to stop, to subside; to remain, to stay behind*

*__**surgo, surgere, surrexi, surrectus**__ ... *to rise, to arise; to rise to a higher level*

*__**tectum, tecti,**__ n. ... (plur. may have sing. meaning) *roof, hall; house, dwelling, shelter* tenebrae, tenebrárum, f. ... (plur. may have sing. meaning) *darkness, shadows*

tremor, tremóris, m. ... *tremor, quake*

trepidatio, trepidatiónis, f. ... *anxiety, agitation*

vagor, vagári, vagátus sum ... *to wander*

vastus, vasta, vastum ... *enormous, turbulent*

§D   Reading.

Pliny the Elder Tries to Sleep amid a Worsening Situation.

Interim e Vesuvio monte pluribus locis latissimae flammae
altaque incendia relucébant, quorum fulgor et claritas tenebris
noctis excitabátur. Ille agrestium trepidatióne ignes relictos
desertasque villas per solitudinem ardére in remedium

5   formidinis dictitábat. Tum se quiéti dedit et quiévit verissimo
quidem somno. Nam meátus animae, qui illi (propter
amplitudinem corporis) gravior et sonantior erat, ab eis, qui
limini obversabantur, audiebátur. Sed area, ex qua diaeta
adibátur, ita iam cinere mixtisque pumicibus oppléta surrexerat,

10 ut si longior in cubiculo mora, exitus negarétur. Excitátus
procédit, seque Pomponiáno ceterisque, qui pervigilaverant,
reddit. In commúne consultant, intra tecta subsistant an in
aperto vagentur. Nam crebris vastisque tremoribus tecta
nutábant, et quasi emóta sedibus suis nunc huc nunc illuc abíre

15 aut referri videbantur. Sub dio rursus (quamquam levium

exesorumque) pumicum casus metuebátur, quod tamen

periculórum collatio elégit.

§E **Notes and Queries.**

(1) **locis:** What kind of ablative? (See *ARA*, Lesson 13, Section H, note to line 8.)—**latissimae:** Degree of adjective?

(3) **excitabátur:** See above, Lesson 12, Section E, note to line 16.—**Ille:** Refers to Pliny the Elder. Of what verb is this the subject?

(3–4) **ignes ... villas ... ardére:** What construction? (Here **ignes** refers not to the volcanic fires but to the wood or coal fires that the rustics were very likely using for domestic / artifactual purposes such as cooking, heating, smithing, and worshiping.)—**relictos desertasque:** Tense, voice, and mood? Subjects of the verbal action?

(4) **solitudinem:** Refers to the unfrequented wilderness or sparsely populated countryside in the vicinity of the volcano.

(4–5) **in remedium formidinis:** Translate *to remedy* or *relieve (their) fear.* What is the literal meaning of these words?

(6) **meátus animae:** Refers to Pliny the Elder's snoring.—**illi:** What kind of dative? (See *ARA*, Lesson 32, Section F, note to line 1.)

(7) **gravior:** Degree of adjective?

(9) **adibátur:** Translate *could be approached.*

(10) **ut ... negarétur:** What construction? (Translate the subjunctive according to sense.)—**si ... mora:** What verb should be supplied in this clause?

(12) **consultant ... subsistant:** What sequence of tenses is illustrated by these verbs? What tense of the subjunctive is used here and what kind of action does it denote in relation to the main verb?

(14) **abíre:** Translate *to move away.*

(15) **referri:** Translate *to be drawn back.*

(16) **quod:** Here the relative refers to the overall concept expressed by the words **pumicum casus metuebátur.**

(17) **elégit:** What meaning of this verb best fits the context? What did Pliny and his friends finally decide to do?

LESSON 17

SEQUENCE OF TENSES: SECONDARY SEQUENCE. PLINY: PLINY THE ELDER GOES TO THE SHORE AND COLLAPSES ON THE BEACH.

§A **Sequence of Tenses: Secondary Sequence.** In the previous lesson, you studied the rule for sequence of tenses, with application to that aspect of the rule concerned with primary sequence. In secondary sequence, as shown in the chart below, the tenses of the indicative expressing past time are followed by the imperfect or pluperfect subjunctive.

	Indicative	**Subjunctive**
Secondary	Imperfect	Imperfect
⇓	Perfect	Pluperfect
	Pluperfect	

In secondary sequence, the imperfect subjunctive denotes action happening at the same time as or after that of the main verb; the pluperfect subjunctive, action before it. In translating the subjunctive in a subordinate clause, continue to do so in a way that shows the time of the action denoted by the subjunctive in relation to the main verb.

§B **Exercise.** Translate the following sentences with secondary sequence into English; then indicate the tense of the subjunctive used and the kind of action it denotes in relation to the main verb:

(1) **Plinius in cubiculum venit ut verissimo somno quiesceret.**

(2) **Plinius Pomponiánum rogávit an ceteri pervigilavissent.**

(3) **Plinius viros et feminas rogábat ne intra tecta subsisterent.**

§C Vocabulary.

abicio, abicere, abiéci, abiectus ... *to throw from; to throw down*

admitto, admittere, admísi, admissus ... *to send to; to admit, to let go; to allow* or *permit* a course of action

adsurgo, adsurgere, adsurrexi, adsurrectus ... *to rise, to rise up, to rise to* one's *feet*

*adversus, adversa, adversum ... *facing, exposed; opposed, unfavorable;* (neut. as substantive) *disaster, catastrophe;* **adversus:** (prep.) *against, to ward off* (+ acc.)

aestuo, aestuáre, aestuávi ... *to be hot, to be inflamed; to blaze, to burn fiercely*

alibi ... *else, elsewhere*

angustus, angusta, angustum ... *narrow, constricted*

*apud ... *near, with, among* (+ acc.); *as for, in the case of* (+ acc.); *in the works of, in the writings of* (+ acc.); *at the house of, in the quarters of* (+ acc.)

aspicio, aspicere, aspexi, aspectus ... *to see, to observe, to look at*

calígo, caliginis, f. ... *darkness; fog, mist; smoke, vapor*

cervícal, cervicális, n. ... *pillow, cushion*

concido, concidere, concidi ... *to fall; to fall down, to collapse*

*cado, cadere, cecidi ... *to fall; to set, to sink; to abate, to lessen, to subside* (+ dat.)

constringo, constringere, constrinxi, constrictus ... *to tie up; to bind, to fasten*

crassus, crassa, crassum ... *thick, dense, heavy*

defunctus, defuncta, defunctum ... *dead, deceased*

ecquid ... *whether*

fax, facis, f. ... *torch*

haurio, hauríre, hausi, haustus ... *to draw* water; *to drink* water

illaesus, illaesa, illaesum ... *unharmed, uninjured*

illic ... *there, in that place*

impóno, imponere, imposui, impositus ... *to put on, to place on*

innítor, inníti, innixus sum ... *to lean on, to support* oneself *on* (+ dat.)

invalidus, invalida, invalidum ... *weak, powerless*

iterum ... *again, a second time*

linteum, lintei, n. ... (plur. may have sing. meaning) *linen, linen-cloth*

*****litus, litoris**, n. ... *beach, shore*

*****lumen, luminis**, n. ... (plur. may have sing. meaning) *light, source of light;* (of the light in one's head) *eye*

munimentum, munimenti, n. ... *defense, protection*

*****novus, nova, novum** ... *new, fresh; strange, unusual;* **novissime:** *last, last in time, for the last time*

obstruo, obstruere, obstruxi, obstructus ... *to build against; to block, to stifle, to obstruct*

odor, odóris, m. ... *smell*

*****operio, operíre, operui, opertus** ... *to cover; to clothe, to dress*

praenuntius, praenuntii, m. ... *harbinger, forerunner* (= something that announces in advance what is coming)

recubo, recubáre ... *to lie back, to lie down*

semel ... *once, a single time; once and no more, once and for all*

servolus, servoli, m. ... *young slave*

stomachus, stomachi, m. ... *esophagus; belly, stomach*

sulpur, sulpuris, n. ... *sulphur*

varius, varia, varium ... *various, different*

Reading.

Pliny the Elder Goes to the Shore and Collapses on the Beach.

Et apud illum quidem ratio ratiónem, apud alios timórem timor

vicit. Cervicalia capitibus imposita linteis constringunt; id

munimentum adversus incidentia fuit. Iam dies alibi; illic nox

omnibus noctibus nigrior densiorque; quam tamen faces multae

5   variaque lumina solvébant. Placuit egredi in litus et ex proximo

aspicere ecquid iam mare admitteret; quod adhuc vastum et

adversum permanébat. Ibi super abiectum linteum recubans,

semel atque iterum frigidam poposcit hausitque. Deinde

flammae flammarumque praenuntius, odor sulpuris, alios in

10   fugam vertunt, excitant illum. Innitens servolis duóbus

adsurrexit et statim concidit (ut ego colligo) crassióre caligine

spiritu obstructo clausoque stomacho, qui illi natúra invalidus et

angustus et frequenter aestuans erat. Ubi dies redditus (is ab eo

quem novissime viderat tertius), corpus inventum integrum,

15   illaesum, opertumque, ut fuerat indútus; habitus corporis

quiescenti quam defuncto similior.

§E   Notes and Queries.

(1) **apud illum . . . apud alios:** That is, in deciding whether or not to
leave the house, Pliny the Elder relied on reason, whereas his friends
gave in to their fear.

(2) **vicit:** Sometimes a verb is used twice, in two different parts of a
sentence, as here, where **vicit** is used first with **ratio ratiónem,** then
with **timórem timor.**

(3) **adversus:** The adjective or the preposition? What is your reason for thinking so?—**incidentia:** Refers to the pumice-stones. What use of the participle?—**Iam dies alibi:** What verb should be supplied in this clause?

(4) **noctibus:** What kind of ablative? (See above, Lesson 3, Section E, note to line 7, on **isto**.)

(5) **lumina:** Refers to lamps or candles or some other source of light, which Pliny and his friends were apparently using in order to help 'loosen' or 'break up' (i.e., enable them to see through) the darkness.

(6) **ecquid . . . admitteret:** What construction? To what course of action does the verb **admitteret** refer? (Show this by supplying an appropriate direct object in your translation.)

(7) **abiectum:** Tense, voice, and mood? Subject of the verbal action?—**recubans:** Tense, voice, and mood? Subject of the verbal action?

(12) **spiritu obstructo:** What construction?—**clausoque stomacho:** Here Pliny the Younger may be confusing the esophagus, which carries food to the stomach, with the trachea, which carries air to the lungs.—**illi:** What kind of dative?

(13) **redditus:** Occasionally a form of the verb *to be* is understood in the perfect passive system, as here, where the form **redditus** is the equivalent of **redditus est** (in this instance, to be translated as active).

(13–14) **is ab eo . . . tertius:** Translate *this (being) the third (day) from that (day)* . . . What specific date (month/day) is indicated by this phrase? (See above, Lesson 13, Section F, note to lines 1–2, on the date used and included in the count forward to this third day.)

(14) **viderat:** The subject is Pliny the Elder.—**inventum:** See above, note to line 13, regarding the understood form of the verb.

(15) **fuerat indútus:** The equivalent of **erat indútus** (see *ARA*, App. G, p. 438, note 4)—itself a variant of **indútus erat** (see *ARA*, Lesson 64, Section F, note to line 1).

(16) **quiescenti:** What use of the participle? (Supply *someone* before the participle in order to fully convey this use.)—**quam:** The relative or the conjunction? What is your reason for thinking so?

(general) During the excavations conducted in the nineteenth and twentieth centuries at the different locations affected by the eruption, archaeologists unearthed the skeletal remains of people preserved in the volcanic ash that destroyed them, with their agonized facial expressions and bodily contortions indicative of their terrible suffering.

LESSON 18

SUBORDINATE CLAUSES IN INDIRECT STATEMENT. SUETONIUS: A SUMMARY OF THE LIFE AND DEATH OF PLINY THE ELDER.

§A **Subordinate Clauses in Indirect Statement.** An indirect statement may be a complex sentence, which contains one or more subordinate clauses (see *ARA,* App. K, p. 478). In an indirect statement consisting of a complex sentence, the main clause takes the accusative and infinitive; the verb in the subordinate clause is in the subjunctive.

> **dicit regem superáre ubi milites contendant,**
>
> *he says that the king conquers when the soldiers hasten.*
>
> **dixit regem superáre ubi milites contenderent,**
>
> *he said that the king was conquering when the soldiers were hastening.*

The tense of the subjunctive generally depends upon the tense of the introductory verb, in accordance with the rule for sequence of tenses (above, Lessons 16–17). In the first sentence, the present subjunctive **contendant** follows **dicit** (primary sequence); in the second, the imperfect subjunctive **contenderent** follows **dixit** (secondary sequence).

§B **Exercise.** Translate the following sentences with subordinate clauses in indirect statement; then indicate the tense of the subjunctive used and the kind of action it denotes in relation to the main verb.

> (1) **Plinius videt pumices cadere dum cervicalia constringant.**
>
> (2) **Aliquis audívit illum rogavisse an mare fugam admitteret.**
>
> (3) **Aliquis narrávit illum concidisse postquam adsurrexisset.**

§C   **Vocabulary.**

absolvo, absolvere, absolvi, absolútus ... *to free* someone (acc.) *from* something (abl.); *to finish, to complete* a project such as a book

administro, administráre, administrávi, administrátus ... *to assist; to manage, to administer*

adversor, adversári, adversátus sum ... *to oppose, to be contrary*

aestus, aestus, m. ... *heat, blaze*

*****bellum, belli,** n. ... *war*

Campania, Campaniae, f. ... the region *Campania*

clades, cladis, f. (gen. plur. **cladium**) ... *disaster, destruction*

comprehendo, comprehendere, comprehendi, comprehensus ... *to grasp firmly; to seize, to capture; to include* in, *to deal with* in

continuus, continua, continuum ... *continuous, uninterrupted*

deficio, deficere, deféci, defectus ... *to let down; to subside, to become weak;* (of the sun) *to undergo an eclipse;* (of soldiers) *to become disaffected* or *discontented*

equester, equestris, equestre ... *equestrian; proper to* or *required of an equestrian*

exploro, exploráre, explorávi, explorátus ... *to ascertain, to investigate*

favilla, favillae, f. ... *ashes*

flagro, flagráre, falgrávi ... *to be ablaze, to be on fire*

fungor, fungi, functus sum ... *to perform, to execute* (+ abl.)

Germánus, Germáni, m. ... *a German*

*****gero, gerere, gessi, gestus** ... *to bear, to carry; to wage, to conduct; to display, to exhibit*

historia, historiae, f. ... *history*

industrius, industria, industrium ... *careful, diligent;* **industrie:** *carefully, diligently*

integritas integritátis, f. ... *wholeness; integrity, uprightness*

*****liber, libri,** m. ... *book, volume; bark* of a tree

matúro, maturáre, maturávi, maturátus ... *to ripen, to mature; to hasten, to advance in time*

militia, militiae, f. ... (plur. may have sing. meaning) *military duty* or *service*

Misenensis, Misenense ... *of Misenum, stationed at Misenum*

naturális, naturále ... *natural*

nex, necis, f. ... *death*

Novocomensis, Novocomense ... *of Novum Comum*

*****opera, operae,** f. ... *work, effort, service;* **operam dare:** *to give* or *devote attention to* (+ dat.)

opprimo, opprimere, oppressi, oppressus ... *to press down; to crush, to destroy; to suffocate, to asphyxiate*

*****otium, otii,** n. ... *leisure*

pertendo, pertendere, pertendi, pertensus ... *to persist, to push on; to continue on* one's *way*

Plinius, Plinii, m. ... *Pliny* (= Pliny the Elder)

procuratio, procuratiónis, f. ... *procuratorship*

pulvis, pulveris, m. ... *dust*

remeo, remeáre, remeávi ... *to return, to go back*

Secundus, Secundi, m. ... *Secundus* (= Pliny's family name)

splendidus, splendida, splendidum ... *bright, shining; distinguished, outstanding*

*****summus, summa, summum** ... (alternate superl. of **superus;** see *ARA,* App. D, p. 419) *highest, very great; top of, surface of; topmost, uppermost;* (fem. sing. as substantive) *sum total, central point;* (neut. sing. as substantive) *surface, topmost layer, uppermost layer*

temere ... *rashly, blindly, recklessly;* **non temere** or **haud temere**: *not easily, not readily, not without care*

umquam ... *ever*

*vel ... *or; even, at least;* **vel . . , vel . . ,** *either . . , or . .*

volúmen, voluminis, n. ... *book, volume*

§D   Reading.

A Summary of the Life and Death of Pliny the Elder.

Lesson 18 contains a summary of the life and death of Pliny the Elder by the Roman historian Suetonius, who (like Pliny the Younger) talks about the eruption of Mt. Vesuvius. In this short passage, Suetonius focuses on Pliny the Elder's distinguished career, as well as the fate that he suffered while attempting to investigate things more closely.

Plinius Secundus Novocomensis, equestribus militiis industrie

functus, procuratiónes quoque splendidissimas et continuas

summa integritáte administrávit. Et tamen liberalibus studiis

tantam operam dedit, ut non temere quis plura in otio

5   scripserit. Itaque bella omnia, quae umquam cum Germánis

gesta sunt, XX voluminibus comprehendit, itemque Naturális

Historiae XXXVII libros absolvit. Periit clade Campaniae. Cum

enim Misenensi classi praeesset, et flagrante Vesuvio ad

explorandas propius causas Liburnica pertendisset, nec

10   adversantibus ventis remeáre posset, vi pulveris ac favillae

oppressus est, vel (ut quidam existimant) a servo suo occísus,

quem, aestu deficiens, ut necem sibi maturáret, oraverat.

(1) **Plinius Secundus:** Pliny the Elder's full name was C. (= Gaius) Plinius Secundus. A Roman name usually consisted of three parts (see *ARA,* Lesson 18, Section H, note to line 1).—**Novocomensis:** Refers to the city called Comum (resettled as Novum Comum), in northern Italy at the Swiss border.—**equestribus:** Refers to the class of Roman citizens beneath the Senate, subject (since 67 B.C.) to a property qualification of 400,000 sesterces (= silver coins). During imperial times individual equestrians served as advisors to the emperors and held various posts in the civil-service administration.

(2) **functus:** Tense, voice, and mood? Subject of the verbal action?—**procuratiónes:** Refers to the office of a procurator, normally open to equestrians, which involved the administration of imperial and senatorial provinces.—**splendidissimas:** Degree of adjective?

(4) **non temere:** These two words should be taken together, in accordance with the vocabulary entry for this idiom.—**quis:** The indefinite pronoun or the interrogative pronoun?

(4–5) **dedit . . . scripserit:** In secondary sequence, the perfect indicative may be followed by the perfect subjunctive when the subjunctive is used in a result clause. In this use of the construction, the perfect subjunctive is regarded as a secondary tense, specifying a result simply as a fact, without referring to the continuation of the action.

(5) **bella . . . cum Germánis:** Refers to the military campaigns that the Romans waged against the Germans, such as those waged by Julius Caesar during the first century B.C.

(6–7) **XX . . . XXXVII:** The Roman numerals **X** = 10, **V** = 5, and **I** = 1.—**Naturális Historiae:** Pliny the Elder's best known literary work—a thirty-seven volume encyclopedia on the natural sciences, interspersed with essays on the accomplishments of the human race.

(7) **Periit:** Translate *he perished.*—**clade:** An ablative of time, here indicating an event during which something took place.—**Campaniae:** The locative case, here meaning *at Campania* (see *ARA,* App. E, p. 426, note 1). The region Campania included the cities of Pompeii, Herculaneum, and Stabiae (see also above, Lesson 13, Section C).—**Cum:** What three verbs does this conjunction introduce?

(8) **Misenensi classi:** See above, Lesson 13, Section E, line 1.—**praeesset:** Translate *he was in charge of.* This verb takes the dative case.—**flagrante Vesuvio:** What construction?

(9) **explorandas:** What verbal form? Case, number, and gender?

(10) **posset:** Translate *he was able.*—**vi:** Of what noun is this a form?

(11) **ut quidam existimant:** Refers to sources that Suetonius used beside the two letters by Pliny the Younger. How does Suetonius's account of Pliny the Elder's death differ from that presented by Pliny the Younger? (See above, Lesson 17, Section D, lines 13–16.)—**occísus:** Occasionally a form of the verb *to be* is understood in the perfect passive system (see above, Lesson 17, Section E, note to line 13).

(12) **quem:** What is the antecedent? Of what verb is this the direct object?—**deficiens:** Tense, voice, and mood? Subject of the verbal action?—**sibi:** To whom does this pronoun refer? (See above, Lesson 14, Section E, note to line 6, on **se,** for a similar use of the reflexive.)—**maturáret, oraverat:** What sequence of tenses is illustrated by these verbs? What tense of the subjunctive is used here and what kind of action does it denote in relation to the main verb? (See above, Lesson 14, Section D, line 7, for the sequence **eriperet, orábat**—where **orábat** appears [as does **oraverat**] after the construction that it introduces.)

LESSON 19

FIRST AND SECOND CONJUGATIONS: FUTURE PASSIVE INDICATIVE. PLINY: PLINY THE YOUNGER CONTINUES TO STUDY DESPITE THE DANGER.

§A **First and Second Conjugations: Future Passive Indicative.** With regard to the future passive system, **amo** will serve as the model for the future passive indicative of first and second conjugation verbs.

Ind. Sing.			
	amábor		**monébor**
⇓	**amaberis**		**moneberis**
	amabitur		**monebitur**
Ind. Plur.	**amabimur**		**monebimur**
⇓	**amabimini**		**monebimini**
	amabuntur		**monebuntur**

The future passive indicative of **amo** and **moneo** *(I will be loved / I will be warned)* consists of the present stem **ama-** or **mone-**, the future indicative infix **-bi-** or **-be-** or **-bu-**, and the present passive endings.

§B **Exercise.** Identify the tense, voice, mood, person, and number of the following verbs and translate (**armo, armáre, armávi, armátus** ... *to arm*; **foveo, fovére, fovi, fotus** ... *to cherish*):

(1) **armábor**   (4) **fovebuntur**

(2) **fovebimur**   (5) **armabátur**

(3) **armaberis**   (6) **fovebimini**

> ***coepi, coepisti, coepit,** etc. ... (perf. ind. of **coepi**, found only in the perf., plup., and fut. perf. tenses) *I began, you began, he / she / it began, etc.;* **coeptus, coepta, coeptum:** *having been begun*

> **constantia, constantiae,** f. ... *steadiness; courage, fearlessness*

> **corripio, corripere, corripui, correptus** ... *to seize, to snatch; to criticize, to find fault with*

> ***debeo, debére, debui, debitus** ... *to owe; to be indebted* or *beholden* to someone (dat.) for something (acc.)

> ***divido, dividere, divísi, divísus** ... *to divide, to separate*

> ***dubito, dubitáre, dubitávi, dubitátus** ... *to doubt, to hesitate, to be uncertain*

> **duodevicesimus, duodevicesima, duodevicesimum** ... *eighteenth*

> **excerpo, excerpere, excerpsi, excerptus** ... *to pick out; to make excerpts* or *extracts* of a literary text

> **formidolósus, formidolósa, formidolósum** ... *alarming, frightful*

> **Hispania, Hispaniae,** f. ... *Spain*

> ***ideo** ... *on that account, for that reason*

> **impendo, impendere, impendi, impensus** ... *to weigh out; to devote, to set aside*

> **imprudentia, imprudentiae,** f. ... *ignorance, inexperience*

> **inquiétus, inquiéta, inquiétum** ... *unquiet, restless*

> **intendo, intendere, intendi, intentus** ... *to stretch out, to spread out;* **intentus, intenta, intentum:** *intent; exerting* oneself; *keenly focused* on, *intensely interested* in (+ acc.)

> **invalesco, invalescere, invalui** ... *to become strong, to become violent*

> ***lego, legere, legi, lectus** ... *to gather; to read, to recite; to choose, to select*

> **Livius, Livii,** m. ... *Livy,* the Roman historian

minus ... (compar. of **parum;** see *ARA*, App. D, p. 421) *less*

modicus, modica, modicum ... *modest, moderate*

nihilum, nihili, n. ... *nothing;* (abl. with compar. word) *not at all, by no degree*

nuper ... *recently, not long ago*

patientia, patientiae, f. ... *patience; apathy, passivity*

praecédo, praecedere, praecessi ... *to go before, to occur earlier*

reliquus, reliqua, reliquum ... *rest, remaining*

remaneo, remanére, remansi ... *to stay, to remain*

segnis, segne ... *slow, sluggish, inactive;* **segniter:** *halfheartedly, un-enthusiastically*

*****somnus, somni,** m. ... (plur. may have sing. meaning) *sleep*

Titus, Titi, m. ... *Titus* (= Livy's given name)

§D   **Reading.**

Pliny the Younger Continues to Study despite the Danger.

Lessons 19–23 contain the narrative portions of the second of Pliny's two letters addressed to the Roman historian Tacitus concerning the eruption of Mt. Vesuvius in 79 A.D. In it Pliny describes how he and his mother attempted to escape an increasingly dangerous situation after his uncle had sailed away in order to investigate the eruption.

Profecto avunculo, ipse reliquum tempus studiis (ideo enim

remanseram) impendi; mox balineum, cena, somnus inquiétus

et brevis. Praecesserat per multos dies tremor terrae, minus

formidolósus quia Campaniae solitus. Illa vero nocte ita invaluit

5   **ut non movéri omnia sed verti crederentur. Irrumpit cubiculum**

meum mater; surgébam invicem, si quiesceret excitatúrus.

Residimus in area domus, quae mare a tectis modico spatio

dividébat. Dubito constantiam vocáre an imprudentiam debeam

(agébam enim duodevicesimum annum): posco librum Titi Livi,

10   et quasi per otium lego, atque etiam (ut coeperam) excerpo.

Ecce amícus avunculi, qui nuper ad eum ex Hispania venerat,

ut me et matrem sedentes (me vero etiam legentem) videt, illíus

patientiam, securitátem meam corripit. Nihilo segnius ego

intentus in librum.

§E   Notes and Queries.

(1) **Profecto avunculo:** What construction? Of what verb is **profecto** a form?

(1–2) **ipse . . . impendi:** Here Pliny again refers to the decision that he had made not to accompany his uncle on the mission to investigate the eruption (see above, Lesson 14, Section D, lines 3–4).

(2–3) **mox . . . brevis:** What verb should be supplied in this sentence?

(4) **Campaniae:** See above, Lesson 18, Section E, note to line 7.—**illa:** What noun does this adjective modify?

(5) **ut . . . crederentur:** What construction?—**movéri . . . verti:** Tense, voice, and mood?

(6) **si quiesceret:** A conditional clause in which the subjunctive should be translated according to sense.—**excitatúrus:** Tense, voice, and mood? (See *ARA*, Lesson 53, Section E, note to line 17.) Subject of the verbal action? What should be supplied as the direct object?

(7) **modico spatio:** Pliny the Elder's house, where Pliny the Younger and his mother were staying at the time of the eruption, was apparently located not far from the shore.

(8) **an . . . debeam:** What construction? (Here **debeam** functions as an auxiliary verb meaning *I ought.*)—**constantiam vocáre:** The noun **constantiam** is in apposition with the direct object of the verb **vocáre**, to be supplied from the overall context.

(9) **duodevicesimum annum:** Pliny the Younger's age at the time of the eruption in 79 A.D. In what year do you calculate that Pliny the Younger was born?—**Titi Livi:** See *ARA,* Lesson 42, Section E, for a description of the Roman historian Livy.

(10) **quasi per otium:** Although the Latin idiom is *as if through leisure,* how would you express it in normal English?—**coeperam:** That is, as Pliny had begun to do before he was interrupted by the tremor.

(12) **sedentes:** Tense, voice, and mood? Subject of the verbal action?—**illíus:** To whom does this pronoun refer? Why can it not refer to Pliny or his uncle?

(13) **segnius:** Degree of adverb? (Make sure that you use a meaning suitable for this word in its adverbial form.)

LESSON 20

THIRD AND FOURTH CONJUGATIONS: FUTURE PASSIVE INDICATIVE. PLINY: PLINY THE YOUNGER LEAVES MISENUM AS PEOPLE EVACUATE.

§A **Third and Fourth Conjugations: Future Passive Indicative.** As you can see from the following chart, **traho** will serve as the model for the future passive indicative of third and fourth conjugation verbs.

Ind. Sing.	trahar	audiar	capiar
⇓	trahéris	audiéris	capiéris
	trahétur	audiétur	capiétur
Ind. Plur.	trahémur	audiémur	capiémur
⇓	trahemini	audiemini	capiemini
	trahentur	audientur	capientur

The future passive indicative of **traho, audio,** and **capio** consists of a variation of the present stem (**traha-/trahe-, audia-/audie-, capia-/capie-**) and the present passive endings (future infix not found here).

§B **Exercise.** Identify the tense, voice, mood, person, and number of the following verbs and translate (**cingo, cingere, cinxi, cinctus** ... *to encircle;* **vincio, vincíre, vinxi, vinctus** ... *to bind*):

(1) **cingéris**

(2) **vincientur**

(3) **cingimini**

(4) **vinciar**

(5) **cingémur**

(6) **vinciétur**

agmen, agminis, n. ... (plur. may have sing. meaning) *band, mass; army, host; crowd, throng*

aliénus, aliéna, aliénum ... *another's; hostile, unfriendly*

animal, animális, n. (gen. plur. **animalium**) ... *animal, living creature*

ater, atra, atrum ... *dark, black*

attonitus, attonita, attonitum ... *struck by lightning; thunderstruck, panic-stricken*

campus, campi, m. ... *field, plain, ground*

circumiaceo, circumiacére, circumiacui ... *to lie around, to lie in the neighborhood*

consisto, consistere, constiti ... *to stop moving, to come to a halt; to set foot, to take* one's *place or position*

dehisco, dehiscere ... *to gape, to yawn; to burst open, to split open*

demum ... *at last, finally*

detineo, detinére, detinui, detentus ... *to hold, to hold back; to hold captive, to cause to remain*

discursus, discursus, m. ... a *running about; discharge, explosion*

dubius, dubia, dubium ... *doubtful, uncertain*

excédo, excedere, excessi ... *to leave, to go out* from, *to depart* from

fulcio, fulcíre, fulsi, fultus ... *to prop up, to support*

fulgur, fulguris, n. ... *flash of lightning*

haréna, harénae, f. ... (plur. may have sing. meaning) *sand*

*hora, horae, f. ... *hour*

horrendus, horrenda, horrendum ... *terrible, dreadful*

igneus, ignea, igneum ... *fiery*

impello, impellere, impuli, impulsus ... *to drive, to drive forward;* (of the wind) *to blow on, to caress roughly*

*ingens, ingentis ... *huge, enormous*

languidus, languida, languidum ... *weak, faint*

latus, lateris, n. ... *side, flank*

maior, maius ... (compar. of **magnus;** see *ARA,* App. D, p. 419) *greater*

*ne ... *lest, that not, in order that not;* **ne . . . quidem:** (emphasizing the intervening word) *not even* (e.g., **ne aurum quidem,** *not even gold*)

*nubes, nubis, f. (gen. plur. **nubium**) ... *cloud*

patior, pati, passus sum ... *to experience; to allow, to permit; to suffer, to endure*

pavor, pavóris, m. ... *fear; panic, terrifying situation*

planus, plana, planum ... *even, flat, level*

praeterea ... *besides, further*

*premo, premere, pressi, pressus ... *to press; to push, to pursue; to bind, to secure; to cover, to conceal*

prodúco, producere, produxi, productus ... *to lead out, to bring forth*

prudentia, prudentiae, f. ... *intelligence; good judgment, rational thinking*

*quasi ... *as if, just as; as it were, so to speak*

quasso, quassáre, quassávi, quassátus ... *to shake repeatedly, to cause* something *to shake violently*

repello, repellere, reppuli, repulsus ... *to drive back* or *away; to drive back* or *away* from; *to spurn, to reject, to rebuff*

resorbeo, resorbére, resorbui ... *to swallow again; to suck back* or *away*

siccus, sicca, siccum ... *dry*

vehiculum, vehiculi, n. ... *vehicle; cart, wagon; chariot, carriage*

*vestigium, vestigii, n. ... *footstep, footprint; trace, track, position*

vibro, vibráre, vibrávi, vibrátus ... *to flash; to hurl out, to shoot out; to* cause something *to flap* or *flutter*

vulgus, vulgi, n. ... *people; crowd, throng*

§D   Reading.

Pliny the Younger Leaves Misenum As People Evacuate.

Iam hora diéi prima, et adhuc dubius et quasi languidus dies.

Iam quassátis circumiacentibus tectis, quamquam in aperto loco,

angusto tamen, magnus et certus ruínae metus. Tum demum

excedere oppido visum. Sequitur vulgus attonitum, quodque in

5   pavóre simile prudentiae, aliénum consilium suo praefert,

ingentique agmine abeuntes premit et impellit. Egressi tecta,

consistimus. Multa ibi miranda, multas formidines patimur.

Nam vehicula, quae prodúci iusserámus, quamquam in

planissimo campo, in contrarias partes agebantur, ac ne

10   lapidibus quidem fulta, in eódem vestigio quiescébant. Praeterea

mare in se resorbéri et tremóre terrae quasi repelli videbámus.

Certe processerat litus multaque animalia maris siccis harénis

detinébat. Ab altero latere nubes atra et horrenda, ignei spiritus

tortis vibratisque discursibus rupta, in longas flammárum

15   figúras dehiscébat; fulguribus illae et similes et maióres erant.

(1) **Iam . . . dies:** What verb should be supplied in this sentence?—**hora . . . prima:** See above, Lesson 13, Section F, note to line 2.

(2) **quassátis . . . tectis:** What construction?

(4) **visum:** The equivalent of **visum est,** the impersonal form of **video** here meaning *it seemed good.*—**vulgus:** Of what four verbs is this the subject?—**quodque:** That is, **quodque est.** What should be supplied as the antecedent of the **quod** in **quodque?**

(5) **praefert:** Translate *prefers* or *preferred*, depending on whether or not you treat this verb as a historical present. Here this verb takes the accusative **aliénum consilium** and the dative **suo** (i.e., **suo consilio**). (Pliny is essentially saying that during a mass panic, people are so frightened that they generally do what someone else tells them to do.)

(6) **abeuntes:** Translate *(us) departing.*

(7) **miranda:** The gerundive of **miror,** here used as a substantive.

(8) **prodúci:** Tense, voice, and mood?

(9–10) **ne . . . quidem:** See the entry for **ne** in the vocabulary of this lesson for the way in which this idiom functions.

(10) **lapidibus:** Placed under the wheels of the vehicles to serve as a brake, although apparently without success.—**fulta:** Tense, voice, and mood? Subject of the verbal action?

(11) **mare . . . resorbéri et . . . repelli videbámus:** Instead of using these words, Pliny could have written the sentence **Diximus: "Mare resorbebitur et repellétur."** If he had chosen to do so, what form of the verbs **resorbeo** and **repello** (tense, voice, mood, person, and number) would he have used and how would you translate this sentence?

(12) **litus:** Of what two verbs is this the subject?—**harénis:** What kind of ablative?

(13) **Ab altero latere:** That is, on the landward side, in contrast to what was happening on the seaward side.—**ignei:** What noun does this adjective modify?

(14) **rupta:** Tense, voice, and mood? Subject of the verbal action?

(15) **fulguribus:** This noun is used with two adjectives. Case and number in relation to the first adjective? Case and number in relation to the second adjective?

LESSON 21

FUTURE PERFECT PASSIVE INDICATIVE. PLINY: PLINY THE YOUNGER IGNORES A WARNING BUT PROTECTS HIS MOTHER.

§A   **Future Perfect Passive Indicative.** With regard to the future perfect passive system, **amo** will serve (as in the future perfect active system) as the model for the future perfect passive indicative of all verbs.

amátus, -a, -um ero
amátus, -a, -um eris
amátus, -a, -um erit
amáti, -ae, -a erimus
amáti, -ae, -a eritis
amáti, -ae, -a erunt

monitus, -a, -um ero, etc.

tractus, -a, -um ero, etc.

audítus, -a, -um ero, etc.

captus, -a, -um ero, etc.

The future perfect passive indicative (*I will have been loved, I will have been warned,* etc.) consists of the perfect passive participle and the future indicative of **sum** (see *ARA,* App. J, for the verb **sum**).

§B   **Exercise.** Identify the tense, voice, mood, person, and number of the following verbs and translate (**doceo, docére, docui, doctus** ... *to teach;* **pingo, pingere, pinxi, pictus** ... *to paint*):

    (1) **doctus eris**   (4) **picti eritis**

    (2) **picta erunt**   (5) **docta eram**

    (3) **doctum erit**   (6) **pictae erimus**

Vocabulary.

abscondo, abscondere, abscondi, absconditus ... *to hide, to conceal*

acer, acris, acre ... *keen, sharp; wild, fierce; excited, spirited;* **acriter:** *keenly, sharply; wildly, fiercely; excitedly, spiritedly*

addo, addere, addidi, additus ... *to add; to increase, to quicken* one's *step* or *pace*

aeger, aegra, aegrum ... *ill, sick; weary, exhausted;* **aegre:** *painfully, grudgingly, reluctantly*

amplector, amplecti, amplexus sum ... *to clasp, to embrace; to take hold of, to seize hold of*

*****bene** ... *well, kindly; at peace, contentedly*

Capreae, Capreárum, f. ... (plur. noun with sing. meaning) *Capri*

cesso, cessáre, cessávi ... *to stop, to cease; to delay, to hesitate*

*****cingo, cingere, cinxi, cinctus** ... *to encircle, to surround; to fasten, to gird up, to strap on*

*****cinis, cineris,** c. ... *ashes*

cogo, cogere, coégi, coactus ... *to force, to drive*

committo, committere, commísi, commissus ... *to send together; to bring about, to allow to happen*

consulo, consulere, consului, consultus ... *to consult* (+ acc.); *to look after the interests of* (+ dat.)

*****contra** ... *against, opposite* (+ acc.); (adv.) *in reply, in return; on the other hand, on the other side*

*****cursus, cursus,** m. ... (plur. may have sing. meaning) a *running; voyage, journey;* **cursu:** (of animals) *at a run, at a gallop*

evádo, evadere, evási ... *to go out; to escape, to get away; to go upward, to come upward*

gradus, gradus, m. ... *step, pace; stage, phase*

incúso, incusáre, incusávi, incusátus ... *to blame, to criticize, to find fault with*

instans, instantis ... *urgent, pressing, insistent;* **instanter:** *urgently, pressingly, insistently*

*modus, modi, m. ... *way, manner;* (abl. sing. + gen.) *in the way* of; (abl. sing. + adj.) *in . . . way;* (abl. plur. + adj.) *in . . . ways*

moror, morári, morátus sum ... *to delay, to tarry; to detain, to hold back*

procurro, procurrere, procurri ... *to run forward; to extend, to project*

proinde ... *therefore, accordingly*

proripio, proripere, proripui, proreptus ... *to seize, to snatch;* (used with the reflexive **se,** which is not translated in this idiom) *to rush off, to hurry off*

rarus, rara, rarum ... *thin, loose; sparse, scattered; unusual, exquisite*

salus, salútis, f. ... *health, safety; salvation, deliverance*

*salvus, salva, salvum ... *safe, well;* **salve:** *safe, well*

superstes, superstitis ... *standing over; surviving* or *remaining alive after someone's death*

tergum, tergi, n. ... (plur. may have sing. meaning) *back, rear; hide, skin*

torrens, torrentis, m. ... *torrent*

ultra ... *beyond, further; any more, any longer*

vos ... (nom. or acc. plur. of **tu**) *you*

§D   **Reading.**

Pliny the Younger Ignores a Warning but Protects His Mother.

Tum vero idem ille ex Hispania amícus acrius et instantius, "Si frater," inquit, "tuus, tuus avunculus vivit, vult esse vos salvos; si periit, superstites voluit. Proinde quid cessátis evadere?"

Respondimus non commissúros nos ut, de salúte illíus incerti,

5   nostrae consulerémus. Non morátus ultra proripit se, effusoque

cursu periculo aufertur. Nec multo post illa nubes descendere

in terras, operíre maria; cinxerat Capreas et absconderat;

Miséni quod procurrit, abstulerat. Tum mater oráre, hortári,

iubére, quoquo modo fugerem; posse enim iuvenem, se et annis

10   et corpore gravem bene moritúram, si mihi causa mortis non

fuisset. Ego contra salvum me nisi una non futúrum; dein

manum eius amplexus, addere gradum cogo. Paret aegre,

incusatque se, quod me morétur. Iam cinis, adhuc tamen

rarus. Respicio: densa calígo tergis imminébat, quae nos

15   (torrentis modo infúsa terrae) sequebátur.

§E   **Notes and Queries.**

(1) **idem . . . amícus:** See above, Lesson 19, Section D, line 11.—**acrius
. . . instantius:** Degree of adverbs?

(2) **tuus, tuus:** To whom is the first **tuus** addressed? To whom is the
second **tuus** addressed?—**vult:** Translate *he wishes* or *he wants.*—
salvos: To whom does this adjective refer? Explain the use of the gender. (See *ARA,* Lesson 28, Section G, note to line 10.)

(3) **periit:** Translate *he has perished.*—**voluit:** Translate *he wished* or
he wanted. What words should be supplied after this verb from earlier in the sentence?

(4) **commissúros nos:** What construction? Tense, voice, and mood of
commissúros (esse)? (See *ARA,* Lesson 59, Section E, note to line 3.)—
illíus: To whom does this pronoun refer? Why can it not refer to Pliny
or his mother?—**incerti:** To whom does this adjective refer? With
what verb(s) should it be connected in order to identify the subject?

(5) **nostrae:** After this adjective supply the noun **salúti.**

(5–6) **effusoque cursu:** Translate *and running as fast as he could.* What is the literal meaning of these words?

(6) **aufertur:** Translate *he is removed from* or *was removed from,* depending on whether or not you treat this verb as a historical present.

(6–7) **descendere . . . operíre:** The present infinitive may be used in historical narrative instead of the imperfect indicative in order to demonstrate a rapid sequence of events (see *ARA,* App. K, p. 470, Historical Infinitive).

(7) **Capreas:** An island off the coast of Campania. (See above, Lesson 18, Section E, note to line 7.)

(8) **abstulerat:** Translate *it had removed from sight.* Supply *land* as the direct object of this verb and as the antecedent of the relative in the clause **Miséni quod procurrit,** which refers to the promontory (a high ridge of land jutting out into the sea) at Misenum.

(8–9) **oráre, hortári, iubére:** Three historical infinitives (see above, note to lines 6–7.) After these infinitives supply the conjunction **ut** in order to introduce the clause **ut . . . fugerem.**

(9) **quoquo:** A form of the indefinite pronoun **quisquis,** here used as an adjective.—**posse . . . iuvenem:** What construction? This construction is introduced by a verb implied by the three historical infinitives **oráre, hortári,** and **iubére.** (Here translate **posse** as *was able*—it being the present active infinitive of the irregular verb **possum.**)

(9–10) **se . . . moritúram:** The same construction as **posse . . . iuvenem** earlier in the sentence, also introduced by a verb implied by the three historical infinitives **oráre, hortári,** and **iubére.**

(11) **fuisset:** Translate *she had been.*—**me . . . non futúrum:** The same construction as **posse . . . iuvenem** in the previous sentence, but with the subject of the implied verb here changed from **mater** to **Ego.** (Translate **futúrum** as *would be*—it being the future active infinitive of the irregular verb **sum.**)—**nisi una:** Although the Latin idiom is *unless together,* how would you express it in normal English?

(13) **quod . . . morétur:** See above, Lesson 11, Section E, note to line 13.

(13–14) **Iam . . . rarus:** What verb should be supplied in this sentence?

(15) **infúsa:** Tense, voice, and mood? Subject of the verbal action?

LESSON 22

CONDITIONAL SENTENCES: INDICATIVE. PLINY: PLINY THE YOUNGER DESCRIBES THE HORRORS OF A MASS PANIC.

§A **Conditional Sentences: Indicative.** Conditional sentences involve a conjecture or supposition concerning reality. They consist of the *protasis,* the subordinate clause stating the condition *(if),* and the *apodosis,* the main clause stating the conclusion *(then).* Two types of conditional sentences use the indicative in the protasis and apodosis:

SIMPLE

| **Protasis** | **Apodosis** |
| si + Ind. | Ind. |

Example: **si rex superat, milites contendunt,** *if the king conquers, the soldiers hasten.*

FUTURE MORE VIVID

| **Protasis** | **Apodosis** |
| si + Fut. Ind. | Fut. Ind. |

Example: **si rex superábit, milites contendent,** *if the king conquers, the soldiers will hasten.*

Simple conditions have the present, imperfect, or perfect indicative in the subordinate clause and the main clause, where the tense of the indicative has its usual meaning. Future more vivid conditions have the future or future perfect indicative in the subordinate clause (translated as present) and the future indicative in the main clause.

§B **Exercise.** Translate the following conditional sentences into English; then indicate (1) the type of condition used, and (2), the tense and mood of the verbs in the protasis and apodosis:

(1) Si nubes in terras descendébat, maria litoraque operiébat.

(2) Si Plinius in oppido manébit, avunculum non inveniet.

(3) Si Plinius ex oppido excédet, matrem ex periculo servábit.

§C   Vocabulary.

advento, adventáre, adventávi, adventátus ... *to come toward; to approach, to draw near*

aeternus, aeterna, aeternum ... *eternal, everlasting*

*__augeo, augére, auxi, auctus__ ... *to increase; to enhance, to strengthen*

comitor, comitári, comitátus sum ... *to accompany*

consído, considere, consédi ... *to sit down; to take* one's *seat; to set up quarters*

deflecto, deflectere, deflexi, deflexus ... *to bend* something *down; to turn aside, to change* one's *direction*

exstinguo, exstinguere, exstinxi, exstinctus ... *to put out;* (in passive) *to die, to perish*

falsus, falsa, falsum ... *false, deceptive;* **falso:** *falsely, mistakenly*

*__fingo, fingere, finxi, fictus__ ... *to form, to shape; to feign, to invent, to contrive*

illúnis, illúne ... *moonless*

indicium, indicii, n. ... *disclosure; proof, evidence*

infans, infantis, c. ... *baby; child*

inquam ... *I say* or *said*

interpretor, interpretári, interpretátus sum ... *to interpret; to take the view* or *position*

*__liberi, liberórum,__ m. ... (plur. noun with plur. meaning) *children; sons*

mentior, mentíri, mentítus sum ... *to lie; to invent, to make up*

miseror, miserári, miserátus sum ... *to bewail; to pity, to have pity for;* (gerundive) **miserandus, miseranda, miserandum:** *to be pitied, to be lamented*

mundus, mundi, m. ... *world, universe*

noscito, noscitáre, noscitávi, noscitátus ... *to try to recognize*

nubilus, nubila, nubilum ... *cloudy;* (neut. plur. as substantive) *clouds*

nusquam ... *nowhere*

obtero, obterere, obtrívi, obtrítus ... *to crush, to trample*

precor, precári, precátus sum ... *to pray for; to beseech, to implore;* (pres. ind. first pers. sing.) *I beseech you*

*qualis, quale ... *as, just as, such as*

*quidem ... *indeed, certainly*

quiritátus, quiritátus, m. ... (plur. may have sing. meaning) *crying, screaming*

relucesco, relucescere, reluxi ... *to grow bright again*

requíro, requirere, requisii, requisítus ... *to seek, to desire; to look for, to try to find; to ask about, to inquire about; to examine carefully, to commit to memory*

*ruo, ruere, rui ... *to rush, to move swiftly; to fall, to collapse, to be destroyed*

sterno, sternere, stravi, stratus ... *to lay out, to spread out; to knock down, to strike down*

terror, terróris, m. ... *terror, fright*

ululátus, ululátus, m. ... (plur. may have sing. meaning) *screaming, shrieking*

*via, viae, f. ... *way, road, path*

vix ... *hardly, scarcely;* **vix tandem:** *only just after all this time*

§D **Reading.**

Pliny the Younger Describes the Horrors of a Mass Panic.

"Deflectámus," inquam, "dum vidémus, ne in via strati

comitantium turba in tenebris obterámur." Vix consederámus,

et nox non qualis illúnis aut nubila, sed qualis in locis clausis

lumine exstincto. Audíres ululátus feminárum, infantum

5 quiritátus, clamóres virórum. Alii parentes alii liberos alii

coniuges vocibus requirébant, vocibus noscitábant. Hi suum

casum, illi suórum miserabantur; erant qui metu mortis

mortem precarentur. Multi ad deos manus tollere; plures

nusquam iam deos ullos aeternamque illam et novissimam

10 noctem mundo interpretabantur. Nec defuérunt qui fictis

mentitisque terroribus vera pericula augérent. Aderant qui

Miséni illud ruisse illud ardére falso sed credentibus

nuntiábant. Paulum reluxit, quod non dies nobis sed

adventantis ignis indicium videbátur; et ignis quidem longius

15 substitit.

§E **Notes and Queries.**

(1) **strati:** Tense, voice, and mood? Subject of the verbal action? With
what other verb(s) should this form be connected in order to identify
the subject? (See above, Lesson 21, Section E, note to line 4, on **incerti**,
for a similar situation involving an adjective.)

(1–2) **Deflectámus . . . ne . . . obterámur:** What use of the subjunctive
is **Deflectámus?** What construction is contained in **ne . . . obterámur?**
Instead of using these words, Pliny could have written the sentence
Si deflectémus . . . non . . . obterémur. Translation of this sentence?
What type of condition is this? Tense and mood of the verbs?

(2) **comitantium:** What use of the participle? Subject to be supplied here? (Make sure that you also pay attention to case and number.)—**consederámus:** Pliny and his mother adopted some kind of crouching posture in order to protect themselves from the falling ashes.

(4) **Audíres:** The subjunctive may be used to state—in someone's opinion—that something is likely, possible, probable, etc. (see *ARA,* Appendix K, p. 472, Potential Subjunctive, and choose the appropriate translation for the tense of the subjunctive used in this sentence).

(5) **Alii . . . alii . . . alii:** These three subjects (referring to three groups of people) share the verbs **requirébant** and **noscitábant,** while taking the direct objects **parentes, liberos,** and **coniuges,** respectively.

(6–7) **Hi . . . illi:** Here the equivalent of **Alii . . . alii,** referring to two groups of people, not necessarily the same people mentioned earlier.

(7) **casum . . . miserabantur:** These words should be used twice, first in the **Hi** clause and then in the **illi** clause.—**suórum:** In the masculine plural, the reflexive adjective is sometimes used as a substantive meaning *his own, her own, their own* family or friends or relatives.

(7–8) **qui . . . precarentur:** What construction? (See above, Lesson 13, Section F, note to lines 7–8.)

(8) **tollere:** The present infinitive may be used in historical narrative instead of the imperfect indicative (see above, Lesson 21, Section E, note to lines 6–7).

(10) **interpretabantur:** What construction does this verb introduce? What element of this construction should be supplied in this sentence?—**defuérunt:** Translate *they were absent.*

(10–11) **qui . . . augérent:** What construction?—**fictis mentitisque:** Tense, voice, and mood? Subject of the verbal action?

(11) **Aderant:** Translate *they were present.*

(12) **illud . . . illud:** Here translate *this part . . . that part,* referring to specific places that were presumably being destroyed at Misenum.—**credentibus:** What use of the participle? Subject to be supplied here? (Make sure that you also pay attention to case and number.)

(13) **nuntiábant:** What construction does this verb introduce? What are the elements of this construction in this sentence?—**quod:** Here the relative refers to the entire statement **Paulum reluxit.**

(14) **adventantis:** Tense, voice, and mood? Subject of the verbal action?

LESSON 23

CONDITIONAL SENTENCES: SUBJUNCTIVE. PLINY: PLINY THE YOUNGER RETURNS TO MISENUM AFTER THE ERUPTION.

§A   **Conditional Sentences: Subjunctive.** Some types of conditional sentences use the subjunctive rather than the indicative. They depict a situation that differs from what actually is the case and usually take the subjunctive in the protasis and apodosis. Three types of conditional sentences that take the subjunctive are presented below:

FUTURE LESS VIVID

Protasis	**Apodosis**
si + Pres. Subj.	Pres. Subj.

Example: **si rex superet, milites contendant,** *if the king should conquer, the soldiers would hasten.*

PRESENT CONTRARY TO FACT

Protasis	**Apodosis**
si + Imperf. Subj.	Imperf. Subj.

Example: **si rex superáret, milites contenderent,** *if the king were conquering, the soldiers would be hastening.*

PAST CONTRARY TO FACT

Protasis	**Apodosis**
si + Plup. Subj.	Plup. Subj.

Example: **si rex superavisset, milites contendissent,** *if the king had conquered, the soldiers would have hastened.*

Future less vivid conditions are usually translated by *should/would,* present contrary to fact conditions by *were/would,* and past contrary to fact conditions by *had/would have.* See *ARA,* App. K, pp. 476–77, for a detailed examination of conditions, including two types that take the subjunctive in the protasis and the indicative in the apodosis.

§B **Exercise.** Translate the following conditional sentences into English; then indicate (1) the type of condition used, and (2), the tense and mood of the verbs in the protasis and apodosis:

    (1) **Si Plinius et mater deflectant, in tenebris non sternantur.**

    (2) **Si Plinius diu consedisset, ululátus feminárum audivisset.**

    (3) **Si Plinius avunculum vidéret, deis multas gratias ageret.**

§C **Vocabulary.**

alioqui ... *otherwise*

curo, curáre, curávi, curátus ... *to care; to care for, to look after*

decédo, decedere, decessi ... *to go away; to fade away, to drift away*

donec ... *until*

effulgeo, effulgére, effulsi ... *to shine, to come out*

excido, excidere, excidi ... *to fall out; to fall or escape or slip away from* (+ dat.)

excutio, excutere, excussi, excussus ... *to shake out, to shake off*

exigo, exigere, exégi, exactus ... *to drive out; to spend* one's time or life

experior, experíri, expertus sum ... *to try out; to undergo, to experience*

fumus, fumi, m. ... *smoke*

glorior, gloriári, gloriátus sum ... *to brag, to boast*

identidem ... *repeatedly*

ludificor, ludificári, ludificátus sum ... *to make* something *seem ludicrous* or *ridiculous*

luridus, lurida, luridum ... *murky, sickly, ghastly*

lymphátus, lympháta, lymphátum ... *crazed, frantic, frenzied*

mortalitas, mortalitátis, f. ... *mortality; humanity, human condition*

*****mox** ... *then, soon, presently*

nebula, nebulae, f. ... *mist, cloud*

nix, nivis, f. ... *snow*

*****nuntius, nuntii,** m. ... *messenger; message, report*

obdúco, obducere, obduxi, obductus ... *to lead to; to cover up, to cover over*

oblído, oblidere, oblísi, oblísus ... *to crush*

occurso, occursáre, occursávi ... *to keep running; to become visible to the eyes*

parum ... *not, not at all; too little, not enough*

persevéro, perseveráre, perseserávi ... *to persist, to continue*

plerique, pleraeque, pleraque ... (plur. adjective used as substantive) *very many*

praevaleo, praevalére, praevalui ... *to be very strong; to prevail, to predominate*

regredior, regredi, regressus sum ... *to return, to go back*

solacium, solacii, n. ... *comfort, consolation*

*****soleo, solére, solitus sum** ... (semi-deponent verb) *to be accustomed (+ inf.);* **solitus, solita, solitum:** *usual, normal, customary*

*****spes, spei,** f. ... *hope*

suspensus, suspensa, suspensum ... *anxious, uncertain*

*****tamquam** ... *as if, just as if*

*****tandem** ... *at last, at length;* (as emphatic affirmation) *I ask you, I beg you*

*****tenebrae, tenebrárum,** f. ... (plur. may have sing. meaning) *darkness, shadows*

tenuo, tenuáre, tenuávi, tenuátus ... *to make thin; to weaken, to diminish*

terrificus, terrifica, terrificum ... *terrifying, frightening*

utcumque ... *in whatever manner, by whatever means possible*

vaticinatio, vaticinatiónis, f. ... *prophecy, prediction*

§D   Reading.

Pliny the Younger Returns to Misenum after the Eruption.

Tenebrae rursus, cinis rursus, multus et gravis. Hunc
identidem adsurgentes excutiebámus; operti alioqui atque etiam
oblísi pondere essémus. Possem gloriári non gemitum mihi,
non vocem parum fortem in tantis periculis excidisse, nisi me

5   cum omnibus, omnia mecum períre (misero, magno tamen
mortalitátis solacio) credidissem. Tandem illa calígo tenuáta
quasi in fumum nebulamve decessit; mox dies verus; sol etiam
effulsit, luridus tamen, qualis esse cum deficit solet.
Occursábant trepidantibus adhuc oculis mutáta omnia altoque

10   cinere tamquam nive obducta. Regressi Misénum, curátis
utcumque corporibus, suspensam dubiamque noctem spe ac
metu exegimus. Metus praevalébat; nam et tremor terrae
perseverábat, et plerique lympháti terrificis vaticinationibus et
sua et aliéna mala ludificabantur. Nobis tamen ne tunc quidem

15   (quamquam et expertis periculum et exspectantibus) abeundi
consilium, donec de avunculo nuntius.

(2) **adsurgentes:** Tense, voice, and mood? Subject of the verbal action?

(2–3) **operti . . . oblísi . . . essémus:** That is, **operti essémus** and **oblísi essémus.** What use of the subjunctive? (See above, Lesson 22, Section E, note to line 4). Pliny could have used **operti essémus** in the sentence **si non adsurrexissémus, operti essémus.** Translation of this sentence? What type of condition is this? Tense and mood of the verbs?

(3–6) **Possem gloriári . . . nisi . . . credidissem:** A mixed conditional sentence in inverted order, with the pluperfect subjunctive in the protasis (**nisi . . . credidissem**) and the imperfect subjunctive in the apodosis (**Possem gloriári,** with **Possem** translated as *I would be able*). What construction do the words **Possem gloriári** introduce? What construction do the words **nisi . . . credidissem** introduce? In the second use of this construction, translate **períre** as *was perishing* and *were perishing* according to whether its subject is singular or plural. (Pliny is essentially saying that he cannot claim to have acted bravely during the eruption as his stoic demeanor might have suggested, inasmuch as he was ultimately taking comfort in the notion that he would not die alone and that everyone else would die along with him.)

(5–6) **misero, magno tamen . . . solacio:** An idiomatic expression in the ablative case. Translate *(it being) a sad, nevertheless great . . .*

(9) **trepidantibus:** Tense, voice, and mood? Subject of the verbal action?—**omnia:** Of what verb is this the subject?

(9–10) **mutáta . . . obducta:** Tense, voice, and mood? Subject of the verbal action?

(10) **Regressi:** Tense, voice, and mood? Subject of the verbal action? Explain the use of the gender.

(10–11) **curátis . . . corporibus:** What construction?

(14) **Nobis:** What kind of dative? What verb should be supplied here?— **ne . . . quidem:** See above, Lesson 20, Section E, note to lines 9–10.

(15) **expertis . . . exspectantibus:** Tense, voice, and mood? Subject of the verbal action?—**abeundi:** Translate *of going away.*

(general) At the end of the second letter on the eruption—as at the end of the first letter—one observes the devastating effect of the volcanic ash on the people whom it destroyed, whose bodies archaeologists unearthed during extensive excavations and attempted to preserve by injecting liquid plaster into the hollows of the hardened ash.

LESSON 24

CONDITIONAL SENTENCES IN INDIRECT STATEMENT.
SUETONIUS: HOW THE EMPEROR TITUS HELPED THE
PEOPLE AFTER THE ERUPTION. CLASSICAL TRADITION:
EDWARD BULWER-LYTTON'S THE LAST DAYS OF POMPEII.

§A **Conditional Sentences in Indirect Statement.** An indirect statement may be a complex sentence, which contains a conditional sentence (see *ARA,* App. K, p. 479). In an indirect statement containing a condition, the main clause of the condition takes the accusative and infinitive; the verb in the subordinate clause is in the subjunctive.

> **dicit si rex superet, milites contendere,**
>
> *he says that if the king conquers, the soldiers hasten.*
>
> **dixit si rex superáret, milites contendere,**
>
> *he said that if the king was conquering, the soldiers were hastening.*

The tense of the subjunctive generally depends upon the tense of the introductory verb, in accordance with the rule for sequence of tenses (see above, Lessons 16–17). In the first sentence, the present subjunctive **superet** follows **dicit** (primary sequence); in the second, the imperfect subjunctive **superáret** follows **dixit** (secondary sequence).

§B **Exercise.** Translate the following sentences with conditional clauses in indirect statement; then indicate the tense of the subjunctive used and the kind of action it denotes in relation to the main verb.

(1) **Plinius putávit si cinerem excuteret, periculum decedere.**

(2) **Plerique credunt si sol effulgeat, verum diem accedere.**

(3) **Plerique clamavérunt si sol deficeret, periculum crescere.**

§C **Vocabulary.**

accido, accidere, accidi ... *to occur, to happen*

affectus, affectus, m. ... *feeling; love, devotion*

afflictus, afflicta, afflictum ... *damaged, destroyed*

alias ... *otherwise, at another time*

attribuo, attribuere, attribui, attribútus ... *to apply, to assign*

complúres, complurium ... (plur. adj. used as substantive) *several*

conflagratio, conflagratiónis, f. ... *eruption*

consuláris, consuláris, m. (gen. plur. **consularium**) ... *ex-consul*

cunctus, cuncta, cunctum ... *all*

curátor, curatóris, m. ... *supervisor, commissioner*

destino, destináre, destinávi, destinátus ... *to fix; to put* or *set aside* something (acc.) for something (dat.); **destinátus, destináta, destinátum:** *fixed; stubborn, obstinate*

divínus, divína, divínum ... *divine*

edictum, edicti, n. ... *edict, decree*

exsto, exstáre, exstiti ... *to stand out; to exist, to be found*

facultas, facultátis, f. ... *power; means, resources*

fortuitus, fortuita, fortuitum ... *disastrous, unfortunate*

heres, herédis, c. ... *heir*

inquíro, inquirere, inquisii, inquisítus ... *to ask about, to inquire about*

matúrus, matúra, matúrum ... *ripe, mature;* **matúre:** *quickly, expeditiously*

medeor, medéri ... *to cure*

morbus, morbi, m. ... *disease, sickness*

numerus, numeri, m. ... *number*

opitulor, opitulári, opitulátus sum ... *to provide help* or *assistance*

*****ops, opis,** f. ... *aid, help, assistance;* (in plur.) *wealth, property, resources*

*****opus, operis,** n. ... *work, labor; effect, function; public works* or *buildings;* **opus est:** *there is need* for (+ abl.)

ordo, ordinis, m. ... *rank, order, succession*

ornamentum, ornamenti, n. ... *ornament, adornment*

*****parens, parentis,** c. ... *parent; father, mother; ancestor, forefather*

pestilentia, pestilentiae, f. ... *plague*

praepóno, praeponere, praeposui, praepositus ... *to put before; to put in charge*

praetorium, praetorii, n. ... *palace, mansion*

publicus, publica, publicum ... *public;* **publice:** *publicly, in public*

quatenus ... *as far as, to what extent*

*****quisque, quidque** (gen. sing. **cuiusque, cuiusque**) ... (see *ARA*, App. C, p. 414, for the declension of this pronoun) *each person, each thing;* (in plur.) *all persons, all things*

restituo, restituere, restitui, restitútus ... *to restore, to rebuild*

restitutio, restitutiónis, f. ... *restoration*

Roma, Romae, f. ... *Rome*

sacrificium, sacrificii, n. ... *sacrifice*

sollicitúdo, sollicitudinis, f. ... *care, concern*

*****sors, sortis,** f. (gen. plur. **sortium**) ... (plur. may have sing. meaning) *oracle, prophecy; fate, fortune, destiny;* **sorte ducere:** *to choose at random, to select at random*

suppeto, suppetere, suppetívi ... *to allow, to permit*

totidem ... *just as many*

triduum, tridui, n. ... *period of three days*

*tristis, triste ... *bitter; sad, gloomy*

*urbs, urbis, f. (gen. plur. **urbium**) ... *city*

§D   Reading.

How the Emperor Titus Helped the People after the Eruption.

Lesson 24 contains a summary by the Roman historian Suetonius of how the emperor Titus dealt with three natural disasters, starting with the eruption of Mt. Vesuvius. In this short passage, Suetonius considers how Titus did everything in his power to alleviate the widespread suffering that resulted from these three catastrophic events.

Quaedam sub eo fortuita ac tristia accidérunt, ut conflagratio

Vesuvii montis in Campania, et incendium Romae per triduum

totidemque noctes, item pestilentia quanta non temere alias. In

iis tot adversis ac talibus, non modo principis sollicitudinem sed

5   etiam parentis affectum unicum praestitit, nunc consolando per

edicta, nunc opitulando quatenus suppeteret facultas. Curatóres

restituendae Campaniae e consularium numero sorte duxit;

bona oppressórum in Vesuvio, quorum herédes non exstábant,

restitutióni afflictárum civitatium attribuit. Urbis incendio nihil

10   publice nisi periisse testátus, cuncta praetoriórum suórum

ornamenta operibus ac templis destinávit, praeposuitque

complúres ex equestri ordine, quo quaeque maturius

peragerentur. Medendae valetudini leniendisque morbis nullam

divínam humanamque opem non adhibuit, inquisíto omni

15   sacrificiórum remediorumque genere.

Notes and Queries.

(1) **Quaedam:** Of what pronoun is this a form? Of what verb is this the subject?—**sub eo:** Refers to Titus, Roman emperor from 79 A.D. to 81 A.D. Although the Latin idiom is *under him,* how would you express it in normal English?—**ut:** Here the conjunction means *such as.*

(3) **quanta non temere alias:** Translate *of a size not easily paralleled.* What is the literal meaning of these words?

(4) **iis:** The equivalent of **eis.**—**adversis:** What use of the adjective?

(5–6) **consolando . . . opitulando:** What verbal form? Case and number?

(6) **quatenus suppeteret:** What construction?

(7) **restituendae Campaniae:** The gerundive is normally used instead of the gerund when the gerund would take a direct object (see *ARA,* Appendix K, p. 471, Gerundive Construction, and choose the appropriate translation for this sentence).—**consularium:** Refers to men who had served as civil and military magistrates for the emperor.

(8) **bona:** What use of the adjective?—**oppressórum:** What use of the participle? Subject to be supplied here?

(9) **Urbis incendio:** Refers to the **incendium Romae** mentioned in line 2, with the ablative here translated *with respect to the fire.*

(10) **nisi periisse:** Translate *except (that he) had been destroyed*—in the sense that he shared in the destruction suffered by the citizens.—**testátus:** Tense, voice, and mood? Subject of the verbal action?

(11) **ornamenta:** Refers to statues, furniture, general decorations, etc.

(12) **equestri:** See above, Lesson 18, Section E, note to line 1.—**quaeque:** Of what pronoun is this a form?—**maturius:** Degree of adverb?

(12–13) **quo . . . peragerentur:** The relative **quo** may be used in a relative clause of purpose (see *ARA,* Lesson 71, Section E, note to line 20).

(13) **Medendae valetudini leniendisque morbis:** See above, note to line 7, on the use of the gerundive instead of the gerund.

(13–14) **nullam . . . non adhibuit:** Translate *(there was) no . . . (that) he did not . . .* to do full justice to the author's praise of the emperor.

(14–15) **inquisíto . . . genere:** What construction?

§F **Classical Tradition.** The eruption of Mt. Vesuvius became a popular literary theme, which was treated by Pliny the Younger and by other authors in the classical world. This memorable event played a part in the historical novel written by Edward Bulwer-Lytton in 1834—*The Last Days of Pompeii*—a novel that has inspired film-adaptations.

The following passage appears in the chapter of this novel in which the great eruption throws into confusion all the activities taking place in the amphitheater in Pompeii. This particular passage contains words and phrases borrowed from Pliny the Younger's letters on the eruption, which Bulwer-Lytton employed as one of his chief sources.

"The eyes of the crowd followed the gesture of the Egyptian and beheld, with ineffable dismay, a vast vapor shooting from the summit of Vesuvius, in the form of a gigantic pine-tree—the trunk, blackness; the branches, fire! a fire that shifted and wavered in its hues with every moment, now fiercely luminous, now of a dull and dying red, that again blazed terrifically forth with intolerable glare!

There was a dead, heart-sunken silence, through which there suddenly broke the roar of the lion, which was echoed back from within the building by the sharper and fiercer yells of its fellow beast. Dread seers were they of the burden of the atmosphere, and wild prophets of the wrath to come!

Then there arose on high the universal shrieks of women; the men stared at each other but were dumb. At that moment they felt the earth shake beneath their feet; the walls of the theater trembled; and beyond in the distance they heard the crash of falling roofs; an instant more and the mountain-cloud seemed to roll toward them, dark and rapid, like a torrent; at the same time it cast forth from its bosom a shower of ashes mixed with vast fragments of burning stone! Over the crushing vines, over the desolate streets, over the amphitheater itself, far and wide, with many a mighty splash in the agitated sea, fell that awful shower!

No longer thought the crowd of justice or of Arbaces; safety for themselves was their sole thought. Each turned to fly—each dashing, pressing, crushing, against the other. Trampling recklessly over the fallen, amid groans and oaths and prayers and sudden shrieks, the enormous crowd vomited itself forth through the numerous passages. Whither should they fly? Some, anticipating a second earthquake, hastened to their homes to load themselves with their most costly goods and escape while it was yet time; others, dreading the showers of ashes that now fell fast, torrent upon torrent, over the streets, rushed under the roofs of the nearest houses or temples or sheds—shelters of any kind—for protection from the terrors of the open air. But darker and larger and mightier spread the cloud above them. It was a sudden and more ghastly Night rushing upon the realm of Noon!"

LESSON 25

SUM AND POSSUM: INDICATIVE. LIVY. LIVY: CORIOLANUS LIBERATES VOLSCIAN TOWNS FROM ROMAN CONTROL.

§A **Sum and Possum: Indicative.** You will now learn the forms of the most important irregular verbs, beginning with **sum** *(to be),* whose principal parts are **sum, esse, fui.** The indicative tenses of **sum** are presented in *ARA,* App. J, pp. 451–52, and are translated *I am, I was, I will be, I was, I had been, I will have been,* respectively.

Memorize the present, imperfect, and future indicative of **sum** (these being irregular); the perfect, pluperfect, and future perfect are regular, formed on the perfect stem. Using *ARA,* App. J, pp. 451–52, compare the corresponding tenses of **possum** *(to be able);* its principal parts are **possum, posse, potui,** with forms similar to those of **sum.**

§B **Exercise.** Translate the following sentences with forms of **sum** and **possum** into English; identify the tense, voice, mood, person, and number of these irregular verb forms:

(1) **Titus erat princeps qui affectum patris praestáre poterat.**

(2) **Ipse est in praetorio, ubi multa ornamenta tradere potest.**

(3) **Idem erit in templo, ubi de pestilentia deos rogáre poterit.**

§C **Livy.** Livy (59 B.C.–17 A.D.), one of Rome's greatest historians, wrote a history of his city, containing stories about famous Romans from legendary times to his own day. Lessons 25–36 contain two of Livy's stories: the first, on Coriolanus's war against Rome (his own country); the second, on the rape of Lucretia by the son of the Roman king.

§D **Vocabulary.**

adimo, adimere, adémi, ademptus ... *to take away; to take* something (acc.) *from* someone (dat.)

aliquanto ... *somewhat, considerably*

Attius, Attii, m. ... *Attius* (= Attius Tullius)

Circeii, Circeiórum, m. ... (plur. noun with sing. meaning) the town *Circeii*

colónus, colóni, m. ... *farmer; settler, colonist*

Corbio, Corbiónis, f. ... the town *Corbio*

Corioli, Coriolórum, m. ... (plur. noun with sing. meaning) the town *Corioli*

*de ... *from* (root meaning); *from, down from* (+ abl.); *about, concerning* (+ abl.); *according to, in keeping with* (+ abl.)

deinceps ... *in succession, one after another*

digredior, digredi, digressus sum ... *to go off, to go away;* (with plur. subject) *to go separate ways*

*dux, ducis, m. ... *leader, guide; general, commander*

efficio, efficere, efféci, effectus ... *to accomplish, to bring about*

expello, expellere, expuli, expulsus ... *to drive out*

exsul, exsulis, c. ... an *exile*

*fallo, fallere, fefelli, falsus ... *to deceive, to mislead; to appease, to satisfy; to disappoint, to fail to measure up to*

imperátor, imperatóris, m. ... *ruler; general, commander*

incito, incitáre, incitávi, incitátus ... *to excite, to arouse*

instígo, instigáre, instigávi, instigátus ... *to incite, to provoke*

Labíci, Labicórum, m. ... (plur. noun with sing. meaning) the town *Labici*

Latínus, Latína, Latínum ... *Latin*

Lavinium, Lavinii, n. ... the town *Lavinium*

Longula, Longulae, f. ... the town *Longula*

Marcius, Marcii, m. ... *Marcius* (= Coriolanus's clan-name)

Mugilla, Mugillae, f. ... the town *Mugilla*

nequaquam ... *not at all, by no means*

Pedum, Pedi, n. ... the town *Pedum*

*__plenus, plena, plenum__ ... *full, full* of (+ gen. or abl.)

Polusca, Poluscae, f. ... the town *Polusca*

*__recipio, recipere, recépi, receptus__ ... *to admit, to receive; to recover, to recapture; to take* or *draw* someone (acc.) to oneself (acc.)

repóno, reponere, reposui, repositus ... *to put back; to place* in

*__res, rei,__ f. ... *thing; matter, affair; situation, circumstance; affairs of state, political structure*

Románus, Romána, Románum ... *Roman;* **Románus, Románi,** m.: a *Roman*

Satricum, Satrici, n. ... the town *Satricum*

sententia, sententiae, f. ... *opinion; decision, judgment*

spons, spontis, f. ... (found only in abl. sing.) *will;* **sua sponte:** *of* one's *own will; voluntarily, spontaneously*

*__sum, esse, fui__ ... *to be*

Tolerium, Tolerii, n. ... the town *Tolerium*

trames, tramitis, m. ... *path, road*

transgredior, transgredi, transgressus sum ... *to go across*

transversus, transversa, transversum ... *running crosswise*

Tullius, Tullii, m. ... *Tullius* (= Attius Tullius)

Vetelia, Veteliae, f. ... the town *Vetelia*

Volscus, Volsca, Volscum ... *Volscian;* **Volscus, Volsci,** m.: a *Volscian*

Coriolanus Liberates Volscian Towns from Roman Control.

Lessons 25–30 contain Livy's account of Coriolanus, the Roman hero who gained fame fighting for Rome and then betrayed her after losing a political battle in the senate. Livy describes how during his self-imposed exile (488 B.C.), Coriolanus joined forces with the Volscians (a people in central Italy) in order to wage war against the Romans.

Ita et sua sponte irárum pleni et incitáti, domos inde digressi

sunt, instigandoque suos quisque populos effecére ut omne

Volscum nomen deficeret. Imperatóres ad id bellum de omnium

populórum sententia lecti, Attius Tullius et Cn. Marcius, exsul

5   Románus, in quo aliquanto plus spei repositum. Quam spem

nequaquam fefellit, ut facile appareret ducibus validiórem quam

exercitu rem Románam esse. Circeios profectus primum,

colónos inde Románus expulit, liberamque eam urbem Volscis

tradidit; inde in Latínam Viam transversis tramitibus

10   transgressus, Satricum, Longulam, Poluscam, Coriolos,

Mugillam, haec Románis oppida adémit; inde Lavinium recépit;

tunc deinceps Corbiónem, Veteliam, Tolerium, Labícos, Pedum

cepit.

§F   Notes and Queries.

(1) **pleni et incitáti**: Case, number, and gender of **pleni**? Tense, voice, and mood of **incitáti**? (Both **pleni** and **incitáti** refer to the Volscians, whom the Romans have angered by ordering them out of Rome at the beginning of public games and festivities.)—**domos**: With respect to the word **domus**, *place to which* is usually expressed by the accusative without a preposition.

(2) **instigandoque:** What verbal form is **instigando?** What is the direct object of this verb?—**quisque ... effecére:** Here the singular **quisque** is used with the plural **effecére,** since the singular form designates the individual complaints of the Volscians. (The perfect active indicative has an alternate third person plural ending in **-ére,** as here, where the form **effecére** is the equivalent of **effecérunt.**)

(2–3) **ut ... deficeret:** What construction? (Compare above, Lesson 2, Section E, note to lines 11–12.)

(3) **nomen:** That is, a race or nationality, in the sense of an ethnically organized group (see *ARA,* Lesson 54, Section H, note to line 3).—**de:** What noun does this preposition govern?

(4) **lecti:** The equivalent of what verb form? (See above, Lesson 17, Section E, note to line 13, and adjust the missing element to fit the participial element **lecti.**)—**Attius Tullius:** The Volscian general who befriended Coriolanus and plotted with him to wage war against the Romans.—**Cn. Marcius:** Coriolanus's full name was Cn. (= Gnaeus) Marcius Coriolanus (see above, Lesson 18, Section E, note to line 1).

(5) **spei:** See *ARA,* App. E, p. 423, Partitive Genitive.—**repositum:** The equivalent of what verb form?—**Quam:** What noun does this adjective modify?

(6) **apparéret:** Used impersonally, meaning *it appeared.* What construction does this verb introduce? What are the elements of this construction in this sentence?—**ducibus:** The ablative of means is sometimes applied to a person.—**validiórem:** Degree of adjective?—**quam:** The relative or the conjunction? What is your reason for thinking so?

(7) **exercitu:** To what other ablative can this ablative be compared?—**Circeios:** See *ARA,* Lesson 29, Section G, note to line 2.—**profectus:** Tense, voice, and mood? Subject of the verbal action?

(10) **Coriolos:** The town that Coriolanus had helped Rome capture five years earlier by an outstanding act of heroism—an achievement that resulted in the Romans conferring on him the nickname Coriolanus.

LESSON 26

SUM AND POSSUM: SUBJUNCTIVE. LIVY: CORIOLANUS ENCAMPS NEAR ROME AND INSTIGATES CIVIL DISCORD.

§A **Sum and Possum: Subjunctive.** The verb **sum** is found in the same four tenses of the subjunctive as are regular verbs, and in general is conjugated in a regular manner. The subjunctive tenses of **sum** are presented in *ARA*, App. J, pp. 453–54, and are translated in accordance with the subjunctive construction in which they appear.

Memorize the present subjunctive of **sum;** the imperfect may be thought of as formed from the present infinitive; the perfect and pluperfect are formed regularly. Using *ARA*, App. J, pp. 453–54, compare the corresponding tenses of **possum** in the subjunctive, which reveal the same regularity or irregularity as the tenses of **sum.**

§B **Exercise.** Identify the tense, voice, mood, person, and number of the following forms of **sum** and **possum:**

(1) **esset**		(4) **possint**	
(2) **potestis**		(5) **fueris**	
(3) **fuissem**		(6) **possémus**	

§C **Vocabulary.**

*ager, agri, m. ... *land, field; territory, countryside*

Cluilius, Cluilia, Cluilium ... *Cluilian*

concordia, concordiae, f. ... *peace, harmony*

consul, consulis, m. ... *consul*

*convenio, conveníre, convéni, conventus ... *to come together, to make an agreement;* (impersonal use) *to be agreed upon;* (use in passive) *to be approached* or *confronted* by someone or something

criminor, crimināri, criminātus sum ... *to make charges* or *accusations* against

discordia, discordiae, f. ... *discord, dissension*

externus, externa, externum ... *outside, external; of something outside, of something external*

***ferox, ferōcis** ... *angry, cruel, fierce*

fossa, fossae, f. ... *ditch, trench*

infensus, infensa, infensum ... *hostile, hostile to* (+ dat.)

intactus, intacta, intactum ... *untouched, undamaged*

***iungo, iungere, iunxi, iunctus** ... *to join, to yoke; to unite, to bring together; to join* someone (acc.) *in marriage* to someone (dat.)

mille (indecl.) ... a *thousand;* **milia, milium, n.:** *thousands*

passus, passus, m. ... *step, pace*

***pater, patris, m.** ... *father;* (sometimes in plur.) *parents; patricians*

patricius, patricii, m. ... *patrician*

***plebs, plebis,** or **plebes, plebéi, f.** ... (collective sing.) *plebeians*

***pono, ponere, posui, positus** ... *to put, to place; to put* or *place aside; to build, to erect; to pitch* a camp; *to arrange* one's hair

populátor, populatóris, m. ... *ravager, plunderer*

populor, populári, populátus sum ... *to ravage, to plunder*

postrémus, postréma, postrémum ... *last, final;* **postrémum:** *finally, last of all*

primóris, primóre ... *first, foremost;* (masc. plur. as substantive) *leaders*

profecto ... *indeed, assuredly, undoubtedly*

quamvis ... *although, even though, however much*

quinque (indecl.) ... *five*

senátus, senátus, m. ... *senate*

sive ... *or if;* **sive . . , sive . . ,** *whether . . , or . .* (e.g., **sive dicit sive audit,** *whether he speaks or listens*)

suspicio, suspicere, suspexi, suspectus ... *to suspect, to distrust;* **suspectus, suspecta, suspectum:** *suspected, distrusted*

tribúnus, tribúni, m. ... *tribune*

vinculum, vinculi, n. ... *bond, link* (= a force or impulse joining people together)

§D   **Reading.**

Coriolanus Encamps near Rome and Instigates Civil Discord.

Postrémum ad urbem a Pedo ducit, et ad fossas Cluilias
(quinque ab urbe milia passuum) castris positis, populátur inde
agrum Románum, custodibus inter populatóres missis, qui
patriciórum agros intactos servárent, sive infensus plebi magis,
5   sive ut discordia inde inter patres plebemque orerétur. Quae
profecto orta esset—adeo tribúni iam ferócem per se plebem
criminando in primóres civitátis instigábant—sed externus
timor, maximum concordiae vinculum, quamvis suspectos
infensosque inter se iungébat animos. Id modo non conveniébat,
10   quod senátus consulesque nusquam alibi spem quam in armis
ponébant, plebes omnia quam bellum malébat.

§E   **Notes and Queries.**

(1) **urbem:** Refers to Rome.—**ducit:** After this verb supply *army.*
Tense, voice, and mood of **ducit?** What use of the tense of this verb?—
fossas Cluilias: Trenches of an unknown origin.

(2) **quinque . . . milia passuum:** Translate *five miles*. What is the literal meaning?—**castris positis:** What construction? (Refers to the temporary shelters that the soldiers erected not far from the city under attack, in this instance Rome.)

(3) **custodibus . . . missis:** What construction?

(3–4) **qui . . . servárent:** The relative **qui** may be used in a relative clause of purpose (see *ARA,* Lesson 64, Section F, note to line 4).

(4) **patriciórum:** The privileged class of Roman citizens, who held the most important political and religious offices during Rome's early history.—**infensus:** Case, number, and gender? To whom does this adjective refer?—**plebi:** The general body of Roman citizens, who were excluded from the most important political and religious offices during Rome's early history.

(5) **orerétur:** In the subjunctive, deponent verbs are normally conjugated like regular verbs (see above, Lesson 1, Section F, note to line 1). However, in the imperfect subjunctive, the deponent verb **orior** is normally conjugated like a third conjugation verb of the **-io** type.— **Quae:** What is the antecedent? Of what verb is this the subject?

(6) **orta esset:** What use of the subjunctive? (See above, Lesson 22, Section E, note to line 4, and *ARA,* Appendix K, p. 472, for the appropriate translation.)—**tribúni:** The magistrates elected by the plebeians, charged with protecting the lives and property of the plebeians.—**per se:** Translate *on their own.* What is the literal meaning? (Here the reflexive phrase probably does not refer back to **tribúni** but goes with **ferócem . . . plebem,** showing that the plebeians are already angry, even without the prodding of their own elected magistrates.)

(7) **criminando:** What verbal form? Case and number?

(7–9) **externus timor . . . iungébat animos:** A moving and powerful statement, which can be applied to all kinds of situations in which people put aside their internal differences in order to overcome a common external enemy.

(8–9) **suspectos infensosque:** What noun do these adjectives modify?

(9) **inter se:** Although the Latin idiom is *among themselves,* how would you express it in normal English?—**modo:** The adverb, not the noun. (Check **modo,** not **modus,** in the Cumulative Vocabulary.)— **conveniébat:** Here this verb is used impersonally. Tense, voice, mood, person, and number?

(10) **senátus consulesque:** The senate was the permanent political assembly of ancient Rome; the consuls were the two supreme civil and military magistrates under the Republic.

(11) **plebes . . . malébat:** Reflects the historic opposition that the plebeians generally expressed toward the policies of the patricians.—**malébat:** Translate *preferred*.

LESSON 27

SUM AND POSSUM: IMPERATIVES, INFINITIVES, PARTICIPLES. LIVY: THE ROMANS SEND ENVOYS TO CORIOLANUS TO NEGOTIATE PEACE.

§A **Sum and Possum: Imperatives, Infinitives, Participles.** The imperative, infinitive, and participial forms of the verb **sum** (occurring in some tenses) are presented in *ARA*, App. J, p. 454. All the imperatives (singular and plural) are translated as (you) *be*; the infinitives— *to be, to have been, to be about to be*; the participle—*going to be*.

Most of the imperatives of **sum** have the stem **es-**; the present infinitive is the second principal part of the verb; the other forms resemble their counterparts in regular verbs. Using *ARA*, App. J, p. 454, compare the corresponding forms of **possum** (where they exist) and be prepared to recognize these forms when they occur in the readings.

§B **Exercise.** Identify the tense, voice, and mood of the following forms of **sum** and **possum**; then translate:

(1) **este**   (4) **poterant**

(2) **potens**   (5) **futúros**

(3) **fuisse**   (6) **potuisse**

§C   **Vocabulary.**

*accipio, accipere, accépi, acceptus ... *to obtain, to receive; to agree to, to consent to*

adnítor, adníti, adnísus sum ... *to lean on; to strive, to exert effort*

atrox, atrócis ... *cruel, harsh; terrible, horrible*

civis, civis, c. (gen. plur. civium) ... *citizen*

conterreo, conterrére, conterrui, conterritus ... *to terrify* or *frighten thoroughly*

distribuo, distribuere, distribui, distribútus ... *to distribute; to station, to position*

exsilium, exsilii, n. ... *exile, banishment*

*****flecto, flectere, flexi, flexus** ... *to bend; to turn* back, *to change* one's course; *to influence* or *prevail upon* one's mind

*****frango, frangere, fregi, fractus** ... *to break, to smash, to crush; to humble, to soften, to weaken*

fruor, frui, fructus sum ... *to enjoy* (+ abl.)

Furius, Furii, m. ... *Furius,* the Roman consul

iniuria, iniuriae, f. ... *wrong, injustice*

inríto, inritáre, inritávi, inritátus ... *to incite, to stir up, to inflame*

insignis, insigne ... *conspicuous, standing out;* (neut. plur. as substantive) *attire, costume, regalia*

labo, labáre, labávi ... *to totter; to waver, to become weak*

legátus, legáti, m. ... *envoy, ambassador*

legio, legiónis, f. ... *legion*

*****locus, loci,** m. (in plur.: **loci, locórum,** m., or **loca, locórum,** n.) ... (plur. may have sing. meaning) *place; area, region*

multitúdo, multitudinis, f. ... *multitude*

Nautius, Nautii, m. ... *Nautius,* the Roman consul

orátor, oratóris, m. ... *speaker; envoy, ambassador*

*****pax, pacis,** f. ... *peace*

*****possum, posse, potui** ... *to be able; to bring* oneself or *have the heart* to do something

praesidium, praesidii, n. ... *defense, protection; garrison, detachment*

recenseo, recensére, recensui, recensus ... *to review, to inspect*

relatio, relatiónis, f. ... *proposal, petition*

seditiósus, seditiósa, seditiósum ... *mutinous, rebellious*

statio, statiónis, f. ... *guard, picket*

supplex, supplicis ... *suppliant;* (masc. as substantive) a *suppliant,* a *supplicant*

*trado, tradere, tradidi, traditus ... *to hand over; to deliver, to entrust; to say, to relate, to report*

vigilia, vigiliae, f. ... *patrol, sentry*

§D   Reading.

The Romans Send Envoys to Coriolanus to Negotiate Peace.

Sp. Nautius iam et Sex. Furius consules erant. Eos recensentes

legiónes, praesidia per muros aliaque (in quibus statiónes

vigiliasque esse placuerat) loca distribuentes, multitúdo ingens

pacem poscentium primum seditióso clamóre conterruit, deinde

5   vocáre senátum, referre de legátis ad Cn. Marcium mittendis

coégit. Accepérunt relatiónem patres, postquam apparuit labáre

plebis animos. Missique de pace ad Marcium, oratóres atrox

responsum rettulérunt: si Volscis ager redderétur, posse agi de

pace; si praeda belli per otium frui velint, memorem se et

10   civium iniuriae et hospitum beneficii adnisúrum, ut appareat

exsilio sibi inritátos non fractos animos esse. Iterum deinde

iídem missi non recipiuntur in castra. Sacerdótes quoque suis

insignibus velátos isse supplices ad castra hostium traditum est,

nihilo magis quam legátos flexisse animum.

(1) **Sp. Nautius et Sex. Furius:** Their full names were Spurius Nautius and Sextus Furius.—**consules:** See above, Lesson 26, Section E, note to line 10.

(1–6) **Eos ... multitúdo ... primum ... conterruit, deinde ... coégit:** A long sentence with a complex word order, carefully constructed around the central grammatical elements cited above. To whom does the pronoun **Eos** refer—the senators or the consuls? To whom does the noun **multitúdo** refer—the patricians or the plebeians?

(1–3) **recensentes ... distribuentes:** Tense, voice, and mood? Subject of the verbal action? Direct objects of the verbal action? (You may supply the conjunction **et** between the two verbal forms cited above.)

(2) **aliaque:** What noun does the adjective **alia** modify?

(3) **placuerat:** Used impersonally, although here not with the dative (check vocabulary entry). What construction does this verb introduce? What are the elements of this construction in this sentence?

(4) **poscentium:** What use of the participle? Subject to be supplied here?

(5) **senátum:** See above, Lesson 26, Section E, note to line 10.—**referre:** Translate *to make a proposal.*—**de legátis ... mittendis:** The gerundive is normally used instead of the gerund when the gerund would take a direct object (see above, Lesson 24, Section E, note to line 7, and *ARA,* Appendix K, p. 471, Gerundive Construction).

(6) **apparuit:** See above, Lesson 25, Section F, note to line 6. What construction does this verb introduce? What are the elements of this construction in this sentence?—**labáre:** That is, becoming weak in their resolve to fight a war against Coriolanus and the Volscians.

(7) **Missique:** Tense, voice, and mood of **Missi?** Subject of the verbal action of **Missi?**

(8) **si ... redderétur, posse:** A conditional sentence in indirect statement (see above, Lesson 24, Section A), here introduced by the words **responsum retulérunt** (translate **rettulérunt** as *brought back*), with the accusative **id** to be supplied before the infinitive **posse.**—**agi:** Tense, voice, and mood?

(9) **praeda:** Case and number? Why is this case used here?

(9–10) **si . . . velint . . . se . . . adnisúrum:** Another conditional sentence in indirect statement (translate **velint** as *they wished*), also introduced by the words **responsum rettulérunt,** with the accusative **se** (referring to Coriolanus, mentioned in line 7) to be supplied before the infinitive **adnisúrum** (see above, Lesson 21, Section E, note to line 4).

(10) **civium iniuriae:** Refers to Coriolanus's rejection by the Romans, leading up to his exile.—**hospitum beneficii:** Refers to Coriolanus's reception by the Volscians, especially by Attius Tullius.—**appareat:** See above, note to line 6, for a similar form of the verb and the construction that it introduces.

(11) **sibi:** The dative may be used to designate the person to whom a statement refers and is governed by the entire sentence rather than any particular word (see *ARA,* App. E, p. 423, Dative of Reference).—**inritátos non fractos animos esse:** These words need to be expanded in Latin in order to become more intelligible. Translate as if the Latin consisted of the words **animos inritátos esse sed non fractos esse.**

(12) **iídem:** Alternate for **eídem.** Of what pronoun is this a form?—**missi:** Tense, voice, and mood? Subject of the verbal action?

(13) **traditum est:** That is, by other authors who had written about the same subject. What construction does this verb introduce two times in this sentence? (In this double use of the construction, make sure that you take **Sacerdótes** first as the subject of **isse** [which should be translated *had gone*] and then as the subject of **flexisse.**)

LESSON 28

VOLO, NOLO, AND MALO: INDICATIVE. LIVY: CORIOLANUS'S MOTHER, WIFE, AND CHILDREN VISIT HIS CAMP.

§A **Volo, Nolo, and Malo: Indicative.** You will now learn the forms of another important irregular verb, the verb **volo** *(to wish),* whose principal parts are **volo, velle, volui.** The indicative tenses of **volo** are presented in *ARA,* App. J, pp. 455–56, and are translated *I wish, I was wishing, I will wish, I wished, I had wished, I will have wished.*

Memorize the present indicative of **volo;** the imperfect and future are regular (like **traho**); the perfect, pluperfect, and future perfect are formed in the usual way. Using *ARA,* App. J, pp. 455–56, compare the corresponding tenses of **nolo** *(to not wish)* and **malo** *(to prefer);* their principal parts are **nolo, nolle, nolui,** and **malo, malle, malui.**

§B **Exercise.** Translate the following sentences with forms of **volo, nolo,** and **malo** into English; identify the tense, voice, mood, person, and number of these irregular verb forms:

> (1) **Plebs bellum gerere non vult sed pacem quaerere mavult.**
>
> (2) **Patres legátos mittere volébant sed agros reddere nolébant.**
>
> (3) **Legáti cum hoste loqui volent, sed iste cum illis loqui nolet.**

§C **Vocabulary.**

*adsum, adesse, adfui ... *to be present, to be present* for (+ dat.)

*agmen, agminis, n. ... (plur. may have sing. meaning) *band, mass; army, host; crowd, throng*

*cognosco, cognoscere, cognóvi, cognitus ... *to learn, to find out, to discover; to recognize* a person whom one already knows

*consilium, consilii, n. ... (plur. may have sing. meaning) *plan, advice; policy, decision; purpose, intention*

Coriolánus, Coriolání, m. ... *Coriolanus*

defendo, defendere, defendi, defensus ... *to defend, to protect*

familiáris, familiáre ... *of the household;* (masc. as substantive) *member of the household*

frustror, frustrári, frustrátus sum ... *to deceive, to mislead*

*in ... *in, into* (root meanings); *into, to, against* (+ acc.); *in order to cause* or *produce* (+ acc.); *in, on, among* (+ abl.); *at, during, in the course of* (+ abl.); *in respect to, when dealing with* (+ abl.); *as embodied in, as represented by* (+ abl.)

*invenio, inveníre, invéni, inventus ... *to come upon; to find, to discover;* **parum inveníre:** *to be at a loss to know, to be unable to find out*

maestitia, maestitiae, f. ... *sadness, sorrow*

maiestas, maiestátis, f. ... *dignity, majesty*

matróna, matrónae, f. ... *matron, married woman*

nepos, nepótis, m. ... *grandchild; grandson*

nurus, nurus, f. ... *daughter-in-law*

obstinátus, obstináta, obstinátum ... *stubborn, obstinate*

offundo, offundere, offúdi, offúsus ... *to pour over; to convey* to, *to communicate* to

parvus, parva, parvum ... *small, little*

pervinco, pervincere, pervíci, pervictus ... *to overcome completely; to persuade* or *prevail upon* someone to do something

*prex, precis, f. ... *prayer, entreaty*

religio, religiónis, f. ... *religion*

Veturia, Veturiae, f. ... *Veturia,* mother of Coriolanus

Volumnia, Volumniae, f. ... *Volumnia,* wife of Coriolanus

Coriolanus's Mother, Wife, and Children Visit His Camp.

Tum matrónae ad Veturiam matrem Corioláni Volumniamque

uxórem frequentes coeunt. Id publicum consilium an muliebris

timor fuerit, parum invenio. Pervicére certe ut et Veturia

(magno natu mulier) et Volumnia (duos parvos ex Marcio

5   ferens filios) secum in castra hostium irent, et quoniam armis

viri defendere urbem non possent, mulieres precibus lacrimisque

defenderent. Ubi ad castra ventum est nuntiatumque Corioláno

est adesse ingens mulierum agmen, is primo—ut qui nec

publica maiestáte in legátis nec in sacerdotibus tanta (offúsa

10   oculis animoque) religióne motus esset—multo obstinatior

adversus lacrimas muliebres erat. Dein familiarium quidam,

qui insignem maestitia inter ceteras cognoverat Veturiam inter

nurum nepotesque stantem, "Nisi me frustrantur," inquit, "oculi,

mater tibi coniunxque et liberi adsunt."

§E   **Notes and Queries.**

(1) **ad Veturiam . . . Volumniamque:** As Rome was bracing for an attack from Coriolanus and the Volscians, Veturia and Volumnia remained at home, where the other matrons decided to pay them a visit in order to see if they could do something to alleviate the crisis.

(2) **coeunt:** Translate *assemble* or *assembled,* depending on whether or not you treat this verb as a historical present.

(2–3) **an . . . fuerit:** What construction? Tense, voice, mood, person, and number of **fuerit**?

(3) **parum invenio:** That is, from other authors who had written about the same subject and who had offered no explanation of their own.—**Pervicére:** The perfect active indicative has an alternate third person plural ending in **-ére** (see above, Lesson 25, Section F, note to line 2). Supply as direct objects of this verb the nouns **Veturia** and **Volumnia** from the subordinate clause that follows—two nouns that you will obviously no longer need to translate as part of the subordinate clause.

(4) **magno natu:** A Latin idiom in the ablative meaning *of great age* or *of advanced years.* (The form **natu** is the supine of **nascor** [see *ARA,* Lesson 49, Section D], used with adjectives to express age.)

(5) **ferens:** Translate *carrying.*—**secum:** To whom does the **se** in this word refer?—**irent:** Translate *they go (= to go).*

(5–6) **quoniam . . . possent:** See above, Lesson 11, Section E, note to line 13. Tense, voice, mood, person, and number of **possent?**

(6) **viri . . . mulieres:** A striking contrast between the two groups of Romans involved in the crisis, both of which attempt to resolve the situation with their own respective embassies.

(7) **ventum est:** Verbs not taking a direct object may be used impersonally in the passive third person singular but should be translated in the active, as here, with **ventum est** (a form of **venio**). The form **ventum est**—which is translated *they came,* or in some contexts *they come*—consists of the supine **ventum** (see *ARA,* Lesson 49, Section D) and the present indicative third person singular of **sum.**

(7–8) **nuntiatumque . . . est:** Here the passive form **nuntiátum est** should be translated in the passive, since it is not the kind of impersonal verb described in the previous note. (What is the indirect object of **nuntiátum est?** What construction does this verb introduce? What are the elements of this construction in this sentence?)

(8–10) **ut qui . . . motus esset:** What construction? Translate **ut qui** with the words *as (being someone) who* or *as (being the kind of man) who.*

(9) **in legátis . . . in sacerdotibus:** What meaning of the preposition best fits the context? What two recent episodes do these phrases call to mind? (See above, Lesson 27, Section D, lines 7–14, for the relevant descriptions.)—**tanta:** What noun does this adjective modify? (See above, Lesson 27, Section E, note to line 2, involving a similar kind of word order.)—**offúsa:** Tense, voice, and mood? Subject of the verbal action?

(10) **obstinatior:** Degree of adjective?

(11) **erat:** Tense, voice, mood, person, and number? Write out the conjugation of **sum** in this tense, voice, and mood.

(13) **stantem:** Tense, voice, and mood? Subject of the verbal action?

(13–14) **Nisi . . . frustrantur . . . adsunt:** What type of condition is this? Tense and mood of the verbs? (See above, Lesson 22, Section A.)

(14) **tibi:** The dative may be used to designate the person to whom a statement refers (see above, Lesson 27, Section E, note to line 11).

LESSON 29

VOLO, NOLO, AND MALO: SUBJUNCTIVE. LIVY: CORIOLANUS'S MOTHER BERATES HIM FOR BETRAYING HIS COUNTRY.

§A   **Volo, Nolo, and Malo: Subjunctive.** The verb **volo** is found in the same four tenses of the subjunctive as are regular verbs, and in general is conjugated in a regular manner. The subjunctive tenses of **volo** are presented in *ARA*, App. J, pp. 457–58, and are translated in accordance with the subjunctive construction in which they appear.

Memorize the present subjunctive of **volo**; the imperfect may be thought of as formed from the present infinitive; the perfect and pluperfect are formed regularly. Using *ARA*, App. J, pp. 457–58, compare the corresponding tenses of **nolo** and **malo** in the subjunctive, which reveal the same regularity or irregularity as the tenses of **volo**.

§B   **Exercise.** Identify the tense, voice, mood, person, and number of the following forms of **volo, nolo,** and **malo:**

      (1) **vellem**   (4) **voluerimus**

      (2) **noluissent**   (5) **nolit**

      (3) **maluisti**   (6) **maluissétis**

§C   **Vocabulary.**

   alo, alere, alui, altus ... *to rear, to nourish*

   amens, amentis ... *crazed, frantic, frenzied*

   complexus, complexus, m. ... an *embrace*

   consterno, consternáre, consternávi, consternátus ... *to alarm, to shock;* (in passive) *to be driven, to be startled*

   gigno, gignere, genui, genitus ... *to beget, to give birth to*

immatúrus, immatúra, immatúrum ... *unripe, immature; untimely, premature*

infélix, infelícis ... *unhappy, unfortunate*

*****felix, felícis** ... *happy, fortunate*

infestus, infesta, infestum ... *hostile, hostile to* (+ dat.)

minax, minácis ... *threatening*

moenia, moenium, n. ... (plur. noun with plur. meaning) *city-walls*

*****-ne** ... (in direct question, attached to the first word of the question but itself not translated) e.g., **amasne puellam?** *do you love the girl?* (in indirect question) *whether, if;* (in double indirect question, appearing once but translated twice) *whether . . , or . .*

*****obvius, obvia, obvium** ... *opposing; toward, up against* (+ dat.); *standing in* one's *way* or *path*

oppugno, oppugnáre, oppugnávi, oppugnátus ... *to attack, to assault*

*****pugno, pugnáre, pugnávi, pugnátus** ... *to fight*

penátes, penatium, m. ... (plur. noun with plur. meaning) the *penates* (= Roman household gods)

pergo, pergere, perrexi ... *to proceed, to continue*

priusquam ... (conj.) *before*

prope ... *near, at hand; only, almost*

*****sedes, sedis, f.** (gen. plur. **sedium**) ... (plur. may have sing. meaning) *seat, place; base, foundation*

senecta, senectae, f. ... *old age*

sino, sinere, sivi, situs ... *to allow, to permit*

*****ut** or **uti** ... *as, when, how, as if, although* (+ ind.); *that, so that, in order that, to the extent that* (+ subj.); **ut . . , sic . . ,** *just as . . , so . . or although . . , nevertheless . .* (+ ind. in both clauses)

*****vita, vitae, f.** ... *life*

§D   Reading.

Coriolanus's Mother Berates Him for Betraying His Country.

Coriolánus (prope ut amens) consternátus ab sede sua cum

ferret matri obviae complexum, mulier in iram ex precibus

versa, "Sine (priusquam complexum accipio) sciam," inquit, "ad

hostem an ad filium venerim, captíva materne in castris tuis

5   sim. In hoc me longa vita et infélix senecta traxit, ut exsulem

te deinde hostem vidérem? Potuisti populári hanc terram, quae

te genuit atque aluit? Non tibi (quamvis infesto animo et mináci

perveneras) ingredienti fines ira cecidit? Non, cum in conspectu

Roma fuit, succurrit: 'Intra illa moenia domus ac penátes mei

10   sunt, mater coniunx liberique'? Ergo ego nisi peperissem, Roma

non oppugnarétur; nisi filium habérem, libera in libera patria

mortua essem. Sed ego nihil iam pati nec tibi turpius quam

mihi miserius possum; nec, ut sum miserrima, diu futúra

sum. De his videris, quos (si pergis) aut immatúra mors aut

15   longa servitus manet."

§E   Notes and Queries.

(1) **consternátus:** Tense, voice, and mood? Subject of the verbal action?

(2) **ferret:** Translate *was about to offer.*—**obviae:** Translate this adjective after the noun that it modifies. What meaning of the adjective best accommodates this word order?

(3) **Sine . . . sciam:** Although the Latin idiom is *Allow (that) I may know,* how would you express it in normal English? (Tense, voice, mood, person, and number of **Sine?** Tense, voice, mood, person, and number of **sciam?**)

(4) **an . . . venerim:** What construction?

(4–5) **captíva materne . . . sim:** What construction? What two elements does **materne** consist of? Tense, voice, mood, person, and number of **sim?** Write out the conjugation of **sum** in this tense, voice, and mood.

(5) **traxit:** See above, Lesson 12, Section E, note to line 16, on the person and number, and translate this verb within the context of a question (i.e., *has long life . . . dragged . . . ?*).

(6) **Potuisti:** Tense, voice, mood, person, and number?

(8) **ingredienti:** Tense, voice, and mood? Subject of the verbal action?—**fines:** Refers to Rome and her borders.

(9) **succurrit:** Supply *this thought* as the subject, referring to the sentence beginning 'Intra illa moenia . . .—**penátes:** The Roman gods who were believed to preside over the destiny of the household.

(10) **sunt:** Tense, voice, mood, person, and number? Write out the conjugation of **sum** in this tense, voice, and mood.

(10–11) **nisi peperissem . . . oppugnarétur:** A mixed conditional sentence, with the pluperfect subjunctive in the protasis and the imperfect subjunctive in the apodosis. Using Lesson 23, Section A (above), translate these subjunctives with the meanings found in the appropriate clauses of the conditions presented in the chart.

(11–12) **nisi . . . habérem . . . mortua essem:** A mixed conditional sentence, with the imperfect subjunctive in the protasis and the pluperfect subjunctive in the apodosis. Using Lesson 23, Section A (above), translate these subjunctives with the meanings found in the appropriate clauses of the conditions presented in the chart.

(12–13) **turpius . . . miserius:** Degree of adjectives?

(13) **ut:** Here **ut** has a concessive force. (If you do not know the meaning of 'concessive', check it in your English dictionary.)—**miserrima:** Degree of adjective? (Translate this adjective twice, first directly after **sum** and again after **futúra sum.**)

(13–14) **futúra sum:** The future active participle combines with the different tenses of **sum** to form the Active Periphrastic Conjugation, designating future or intended action (see *ARA*, App. K, p. 471). In this sentence, the future active participle of **sum** combines with the present indicative first person singular of **sum** to form the Active Periphrastic verb-form meaning *I am going to be.*

(14) **his:** To whom does this pronoun refer? (See above, Lesson 28, Section D, lines 4–5.) In answering this question, assume that the above pronoun does not designate a group consisting of both sexes.— **videris:** A hortatory subjunctive, in which the perfect tense is translated as the present (i.e., *you should see* or *you should take care,* in the sense of showing concern about some person or some situation).

(14–15) **aut immatúra mors aut longa servitus manet:** A line of verse written in iambic senarii—a meter used in Greek tragedy—which Livy here employs in order to conclude the speech on a dramatic note. What strategy does Coriolanus's mother employ in the final sentence of her speech in order to convince her son not to proceed any further with his plans to wage war against his country and his countrymen?

LESSON 30

VOLO, NOLO, AND MALO: IMPERATIVES, INFINITIVES, PARTICIPLES. LIVY: CORIOLANUS SPARES ROME AND IS PUNISHED BY THE VOLSCIANS.

§A **Volo, Nolo, and Malo: Imperatives, Infinitives, Participles.** The infinitive and participial forms of **volo** are presented in *ARA*, App. J, p. 458 (imperative forms are not found for this irregular verb). Of the infinitive and participial forms presented in the text, the infinitives are translated *to wish, to have wished;* and the participle, *wishing.*

The present infinitive of **volo** is the second principal part of the verb; the other forms resemble their counterparts in regular verbs and are formed in the usual way. Using *ARA*, App J, p. 458, compare the corresponding forms of **nolo** and **malo,** and using *ARA*, App. J, p. 458, note 4, consider how the present imperatives of **nolo** are used.

§B **Exercise.** Identify the tense, voice, and mood of the following forms of **volo, nolo,** and **malo;** then translate:

    (1) **volens**   (4) **volébant**

    (2) **nolíte**   (5) **nolentem**

    (3) **malle**   (6) **maluisse**

§C **Vocabulary.**

abdúco, abducere, abduxi, abductus ... *to lead away*

adiungo, adiungere, adiunxi, adiunctus ... *to join to, to attach to;* (of an army) *to join* or *attach* oneself as an ally

aedifico, aedificáre, aedificávi, aedificátus ... *to build*

Aequus, Aequa, Aequum ... *Aequian;* **Aequus, Aequi,** m.: an *Aequian*

*amplector, amplecti, amplexus sum ... *to clasp, to embrace; to take hold of, to seize hold of*

antiquus, antiqua, antiquum ... *ancient*

*atrox, atrócis ... *cruel, harsh; terrible, horrible*

auctor, auctóris, m. ... *author, authority; advocate, instigator, perpetrator*

certámen, certaminis, n. ... *dispute, rivalry; contest, struggle*

comploratio, comploratiónis, f. ... *mourning, lamentation*

conficio, conficere, conféci, confectus ... *to make together; to defeat, to destroy*

coniungo, coniungere, coniunxi, coniunctus ... *to join to, to attach to; (of an army) to join* or *combine* into a single force

dedico, dedicáre, dedicávi, dedicátus ... *to dedicate*

dimitto, dimittere, dimísi, dimissus ... *to send away*

Fabius, Fabii, m. ... *Fabius,* the Roman historian

*fletus, fletus, m. ... *crying, weeping;* (as the result of the crying or weeping) *tears*

*fortúna, fortúnae, f. ... *fortune;* (as proper noun) **Fortúna:** the goddess *Fortune*

gloria, gloriae, f. ... *fame, glory*

haud ... *not, not at all*

hinc ... *hence, from here, on this side*

*invideo, invidére, invídi, invísus ... *to cast a spell* or *evil eye on; to begrudge* someone (dat.) something (acc. or abl.); *to begrudge* someone (acc.) to do something (inf.)

invidia, invidiae, f. ... *envy, jealousy; resentment, indignation*

*laus, laudis, f. ... *praise; award, prize; honor, renown*

letum, leti, n. ... *death*

monumentum, monumenti, n. ... *memorial, monument*

obtrectatio, obtrectatiónis, f. ... *detraction, disparagement*

perniciósus, perniciósa, perniciósum ... *ruinous, destructive*

pertinax, pertinácis ... *stubborn, obstinate*

*saepe ... *often*

seditio, seditiónis, f. ... *mutiny, rebellion*

senectus, senectútis, f. ... *old age*

senex, senis ... *old;* (masc. sing. as substantive) *old man*

usurpo, usurpáre, usurpávi, usurpátus ... *to use, to usurp; to utter, to mention*

§D   Reading.

Coriolanus Spares Rome and Is Punished by the Volscians.

Uxor deinde ac liberi amplexi, fletusque ab omni turba
mulierum ortus, et comploratio sui patriaeque fregére tandem
virum. Complexus inde suos dimittit, et ipse retro ab urbe
castra movit. Abductis deinde legionibus ex agro Románo,

5   invidia rei oppressum perisse tradunt alii alio leto. Apud
Fabium, longe antiquissimum auctórem, usque ad senectútem
vixisse eundem invenio. Refert certe hanc saepe eum exacta
aetáte usurpasse vocem, multo miserius seni exsilium esse.
Non invidérunt laude sua mulieribus viri Románi—adeo sine

10   obtrectatióne gloriae aliénae vivebátur. Monumento quoque quod
esset, templum Fortúnae Muliebri aedificátum dedicatumque est.
Rediére deinde Volsci adiunctis Aequis in agrum Románum,

sed Aequi Attium Tullium haud ultra tulére ducem. Hinc ex
certamine Volsci Aequíne imperatórem coniuncto exercitui
15 darent, seditio deinde atrox proelium ortum. Ibi fortúna populi
Románi duos hostium exercitus haud minus pernicióso quam
pertináci certamine confécit.

§E   **Notes and Queries.**

(1–2) **Uxor . . . liberi . . . fletusque . . . comploratio:** An extended subject consisting of four nouns, which identify the people visiting the
camp and the actions displayed by them.

(1) **amplexi:** Tense, voice, and mood? Subject of the verbal action?
Explain the use of the gender.

(2) **comploratio sui patriaeque:** When a noun has a verbal meaning,
the genitive may be used with it to denote the object of the verbal action (see *ARA*, App. E, p. 423, Objective Genitive). Here the noun
comploratio is used with the objective genitives **sui** and **patriae,**
which should be translated as *for themselves* and *for their country.*—
fregére: See above, Lesson 25, Section F, note to line 2.

(3) **Complexus:** Tense, voice, and mood? Subject of the verbal action?—**suos:** In the masculine plural, the reflexive adjective is sometimes used as a substantive (see above, Lesson 22, Section E, note to
line 7).

(4) **Abductis . . . legionibus:** What construction?

(5) **invidia rei:** The ablative may be used to designate the cause of an
action (see *ARA*, App. E, p. 425, Ablative of Cause), as here, where
the phrase **invidia rei** should be translated as *because of resentment
over the situation.*—**tradunt:** This verb introduces an indirect statement, in which the accusative **eum** (understood) is subject of the infinitive **perisse** (to be translated as *perished*) and subject of the verbal
action of the participle **oppressum.**—**alii alio leto:** The pronoun **alius**
may be repeated in a case other than the nominative in order to express a double statement, as here, where **alii alio leto** means *some
(authors) . . . by one death, other (authors) . . . by another death.*

(6) **Fabium:** Refers to Fabius Pictor, a Roman historian of the third
century B.C., who wrote a history of Rome in Greek, which Livy apparently used when he was researching the story of Coriolanus.—
antiquissimum: Degree of adjective?

(7) **eundem:** Of what pronoun is this a form?—**invenio:** What construction does this verb introduce? What are the elements of this construction in this sentence?—**Refert:** Translate *He reports.*

(7–8) **eum . . . usurpasse:** What construction? What is the uncontracted form of **usurpasse?**—**exacta aetáte:** What construction? Translate *in old age* or *at the end of his life.* What is the literal meaning of these words?—**hanc . . . vocem:** Refers to the saying paraphrased in the indirect statement **multo miserius seni exsilium esse.** (In contrast to this obscure account of how Coriolanus spent his declining years as an unhappy exile unable to return to his native land, the Greek historians Plutarch and Dionysius of Halicarnassus—who provide the more usual account—report that the Volscians assassinated Coriolanus for betraying them during the war against Rome.)

(10) **vivebátur:** Verbs not taking a direct object may be used impersonally in the passive third person singular but should be translated in the active (see above, Lesson 28, Section E, note to line 7).

(10–11) **Monumento . . . quod esset:** Here the relative **quod** has its antecedent (actually its postcedent) in the noun **templum.** Tense, voice, mood, person, and number of **esset?** How can you reflect the mood of this verb in your translation? What kind of dative is **Monumento?** (See *ARA,* Lesson 48, Section D, note to line 12.)

(11) **templum:** This temple was built several miles outside Rome on the Via Latina—the very road that Coriolanus used when he led the march against his country (see above, Lesson 25, Section E, line 9)—and was dedicated to the goddess Fortune for helping the women bring the crisis instigated by Coriolanus to a successful conclusion. The title **Fortúna Muliebris** *(Women's Fortune)*—one of a number of titles that the Romans used to address the goddess who granted good fortune to deserving people—may also have signified the very name of the temple that the Romans erected as a tribute to the women who succeeded in dissuading Coriolanus from attacking their homeland.

(12) **Rediére:** Translate *returned.*—**Aequis:** Like the Volscians, a people in central Italy, who also felt threatened by the Romans and their conquests.

(13) **Attium Tullium:** See above, Lesson 25, Section F, note to line 4, on this general.—**tulére:** Translate *put up with* or *wished to have.* (Although Livy does not explain why the Aequians refused to accept Attius Tullius as the leader of the joint expedition to Roman territory, one may surmise that they no longer had confidence in the Volscian general after the experience with Coriolanus and that they wanted someone else to lead the new vigorous offensive against the Romans.)

(14–15) **Volsci Aequíne ... darent:** What construction? What two elements does **Aequíne** consist of?

(15) **ortum:** The equivalent of what verb form? (See above, Lesson 17, Section E, note to line 13.)

(general) The Coriolanus episode deals with one small aspect of an extended struggle between Rome and other peoples living in Italy—one that began with the establishment of the Republic, gave rise to a series of wars spanning several centuries, and ended in the assertion of Rome's supremacy as head of a confederacy embracing all of Italy.

LESSON 31

FERO: INDICATIVE. LIVY: LUCRETIA IS PRAISED FOR BEING THE MODEL ROMAN WIFE.

§A **Fero: Indicative.** You will now learn the forms of another important irregular verb, the verb **fero** *(to carry)*, whose principal parts are **fero, ferre, tuli, latus.** The indicative tenses of **fero** are presented in *ARA,* App. J, pp. 459–60, and (in the active) are translated *I carry, I was carrying, I will carry, I carried, I had carried, I will have carried.*

Memorize the present active indicative of **fero;** the imperfect and future are regular (like **traho**); the perfect, pluperfect, and future perfect are formed in the usual way. Using *ARA,* App. J, pp. 459–60, compare the corresponding tenses of **fero** in the passive indicative, which reveal the same regularity or irregularity as the active tenses.

§B **Exercise.** Translate the following sentences with forms of **fero** into English; identify the tense, voice, mood, person, and number of these irregular verb forms:

    (1) **Mater duos parvos filios fert; ad castra Corioláni feruntur.**

    (2) **Ab patre in castris lati sunt; hos manibus tulit et sustulit.**

    (3) **Mater hos ex castris ferébat; ad urbem Romam ferebantur.**

§C **Vocabulary.**

accendo, accendere, accendi, accensus ... *to set on fire; to heat up, to intensify; to stir up, to instigate*

*adventus, adventus, m. ... *arrival*

aedes, aedis, f. (gen. plur. **aedium**) ... (plur. may have sing. meaning) *house; room, hall*

aequális, aequális, c. ... *peer, companion*

ancilla, ancillae, f. ... *maidservant*

avolo, avoláre, avolávi ... *to fly away; to rush off*

benignus, benigna, benignum ... *kind, generous;* **benigne:** *kindly, generously*

castitas, castitátis, f. ... *purity, chastity, fidelity*

cito, citáre, citávi, citátus ... *to excite, to arouse*

Collatia, Collatiae, f. ... the town *Collatia*

Collatínus, Collatíni, m. ... *Collatinus,* husband of Lucretia

comis, come ... *kind, courteous;* **comiter:** *kindly, courteously*

conscendo, conscendere, conscendi ... *to climb, to mount, to ascend*

*cum ... (conj.) *when, since, although;* **cum . . , tum . . ,** *both . . , and . . or not only . . , but also . . or while . . , at the same time . .*

deditus, dedita, deditum ... *devoted* to, *attentive* to (+ dat.)

Egerius, Egerii, m. ... *Egerius,* father of Collatinus

excipio, excipere, excépi, exceptus ... *to take out; to gather, to pick up; to except, to exclude; to receive, to welcome*

*forte ... *by chance, as it happened*

haudquaquam ... *not at all, by no means*

incalesco, incalescere, incalui ... *to grow hot, to become heated*

ingenium, ingenii, n. ... (plur. may have sing. meaning) *talent; character, disposition*

insum, inesse, infui ... *to be in; to be present, to be at hand*

invíso, invisere, invísi, invísus ... *to visit; to look at, to observe*

iuvenális, iuvenále ... *youthful, of* one's *youth*

iuventa, iuventae, f. ... *youth*

lana, lanae, f. ... *wool; spinning*

Lucretia, Lucretiae, f. ... *Lucretia,* wife of Collatinus

lucubro, lucubráre, lucubrávi ... *to work by lamplight*

ludus, ludi, m. ... *play; game, prank*

lusus, lusus, m. ... *play; amusement, entertainment*

marítus, maríti, m. ... *husband; partner, helpmate*

mentio, mentiónis, f. ... *mention*

*****muliebris, muliebre** ... *womanly; of a woman, of the women; involving the women, concerning the women*

necopinátus, necopináta, necopinátum ... *unexpected*

nocturnus, nocturna, nocturnum ... *nocturnal*

occurro, occurrere, occurri ... *to run; to become visible* to the eyes

*****paucus, pauca, paucum** ... (adj. usually found in plur.) *few*

penes ... *worthy of bestowment on, worthy of conferment on* (+ acc.)

poto, potáre, potávi, potátus ... *to drink*

quantum ... (adv.) *as much as; how much, to what extent*

quin ... *why not? (= why don't? why doesn't?)*

*****regius, regia, regium** ... *royal*

sanus, sana, sanum ... *well, healthy;* **sane:** *certainly, by all means*

serus, sera, serum ... *late*

*****specto, spectáre, spectávi, spectátus** ... *to look at, to observe;* **spectátus, spectáta, spectátum:** *proven, tested; reliable, believable*

stupro, stupráre, stuprávi, stuprátus ... *to rape, to ravish, to violate*

Tarquinius, Tarquinii, m. ... *Tarquinius* (= Sextus Tarquinius)

tero, terere, trivi, tritus ... *to rub; to wear out; to while away* time

vigor, vigóris, m. ... *vigor, energy*

§D Reading.

Lucretia Is Praised for Being the Model Roman Wife.

Lessons 31–36 contain Livy's account of Lucretia, the Roman heroine who was raped in her own home by Sextus Tarquinius, the son of the Roman king Tarquinius Superbus. Livy describes how during a campaign involving the town Ardea (510 B.C.), Sextus violated the wife of his colleague, sparking an uprising against the king and his family.

Forte potantibus his apud Sex. Tarquinium, ubi et Collatínus

cenábat Tarquinius (Egerii filius), incidit de uxoribus mentio;

suam quisque laudáre miris modis. Inde, certamine accenso,

Collatínus negat verbis opus esse; paucis id quidem horis posse

5   sciri quantum ceteris praestet Lucretia sua. "Quin, si vigor

iuventae inest, conscendimus equos invisimusque praesentes

nostrárum ingenia? Id cuique spectatissimum sit quod

necopináto viri adventu occurrerit oculis." Incaluerant vino;

"Age sane!" omnes; citátis equis avolant Romam. Quo cum

10   (primis se intendentibus tenebris) pervenissent, pergunt inde

Collatiam, ubi Lucretiam haudquaquam ut regias nurus (quas

in convivio lusuque cum aequalibus viderant tempus terentes),

sed nocte sera deditam lanae inter lucubrantes ancillas in

medio aedium sedentem inveniunt. Muliebris certaminis laus

15   penes Lucretiam fuit. Adveniens vir Tarquiniique excepti

benigne; victor marítus comiter invitat regios iuvenes. Ibi Sex.

Tarquinium mala libído Lucretiae per vim stuprandae capit;

cum forma tum spectáta castitas incitat. Et tum quidem ab

nocturno iuvenáli ludo in castra redeunt.

§E   **Notes and Queries.**

(1) **potantibus his:** What construction? (The pronoun **his** refers to the Roman leaders, relaxing in camp during a respite from the assault on Ardea.)—**Sex. Tarquinium:** His full name was Sextus Tarquinius (= son of Lucius Tarquinius Superbus, the seventh king of Rome).

(1–2) **Collatínus . . . Tarquinius:** His full name was Lucius Tarquinius Collatinus (= husband of Lucretia).

(3) **suam:** What noun should be supplied after this adjective?—**laudáre:** See above, Lesson 21, Section E, note to lines 6–7.

(4) **negat:** What construction does this verb introduce?—**id . . . posse:** What construction? Tense, voice, and mood of **posse?** (This construction is introduced by a verb implied by the verb **negat.**)

(7) **nostrárum:** What noun should be supplied after this adjective?—**Id cuique spectatissimum sit:** Although the Latin idiom is *let that be most believable to each person,* how would you express it in normal English?—**quod:** What is the antecedent? Of what verb is this the subject?

(9) **Age sane:** An idiom combining the imperative **Age** and the adverb **sane** meaning *come now* or *away then.*—**omnes:** What verb should be supplied after this word to introduce the quotation **Age sane?**—**Quo:** The adverb or the pronoun?

(10) **intendentibus tenebris:** What construction? What time of day is indicated by these words?

(11) **Lucretiam:** Of what verb is this the direct object?—**ut:** Translate *like* in accordance with colloquial usage.

(12) **terentes:** Tense, voice, and mood? Subject of the verbal action?

(15) **vir:** Refers to Collatinus.—**Tarquiniique:** Refers to Sextus and the men accompanying him.

(16) **victor:** Here this noun is used as an adjective meaning *victorious.*

(17) **Lucretiae . . . stuprandae:** See above, Lesson 24, Section E, note to line 7, and *ARA,* Appendix K, p. 471, Gerundive Construction.

(19) **redeunt:** Translate *they return* or *returned,* depending on whether or not you treat this verb as a historical present.

LESSON 32

FERO: SUBJUNCTIVE. LIVY: LUCRETIA IS RAPED IN HER HOME BY SEXTUS TARQUINIUS.

§A **Fero: Subjunctive.** The verb **fero** is found in the same four tenses of the subjunctive (in both voices) as are regular verbs, and in general is conjugated in a regular manner. The subjunctive tenses of **fero** are presented in *ARA*, App. J, pp. 461–62, and are translated in accordance with the subjunctive construction in which they appear.

The present active subjunctive of **fero** follows **traho**; the imperfect may be thought of as formed from the present infinitive; the perfect and pluperfect are formed regularly. Using *ARA*, App. J, pp. 461–62, compare the corresponding tenses of **fero** in the passive subjunctive, which reveal the same regularity or irregularity as the active tenses.

§B **Exercise.** Identify the tense, voice, mood, person, and number of the following forms of **fero**:

(1) **ferres**

(2) **ferámur**

(3) **tulerit**

(4) **latae sunt**

(5) **ferátis**

(6) **latus essem**

§C **Vocabulary.**

adulterium, adulterii, n. ... *adultery*

Ardea, Ardeae, f. ... the town *Ardea*

*****circa** ... *around* (+ acc.); *around* (as adv.)

comes, comitis, c. ... *comrade, companion*

*****cum** ... (prep.) *with* (+ abl.); *next to, at the side of* (+ abl.)

decus, decoris, n. ... *honor, dignity; beauty, splendor*

dedecus, dedecoris, n. ... *dishonor, disgrace*

emitto, emittere, emísi, emissus ... *to send out; to discharge; to speak* a word, *to utter* a sound

fateor, fatéri, fassus sum ... *to admit, to confess; to declare, to profess*

***ferrum, ferri,** n. ... *iron, steel; sword, weapon*

fidélis, fidéle ... *faithful, trustworthy*

ignárus, ignára, ignárum ... *ignorant, not knowing; blind, casual, accidental*

inclino, inclináre, inclinávi, inclinátus ... *to bend, to turn; to incline to change, to persuade to give in*

inscius, inscia, inscium ... *not knowing; unknowing, unwitting*

intericio, intericere, interiéci, interiectus ... *to throw between;* (in passive) *to pass, to intervene*

iugulo, iuguláre, iugulávi, iugulátus ... *to cut the throat of; to kill, to murder*

maestus, maesta, maestum ... *sad, sorrowful; distressed, disturbed*

minae, minárum, f. ... (plur. noun with plur. meaning) *threats*

***morior, mori, mortuus sum** (fut. act. part. **moritúrus**) ... *to die;* **mortuus, mortua, mortuum:** *dead*

pavidus, pavida, pavidum ... *alarmed, startled, frightened*

pudicitia, pudicitiae, f. ... *purity, chastity, fidelity*

***satis** ... *enough*

***sinister, sinistra, sinistrum** ... *left;* (fem. sing. as substantive) *left hand;* **sinistra:** (adv.) *on the left*

sopio, sopíre, sopívi, sopítus ... *to be asleep*

tutus, tuta, tutum ... *safe, secure; affording protection*

***velut** ... *as if, just as; as it were, so to speak*

verso, versáre, versávi, versátus ... *to turn, to open; to keep turning, to keep pressuring*

victrix, victrícis ... *victorious, triumphant*

§D   **Reading.**

Lucretia Is Raped in Her Home by Sextus Tarquinius.

Paucis interiectis diébus, Sex. Tarquinius (inscio Collatíno) cum

comite uno Collatiam venit. Ubi exceptus benigne ab ignáris

consilii, cum post cenam in hospitále cubiculum deductus esset,

amóre ardens, postquam satis tuta circa sopitique omnes

5   videbantur, stricto gladio ad dormientem Lucretiam venit,

sinistraque manu mulieris pectore oppresso, "Tace, Lucretia,"

inquit, "Sex. Tarquinius sum; ferrum in manu est; moriére, si

emiseris vocem." Cum pavida ex somno mulier nullam opem

(prope mortem imminentem) vidéret, tum Tarquinius fatéri

10   amórem, oráre, miscére precibus minas, versáre in omnes

partes muliebrem animum. Ubi obstinátam vidébat et ne mortis

quidem metu inclinári, addit ad metum dedecus: cum mortua

iugulátum servum nudum positúrum ait, ut in sordido adulterio

necáta dicátur. Quo terróre cum vicisset obstinátam pudicitiam

15   velut victrix libído, profectusque inde Tarquinius ferox expugnáto

decore muliebri esset, Lucretia (maesta tanto malo) nuntium

Romam eundem ad patrem Ardeamque ad virum mittit, ut cum

singulis fidelibus amícis veniant; ita facto maturatoque opus

esse, rem atrócem incidisse.

(1) **interiectis diébus:** What construction?—**inscio Collatíno:** See *ARA,* Lesson 28, Section G, note to line 8.

(2) **Ubi:** Here the equivalent of **Ibi.**—**exceptus:** Tense, voice, and mood? Subject of the verbal action?—**ignáris:** This adjective refers to members of Lucretia's household. Show this by supplying an appropriate pronoun before this adjective.

(4) **circa:** Here the adverb is used as a substantive meaning *all things around.*

(7–8) **moriére, si emiseris:** What type of condition is this? Tense and mood of the verbs? (See above, Lesson 22, Section A.) Deponent verbs have an alternate future indicative second person singular in **-re,** as here, where **moriére** is alternate for **moriéris.**

(8–9) **Cum . . . tum:** Check the conjunction **cum** for this combination. What meaning of this combination best fits the context?

(9–10) **fatéri . . . oráre, miscére . . . versáre:** What use of the infinitive is illustrated here?

(11) **vidébat:** What construction does this verb introduce? What elements of this construction are understood in this sentence? (See above, Lesson 4, Section E, note to lines 2–3, for this kind of sentence and the elements of this construction to be supplied from the context.)

(11–12) **ne . . . quidem:** See above, Lesson 20, Section E, note to lines 9–10.

(12) **inclinári:** The equivalent of **eam inclinári.** What construction? Tense, voice, and mood of **inclinári?**—**cum mortua:** What meaning of the preposition **cum** best fits the context? What pronoun should be supplied before the adjective **mortua** to show that it refers to Lucretia?

(13) **iugulátum:** That is, murdered by Tarquinius himself or someone ordered by him to commit the murder.—**positúrum:** The equivalent of **se positúrum esse.** What construction? Tense, voice, and mood of **positúrum esse?** (See above, Lesson 21, Section E, note to line 4.)

(14) **dicátur:** This verb has Lucretia as its subject and is followed by **necáta (esse),** which functions here strictly as a complementary infinitive (see *ARA,* Lesson 10, Section F).—**Quo:** What noun does this adjective modify?

(15) **velut victrix libído:** That is, **libído velut victrix.**

(15–16) **profectusque . . . esset:** The words **profectus** and **esset** should be taken together as a single verb form.

(16) **tanto malo:** Translate *by such a dreadful ordeal* or *by such a terrifying experience.* What use of the adjective **malus?** Literal meaning of this use of the adjective?

(17) **patrem . . . virum:** Although in a state of shock, Lucretia sends for the two men whom she trusts the most—they being in two different places at the time of her violation.

(18) **facto maturatoque:** Translate *deed and haste* or *action and speed.* Identify the forms joined by **-que** and give their literal meaning.

(18–19) **opus esse, rem . . . incidisse:** What construction occurs two times in the part of the sentence cited in this note? (This construction is introduced by a verb implied by the words **nuntium . . . mittit.**)

LESSON 33

FERO: IMPERATIVES, INFINITIVES, PARTICIPLES. LIVY: LUCRETIA REVEALS HER ORDEAL AND THEN COMMITS SUICIDE.

§A **Fero: Imperatives, Infinitives, Participles.** The imperative, infinitive, and participial forms of the verb **fero** (occurring in some tenses) are presented in *ARA*, App. J, p. 462. The active imperatives are translated as (you) *carry;* the infinitives—*to carry, to have carried, to be about to carry;* the participles—*carrying, going to carry.*

The present active infinitive of **fero** is the second principal part of the verb; the other active infinitive and participial forms resemble their counterparts in regular verbs. Using *ARA,* App. J, p. 462, compare the corresponding forms of **fero** in the passive and be prepared to recognize these forms whenever they occur in the readings.

§B **Exercise.** Identify the tense, voice, and mood of the following forms of **fero;** then translate:

(1)	**ferte**	(4)	**ferri**
(2)	**tulistis**	(5)	**ferentem**
(3)	**ferendus**	(6)	**latúras esse**

§C **Vocabulary.**

abdo, abdere, abdidi, abditus ... *to hide, to conceal; to bury, to plunge*

absum, abesse, afui ... *to be absent, to be away*

adulter, adulteri, m. ... *adulterer; lecher, debaucher*

amitto, amittere, amísi, amissus ... *to send away; to let go, to lose*

armo, armáre, armávi, armátus ... *to arm, to provide with weapons;*
    armátus, armáta, armátum: *armed, provided with weapons*

aufero, auferre, abstuli, ablátus ... *to carry off, to take away; to take away* something (acc.) *from* someone (dat.)

*fero, ferre, tuli, latus ... *to carry; to bear, to bring; to bear away* or *off* or *along; to say, to relate, to report;* (in passive or with reflexive) *to move, to proceed, to make* one's *way*

Brutus, Bruti, m. ... *Brutus,* Lucius Tarquinius's nephew

*ceterus, cetera, ceterum ... *other,* the *rest;* **ceterum:** (adv.) *but, however, moreover*

conclámo, conclamáre, conclamávi ... *to shout loudly, to scream in horror*

cor, cordis, n. ... *heart*

*cubiculum, cubiculi, n. ... *bedroom*

culpa, culpae, f. ... *fault, blame; sin, wrongdoing*

culter, cultri, m. ... *knife*

defígo, defigere, defixi, defixus ... *to thrust, to plunge*

delictum, delicti, n. ... *crime, outrage*

*dexter, dextra, dextrum ... *right;* (fem. sing. as substantive) *right hand;* **dextra:** (adv.) *on the right*

etsi ... *even if, although*

exemplum, exempli, n. ... *example*

impúne ... *without punishment;* **impúne ferre:** *to do* something *without punishment*

insons, insontis ... *innocent, guiltless*

Iunius, Iunii, m. ... *Iunius* (= Brutus's clan-name)

Lucretius, Lucretii, m. ... *Lucretius,* father of Lucretia

*minimus, minima, minimum ... (superl. of **parvus;** see *ARA,* App. D, p. 419) *smallest;* **minime:** *very little; not at all, not in the least*

moribundus, moribunda, moribundum ... *dying*

noxa, noxae, f. ... *guilt, wrongdoing*

oborior, oboríri, obortus sum ... *to rise up, to well up*

peccátum, peccáti, n. ... *sin, crime*

pestifer, pestifera, pestiferum ... *destructive, destructive* to (+ dat.)

prolábor, prolábi, prolapsus sum ...*to fall forward; to give way, to collapse*

*quaero, quaerere, quaesii, quaesítus ... *to seek, to search for; to seek to know, to ask a question*

supplicium, supplicii, n. ... *entreaty; punishment*

tantum ... (adv.) *just, only; so much, to such an extent*

testis, testis, c. (gen. plur. **testium**) ... *witness*

*ullus, ulla, ullum (gen. sing. **ullíus, ullíus, ullíus**) ... *any;* (as substantive) *anyone, anything*

Valerius, Valerii, m. ... *Valerius,* son of Volesus

Volesus, Volesus, m. ... *Volesus,* father of Valerius

§D   **Reading.**

Lucretia Reveals Her Ordeal and Then Commits Suicide.

Sp. Lucretius cum P. Valerio (Volesi filio), Collatínus cum L.
Iunio Bruto venit, cum quo forte Romam rediens ab nuntio
uxóris erat conventus. Lucretiam sedentem maestam in
cubiculo inveniunt. Adventu suórum lacrimae obortae;
5   quaerentique viro "Satin salve?" "Minime," inquit, "quid enim
salvi est mulieri amissa pudicitia? Vestigia viri aliéni,
Collatíne, in lecto sunt tuo; ceterum corpus est tantum

violátum, animus insons; mors testis erit. Sed date dextras

fidemque haud impúne adultero fore! Sex. est Tarquinius qui

10   hostis pro hospite prióre nocte vi armátus mihi sibique—si vos

viri estis—pestiferum hinc abstulit gaudium." Dant ordine

omnes fidem; consolantur aegram animi avertendo noxam ab

coacta in auctórem delicti: mentem peccáre, non corpus, et unde

consilium afuerit, culpam abesse. "Vos," inquit, "videritis quid

15   illi debeátur; ego me etsi peccáto absolvo, supplicio non libero;

nec ulla deinde impudíca Lucretiae exemplo vivet." Cultrum,

quem sub veste abditum habébat, eum in corde defigit,

prolapsaque in vulnus moribunda cecidit. Conclámat vir

paterque.

§E   Notes and Queries.

(1) **Sp. Lucretius:** His full name was Spurius Lucretius Tricipitinus (= father of Lucretia).—**P. Valerio:** His full name was Publius Valerius, about whom nothing is known.

(1–2) **L. Iunio Bruto:** His full name was Lucius Iunius Brutus (= nephew of Lucius Tarquinius Superbus, the seventh king of Rome).

(2) **rediens:** Translate *returning.*

(3–4) **Lucretiam sedentem . . . inveniunt:** In what other context does Livy use these words? (See above, Lesson 31, Section D, lines 11–14.)

(4) **suórum:** See above, Lesson 22, Section E, note to line 7.—**obortae:** The equivalent of what verb form?

(5) **quaerentique viro "Satin salve?" "Minime," inquit:** These words need to be rearranged in Latin in order to become more intelligible. Translate as if the Latin followed the order **inquitque viro quaerenti "Satin salve?" "Minime . . .** Indirect object of **inquit?** Tense, voice, and mood of **quaerenti?** Subject of the verbal action of **quaerenti?** What meaning of **quaerenti** best fits the context, where it introduces the question **"Satin salve?"** (Assume that **Satin salve? = Satisne salve es?**)

(6) **salvi:** See above, Lesson 25, Section F, note to line 5, on **spei.— amissa pudicitia:** What construction?

(8) **erit:** Tense, voice, mood, person, and number? Write out the conjugation of **sum** in this tense, voice, and mood.

(8–9) **date dextras fidemque:** That is, as a sign of unity or agreement. What construction do these words introduce? What are the elements of this construction in this sentence? (In translating this construction, supply the accusative **id** before the infinitive **fore**—the alternate future infinitive of **sum** [see *ARA,* App. J, p. 454, note 2].)

(9) **Sex. est Tarquinius qui:** Do not translate *Sextus is the Tarquin who.* There is no reason to think that Lucretia would have focused on the Tarquins as the perpetrators of the rape, since they had never threatened her but had actually praised her on the night of their visit. In accordance with the context, at the point of disclosing her ordeal to her father and husband, she would simply name the person who had raped her, of all the possible males in Rome who might have done it.

(11) **pestiferum:** Translate this adjective after the noun that it modifies and before the words **mihi sibique** in order to do full justice to the point that the speaker is making.—**ordine:** That is, one after another.

(12) **aegram:** To whom does this adjective refer? Show this by supplying an appropriate pronoun before this adjective.—**avertendo:** What verbal form? Case and number?

(13) **coacta:** Tense, voice, and mood? What should be supplied as subject of the verbal action?—**mentem peccáre:** What construction? (This construction is introduced by a verb implied by the verb **consolantur.**)

(14) **afuerit:** Tense, voice, mood, person, and number? Explain the use of the mood (see above, Lesson 18, Section A).—**videritis:** See above, Lesson 29, Section E, note to line 14.

(16) **vivet:** Tense, voice, mood, person, and number?

LESSON 34

EO: INDICATIVE. LIVY: BRUTUS TAKES AN OATH TO AVENGE THE DEATH OF LUCRETIA.

§A   **Eo: Indicative.** You will now learn the forms of another irregular verb deserving special attention, the verb **eo** *(to go)*, whose principal parts are **eo, ire, ivi** or **ii.** The indicative tenses of **eo** are presented in *ARA*, App. J, p. 463, and are translated *I go, I was going, I will go, I went, I had gone, I will have gone.*

Memorize the present indicative of **eo**; the imperfect and future resemble **amo**; the perfect, pluperfect, and future perfect are formed in the usual way. Using *ARA*, App. J, p. 463, examine the contracted forms of **eo** for the perfect, pluperfect, and future perfect (in parentheses after the uncontracted forms).

§B   **Exercise.** Translate the following sentences with forms of **eo** into English; identify the tense, voice, mood, person, and number of these irregular verb forms:

(1) **Iam pater in cubiculum ivit; tum vir et duo amíci iérunt.**

(2) **Iam viri ad Lucretiam eunt; femina ad patrem et virum it.**

(3) **Illa ibat ut cultrum caperet; hi ibant ut cultrum auferrent.**

§C   **Vocabulary.**

audeo, audére, ausus sum ... (semi-deponent verb) *to dare* (+ acc. or inf.)

castigátor, castigatóris, m. ... *chider, scolder*

castus, casta, castum ... *pure, chaste, untouched*

concieo, conciére, concívi, concítus ... *to collect, to attract; to incite, to provoke*

*cruor, cruóris, m. ... *blood; murder, slaughter*

defero, deferre, detuli, delátus ... *to carry to, to bring to; to carry down, to bring down*

dehinc ... *from here; after this, from now on*

effero, efferre, extuli, elátus ... *to carry out, to bring out; to lift up, to raise high;* (used with the reflexive pronoun **se,** which is not translated in this idiom) *to rise* or *appear* or *move up in the sky*

exsequor, exsequi, exsecútus sum ... *to pursue, to punish*

extraho, extrahere, extraxi, extractus ... *to drag out, to draw out*

*fio, fieri, factus sum ... (see *ARA,* App. J, pp. 466–68, for the conjugation of this irregular verb) *to become, to happen; to be made, to be built*

hostílis, hostíle ... *hostile, unfriendly*

indignitas, indignitátis, f. ... *outrage, heinousness*

iners, inertis ... *useless, spiritless; lazy, inactive, slow-moving*

luctus, luctus, m. ... (plur. may have sing. meaning) *mourning, lamentation*

*moveo, movére, movi, motus ... *to move; to incite, to provoke*

occupo, occupáre, occupávi, occupátus ... *to seize, to occupy*

prae ... *before, in front of* (+ abl.); *because of, on account of* (+ abl.)

praecipio, praecipere, praecépi, praeceptus ... *to advise, to instruct*

querella, querellae, f. ... *lament, protest, complaint*

queror, queri, questus sum ... *to lament, to protest, to complain about*

*quisquam, quicquam (gen. sing. **cuiusquam, cuiusquam**) ... (indefinite pronoun) *anyone, anything*

scelerátus, sceleráta, scelerátum ... *wicked, accursed*

stirps, stirpis, f. ... *root, stock, offspring*

stupeo, stupére, stupui ... *to be stunned, to be astounded* (+ abl.)

*superbus, superba, superbum ... *proud, arrogant; exultant* in, *glory-ing* in

Tarquinius, Tarquinii, m. ... *Tarquinius* (= Lucius Tarquinius)

*voco, vocáre, vocávi, vocátus ... *to call, to call upon*

voluntarius, voluntaria, voluntarium ... *voluntary;* (masc. sing. as substantive) *volunteer*

*vulnus, vulneris, n. ... *wound, injury;* (as the prospective source of a wound) *weapon*

§D   **Reading.**

Brutus Takes an Oath to Avenge the Death of Lucretia.

Brutus (illis luctu occupátis) cultrum ex vulnere Lucretiae

extractum manante cruóre prae se tenens, "Per hunc," inquit,

"castissimum ante regiam iniuriam sanguinem iuro—vosque, di,

testes facio—me L. Tarquinium Superbum cum sceleráta

5   coniuge et omni liberórum stirpe (ferro, igni, quacumque dehinc

vi possim) exsecutúrum, nec illos nec alium quemquam regnáre

Romae passúrum." Cultrum deinde Collatíno tradit, inde

Lucretio ac Valerio, stupentibus miraculo rei, unde novum in

Bruti pectore ingenium. Ut praeceptum erat, iurant; totique, ab

10   luctu versi in iram, Brutum iam inde ad expugnandum

regnum vocantem sequuntur ducem. Elátum domo Lucretiae

corpus in forum deferunt; concientque miraculo (ut fit) rei novae

atque indignitáte homines. Pro se quisque scelus regium ac vim

queruntur. Movet cum patris maestitia, tum Brutus castigátor

15   lacrimárum atque inertium querellárum, auctorque—quod viros,

quod Romános decéret—arma capiendi adversus hostilia ausos.

Ferocissimus quisque iuvenum cum armis voluntarius adest;

sequitur et cetera iuventus.

§E   Notes and Queries.

(1) **illis . . . occupátis:** What construction? To whom does the pronoun **illis** refer? (Give the names of these individuals.)

(2) **extractum:** Tense, voice, and mood? Subject of the verbal action?—**hunc:** What noun does this adjective modify?

(3) **castissimum:** Translate this adjective after the noun that it modifies and before the phrase **ante regiam iniuriam** in order to do full justice to the point that the speaker is making.—**iuro:** What construction does this verb introduce? What are the elements of this construction in this sentence?

(3–4) **vosque . . . facio:** Here the speaker addresses the gods directly—as one would expect a Roman to do in the course of taking an oath—a parenthetical remark that (along with the verb **iuro**) helps introduce the main construction of the sentence.

(4) **L. Tarquinium Superbum:** His full name was Lucius Tarquinius Superbus, the seventh king of Rome—nicknamed Tarquin the Proud because of his haughty and arrogant behavior.

(4–5) **sceleráta coniuge:** Refers to Tullia, Lucius Tarquinius's former sister-in-law—who persuaded him to murder her husband Arruns Tarquinius and her father Servius Tullius, the sixth king of Rome, in order that she might marry him and become his queen.

(5) **omni liberórum stirpe:** Refers to Lucius Tarquinius's three sons Titus, Arruns, and Sextus—the last (and youngest) of whom Brutus wished to punish most of all inasmuch as he had raped Lucretia and in doing so had ultimately caused her to commit suicide.

(6) **possim:** Tense, voice, mood, person, and number? Explain the use of the mood (see above, Lesson 18, Section A).

(7) **passúrum:** The equivalent of the construction **me passúrum esse.** See also above, Lesson 32, Section E, note to line 13, on **positúrum.—Cultrum . . . tradit:** Here Brutus passes the knife from one man to another, which is used in this scene as a symbol to ratify their oath, in the way that the Bible is used in modern society in a court of law.

(8–9) **novum in . . . pectore ingenium:** Until this moment Brutus had assumed the appearance of stupidity and passivity in order that he might not become suspect in the eyes of the king. In this regard, he had even accepted the nickname Brutus ("Dummy" or "Dullard"), all the time carefully concealing his clever and aggressive nature.

(10) **expugnandum:** What verbal form? Case, number, and gender?

(11) **vocantem:** Tense, voice, and mood? Subject of the verbal action? What should be supplied as direct object?—**Elátum:** Of what verb is this a form?—**domo:** See above, Lesson 14, Section E, note to line 4.

(12) **forum:** See above, Lesson 7, Section E, note to line 3.—**fit:** A form of the irregular verb **fio.** Tense, voice, mood, person, and number of **fit?** (See *ARA,* App. J, pp. 466–68, for the conjugation of this irregular verb.)

(13) **homines:** Refers to nameless spectators. Of what verb is this the direct object?

(13–14) **quisque . . . queruntur:** See above, Lesson 25, Section F, note to line 2.

(14) **Movet:** Has as its subject first **maestitia,** then **Brutus.** Supply *onlookers* or *spectators* as its direct object.—**cum . . . tum:** See above, Lesson 32, Section E, note to lines 8–9.

(15–16) **auctorque . . . arma capiendi:** Here the noun **auctor** introduces the phrase **arma capiendi.** What verbal form is **capiendi?** Case and number of this form?—**quod . . . quod . . . decéret:** What construction? Meaning of the relative here? (The form **decéret,** which means *was fitting for* or *was proper for,* is the imperfect subjunctive of the impersonal verb **decet** [see above, Lesson 1, Section F, note to line 10].)

(16) **adversus hostilia ausos:** The preposition **adversus** has as its object the verbal form **ausos**—the perfect passive participle of the semideponent verb **audeo** (see above, Lesson 3, Section E, note to line 1). The participial form **ausos** is here used as a substantive meaning *those having dared,* which has as its own object the adjective **hostilia,** itself used as a substantive to refer to the atrocities of the royal family.

LESSON 35

EO: SUBJUNCTIVE. LIVY: BRUTUS MARCHES TO ROME AND INCITES THE ROMAN PEOPLE.

§A   **Eo: Subjunctive.** The verb **eo** is found in the same four tenses of the subjunctive (only in the active) as are regular verbs, and in general is conjugated in a regular manner. The subjunctive tenses of **eo** are presented in *ARA*, App. J, p. 464, and are translated in accordance with the subjunctive construction in which they appear.

     The present subjunctive of **eo** follows **traho;** the imperfect may be thought of as formed from the present infinitive; the perfect and pluperfect are formed regularly. Using *ARA*, App. J, p. 464, examine the contracted forms of **eo** for the perfect and pluperfect (as with the indicative, in parentheses after the uncontracted forms).

§B   **Exercise.** Identify the tense, voice, mood, person, and number of the following forms of **eo:**

       (1) **ires**   (4) **eámus**

       (2) **ibunt**   (5) **iverim**

       (3) **ierit**   (6) **iissétis**

§C   **Vocabulary.**

     advoco, advocáre, advocávi, advocátus ... *to summon*

     anteeo, anteíre, anteívi or **anteii** ... *to go before; to take the lead, to march at the head of* a procession

     ***eo, ire, ivi** or **ii** ... *to go, to proceed*

     bellátor, bellatóris, m. ... *warrior*

     ***caedes, caedis,** f. (gen. plur. **caedium**) ... (plur. may have sing. meaning) *murder, slaughter; blood* (shed in killing)

*celer, celeris, celere ... *swift, speedy;* (masc. plur. as substantive) the *celeres* (= the cavalry)

cloáca, cloácae, f. ... *sewer*

*curro, currere, cucurri ... *to run; to hurry, to hasten*

demergo, demergere, demersi, demersus ... *to plunge, to submerge; to send below or underground*

exhaurio, exhauríre, exhausi, exhaustus ... *to draw out; to drain out, to clean out*

*facio, facere, feci, factus ... *to do, to make; to cause, to produce, to bring about*

incédo, incedere, incessi ... *to go; to advance, to proceed*

indignus, indigna, indignum ... *unworthy, undeserving; unworthy of, undeserving of (+ gen. or abl.); shameful, shocking, outrageous;* **indigne:** *unworthily, undeservedly, outrageously*

invoco, invocáre, invocávi, invocátus ... *to invoke*

*labor, labóris, m. ... *work, toil; struggle, hardship*

lapicída, lapicídae, m. ... *stone-cutter*

magistrátus, magistrátus, m. ... *office, official position*

minor, minus ... (compar. of **parvus;** see *ARA,* App. D, p. 419) *smaller*

miserabilis, miserabile ... *pitiable, deplorable*

miseria, miseriae, f. ... *trouble, distress*

nefandus, nefanda, nefandum ... *unspeakable; abominable, despicable*

opifex, opificis, m. ... *artisan, workman*

oratio, oratiónis, f. ... *speech;* **oratiónem habére:** *to make a speech*

orbitas, orbitátis, f. ... *bereavement*

praeco, praecónis, m. ... *crier, herald*

quacumque ... *whenever, wherever*

reor, reri, ratus sum ... *to think, to believe*

*simul ... (conj.) *as soon as, at the same time as;* (as adv.) *along, to-gether, at the same time*

stuprum, stupri, n. ... *violation, defilement*

superbia, superbiae, f. ... *pride, arrogance*

Tricipitinus, Tricipitini, m. ... *Tricipitinus* (= Lucretius's family name)

Tullius, Tullii, m. ... *Tullius* (= Servius Tullius)

tumultus, tumultus, m. ... *confusion, disturbance*

ultor, ultóris, m. ... *avenger*

§D   **Reading.**

Brutus Marches to Rome and Incites the Roman People.

Inde, praesidio relicto Collatiae ad portas, custodibusque datis ne

quis eum motum regibus nuntiáret, ceteri armáti, duce Bruto,

Romam profecti. Ubi eo ventum est, quacumque incédit armáta

multitúdo, pavórem ac tumultum facit. Rursus ubi anteíre

5   primóres civitátis vident, quidquid sit haud temere esse rentur.

Nec minórem motum animórum Romae tam atrox res facit

quam Collatiae fecerat. Ergo ex omnibus locis urbis in forum

curritur. Quo simul ventum est, praeco ad tribúnum celerum

(in quo tum magistrátu forte Brutus erat) populum advocávit.

10   Ibi oratio habita (nequaquam eius pectoris ingeniique quod

simulátum ad eam diem fuerat) de vi ac libidine Sex. Tarquini, de stupro infando Lucretiae et miserabili caede, de orbitáte

Tricipitini, cui morte filiae causa mortis indignior ac

miserabilior esset. Addita superbia ipsíus regis, miseriaeque et

15 labóres plebis in fossas cloacasque exhauriendas demersae.

Romános homines—victóres omnium circa populórum—opifices

ac lapicídas pro bellatoribus factos. Indigna Ser. Tulli regis

memoráta caedes, et invecta corpori patris nefando vehiculo

filia, invocatique ultóres parentum di.

§E Notes and Queries.

(1) **praesidio relicto:** What construction?

(1–2) **ne . . . nuntiáret:** What construction?

(2) **regibus:** Here the noun **regibus** does not mean *to the kings* but *to the royal family,* referring to Lucius Tarquinius and his wife Tullia (see above, Lesson 34, Section E, note to line 4 and note to lines 4–5).— **duce Bruto:** See *ARA,* Lesson 42, Section D, note to line 9.

(3) **profecti:** The equivalent of what verb form?—**ventum est:** See above, Lesson 28, Section E, note to line 7.

(5) **vident:** What construction does this verb introduce? What are the elements of the construction introduced by this verb? (Understand **homines,** referring to nameless spectators, as the subject of the verb **vident.**)—**rentur:** What construction does this verb introduce? What are the elements of the construction introduced by this verb? (Here **quidquid sit** functions as the first element of the construction introduced by **rentur.**)

(6–7) **tam . . . quam:** Here **tam** and **quam** are not used in the combination meaning *as . . . as.* Check these words separately and choose the meanings that best fit the context.

(8) **curritur:** See also above, Lesson 28, Section E, note to line 7.— **tribúnum celerum:** The tribune of the celeres represented the members of the cavalry, who apparently were the historical predecessors of the equestrians (see above, Lesson 18, Section E, note to line 1).

(9) **quo:** What noun does this adjective modify?

(10) **habita:** The equivalent of what verb form?—**nequaquam eius pectoris ingeniique:** See above, Lesson 34, Section E, note to lines 8–9.

(11) **simulátum . . . fuerat:** See above, Lesson 17, Section E, note to line 15.

(13) **Tricipitini:** See above, Lesson 33, Section E, note to line 1.—**morte:** What kind of ablative? (See above, Lesson 3, Section E, note to line 7, on **isto.**)

(14) **esset:** Here the subjunctive is used, since the relative clause does not express the opinion of the writer but the opinion of the speaker.—**Addita:** That is, added to the speech. Of what verb form is **Addita** the equivalent? By what series of subjects is **Addita** followed?

(15) **in fossas cloacasque exhauriendas:** See above, Lesson 24, Section E, note to line 7. (Under the reign of Lucius Tarquinius, the plebeians had been ordered to construct and clean out Rome's main sewers.)—**demersae:** Tense, voice, and mood? Subject of the verbal action?

(16–17) **homines . . . factos:** What construction? (This construction is introduced by a verb implied by **Addita.**) Of what verb is **factos** a form? (It is not a form of **facio** but of an irregular verb related to **facio.**)

(17) **Ser. Tulli:** His full name was Servius Tullius, the sixth king of Rome (see above, Lesson 34, Section E, note to lines 4–5).

(18) **memoráta:** Compare above, note to line 14, on **Addita.** Of what verb form is **memoráta** the equivalent? By what series of subjects is **memoráta** followed?

(18–19) **invecta corpori patris nefando vehiculo filia:** After the murder of Servius Tullius by Lucius Tarquinius, Tullia contributed to the horror by actually driving her chariot over the body of her father.

(19) **ultóres parentum di:** Refers to the three Furies. See *ARA*, Lesson 51, Section F, note to line 10, on their function.

LESSON 36

EO: IMPERATIVES, INFINITIVES, PARTICIPLES. LIVY: BRUTUS LIBERATES THE CITY AND EXPELS THE ROYAL FAMILY. CLASSICAL TRADITION: SHAKESPEARE'S CORIOLANUS.

§A **Eo: Imperatives, Infinitives, Participles.** The imperative, infinitive, and participial forms of the verb **eo** (occurring in some tenses) are presented in *ARA*, App. J, p. 465. All the imperatives (singular and plural) are translated as (you) *go;* the infinitives—*to go, to have gone, to be about to go;* the participles—*going, going to go.*

Most of the imperatives of **eo** have the stem **i-;** the present infinitive is the second principal part of the verb; the other forms resemble their counterparts in regular verbs. Using *ARA*, App. J, p. 465, examine these forms, especially the present participle **iens, euntis**—which has the stem **eu-** in all cases except the nominative singular.

§B **Exercise.** Identify the tense, voice, and mood of the following forms of **eo;** then translate:

(1) **ire**

(2) **iisse**

(3) **euntem**

(4) **ite**

(5) **itúras**

(6) **itúros esse**

§C **Vocabulary.**

abrogo, abrogáre, abrogávi, abrogátus ... *to take away* from; *to revoke, to rescind*

__armo, armáre, armávi, armátus ... to arm, to provide with weapons;__ **armátus, armáta, armátum:** *armed, provided with weapons*

Caere, Caeritis, n. ... the town *Caere*

*comprimo, comprimere, compressi, compressus ... *to rape, to ravage, to violate; to crush, to subdue, to suppress*

concito, concitáre, concitávi, concitátus ... *to incite, to stir up*

diversus, diversa, diversum ... *different; opposite, separate*

Etruscus, Etrusci, m. ... an *Etruscan*

exsecror, exsecrári, exsecrátus sum ... *to curse*

exsulo, exsuláre, exsulávi, exsulátus ... *to be an exile, to live in exile*

furia, furiae, f. ... *frenzy, madness;* (in plur.) the *Furies*

Gabii, Gabiórum, m. ... (plur. noun with sing. meaning) the town *Gabii*

*imperium, imperii, n. ... (plur. may have sing. meaning) *order, command; power, authority; empire, dominion*

*incendo, incendere, incendi, incensus ... *to set on fire; to inflame, to provoke*

indíco, indicere, indixi, indictus ... *to proclaim, to declare*

instituo, instituere, institui, institútus ... *to arrange, to establish; to appoint, to designate*

*inter ... *among, between* (+ acc.); *amid, in the midst of* (+ acc.); *in between, in their midst* (as adv.)

iunior, iunióris, m. ... *younger man;* (in plur.) *younger men* (= the juniors)

*laetus, laeta, laetum ... *happy, joyful*

liberátor, liberatóris, m. ... *liberator*

perfero, perferre, pertuli, perlátus ... *to carry through; to convey, to deliver; to endure, to suffer, to withstand*

perpello, perpellere, perpuli, perpulsus ... *to drive; to urge, to incite*

porta, portae, f. ... *gate*

praefectus, praefecti, m. ... *prefect*

profugio, profugere, profúgi ... *to flee* from, *to run away* from

rapína, rapínae, f. ... (plur. may have sing. meaning) *pillage, plunder*

refero, referre, rettuli, relátus ... *to carry back; to relate, to report*

scriptor, scriptóris, m. ... *writer; author, authority*

simultas, simultátis, f. (gen. plur. **simultatium**) ... *labor, contest; dispute, quarrel*

subicio, subicere, subiéci, subiectus ... *to place under, to put under one's control; to bring to the fore, to cause to come forward*

trepidus, trepida, trepidum ... *alarmed, agitated*

Tullia, Tulliae, f. ... *Tullia,* Lucius Tarquinius's wife

*vetus, veteris ... *old, ancient*

§D   **Reading.**

Brutus Liberates the City and Expels the Royal Family.

His atrocioribusque, credo, aliis (quae praesens rerum

indignitas—haudquaquam relátu scriptoribus facilia—subiécit)

memorátis, incensam multitudinem perpulit ut imperium regi

abrogáret exsulesque esse iubéret L. Tarquinium cum coniuge

5   ac liberis. Ipse, iunioribus (qui ultro nomina dabant) lectis

armatisque, ad concitandum inde adversus regem exercitum,

Ardeam in castra est profectus. Imperium in urbe Lucretio,

praefecto urbis iam ante ab rege institúto, relinquit. Inter hunc

tumultum Tullia domo profúgit, exsecrantibus (quacumque

10   incedébat) invocantibusque parentum furias viris mulieribusque.

Harum rerum nuntiis in castra perlátis, cum (re nova trepidus) rex pergeret Romam ad comprimendos motus, flexit viam Brutus (senserat enim adventum) ne obvius fieret. Eodemque fere tempore diversis itineribus Brutus Ardeam, Tarquinius

15   Romam venérunt. Tarquinio clausae portae exsiliumque indictum; liberatórem urbis laeta castra accepére; exactique inde liberi regis. Duo patrem secúti sunt, qui exsulátum Caere in Etruscos iérunt. Sex. Tarquinius, Gabios (tamquam in suum regnum) profectus, ab ultoribus veterum simultatium (quas sibi

20   ipse caedibus rapinisque concierat) est interfectus.

§E   **Notes and Queries.**

(1–3) **His atrocioribusque . . . aliis . . . memorátis:** What construction? To what things does the pronoun **His** refer? (See above, Lesson 35, Section D, lines 10–19.) What degree of adjective is **atrocioribus** and with what pronoun (**His** or **aliis**) does this adjective go?

(1) **credo:** Here this verb does not introduce an indirect statement but is inserted almost parenthetically, as a side comment by the author.

(2) **indignitas:** That is, the outrage concerning Lucretia. Of what verb is **indignitas** the subject?—**relátu scriptoribus facilia:** The adjective **facilia** (agreeing with **quae**) is followed by the dative **scriptoribus** and the verbal form **relátu**. What verbal form is **relátu**? Case and number of **relátu**? (See *ARA*, Lesson 49, Section D, for this verbal form.)

(3–4) **ut . . . abrogáret . . . iubéret:** What construction?

(5) **iunioribus:** In ancient Rome, the **iunióres**—men between the ages of seventeen and forty-five—were regarded as fit for military service.

(6) **concitandum:** What verbal form? Case, number, and gender?

(8) **praefecto urbis:** The person (in this instance, Lucretius) who governed the city in the absence of the king and dealt with law, business, and any possible emergency.

(9–10) **exsecrantibus . . . invocantibusque . . . viris mulieribusque:** What construction? How does this example of the construction seem a little different from the usual kind?

(10) **parentum furias:** See above, Lesson 35, Section E, note to line 19.

(12) **comprimendos:** What verbal form? Case, number, and gender?—**flexit viam:** Although the Latin idiom is *changed the road,* how would you express it in normal English?

(13) **ne obvius fieret:** Translate *lest he meet him.* What is the literal meaning? Tense, voice, mood, person, and number of **fieret?**

(15) **clausae:** The equivalent of what verb form?

(16) **indictum:** See above, note to line 15.—**accepére:** See above, Lesson 25, Section F, note to line 2.

(17) **Duo:** Refers to Titus and Arruns (see above, Lesson 34, Section E, note to line 5).—**exsulátum:** What verbal form? Case and number? (See above, note to line 2, for this verbal form but in another case.)

(17–18) **in Etruscos:** Lucius Tarquinius decided to take refuge with the Etruscans (a people in northern Italy), since he himself—like the kings who preceded him—was of Etruscan origin.

(18) **iérunt:** Tense, voice, mood, person, and number?

(20) **caedibus rapinisque:** Sextus Tarquinius had once helped his father conquer Gabii—first by tricking the Gabini into believing that he was deserting to their side, then by acquiring their trust in him as leader in the war against the Romans, and finally by executing the leaders of the Gabini as soon as he had consolidated his power.

(general) The Lucretia episode relates the final incident in a series of atrocities prompting Rome to expel the last of her Etruscan kings—resulting in the election of Brutus and Collatinus as the first two consuls and the establishment of the Republic, a system of government under which the Roman people lived for almost five hundred years.

§F   **Classical Tradition.** The Coriolanus and Lucretia stories became popular literary themes, both of which were adapted by a number of classical and post-classical authors. These two dramatic narratives strongly influenced Shakespeare, who preserved the classical story lines in his play *Coriolanus* and in his poem *Rape of Lucrece.*

For his *Coriolanus,* Shakespeare relied not so much on Livy's Latin narrative but to a greater degree on Sir Thomas North's translation of the Greek historian Plutarch. In the following passage from this famous tragedy, Coriolanus addresses his mother, his wife, and the Volscian general Tullius Aufidius (Shakespeare's Attius Tullius).

CORIOLANUS   O mother, mother!
    What have you done? Behold, the heavens do ope,
    The gods look down, and this unnatural scene
    They laugh at. O my mother, mother! O!
    You have won a happy victory to Rome;
    But, for your son—believe it, O, believe it!—
    Most dangerously you have with him prevailed,
    If not most mortal to him. But let it come.
    Aufidius, though I cannot make true wars,
    I'll frame convenient peace. Now, good Aufidius,
    Were you in my stead, would you have heard
    A mother less? Or granted less, Aufidius?
AUFIDIUS
    I was moved withal.
CORIOLANUS   I dare be sworn you were!
    And, sir, it is no little thing to make
    Mine eyes to sweat compassion. But, good sir,
    What peace you'll make, advise me. For my part,
    I'll not to Rome, I'll back with you; and pray you
    Stand to me in this cause. O mother! Wife!
AUFIDIUS [Aside.]
    I am glad thou hast set thy mercy and thy honor
    At difference in thee. Out of that I'll work
    Myself a former fortune.
CORIOLANUS   Ay, by and by;
    But we will drink together; and you shall bear
    A better witness back than words, which we
    On like conditions will have countersealed.
    Come, enter with us. Ladies, you deserve
    To have a temple built you. All the swords
    In Italy, and her confederate arms,
    Could not have made this peace.

LESSON 37

CATULLUS. METER: HENDECASYLLABICS. CATULLUS: CATULLUS MOURNS THE DEATH OF LESBIA'S SPARROW.

§A   **Catullus.** Catullus (84 B.C.–54 B.C.), one of Rome's greatest lyric poets, became famous for his love poems, many of them centering on the woman whom he calls Lesbia. Lessons 37–48 contain a series of poems reflecting the different sides of this writer, which (when taken together) afford a microcosm of his poetry, a glimpse into his world.

§B   **Meter: Hendecasyllabics.** Catullus composed his poems in verse—a patterned flow of sounds—and did so in a variety of meters, including the verse-form called *hendecasyllabics*. You will now learn some basic facts about poetic form in order to prepare you for this and other metrical patterns exhibited by the poems that appear in this textbook.

In classical literary texts, poetic form consists of a rhythmic pattern, based on the number and kinds of metrical feet (groups of syllables) found in a particular line of verse. Unlike English poetry, which is based on accent, Latin poetry is based on quantity, which (whatever the meter) involves a patterned succession of long and short syllables.

A syllable is long if it contains (1) a long vowel, or (2) a diphthong, or (3) a vowel followed by two consonants (see *ARA,* Lesson 3, Section F, for the rules concerning accents). However, in other instances the syllable may be short, such as when a short vowel is followed by another vowel or when a short vowel is followed by a single consonant.

The poet may sometimes use a long syllable instead of a short syllable and a short syllable instead of a long syllable, involving many exceptions to the rules presented above. Final syllables ending in a vowel, diphthong, or an **m** are not pronounced but are said to be elided (that is, slurred over) whenever the next word begins with a vowel or an **h.**

As for hendecasyllabics—a meter often used by Catullus—each line consists of eleven syllables, which are divided into five metrical feet (– designates a long syllable, ◡ a short syllable, × a long or short one):

$$- - \mid - \cup \cup \mid - \cup \mid - \cup \mid - \times$$

Now consider the first three lines of the reading in this lesson—lines that have been scanned (that is, marked off to show the long and short syllables), with the elided syllables enclosed in parentheses:

– – | – ∪ ∪ | – ∪ | – ∪ | – ∪

Lugét(e), o Veneres Cupidinesque,

– – | – ∪ ∪ | – ∪ | – ∪ | – ∪

et quant(um) est hominum venustiórum!

– – | – ∪ ∪ | – ∪ | – ∪ | – –

Passer mortuus est meae puellae,

§C   **Vocabulary.**

*bellus, bella, bellum ... *pretty, charming, attractive*

circumsilio, circumsilíre ... *to hop around, to jump around*

*cupído, cupidinis, m. ... *desire, carnal desire;* (as proper noun) **Cupído:** the god *Cupid*

*deliciae, deliciárum, f. ... (plur. noun with sing. meaning) *darling, delight; allurement, enticement*

devoro, devoráre, devorávi, devorátus ... *to eat, to swallow*

*fleo, flere, flevi ... *to cry, to weep; to cry for, to weep for*

*gremium, gremii, n. ... *lap, bosom*

mellítus, mellíta, mellítum ... *honey-sweet*

misellus, misella, misellum ... *sad little, poor little, wretched little*

o ... (interjection) *oh!*

ocellus, ocelli, m. ... *little eye*

Orcus, Orci, m. ... the god *Orcus*

*passer, passeris, m. ... *sparrow*

pipio, pipiáre ... *to chirp*

*puella, puellae, f. ... *girl; mistress, sweetheart*

redeo, redíre, redívi or **redii** ... *to go back, to return;* (of the sun) *to rise again*

rubeo, rubére ... *to be red*

tenebricósus, tenebricósa, tenebricósum ... *dark, gloomy*

turgidulus, turgidula, turgidulum ... *tiny swollen*

Venus, Veneris, f. ... *Venus*

venustus, venusta, venustum ... *pretty, charming, attractive*

vobis ... (dat. or abl. plur. of **tu**) *to/for you* or *by/with you*

§D **Reading.** Although the usual stress accents will continue to appear over the words, one should realize that if he/she reads in meter, the beat will depend not on the accents but on the quantity of the syllables.

Catullus Mourns the Death of Lesbia's Sparrow.

Lessons 37–39 contain poems by Catullus dealing with love, especially his love for Lesbia, a pseudonym for Clodia (the wife of the urban magistrate Q. Caecilius Metellus). The poems in these lessons are all written in hendecasyllabics—the meter normally used by Catullus for light and intimate themes, and those having a humorous subject.

Lugéte, o Veneres Cupidinesque,

et quantum est hominum venustiórum!

Passer mortuus est meae puellae,

passer, deliciae meae puellae,

5   quem plus illa oculis suis amábat.

Nam mellítus erat, suamque norat

ipsam tam bene quam puella matrem.

Nec sese a gremio illíus movébat,

sed circumsiliens modo huc modo illuc,

10   ad solam dominam usque pipiábat.

Qui nunc it per iter tenebricósum

illuc, unde negant redíre quemquam.

At vobis male sit, malae tenebrae

Orci, quae omnia bella devorátis:

15 tam bellum mihi passerem abstulistis.

O factum male! O miselle passer!

Tua nunc opera meae puellae

flendo turgiduli rubent ocelli.

§E   Notes and Queries.

(1) **Lugéte:** Tense, voice, mood, person, and number?—**Veneres Cupidinesque:** A common jingle or proverbial expression, playing upon an early mythological account of there being more than one Venus and more than one Cupid.

(2) **quantum est hominum:** Translate *whatever people there are.* What is the literal meaning of these words?—**venustiórum:** Degree of adjective? Modifies what noun?

(5) **oculis:** What kind of ablative?

(6) **norat:** A form of the verb **nosco.** What is the uncontracted form?

(6–7) **suamque . . . ipsam:** After these words supply *mistress.*

(7) **puella matrem:** Between these words supply *knows.*

(8) **sese:** An alternate form of the accusative **se** (see *ARA,* App. C, p. 408).

(9) **circumsiliens:** Tense, voice, and mood? Subject of the verbal action?

(11) **it:** Of what verb is this a form? Tense, voice, mood, person, and number?—**per iter tenebricósum:** Although Catullus here describes Lesbia's sparrow as traveling to the land of the dead, one should not assume that the Romans seriously thought of their household pets as taking such a journey.

(12) **negant:** What construction does this verb introduce? What are the elements of this construction in this sentence?

(13) **vobis male sit:** See above, Lesson 10, Section E, note to line 8.

(14) **Orci:** Refers to the god of the underworld or possibly the underworld itself.

(15) **abstulistis:** Of what verb is this a form? Tense, voice, mood, person, and number?

(16) **factum male:** A Latin idiom meaning *what a pity* or *what a shame.*—**miselle:** Catullus has a propensity for using diminutives (see *ARA,* Lesson 15, Section D, Lesson 22, Section D, and Lesson 23, Section D).—**passer:** Case and number? Function of this case?

(17) **opera:** What kind of ablative?

(18) **flendo:** What verbal form? Case and number?—**turgiduli . . . ocelli:** See above, note to line 16, on Catullus's propensity for using diminutives.

LESSON 38

CATULLUS: CATULLUS ASKS LESBIA FOR COUNTLESS
KISSES; CATULLUS INVITES FABULLUS TO A SPECIAL
DINNER.

§A   **Vocabulary.**

adfero, adferre, attuli, adlátus ... *to bring to, to bring along*

aestimo, aestimáre, aestimávi, aestimátus ... *to think, to realize; to value* or *assess* something (acc.) at something (gen.)

*amor, amóris, m. ... (plur. may have sing. meaning) *love, desire; lover,* one's *beloved;* (as proper noun) **Amor:** the god *Love*

aranea, araneae, f. ... *spider; cobweb*

as, assis, m. ... *coin; cent, penny*

*basium, basii, n. ... *kiss*

cachinnus, cachinni, m. ... (plur. may have sing. meaning) *laugh, laughter*

*candidus, candida, candidum ... *white, bright; fair, lovely, beautiful*

Catullus, Catulli, m. ... *Catullus,* the Roman poet

*cena, cenae, f. ... *dinner*

*ceno, cenáre, cenávi ... *to eat, to dine*

*centum (indecl.) ... a *hundred*

conturbo, conturbáre, conturbávi, conturbátus ... *to mix up, to confound, to throw into disorder*

elegans, elegantis ... *elegant, graceful, tasteful*

Fabullus, Fabulli, m. ... *Fabullus,* friend of Catullus

faveo, favére, favi ... *to favor, to be favorable* to (+ dat.)

Lesbia, Lesbiae, f. ... *Lesbia,* mistress of Catullus

lux, lucis, f. ... *light; day, daylight; sheen, splendor;* **sub luce:** *at daybreak*

merus, mera, merum ... *pure, sheer*

***mille** (indecl.) ... a *thousand;* **milia, milium, n.:** *thousands*

nasus, nasi, m. ... *nose*

occido, occidere, occidi ... *to die, to perish;* (of the sun) *to set, to go down*

olfacio, olfacere, olféci, olfactus ... *to smell, to sniff*

perpetuus, perpetua, perpetuum ... *continuous, everlasting;* **in perpetuum:** *forever, for all time*

rumor, rumóris, m. ... (plur. may have sing. meaning) *talk, rumor, gossip*

sacculus, sacculi, m. ... *small bag; purse, money-bag*

sal, salis, m. ... *salt; wit, humor*

seu ... *or if*

sevérus, sevéra, sevérum ... *stern, strict, severe*

suavis, suave ... *sweet, pleasant*

unguentum, unguenti, n. ... *perfume; scent, essence*

§B   Reading.

Catullus Asks Lesbia for Countless Kisses.

Vivámus, mea Lesbia, atque amémus,

rumoresque senum severiórum

omnes uníus aestimémus assis.

Soles occidere et redíre possunt:

5   nobis, cum semel occidit brevis lux,

nox est perpetua una dormienda.

Da mi basia mille, deinde centum,

dein mille altera, dein secunda centum,

deinde usque altera mille, deinde centum!

10   Dein, cum milia multa fecerimus,

conturbabimus illa, ne sciámus,

aut ne quis malus invidére possit,

cum tantum sciat esse basiórum.

Catullus Invites Fabullus to a Special Dinner.

Cenábis bene, mi Fabulle, apud me

paucis (si tibi di favent) diébus,

si tecum attuleris bonam atque magnam

cenam, non sine candida puella

5   et vino et sale et omnibus cachinnis.

Haec si (inquam) attuleris, venuste noster,

cenábis bene; nam tui Catulli

plenus sacculus est araneárum.

Sed contra accipies meros amóres,

10   seu quid suavius elegantiusve est:

nam unguentum dabo, quod meae puellae

donárunt Veneres Cupidinesque,

quod tu cum olfacies, deos rogábis,

totum ut te faciant, Fabulle, nasum.

§C   **Notes and Queries.**

First Passage

(1) **Vivámus . . . amémus:** What use of the subjunctive?

(2) **senum severiórum:** Refers to old people who are unusually critical and no longer capable of falling in love or having a good time.

(3) **uníus . . . assis:** The genitive may be used to designate the price at which something is valued or assessed (compare above, Lesson 7, Section E, note to line 15).

(4) **Soles:** Here the plural is used to indicate that each day has a different sun.—**possunt:** Of what verb is this a form? Tense, voice, mood, person, and number?

(5) **brevis lux:** Refers to the short life span allotted to human beings.

(5–6) **est . . . dormienda:** The gerundive may combine with the different tenses of **sum** to form the Passive Periphrastic Conjugation, designating the idea of obligation or necessity (see *ARA*, App. K, p. 471). The passive periphrastic may be used with the dative of agent, as here with **nobis . . . est . . . dormienda,** and (if used impersonally) should be translated in the active (i.e., *we must sleep*).

(7) **Da:** Tense, voice, mood, person, and number?

(10) **fecerimus:** Tense, voice, mood, person, and number? (See above, Lesson 15, Section A).

(11) **conturbabimus:** Tense, voice, and mood? Write out the conjugation of **conturbo** in this tense, voice, and mood.—**ne sciámus:** What construction?

(13) **basiórum:** See above, Lesson 25, Section F, note to line 5.

Second Passage

(1–3) **Cenábis . . . si . . . attuleris:** What type of condition? Tense and mood of the verbs?

(1) **mi:** Here the vocative singular of the adjective **meus.**

(2) **diébus:** What kind of ablative?

(6) **noster:** The words **nos** and **noster** may be used by a single person in speaking of himself/herself in order to convey a formal, impersonal, or self-depreciating tone. (In this sentence, after the adjective **noster** supply *guest* or *friend*—as in above, Lesson 2, Section E, note to line 13, although there the adjective retains its plural meaning.)

(8) **plenus . . . araneárum:** A colloquial expression designating utter emptiness and destitution.

(9) **contra:** That is, in return for bringing the food.—**accipies:** Tense, voice, mood, person, and number?—**meros amóres:** That is, the very essence of love or something really worth loving.

(10) **suavius elegantiusve:** Degree of adjectives?

(11) **unguentum:** Refers to a smell associated with Catullus's mistress, that of her perfume or her bodily scent or essence.

(12) **donárunt:** What is the uncontracted form of this verb?—**Veneres Cupidinesque:** See above, Lesson 37, Section E, note to line 1.

(14) **ut . . . faciant:** What construction?—**totum . . . nasum:** That is, Fabullus will become so enamored of the girl's **unguentum** that he will not want to do anything other than to smell it.

LESSON 39

CATULLUS: SEPTIMIUS AND ACME PLEDGE THEIR
MUTUAL LOVE.

§A   Vocabulary.

Acme, Acmes, f. (acc. sing. **Acmen**) ... the girl *Acme*

approbatio, approbatiónis, f. ... *assent, approval*

assiduus, assidua, assiduum ... *constant, continuous;* **assidue:** *constantly, continuously*

auspicátus, auspicáta, auspicátum ... *auspicious, favorable*

auspicium, auspicii, n. ... *augury; omen, portent*

*****beátus, beáta, beátum** ... *happy, blessed, fortunate*

Britannia, Britanniae, f. ... *Britain*

caesius, caesia, caesium ... *gray-eyed*

ebrius, ebria, ebrium ... *drunk; drunk with love*

India, Indiae, f. ... *India*

Libya, Libyae, f. ... *Libya*

*****malo, malle, malui** ... *to prefer*

medulla, medullae, f. ... (plur. may have sing. meaning) *marrow, inmost part*

*****mollis, molle** ... *soft, gentle*

mutuus, mutua, mutuum ... *mutual;* **mutuo:** *mutually, in turn*

*****ni** or **nisi** ... *if not, unless; except*

*os, oris, n. ... (plur. may have sing. meaning) *mouth; face, head; opening, aperture*

*paro, paráre, parávi, parátus ... *to prepare; to furnish, to provide*

*perdo, perdere, perdidi, perditus ... *to lose, to ruin, to destroy; to use without purpose, to waste* one's *time on;* **perditus, perdita, perditum:** *lost, ruined, destroyed;* **perdite:** *desperately, without restraint*

pereo, períre, perívi or **perii** ... *to die, to perish; to be ruined, to be destroyed*

plurimum ... (superl. of **multum;** see *ARA,* App. D, p. 421) *very much, most of all*

porro ... *in the future, in time to come*

potis or **pote** (indecl.) ... *able, possible*

purpureus, purpurea, purpureum ... *purple, dark red; gleaming, beautiful*

reflecto, reflectere, reflexi, reflexus ... *to bend back; to turn back, to turn around*

Septimius, Septimii, m. ... the boy *Septimius;* **Septimillus, Septimilli,** m.: *little Septimius*

servio, servíre, servívi ... *to serve, to be a slave to* (+ dat.)

sternuo, sternuere, sternui ... *to sneeze*

suavior, suaviári, suaviátus sum ... *to kiss*

Syria, Syriae, f. ... *Syria*

torreo, torrére, torrui, tostus ... *to burn, to parch, to roast*

§B   **Reading.**

Septimius and Acme Pledge Their Mutual Love.

Acmen Septimius suos amóres

tenens in gremio "Mea" inquit "Acme,

ni te perdite amo atque amáre porro

omnes sum assidue parátus annos

5   quantum qui pote plurimum períre,

solus in Libya Indiaque tosta

caesio veniam obvius leóni."

Hoc ut dixit, Amor (sinistra ut ante

dextra) sternuit approbatiónem.

10   At Acme, leviter caput reflectens,

et dulcis pueri ebrios ocellos

illo purpureo ore suaviáta,

"Sic" inquit "mea vita Septimille,

huic uni domino usque serviámus,

15   ut multo mihi maior acriorque

ignis mollibus ardet in medullis."

Hoc ut dixit, Amor (sinistra ut ante

dextra) sternuit approbatiónem.

Nunc, ab auspicio bono profecti,

20   mutuis animis amant amantur.

Unam Septimius misellus Acmen

mavult quam Syrias Britanniasque;

uno in Septimio fidélis Acme

facit delicias libidinesque.

25   Quis ullos homines beatióres

vidit, quis Venerem auspicatiórem?

(1) **Acmen Septimius:** The names of the lovers—who may be real or fictitious—suggest that the boy is Roman and the girl is Greek.

(2) **tenens:** Tense, voice, and mood? Subject of the verbal action?

(4) **omnes:** What noun does this adjective modify?—**sum . . . parátus:** See above, Lesson 2, Section E, note to line 4.—**annos:** *Duration of time* is normally denoted by the accusative case without a preposition (see *ARA,* Lesson 32, Section F, note to line 8).

(5) **qui:** Supply *anyone* as the antecedent.—**pote:** Here the equivalent of **pote est.**

(6) **tosta:** Tense, voice, and mood? Subject of the verbal action?

(7) **caesio:** What noun does this adjective modify?—**veniam:** An example of the optative subjunctive, used to express a wish on the part of the speaker (see *ARA,* App. K, p. 472).—**leóni:** In Catullus's day, lions were found not only in Africa but also in Asia.

(8–9) **sinistra . . . dextra:** Although either adverb may be translated first in relation to the phrase **ut ante,** the adverb **sinistra** is usually translated before this phrase and the adverb **dextra** after this phrase.

(9) **sternuit approbatiónem:** A favorable omen, implying divine approbation of the romantic declaration just expressed by Septimius to his beloved Acme, where one may imagine Cupid sneezing first on one side and then on the other side in rapid succession and with equal enthusiasm.

(13) **vita:** Here the noun is applied to Septimius himself, as a term of endearment.—**Septimille:** Into what kind of word (according to its suffix) has Catullus converted this name?

(14) **domino:** To whom does this word refer? (Give the name of this individual.)—**serviámus:** See above, note to line 7, on this use of the subjunctive.

(15) **mihi:** See above, Lesson 27, Section E, note to line 11.

(16) **ignis:** See above, Lesson 4, Section E, note to line 13.

(17–18) **Hoc . . . approbatiónem:** Which two lines of this poem does Catullus repeat word for word? To whose romantic declaration does the favorable omen now apply?

(19) **profecti:** Tense, voice, and mood? Subject of the verbal action? Explain the use of the gender.

(22) **mavult:** Of what verb is this a form? Tense, voice, mood, person, and number?—**Syrias Britanniasque:** Here the plural is used instead of the singular in order to express Septimius's extravagant love for Acme.

(24) **facit delicias:** Although the Latin idiom is *makes delight,* how would you express it in normal English?

(26) **vidit:** What use of the perfect tense?—**quis:** What verb should be supplied after this pronoun?

LESSON 40

METER: CHOLIAMBICS. CATULLUS: CATULLUS BIDS LESBIA A BITTER FAREWELL.

§A   **Meter: Choliambics.** Catullus also composed poems in *choliambics*—a variation of the iambic trimeter, the meter used in the spoken parts of Greek tragedy and elsewhere. The iambic foot consists of a short syllable followed by a long syllable; the iambic metron consists of two iambic feet; three iambic metra make up a line of iambic trimeter:

$$x - \smile - \mid x - \smile - \mid x - \smile -$$

As you can see from the above diagram, a long or short syllable is permitted in the first position of each iambic metron—a pattern that carries over into choliambics. Yet the choliambic meter also substitutes a long for the last short, disrupting the rhythmic flow of iambs at the end of the line (choliambics actually means *limping iambs*):

$$x - \smile - \mid x - \smile - \mid x - - x$$

Now consider the first three lines of the reading in this lesson—lines that have been scanned for the metrical pattern and that illustrate their flexibility with respect to admitting long and short syllables:

$$\smile - \smile - \mid \smile - \smile - \mid \smile - - \smile$$

Miser Catulle, desinas ineptíre,

$$- - \smile - \mid \smile - \smile - \mid \smile - - -$$

et quod vides perisse perditum ducas.

$$- - \smile - \mid - - \smile - \mid \smile - - -$$

Fulsére quondam candidi tibi soles.

§B   **Vocabulary.**

adeo, adíre, adii ... *to go near, to approach*

basio, basiáre, basiávi, basiátus ... *to kiss*

*desino, desinere, desii ... *to stop, to cease*

*doleo, dolére, dolui ... *to grieve*

*fulgeo, fulgére, fulsi ... *to flash, to gleam, to shine*

impotens, impotentis ... *powerless; out of control, lacking in control*

ineptio, ineptíre ... *to be silly, to act foolishly*

invítus, invíta, invítum ... *unwilling, not wishing, against* one's *will*

iocósus, iocósa, iocósum ... *funny, humorous; joyous, pleasurable*

labellum, labelli, n. ... *lip*

mordeo, mordére, momordi, morsus ... *to bite*

*nolo, nolle, nolui ... *to not wish, to be unwilling*

*nullus, nulla, nullum (gen. sing. nullíus, nullíus, nullíus) ... *no, not any;* (used with adv. force) *not at all, in no respect;* (masc./fem. as substantive) *no man, no woman*

*obdúro, obduráre, obdurávi, obdurátus ... *to be hard; to hold out, to stand firm*

quondam ... *once, formerly*

scelestus, scelesta, scelestum ... *wicked, accursed*

sector, sectári, sectátus sum ... *to follow eagerly; to chase, to pursue, to run after*

vae ... (interjection) *woe!*

ventito, ventitáre, ventitávi ... *to keep coming, to come frequently or repeatedly*

*volo, velle, volui ... *to wish, to be willing*

Catullus Bids Lesbia a Bitter Farewell.

Lessons 40–42 contain poems by Catullus expressing his contempt for Lesbia and her lusty lovers, thus revealing the angry and vicious aspect of the poet's personality. The poems in these lessons are all written in choliambics—the meter used by Catullus for satirical purposes, with its halting lines serving as a vehicle for his vehemence.

Miser Catulle, desinas ineptíre,

et quod vides perisse perditum ducas.

Fulsére quondam candidi tibi soles,

cum ventitábas quo puella ducébat,

5   amáta nobis quantum amabitur nulla.

Ibi illa multa cum iocósa fiébant,

quae tu volébas nec puella nolébat,

fulsére vere candidi tibi soles.

Nunc iam illa non vult: tu quoque †impote … †

10   Nec quae fugit sectáre, nec miser vive,

sed obstináta mente perfer, obdúra!

Vale, puella! Iam Catullus obdúrat.

Nec te requíret, nec rogábit invítam.

At tu dolébis, cum rogaberis nulla.

15   Scelesta, vae te! Quae tibi manet vita?

Quis nunc te adíbit? Cui videberis bella?

Quem nunc amábis? Cuius esse dicéris?

Quem basiábis? Cui labella mordébis?

At tu, Catulle, destinátus obdúra!

§D   **Notes and Queries.**

(1) **Catulle:** Case and number? Function of this case? (By addressing himself, Catullus dramatizes his awareness of a conflict within himself.)—**desinas:** A variation of the hortatory subjunctive, where the poet uses the second person *(you should . . .)* rather than the more customary first person *(let us . . .)* or third person *(let them . . .).*

(2) **ducas:** After this verb—the same variation of the hortatory subjunctive mentioned above, note 1—first translate **perditum** (supply *as* or *to be* between them), then the relative clause **quod vides perisse** (see *ARA,* App. J, p. 465, note 6, for the contracted form **perisse**).

(3) **Fulsére:** Tense, voice, mood, person, and number?—**soles:** See above, Lesson 38, Section C, First Passage, note to line 4.

(5) **nobis:** The words **nos** and **noster** may be used by a single person in speaking of himself/herself (see above, Lesson 38, Section C, Second Passage, note to line 6). The form **nobis** is a dative of agent, here used not with the passive periphrastic but with the perfect passive participle **amáta** (see above, Lesson 38, Section C, First Passage, note to lines 5–6).—**amabitur:** Tense, voice, mood, person, and number? Write out the conjugation of **amo** in this tense, voice, and mood.

(6) **Ibi:** Refers to the place where Catullus and Lesbia would meet, as implied by the adverb **quo** in line 4.—**illa multa . . . iocósa:** Refers to the amatory pleasures that Catullus and Lesbia probably shared during their rendezvous.—**fiébant:** Of what verb is this a form? Tense, voice, mood, person, and number?

(7) **volébas:** Tense, voice, mood, person, and number? Write out the conjugation of **volo** in the present tense of this voice and mood.

(8) **fulsére . . . soles:** Which line of this poem does Catullus repeat almost word for word? What single change does he make in this line the second time that he employs it?

(9) **†impote . . . †:** A corruption in the text, since the line is metrically incomplete as it stands and since one cannot tell what Catullus is saying to himself at the end of it. The scholar Avanzi suggested the emendation **impotens noli**—the reading adopted by most editors—which fills out the line metrically with a remark that fits the context. (For the adjective **impotens,** see the entry in this lesson vocabulary; for the imperative **noli,** see *ARA,* App. J, p. 458, note 4, and understand the infinitive **esse** with this form.)

(10) **sectáre:** See above, Lesson 8, Section E, note to line 7. (The direct object of this verb, which must be supplied from the context, also serves as the antecedent of the relative **quae.**)

(11) **perfer:** Of what verb is this a form? Tense, voice, mood, person, and number?

(13) **requíret:** Tense, voice, mood, person, and number? Write out the conjugation of **requíro** in this tense, voice, and mood.—**rogábit:** What should be supplied as the direct object?

(14) **rogaberis:** Tense, voice, mood, person, and number? Write out the conjugation of **rogo** in this tense, voice, and mood.—**nulla:** Here the adjective is used with adverbial force.

(15) **vae te:** A Latin idiom meaning *woe to you* or *curses on you.*

(16) **adíbit:** Of what verb is this a form? Tense, voice, mood, person, and number?

(17) **dicéris:** Tense, voice, mood, person, and number? Write out the conjugation of **dico** in this tense, voice, and mood.

LESSON 41

CATULLUS: CATULLUS ATTACKS LESBIA AND HER LUSTY LOVERS.

§A   Vocabulary.

atqui ... *and yet, nevertheless*

*****barba, barbae**, f. ... *beard*

capillátus, capilláta, capillátum ... *long-haired*

Celtiberia, Celtiberiae, f. ... the region *Celtiberia*

confutuo, confutuere, confutui ... *to have sex with*

continens, continentis ... *unbroken, continuous;* **continenter**: *in a row, in close succession*

contubernális, contubernális, c. ... *tent-mate; fellow-barfly, fellow-drinker*

cuniculósus, cuniculósa, cuniculósum ... *rabbit-filled*

defrico, defricáre, defricui, defricátus ... *to rub or brush thoroughly*

*****dens, dentis**, m. (gen. plur. **dentium**) ... *tooth;* (collective sing.) *teeth*

Egnatius, Egnatii, m. ... the Spaniard *Egnatius*

frons, frontis, f. (gen. plur. **frontium**) ... *brow, forehead; front, facade*

*****fugio, fugere, fugi** ... *to flee, to run away; to flee* from, *to run away* from

Hibérus, Hibéra, Hibérum ... *Spanish*

hircus, hirci, m. ... *goat*

*indignus, indigna, indignum ... *unworthy, undeserving; unworthy of, undeserving* of (+ gen. or abl.); *shameful, shocking, outrageous;* **indigne:** *unworthily, undeservedly, outrageously*

insulsus, insulsa, insulsum ... *unsalted; dull, boring, stupid*

irrumo, irrumáre, irrumávi ... *to perform oral sex on*

istic ... *there, there by you*

licet, licére, licuit ... (impersonal verb) **licet** = *it is allowed,* **licére** = *to be allowed,* **licuit** = *it was allowed*

mentula, mentulae, f. ... *penis, phallus*

moechus, moechi, m. ... *adulterer; lecher, debaucher*

opácus, opáca, opácum ... *shady; thick, bushy*

pila, pilae, f. ... *pillar, column*

pilleátus, pilleáta, pilleátum ... *wearing a felt cap*

*praeter ... *beyond; except, except for; more than, apart from* (+ acc.)

pusillus, pusilla, pusillum ... *very small; unimportant, insignificant*

*puto, putáre, putávi, putátus ... *to think, to believe; to regard* as, *to consider* to be

salax, salácis ... *lusty, lecherous*

*scribo, scribere, scripsi, scriptus ... *to write; to write on* something (acc.) to someone (dat.); *to write on* something (acc.) to someone (dat.) with something (abl.)

semitarius, semitaria, semitarium ... *back-alley, back-street*

sessor, sessóris, m. ... *sitter* (= one sitting or seated)

sopio, sopiónis, m. ... (plur. may have sing. meaning) *penis, phallus*

taberna, tabernae, f. ... *inn, tavern*

urína, urínae, f. ... *urine*

§B   Reading.

Catullus Attacks Lesbia and Her Lusty Lovers.

Salax taberna vosque contubernáles,

a pilleátis nona fratribus pila:

solis putátis esse mentulas vobis,

solis licére quidquid est puellárum

5   confutuere et putáre ceteros hircos?

An continenter quod sedétis insulsi

centum an ducenti, non putátis ausúrum

me una ducentos irrumáre sessóres?

Atqui putáte! Namque totíus vobis

10   frontem tabernae sopionibus scribam.

Puella nam mi—quae meo sinu fugit,

amáta tantum quantum amabitur nulla,

pro qua mihi sunt magna bella pugnáta—

consédit istic. Hanc boni beatique

15   omnes amátis, et quidem (quod indignum est)

omnes pusilli et semitarii moechi—

tu praeter omnes, une de capillátis,

cuniculósae Celtiberiae fili,

Egnáti, opáca quem bonum facit barba

20   et dens Hibéra defricátus urína.

(1) **taberna:** The equivalent of a present-day bar.—**contubernáles:** The equivalent of our present-day barflies.

(2) **nona . . . pila:** In apposition with **taberna,** identified by the pillar standing in front of it, which was designed to advertise its services.—**pilleátis . . . fratribus:** Refers to Castor and Pollux, the twin brothers of classical mythology, frequently represented in ancient art and on ancient coins as wearing felt caps. In this context, however, the phrase refers to the temple of Castor and Pollux, which stood on the south side of the Roman Forum near the Palatine Hill.

(3) **solis:** This adjective modifies the pronoun **vobis.**—**putátis:** Tense, voice, mood, person, and number? What construction does this verb introduce? What are the elements of this construction in this sentence?—**vobis:** What kind of dative?

(4) **solis:** Before this adjective supply the pronoun **vobis.**—**licére:** Before this infinitive supply the verb **putátis** from the previous line.—**quidquid est puellárum:** Although the Latin idiom is *whatever there is of girls,* how would you express it in normal English?

(5) **ceteros hircos:** Here Catullus accuses the barflies of regarding all other men as goatish, that is, unrefined and unsophisticated.

(7) **putátis:** What construction does this verb introduce? What are the elements of this construction in this sentence?—**ausúrum:** That is, **ausúrum esse,** a form of the semi-deponent verb **audeo.** Check this verb in the Cumulative Vocabulary for the appropriate meaning.

(8) **irrumáre:** In Catullus's day, the Romans apparently considered this kind of sexual act insulting to those on whom it was performed.

(9) **putáte:** Tense, voice, mood, person, and number?

(10) **sopionibus:** This noun may be dative in apposition with **vobis** in line 9 (referring insultingly to the barflies themselves as penises), or ablative denoting the instrument to be used to insult them (implying that Catullus will urinate on the tavern with his penis), or ablative denoting the pornography to be used to embarrass them (implying that Catullus will scribble pictures of penises all over the tavern).—**scribam:** Tense, voice, mood, person, and number? Check this verb in the lesson vocabulary and show how it may be used to accommodate the three possible ways of translating **sopionibus** in this sentence.

(11) **mi:** Of what pronoun is this dative an alternate form? Check this pronoun in the Cumulative Vocabulary for the uncontracted form.

(12) **amáta . . . nulla:** In what other poem does Catullus use this line? What single difference exists between the two versions of this line?

(13) **mihi:** Here a dative of agent, used with the perfect passive indicative **sunt . . . pugnáta** (compare above, Lesson 40, Section D, note to line 5).—**magna bella:** Refers to the enormous difficulties that probably accompanied Catullus's liaison with Lesbia, a married woman of considerable social position.

(14) **consédit:** What use of the perfect tense?—**boni beatique:** The first group of Lesbia's lovers, men of substance and social standing.

(15) **amátis:** Tense, voice, mood, person, and number?

(16) **pusilli et semitarii moechi:** The second group of Lesbia's lovers, demonstrating that Lesbia lacks taste and discrimination.

(17) **une:** Vocative of **unus.**—**capillátis:** What use of the adjective? (In Catullus's day, if young men wore their hair long, they were generally regarded as foppish and affected.)

(18) **cuniculósae Celtiberiae:** Celtiberia, a region in central Spain, abounded in rabbits that had long, soft hair—something with which any **capillátus** could easily associate.

(18–19) **fili, Egnáti:** Case and number? Function of this case?

(19) **opáca . . . bonum facit barba:** A sarcastic comment on Egnatius's attempt to cultivate a beard in his seemingly futile aspiration to become respectable.

(20) **dens . . . defricátus urína:** A sarcastic comment on Egnatius's habit of brushing his teeth according to a peculiar Celtiberian custom (a custom corroborated elsewhere by the Greek historians Strabo and Diodorus Siculus).

LESSON 42

CATULLUS: CATULLUS ATTACKS EGNATIUS FOR ALWAYS
SMILING.

§A   Vocabulary.

*ater, atra, atrum ... *dark, black*

attingo, attingere, attigi, attactus ... *to touch; to touch on, to mention briefly*

*tango, tangere, tetigi, tactus ... *to touch; to examine, to explore*

bibo, bibere, bibi ... *to drink*

Celtiber, Celtibri, m. ... a *Celtiberian*

dentátus, dentáta, dentátum ... *toothy*

*excito, excitáre, excitávi, excitátus ... *to cause to move; to excite, to stir up; to arouse, to awaken; to heighten, to intensify*

expolítus, expolíta, expolítum ... *smooth, polished*

gingíva, gingívae, f. ... (collective sing.) *gums*

ineptus, inepta, ineptum ... *silly, foolish*

Lanuvínus, Lanuvíni, m. ... a *Lanuvinian*

lotium, lotii or loti, n. ... *urine*

meio, meiere, minxi ... *to urinate; to excrete* something (acc.) *during urination*

*morbus, morbi, m. ... *disease, sickness*

obésus, obésa, obésum ... *fat, plump*

orbus, orba, orbum ... *deprived; bereft, bereaved*

*pinguis, pingue ... *fat; covered* with; *well-laden, sumptuous*

pius, pia, pium ... *pious; dutiful, devoted*

praedico, praedicáre, praedicávi, praedicátus ... *to declare, to pro-claim*

purus, pura, purum ... *pure, clean;* **puriter:** *in a pure or clean man-ner*

*quare ... (relative adv.) *why, wherefore, for which reason;* (interroga-tive adv.) *why? wherefore? for which reason?*

quilubet, quaelubet, quidlubet ... (indefinite relative pronoun) *anyone at all, anything at all; whoever you please, whatever you please*

renideo, renidére ... *to shine; to grin, to smile*

reus, rei, m. ... *culprit;* the *accused,* the *defendant*

risus, risus, m. ... *laughter;* a *grin,* a *smile*

rogus, rogi, m. ... *funeral pyre*

russus, russa, russum ... *red*

Sabínus, Sabíni, m. ... a *Sabine*

subsellium, subsellii, n. ... *seat, bench*

Tiburs, Tiburtis, m. ... a *Tiburtine*

Transpadánus, Transpadáni, m. ... a *Transpadine*

ubicumque ... *wherever, in whatever place*

Umber, Umbri, m. ... an *Umbrian*

urbánus, urbána, urbánum ... *of the city, from the city; refined, sen-sitive, sophisticated*

usquequaque ... *all over the place, in every possible situation*

*vester, vestra, vestrum ... (possessive adj. related to **vos**) *your*

Catullus Attacks Egnatius for Always Smiling.

Egnatius, quod candidos habet dentes,

renídet usquequaque. Si ad rei ventum est

subsellium, cum orátor excitat fletum,

renídet ille. Si ad pii rogum fili

5   lugétur, orba cum flet unicum mater,

renídet ille. Quidquid est, ubicumque est,

quodcumque agit, renídet. Hunc habet morbum,

neque elegantem (ut arbitror) neque urbánum.

Quare monendum est † ... † mihi, bone Egnáti:

10   si urbánus esses aut Sabínus aut Tiburs

aut pinguis Umber aut obésus Etruscus

aut Lanuvínus ater atque dentátus

aut Transpadánus (ut meos quoque attingam)

aut quilubet qui puriter lavit dentes,

15   tamen renidére usquequaque te nollem.

Nam risu inepto res ineptior nulla est.

Nunc Celtiber † ... †. Celtiberia in terra,

quod quisque minxit, hoc sibi solet mane

dentem atque russam defricáre gingívam,

20   ut, quo iste vester expolitior dens est,

hoc te amplius bibisse praedicet loti.

§C   **Notes and Queries.**

(1) **Egnatius:** See also above, Lesson 41, Section B, lines 17–20, for Catullus's earlier reference to this individual.

(2) **renídet:** Egnatius's offensive habit. Tense, voice, mood, person, and number of **renídet?**—**ventum est:** How should this verb form be translated? (See above, Lesson 28, Section E, note to line 7.)

(2–3) **ad rei . . . subsellium:** This scene occurs in a courtroom, where Egnatius has come to support the defendant. (Here the word **rei** is not a form of **res** but a form of **reus,** listed in the lesson vocabulary.)

(3) **orátor:** Refers to a speaker for the defendant.

(4) **ad . . . rogum fili:** This scene occurs at a funeral, where Egnatius has come to pay his respects to the deceased. (In this context the word **fili** is a contracted version of the genitive singular of the noun **filius.**) At a Roman funeral, the body of the deceased would be cremated on a funeral pyre with the mourners present and actually looking on.

(5) **lugétur:** How should this verb form be translated? (See also above, Lesson 28, Section E, note to line 7.)—**unicum:** What noun should be supplied after this adjective?

(6) **Quidquid est:** That is, whatever the occasion.

(7) **morbum:** To what 'disease' does this word refer?

(8) **urbánum:** Here the adjective is used figuratively, demonstrating Catullus's fondness for sensitive and sophisticated people.

(9) **monendum est † . . . † mihi:** The gerundive may be used in the Passive Periphrastic Conjugation, sometimes with the dative of agent (see also above, Lesson 38, Section C, First Passage, note to lines 5–6). A corruption exists in the text, since this line is metrically short by one syllable in the manuscript; **te** is generally inserted at this point in the text, where it functions as direct object of the impersonal verb.— **bone Egnáti:** Case and number? Function of this case? The adjective **bone** is used sarcastically, as it was in Catullus's earlier description of this individual (compare above, Lesson 41, Section B, line 19).

(10–15) **si . . . esses . . . tamen . . . nollem:** What type of condition is this? Tense and mood of the verbs? (See above, Lesson 23, Section A.) Catullus is essentially saying by means of this extended condition that even if Egnatius were a Roman or someone who could claim a cultural connection with one of the Italian peoples mentioned, he would still regard Egnatius's habit of smiling as somewhat offensive.

(10) **urbánus:** Here the adjective is used literally (compare above, note to line 8), with specific reference to Rome (see also above, Lesson 26, Section E, note to line 1).—**Sabínus:** The Sabines were a people who lived northeast of Rome.—**Tiburs:** The Tiburtines were a people who lived northeast of Rome.

(11) **Umber:** The Umbrians were a people who lived northeast of Rome.—**Etruscus:** The Etruscans were a people who lived in northern Italy, who brought about the most advanced civilization in Italy before the rise of Rome and who (while their kings ruled Rome) exerted a significant influence on Roman civil, military, and cultural institutions (see also above, Lesson 36, Section E, note to lines 17–18).

(12) **Lanuvínus:** The Lanuvinians were a people who lived south of Rome.

(13) **Transpadánus:** Refers to any person who lived north of the Po, the longest river in Italy, well-known for its numerous tributaries.—**ut . . . attingam:** A purpose clause in which the writer expresses the purpose underlying his own statement rather than the purpose of any particular action being described elsewhere in the sentence. (Although Catullus lived in Rome, he here refers to his own countrymen as Transpadine, since he was born in the northern town of Verona, which he supposedly revisited on a number of occasions.)—**meos:** What noun should be supplied with this adjective? (See above, Lesson 22, Section E, note to line 7, for a similar use of the reflexive.)

(16) **risu:** What kind of ablative?

(17) **Nunc:** Here this adverb means *as it is* or *as matters stand.*—**Celtiber . . . Celtiberia:** See above, Lesson 41, Section C, note to line 18, for Catullus's earlier reference to Egnatius's Spanish background.—**† . . . †:** A corruption in the text, since this line is metrically short by one syllable in the manuscript; **es** is generally inserted at this point, where it functions as the main verb and has Egnatius as its subject.

(18) **quod . . . hoc:** Translate *(that) which . . . with this.*—**sibi:** What kind of dative?

(19) **russam . . . gingívam:** Implies that the typical Celtiberian would brush his gums until they became inflamed.

(20–21) **ut . . . praedicet:** What construction?—**quo . . . hoc:** Translate *by what degree . . . by this degree.*

(20) **vester:** Here the adjective **vester** is used instead of the adjective **tuus,** because Egnatius's teeth are regarded not simply as his own teeth but as representative of those of his countrymen.

(21) **te . . . bibisse:** What construction?—**amplius . . . loti:** See above, Lesson 41, Section C, note to line 20, for Catullus's earlier reference to this mouthwash, as used by Egnatius while cleaning his teeth. (Here Catullus concludes his attack on Celtiberian dental hygiene, where he implies either that Egnatius simply put urine in his mouth in order to brush his teeth, or that he may have accidentally swallowed some of the urine while holding it in his mouth, or that he may have deliberately swallowed some of it while brushing and gargling.)

LESSON 43

METER: ELEGIAC COUPLETS. CATULLUS: CATULLUS APOLOGIZES TO JUVENTIUS FOR KISSING HIM.

§A   **Meter: Elegiac Couplets.** Catullus also composed poems in *elegiac couplets*—each consisting of a hexameter (a line divided into six feet) and a pentameter (a line divided into five feet). In both the hexameter and the pentameter, the dactylic foot plays an important part—each dactyl consisting of a long syllable followed by two short syllables:

– ∪ ∪ | – ∪ ∪ | – ∪ ∪ | – ∪ ∪ | – ∪ ∪ | – ×

– ∪ ∪ | – ∪ ∪ | – || – ∪ ∪ | – ∪ ∪ | ×

In the hexameter, two shorts can be replaced by a long in any foot except the fifth foot; in the pentameter, two shorts can be replaced by a long only in the first or second foot. As you can see from the diagram, a pentameter consists of two halves, each containing two and a half feet, with a break in the middle of the line (as shown by the symbol ||).

Now consider the first four lines of the reading in this lesson—lines that have been scanned for their metrical pattern and that illustrate their flexibility with respect to admitting long and short syllables:

– ∪ ∪ | – ∪ ∪ | – – | – – | – ∪ ∪ | – –

Surripui tibi, dum ludis, mellíte Iuventi,

– ∪ ∪ | – – | – || – ∪ ∪ | – ∪ ∪ | –

suaviolum dulci dulcius ambrosia.

– – | – – | – ∪ ∪ | – – | – ∪ ∪ | – ∪

Ver(um) id non impúne tuli: namqu(e) amplius horam

– – | – – | – || – ∪ ∪ | – ∪ ∪ | ∪

suffix(um) in summa me memin(i) esse cruce,

§B   **Vocabulary.**

abstergeo, abstergére, abstersi, abstersus ... *to wipe off, to wipe clean*

ambrosia, ambrosiae, f. ... *ambrosia*

articulus, articuli, m. ... *joint; finger*

commeio, commeiere, comminxi, commictus ... *to defile with urine;*
   commictus, commicta, commictum: *defiled, polluted*

contraho, contrahere, contraxi, contractus ... *to draw together; to*
   catch, to contract

*crux, crucis, f. ... *cross*

*demo, demere, dempsi, demptus ... *to remove, to take away*

dilútus, dilúta, dilútum ... *diluted, cleaned*

*dulcis, dulce ... *sweet; delightful*

elleborum, ellebori, n. ... the plant *hellebore*

*excrucio, excruciáre, excruciávi, excruciátus ... *to torment, to tor-*
   ture

gutta, guttae, f. ... *drop* of water

Iuventius, Iuventii, m. ... the boy *Juventius*

*ludo, ludere, lusi ... *to play, to have fun; to tease, to trifle with*

lupa, lupae, f. ... *she-wolf; whore, prostitute*

memini, meminisse ... (perf. act. ind. first pers. sing. and perf. act.
   inf. of the defective verb **memini,** translated with pres. force)
   memini = *I remember;* **meminisse** = *to remember*

*numquam ... *never*

posthac ... *hereafter, from now on*

purgo, purgáre, purgávi, purgátus ... *to clean, to clear away; to ex-*
   cuse oneself; *to apologize for* oneself

saevitia, saevitiae, f. ... *cruelty, fierceness, savageness*

salíva, salívae, f. ... *saliva, spittle*

spurcus, spurca, spurcum ... *dirty, filthy*

suaviolum, suavioli, n. ... *little kiss*

suffígo, suffigere, suffixi, suffixus ... *to fix up, to fasten, to attach*

surripio, surripere, surripui, surreptus ... *to steal; to steal* something (acc.) *from* someone (dat.)

tantillus, tantilla, tantillum ... *so small;* (neut. sing. as substantive) *so small a quantity*

*verus, vera, verum ... *true;* **verum, veri,** n.: *truth;* **vere** or **vero:** *truly, in truth;* **verum** (conj.): *but, but at the same time*

§C   **Reading.**

Catullus Apologizes to Juventius for Kissing Him.

Lessons 43–45 contain poems by Catullus expressing his affection or contempt for various people, pieces that continue to exhibit his absorption with romantic emotion. The poems in these lessons are all written in elegiac couplets—the meter used by Catullus (and other Roman poets of his day) primarily for erotic subjects and themes.

Surripui tibi, dum ludis, mellíte Iuventi,

　　suaviolum dulci dulcius ambrosia.

Verum id non impúne tuli: namque amplius horam

　　suffixum in summa me memini esse cruce,

5　**dum tibi me purgo, nec possum fletibus ullis**

　　tantillum vestrae demere saevitiae.

Nam simul id factum est, multis dilúta labella

　　guttis abstersti omnibus articulis,

ne quicquam nostro contractum ex ore manéret,

10　**tamquam commictae spurca salíva lupae.**

Praeterea infesto miserum me tradere Amóri

non cessasti omnique excruciáre modo,

ut mi ex ambrosia mutátum iam foret illud

suaviolum tristi tristius elleboro.

15 Quam quoniam poenam misero propónis amóri,

numquam iam posthac basia surripiam.

§D   Notes and Queries.

(1) **dum ludis:** See *ARA,* Lesson 10, Section J, note to lines 4–5.—
Iuventi: Case and number? Function of this case? (The name of the
boy—who may be real or fictitious—suggests that he may have come
from a very distinguished Roman family, the Juventii.)

(2) **ambrosia:** What kind of ablative? (This word refers to the food of
the gods, believed to impart immortality to those who consumed it.)

(3) **Verum:** The conjunction, not the substantive.—**tuli:** Tense, voice,
mood, person, and number? Conjugate **fero** in the present tense of
this voice and mood.—**horam:** See above, Lesson 39, Section C, note to
line 4.

(4) **memini:** What construction does this verb introduce? What are the
elements of this construction in this sentence? (Keep in mind that
suffixum and **esse** should be taken together as a single verb form.)—
in summa . . . cruce: The Romans executed slaves and criminals by
crucifying them, generally beating them and requiring them to carry
their cross to the place of crucifixion. Here Catullus refers to this
practice figuratively, in the sense of wanting Juventius to understand that he (the poet) had suffered great emotional stress.

(5) **possum:** Tense, voice, mood, person, and number?

(6) **vestrae:** Here the adjective **vester** is used instead of the adjective
tuus, because Juventius's cruelty is regarded not simply as his own
cruelty but as representative of that of boys like him (see also above,
Lesson 42, Section C, note to line 20).

(8) **abstersti:** What is the uncontracted form?

(9) **ne . . . manéret:** What construction?—**nostro:** See above, Lesson
38, Section C, Second Passage, note to line 6.

(12) **cessasti:** What is the uncontracted form?—**modo:** The noun, not the adverb.

(13) **ut ... mutátum ... foret:** What construction? (Keep in mind that **mutátum** and **foret** should be taken together as a single verb form, and that **foret** is the alternate imperfect subjunctive third person singular of **sum** [see *ARA*, App. J, p. 453].)

(14) **elleboro:** What kind of ablative? (This word refers to a plant that was used for medicinal purposes, especially to help cure insanity.)

(15) **Quam:** What noun does this adjective modify?

(16) **surripiam:** Tense, voice, mood, person, and number?

LESSON 44

CATULLUS: CATULLUS ATTACKS RUFUS FOR HIS BODY ODOR; CATULLUS BIDS FAREWELL TO HIS DECEASED BROTHER.

§A   Vocabulary.

adloquor, adloqui, adlocútus sum ... *to speak to, to address*

admíror, admirári, admirátus sum ... *to wonder, to be amazed*

aequor, aequoris, n. ... *level surface; sea* (as level and smooth)

ala, alae, f. ... *wing; arm, arm-pit*

aveo, avére ... *to be well;* **ave:** (imperative sing.) *hail!*

bestia, bestiae, f. ... *beast*

caper, capri, m. ... *goat; goatish-smell*

crudélis, crudéle ... *cruel, fierce, savage*

cubo, cubáre, cubui ... *to lie down* with; *to have sex* with

cur ... *why?*

*__**dono, donáre, donávi, donátus** ... *to give, to present, to provide*

fabula, fabulae, f. ... *story; rumor, gossip*

femur, femoris, n. ... *thigh*

fraternus, fraterna, fraternum ... *brotherly, of a brother*

*__**gens, gentis,** f. (gen. plur. **gentium**) ... *race, stock; nation, people*

habito, habitáre, habitávi, habitátus ... *to inhabit; to live, to dwell*

heu ... (interjection) *alas!*

inferiae, inferiárum, f. ... (plur. noun with plur. meaning) *rites for the dead*

*interea ... *meanwhile; anyhow, at any rate*

labefacto, labefactáre, labefactávi, labefactátus ... *to weaken, to make unsteady; to corrupt, to cause to waver*

laedo, laedere, laesi, laesus ... *to hurt; to strike, to injure*

*lapis, lapidis, m. ... *stone; precious stone (= gem or jewel)*

*mirus, mira, mirum ... *amazing, astonishing;* (in negative context) not *surprising,* not *unexpected*

*multus, multa, multum ... (sing.) *much,* (plur.) *many;* **multo** or **multum:** *much, by much, greatly*

mutus, muta, mutum ... *silent*

*nequiquam ... *in vain*

perlucidulus, perlucidula, perlucidulum ... *translucent, transparent*

pestis, pestis, f. (gen. plur. **pestium**) ... *plague, disease*

priscus, prisca, priscum ... *ancient*

quandoquidem ... *since, because*

Rufus, Rufi, m. ... *Rufus* (perhaps Caelius Rufus)

suppóno, supponere, supposui, suppositus ... *to place under; to place something (acc.) under someone (dat.)*

tener, tenera, tenerum ... *tender, delicate*

trux, trucis ... *cruel, fierce, savage*

valles, vallis, f. (gen. plur. **vallium**) ... (plur. may have sing. meaning) *valley; hollow, cavity*

veho, vehere, vexi, vectus ... *to carry;* (in passive) *to travel, to journey*

§B   Reading.

Catullus Attacks Rufus for His Body Odor.

Noli admirári quare tibi femina nulla,

    Rufe, velit tenerum supposuisse femur,

non si illam rarae labefactes munere vestis

    aut perluciduli deliciis lapidis.

5   Laedit te quaedam mala fabula, qua tibi fertur

    valle sub alárum trux habitáre caper.

Hunc metuunt omnes, neque mirum: nam mala valde est

    bestia, nec quicum bella puella cubet.

Quare aut crudélem nasórum interfice pestem,

10   aut admirári desine cur fugiunt!

Catullus Bids Farewell to His Deceased Brother.

Multas per gentes et multa per aequora vectus,

    advenio has miseras, frater, ad inferias,

ut te postrémo donárem munere mortis

    et mutam nequiquam adloquerer cinerem.

5   Quandoquidem fortúna mihi tete abstulit ipsum—

    heu miser indigne frater adempte mihi—

nunc tamen interea haec, prisco quae more parentum

    tradita sunt tristi munere ad inferias,

accipe fraterno multum manantia fletu,

10   atque in perpetuum, frater, ave atque vale!

First Passage

(1) **Noli admirári:** For the imperative **noli,** see *ARA,* App. J, p. 458, note 4, and above, Lesson 40, Section D, note to line 9.

(1–2) **quare . . . velit:** What construction? Tense, voice, mood, person, and number of **velit?** Write out the conjugation of **volo** in this tense, voice, and mood.

(2) **Rufe:** Possibly Caelius Rufus, a statesman/politician of Catullus's day, who is believed to have succeeded Catullus as Lesbia's lover.—**supposuisse:** Here the equivalent of the present active infinitive.

(3) **si . . . labefactes:** The protasis of a future less vivid condition (see above, Lesson 23, Section A), here used by itself after **Noli admirári.**

(5) **quaedam:** What noun does this adjective modify?—**tibi:** What kind of dative?—**fertur:** Here the equivalent of **dicitur** (see above, Lesson 32, Section E, note to line 14). Tense, voice, mood, person, and number of **fertur?** What meaning of **fertur** should be used in this context?

(6) **trux . . . caper:** Apparently Rufus did not bathe frequently or use deodorants to get rid of his body odor.

(8) **quicum . . . cubet:** Here the equivalent of **cum qua . . . cubet.** What construction do these words constitute? (Keep in mind that in this construction **cum** is the preposition, not the conjunction.)

(9) **interfice:** Tense, voice, mood, person, and number?

(10) **cur fugiunt:** An indirect question exhibiting an archaic and colloquial use of the indicative instead of the subjunctive.

Second Passage

(1) **vectus:** Tense, voice, and mood? Subject of the verbal action?

(2) **inferias:** Refers to the religious ceremony in honor of the dead conducted at the grave-site of the deceased person.

(2–3) **advenio . . . donárem:** In primary sequence, the present indicative may be followed by the imperfect subjunctive when the subjunctive is used in a purpose clause. Here the imperfect subjunctive is regarded as a primary tense, since its action belongs to the present even though the purpose behind it belongs to the past.

(3) **postrémo . . . munere mortis:** Refers to the final duty to be performed for and/or the final gift to be dedicated to the deceased person.

(4) **adloquerer:** Tense, voice, mood, person, and number? (See above, Lesson 1, Section F, note to line 1, on **hortarétur.**)

(5) **mihi:** What kind of dative?—**tete:** An alternate form of **te.**

(6) **adempte:** The perfect passive participle of **adimo,** here used in the vocative case in agreement with **frater.**

(7) **haec:** Refers to the actual offerings (wine, honey, flowers, etc.) dedicated to the deceased person during the religious ceremony.—**more:** Of what noun—**mos** or **mora**—is this a form?

(8) **munere:** Here the ablative functions in the same way as the dative when it expresses purpose (see *ARA,* Lesson 48, Section D, note to line 12).

(9) **accipe:** What is the subject of this verb? What is the direct object of this verb?—**manantia:** Tense, voice, and mood? Subject of the verbal action?

LESSON 45

CATULLUS: CATULLUS PRAYS FOR HIS RELEASE FROM LESBIA.

§A   **Vocabulary.**

abútor, abúti, abúsus sum ... *to use up; to abuse, to exploit* (+ abl.)

artus, artus, m. ... *limb* of the body

benefactum, benefacti, n. ... *service, good deed*

cogito, cogitáre, cogitávi, cogitátus ... *to think, to consider*

*****credo, credere, credidi, creditus** ... *to believe; to entrust* (+ dat.)

*****deus, dei,** m. (nom. plur. **dei, dii, di;** dat./abl. plur. **deis, diis, dis**) ... *god*

*****difficilis, difficile** ... *difficult;* **difficiliter:** *with difficulty*

diligo, diligere, dilexi, dilectus ... *to love, to cherish*

*****divus, divi,** m. (gen. plur. **divórum** or **divum**) ... *god*

extrémus, extréma, extrémum ... *outermost; last, last of all; extremely urgent* or *desperate*

foedus, foederis, n. ... *compact, covenant*

imus, ima, imum ... (alternate superl. of **inferus;** see *ARA,* App. D, p. 419) *lowest, very low; bottom of, bottommost part of*

ingrátus, ingráta, ingrátum ... *thankless, ungrateful;* **ingráte:** *unwillingly, ungratefully*

istinc ... *from there; from the situation* one is *in*

laetitia, laetitiae, f. ... (plur. may have sing. meaning) *happiness*

*mens, mentis, f. (gen. plur. **mentium**) ... *mind, heart; frame of mind; purpose, intention*

*numen, numinis, n. ... (plur. may have sing. meaning) *majesty, divinity, divine power*

offirmo, offirmáre, offirmávi, offirmátus ... *to become firm, to become resolute*

pernicies, perniciéi, f. ... *ruin, destruction*

*potis or **pote** (indecl.) ... *able, possible*

pudícus, pudíca, pudícum ... *pure, chaste, faithful*

qualubet ... *no matter how, somehow or other*

recordor, recordári, recordátus sum ... *to recall, to recollect*

redúco, reducere, reduxi, reductus ... *to lead back; to draw back, to pull back*

sanctus, sancta, sanctum ... *holy, sacred, blessed*

subrépo, subrepere, subrepsi, subreptus ... *to creep* into or under; *to crawl* into or under

taeter, taetra, taetrum ... *foul, horrible*

torpor, torpóris, m. ... *numbness, paralysis*

vestrum ... (gen. plur. of **tu**) *of you*

voluptas, voluptátis, f. ... *pleasure, enjoyment*

§B   **Reading.**

Catullus Prays for His Release from Lesbia.

Siqua recordanti benefacta prióra voluptas

    est homini, cum se cogitat esse pium,

nec sanctam violasse fidem, nec foedere in ullo

    divum ad fallendos numine abúsum homines,

5   multa paráta manent in longa aetáte, Catulle,

        ex hoc ingráto gaudia amóre tibi.

    Nam quaecumque homines bene cuiquam aut dicere possunt

        aut facere, haec a te dictaque factaque sunt.

    Omnia quae ingrátae periérunt credita menti.

10   Quare iam te cur amplius excrucies?

    Quin tu animo offirmas atque istinc teque redúcis,

        et dis invítis desinis esse miser?

    Difficile est longum subito deponere amórem;

        difficile est, verum hoc qualubet efficias:

15   una salus haec est, hoc est tibi pervincendum,

        hoc facias, sive id non pote sive pote.

    O di, si vestrum est miseréri, aut si quibus umquam

        extrémam iam ipsa in morte tulistis opem,

    me miserum aspicite et, si vitam puriter egi,

20   eripite hanc pestem perniciemque mihi,

    quae mihi subrépens imos (ut torpor) in artus

        expulit ex omni pectore laetitias!

    Non iam illud quaero, contra me ut diligat illa,

        aut (quod non potis est) esse pudíca velit.

25   Ipse valére opto et taetrum hunc deponere morbum.

        O di, reddite mi hoc pro pietáte mea!

§C   Notes and Queries.

(1) **Siqua:** This word = **Si + qua** (the adjective form of the indefinite pronoun **quis** in the nominative singular feminine).—**recordanti:** Tense, voice, and mood? Subject of the verbal action?

(2) **homini:** Here this noun does not refer to any specific individual.—**cogitat:** What construction does this verb introduce three times in this sentence? What element of this construction should be supplied in the second and third occurrences of this construction?

(3) **violasse:** What is the uncontracted form?

(4) **fallendos:** What verbal form? Case, number, and gender?—**abúsum:** The equivalent of **abúsum esse.** What is the direct object of this verb? In what case does the direct object of this verb appear?

(5) **multa:** What noun does this adjective modify?—**paráta:** Tense, voice, and mood? Subject of the verbal action? (The queries about **multa** and **paráta** point to the same noun, which you should not have any trouble finding if you pay attention to the endings of the words.)

(9) **ingrátae:** What noun does this adjective modify?—**credita:** Here the equivalent of **credita sunt.**

(10) **te:** See above, Lesson 8, Section E, note to line 9.—**excrucies:** An example of the deliberative subjunctive, used in questions or deliberations relating to future or past action (see *ARA,* App. K, p. 472).

(11) **teque:** Although this word may seem a little awkward coming directly after **atque,** the **-que** in **teque** (introducing **redúcis**) may be regarded as complementing the **et** in line 12 (introducing **desinis**).

(12) **dis invítis:** See *ARA,* Lesson 28, Section G, note to line 8.—**desinis esse miser:** Compare above, Lesson 40, Section C, line 1.

(13) **Difficile est longum subito deponere amórem:** A moving and poignant statement, applicable to any relationship in which lovers decide to go their separate ways even though they may still care deeply about the other person.

(14) **verum:** See above, Lesson 43, Section D, note to line 3.—**efficias:** See above, Lesson 40, Section D, notes to lines 1 and 2.

(15) **est tibi pervincendum:** For the Passive Periphrastic Conjugation, see above, Lesson 38, Section C, First Passage, note to lines 5–6.

(16) **pote . . . pote:** See above, Lesson 39, Section C, note to line 5.

(17) **si vestrum est:** Translate *if it is in your power.* What is the literal meaning?

(18) **ipsa in morte:** Translate *on the brink of death.* What is the literal meaning?

(19) **egi:** Of what verb—**ago** or **egeo**—is this a form? Tense, voice, mood, person, and number of this form?

(23) **illud:** Directly explained by the clause **contra me ut diligat illa.**—**contra:** The adverb, not the preposition.—**illa:** Refers to Lesbia, to whom Catullus has been alluding throughout this poem.

(25) **morbum:** To what 'disease' does this word refer?

LESSON 46

METER: DACTYLIC HEXAMETERS. CATULLUS: THE BOYS AND GIRLS PREPARE FOR A SINGING-CONTEST.

§A **Meter: Dactylic Hexameters.** Catullus also composed long poems in *dactylic hexameters,* the meter used in Greek and Latin epic, such as Homer's *Iliad* and *Odyssey,* and Vergil's *Aeneid.* You have already observed the form of the dactylic hexameter in connection with your examination of the elegiac couplet (see above, Lesson 43, Section A):

– ◡ ◡ | – ◡ ◡ | – ◡ ◡ | – ◡ ◡ | – ◡ ◡ | – ×

Now consider the first five lines of the reading in this lesson—lines that have been scanned for their metrical pattern and that illustrate their flexibility with respect to admitting long and short syllables:

– ◡ ◡ | – ◡ ◡ | – – | – ◡ ◡ | – ◡ ◡ | – –

Vesper adest, iuvenes, consurgite! Vesper Olympo

– – | – ◡ ◡ | – – | – – | – ◡ ◡ | – ◡

exspectáta diu vix tandem lumina tollit.

– ◡ ◡ | – – | – – | – – | – ◡ ◡ | – –

Surgere iam tempus, iam pinguis linquere mensas;

– ◡ ◡ | – – | – – | – – | – ◡ ◡ | – ◡

iam veniet virgo, iam dicétur Hymenaeus.

– – | – ◡ ◡ | – – | – ◡ ◡ | – ◡ ◡ | – ◡

Hymen o Hymenae(e), Hymen ades o Hymenaee!

§B **Vocabulary.**

cerno, cernere, crevi, cretus ... *to sift; to see, to observe*

consurgo, consurgere, consurrexi, consurrectus ... *to rise up, to stand up*

converto, convertere, converti, conversus ... *to turn, to change; to direct* one's *mind* toward an activity

*cura, curae, f. ... *care; anxiety, concern; heartache, lovesickness*

exsilio, exsilíre, exsilui ... *to leap up, to spring up*

frustra ... *in vain*

Hymen, Hymenis, or **Hymenaeus, Hymenaei,** m. ... the god *Hymen* or *Hymenaeus* (= god of marriage)

*igitur ... *then, therefore*

*incipio, incipere, incépi, inceptus ... *to begin*

*innuptus, innupta, innuptum ... *unmarried;* (fem. plur. as substantive) *unmarried women* (= maidens)

*ius, iuris, n. ... *law, right;* **iure:** *justly, rightly*

labóro, laboráre, laborávi, laborátus ... *to work; to toil, to struggle*

linquo, linquere, liqui ... *to leave*

meditor, meditári, meditátus sum ... (perf. participle may have pass. meaning) *to think over; to ponder, to consider; to practice, to rehearse*

memorabilis, memorabile ... *memorable, worthy of memory*

mensa, mensae, f. ... *table*

nimírum ... *indeed, certainly*

Noctifer, Noctiferi, m. ... the *Evening-Star*

Oetaeus, Oetaea, Oetaeum ... *Oetaean* (= of Mount Oeta)

Olympus, Olympi, m. ... the mountain *Olympus;* (in general) *sky, heaven*

palma, palmae, f. ... *palm-tree, palm-branch; glory, honor, victory*

*par, paris ... *equal, similar; suitable, appropriate;* **pariter:** *equally, similarly; together, at the same time*

penitus ... *deeply, deep inside*

pernix, pernícis ... *swift, quick;* **perniciter:** *swiftly, quickly*

*requíro, requirere, requisii, requisítus ... *to seek, to desire; to look for, to try to find; to ask about, to inquire about;* (of verses) *to examine carefully, to commit to memory*

saltem ... *at least, in any case*

Vesper, Vesperi, m. ... the *Evening-Star*

§C   **Reading.**

The Boys and Girls Prepare for a Singing-Contest.

Lessons 46–48 contain a poem by Catullus in the form of a wedding-song, in which a chorus of young men and a chorus of young women express their views on marriage. This lively, spirited singing-contest is written in dactylic hexameters—the meter used by the Romans for epic themes but here used by Catullus for a more personal subject.

Young Men

Vesper adest, iuvenes, consurgite! Vesper Olympo

exspectáta diu vix tandem lumina tollit.

Surgere iam tempus, iam pinguis linquere mensas;

iam veniet virgo, iam dicétur Hymenaeus.

5   **Hymen o Hymenaee, Hymen ades o Hymenaee!**

Young Women

Cernitis, innuptae, iuvenes? Consurgite contra!

Nimírum Oetaeos ostendit Noctifer ignes.

Sic certest; viden ut perniciter exsiluére?

Non temere exsiluére: canent quod vincere par est.

10   **Hymen o Hymenaee, Hymen ades o Hymenaee!**

Non facilis nobis, aequáles, palma paráta est.

Aspicite, innuptae secum ut meditáta requírunt!

Non frustra meditantur: habent memorabile quod sit;

nec mirum, penitus quae tota mente labórant.

15 Nos alio mentes, alio divisimus aures;

iure igitur vincémur: amat victoria curam.

Quare nunc animos saltem convertite vestros!

Dicere iam incipient, iam respondére decébit.

Hymen o Hymenaee, Hymen ades o Hymenaee!

§D Notes and Queries.

(1) **adest:** Of what verb is this a form? Tense, voice, mood, person, and number?—**iuvenes, consurgite:** Here the leader of the young men exhorts his peers to rise from their dining-tables at the conclusion of the wedding-feast in order to participate in a singing-contest with the young women.—**Olympo:** A variation of the ablative of place where, applied to a mountain (see *ARA,* Lesson 41, Section F, note to line 9).

(2) **exspectáta:** Tense, voice, and mood? Subject of the verbal action?

(3) **tempus:** The equivalent of **tempus est.**—**pinguis:** See *ARA,* App. C, p. 403, note 11, and p. 404, note 12.

(4) **iam veniet virgo:** Refers to the imminent arrival of the bride in her future home, where she will very likely find the groom sitting on the marriage-couch or still participating in the wedding-feast.—**dicétur:** Tense, voice, mood, person, and number? Conjugate **dico** in this tense, voice, and mood.

(5) **Hymen o Hymenaee, Hymen ades o Hymenaee:** This jubilant refrain, in which the god is invoked by the chorus, is repeated at various intervals throughout the singing-contest and serves to separate the words of the young men from the words of the young women.—**ades:** Of what verb is this a form? Tense, voice, mood, person, and number? (See *ARA,* App. J, p. 454, for a clue to the form of this verb.)

(6) **innuptae . . . Consurgite:** Here the leader of the young women exhorts her peers to rise from their dining-tables at the conclusion of the wedding-feast in order to participate in a singing-contest with the young men.

(7) **Oetaeos . . . ignes:** Here the Evening-Star is described as a celestial body emitting fire, whose rising was traditionally associated with Mount Oeta, a mountain in central Greece.

(8) **certest:** The equivalent of **certe est.**—**viden:** The equivalent of **videsne.** What two elements does **videsne** consist of? (This form of the verb may be used in the singular to address more than one person.)—**exsiluére:** Supply **iuvenes** as the subject of this verb. Tense, voice, mood, person, and number of **exsiluére?**

(9) **canent:** Tense, voice, mood, person, and number?—**quod:** Supply *something* as the antecedent of the relative.—**vincere par est:** Points to the highly competitive nature of the singing-contest, in which each side attempts to surpass the verses composed by the other side.

(11) **facilis:** What noun does this adjective modify?—**palma:** In different contests in the classical world, the palm-branch was generally placed in the hands of the victor, thus functioning as the traditional symbol of victory.

(12) **meditáta:** The perfect passive participle of **meditor,** here used as a substantive and the direct object of **requírunt.** Although the Latin idiom is *things having been practiced,* how would you express it in normal English?

(13) **quod:** See above, note to line 9, on the antecedent to be supplied.

(14) **quae . . . labórant:** Here the relative is used in a causal sense—*since they struggle . . .*

(15) **alio . . . alio:** Here translate *in one direction . . . in another direction.*—**mentes . . . divisimus aures:** Although the verb is in the active voice, with the two nouns functioning as its direct objects, perhaps translate the verb in the passive voice, with the two nouns functioning as its subjects.

(16) **vincémur:** Tense, voice, mood, person, and number?

(17) **animos . . . convertite:** Toward what activity is this utterance directed? Make sure that you show this in your translation.

(18) **incipient:** What is the subject of this verb? Tense, voice, mood, person, and number?—**decébit:** The future indicative of the impersonal verb **decet** (see above, Lesson 1, Section F, note to line 10).

LESSON 47

CATULLUS: THE BOYS AND GIRLS SING ABOUT THE SUBJECT OF MARRIAGE.

§A   **Vocabulary.**

*ardeo, ardére, arsi ... *to burn, to be on fire; to burn with anger, to burn with desire*

ardor, ardóris, m. ... *fire, flame; flash, gleam*

avello, avellere, avelli, avulsus ... *to tear away; to tear away* from; *to tear away* something (acc.) from something (abl.)

*caelum, caeli, n. ... *sky, heaven*

*carpo, carpere, carpsi, carptus ... *to pluck, to seize; to carp at, to criticize*

*conubium, conubii, n. ... (plur. may have sing. meaning) *marriage, marriage-proposal*

*crudélis, crudéle ... *cruel, fierce, savage*

custodia, custodiae, f. ... *guard*

despondeo, despondére, despondi, desponsus ... *to pledge, to promise*

Eóus, Eói, m. ... *Dawn* (= the Morning-Star)

firmo, firmáre, firmávi, firmátus ... *to strengthen; to confirm, to make good*

fur, furis, c. ... *thief*

Hesperus, Hesperi, m. ... the *Evening-Star*

iucundus, iucunda, iucundum ... *pleasant, delightful*

*lateo, latére, latui ... *to hide; to lie hidden, to be concealed; to escape notice* or *detection*

libet, libére, libuit ... (impersonal verb) libet = *it is pleasing,* libére = *to be pleasing,* libuit = *it was pleasing*

luceo, lucére, luxi ... *to shine*

pango, pangere, pepigi, pactus ... *to fix, to fasten; to arrange, to agree upon*

questus, questus, m. ... *protest, complaint*

retineo, retinére, retinui, retentus ... *to hold back; to hold fast, to cling tightly*

tacitus, tacita, tacitum ... *silent*

*vigilo, vigiláre, vigilávi, vigilátus ... *to be awake, to stay awake*

§B   **Reading.**

The Boys and Girls Sing about the Subject of Marriage.

Young Women

Hespere, quis caelo fertur crudelior ignis?—

qui natam possis complexu avellere matris,

complexu matris retinentem avellere natam,

et iuveni ardenti castam donáre puellam.

5   Quid faciunt hostes capta crudelius urbe?

Hymen o Hymenaee, Hymen ades o Hymenaee!

Young Men

Hespere, quis caelo lucet iucundior ignis?—

qui desponsa tua firmes conubia flamma,

quae pepigére viri, pepigérunt ante parentes,

10   **nec iunxére priusquam se tuus extulit ardor.**

Quid datur a divis felíci optatius hora?

Hymen o Hymenaee, Hymen ades o Hymenaee!

Young Women

Hesperus e nobis, aequáles, abstulit unam.

† . . . .

Young Men

. . . . †

Namque tuo adventu vigilat custodia semper.

15   **Nocte latent fures, quos idem saepe revertens,**

Hespere, mutáto comprendis nomine Eóus.

At libet innuptis ficto te carpere questu.

Quid tum, si carpunt, tacita quem mente requírunt?

Hymen o Hymenaee, Hymen ades o Hymenaee!

§C   **Notes and Queries.**

(1) **Hespere:** At this point the Evening-Star is invoked, since he oversees marriage-contracts and marriage-ceremonies.—**quis:** The interrogative may be used as an adjective, as here, where **quis** modifies **ignis.**—**caelo:** Ablative of comparison or place where? (Use the overall context to help you determine which makes more sense.)—**fertur:** Tense, voice, mood, person, and number?—**ignis:** See above, Lesson 46, Section D, note to line 7.

(2) **qui . . . possis:** What construction? Antecedent of the relative?

(5) **Quid:** Here the interrogative modifies **crudelius.**—**capta . . . urbe:** Here the young women compare their fate on their wedding-night to that generally experienced by the women of their day at the hands of the enemy during the conquest of a city.

(7) **quis:** See above, note to line 1, on this use of the interrogative.—**caelo:** See above, note to line 1, on this use of the ablative.

(8) **qui . . . firmes:** See above, note to line 2, for this same construction.—**desponsa:** Tense, voice, and mood? Subject of the verbal action?

(9) **pepigére:** Tense, voice, mood, person, and number?—**ante:** The adverb, not the preposition.

(11) **Quid:** Here the interrogative modifies **optatius,** the perfect passive participle of the verb **opto,** used as a substantive in the comparative degree and meaning *more hopeful omen* or *more hopeful sign.*—**hora:** What kind of ablative?

(13) **e nobis . . . unam:** To whom do these words refer?—**abstulit:** Of what verb is this a form? Tense, voice, mood, person, and number?

(13–14) **Hesperus . . . Namque:** A corruption occurs in the text between lines 13 and 14, one involving the loss of most of this section on the young women's contribution to the singing-contest and some of this section on the young men's contribution to the singing-contest. In the missing lines sung by the young women, the young women very likely described Hesperus as a negative force and as a friend of thieves—a subject eventually considered by the young men in the surviving portion of their response. In the missing lines sung by the young men, the young men very likely invoked Hesperus as some kind of positive and protective force, before proceeding to describe him in greater detail as an enemy of thieves and as the bringer of dawn.

(14) **tuo adventu:** Refers to the arrival of the Evening-Star, whom the young men continue to address in the surviving portion of the text.—**vigilat custodia:** Refers to the guards maintained by property-owners to protect their possessions or possibly to certain public officials responsible in Catullus's day for keeping some kind of peace at night. (Although not an actual police force in the modern sense of the word, the **tresviri nocturni**—a triumvirate responsible for the safety of the city during the nocturnal hours—could arrest and imprison thieves.)

(15) **idem:** To whom does this pronoun refer?—**revertens:** Tense, voice, and mood? Subject of the verbal action? (The queries about **idem** and **revertens** point to the same subject, which you should not have any trouble finding if you pay attention to the endings of the words.)

(16) **Hespere . . . Eóus:** That is, Hesperus (the Evening-Star) ironically turns up under a different identity, as Eous (the Morning-Star), in which aspect he exposes (like a professional informer) the very thieves who regard him as their protector and accomplice in crime. (In Catullus's day, certain planets were mistakenly called evening-'stars' or morning-'stars'—as is still the case—because they shine brightly at dusk and at dawn, becoming visible in the western sky shortly after sunset or in the eastern sky shortly before sunrise.)—**comprendis:** Contracted for **comprehendis.**

(17) **ficto . . . questu:** According to Catullus, what does this phrase imply about the real attitude of the young women toward the Evening-Star and ultimately toward the institution of marriage?

(18) **Quid tum:** Translate *what then* or *so what.*—**carpunt:** What should be supplied as the direct object of this verb?—**tacita . . . mente requírunt:** See above, note to line 17, for exactly the same attitude.

LESSON 48

CATULLUS: THE BOYS AND GIRLS SING ABOUT THE FLOWER AND THE VINE. CLASSICAL TRADITION: ALFRED TENNYSON'S HENDECASYLLABICS.

§A   **Vocabulary.**

adipiscor, adipisci, adeptus sum ... *to obtain, to acquire*

agricola, agricolae, m. ... *farmer*

aratrum, aratri, n. ... *plow*

arvum, arvi, n. ... *field*

*aura, aurae, f. ... *wind, breeze; (in plur.) sky, heaven*

*carus, cara, carum ... *dear, dear to (+ dat.)*

colo, colere, colui, cultus ... *to inhabit; to tend, to cultivate*

contingo, contingere, contigi, contactus ... *to touch, to come into contact with*

convello, convellere, convelli, convulsus ... *to pull up, to uproot; to wrench* from, *to dislodge* from

defloresco, deflorescere, deflorui ... *to shed blossom; to fade, to wither*

dos, dotis, f. ... *dowry*

*dum ... *while, until, as long as;* dum . . , dum . . , *as long as . . , so long . .*

educo, educáre, educávi, educátus ... *to rear, to bring up; to produce, to bring forth*

extollo, extollere ... *to lift up, to raise up*

flagellum, flagelli, n. ... *lash, whip; shoot* of a vine

flos, floris, m. ... *flower; chastity, virginity*

gener, generi, m. ... *son-in-law*

hortus, horti, m. ... (plur. may have sing. meaning) *garden*

*iam ... *now, already; soon, presently;* **iam iam:** *now indeed;* **iam iamque:** *now at any moment;* **iam . . , iam . . ,** *now . . , now . . or first . . , then . .*

ignótus, ignóta, ignótum ... *unknown*

imber, imbris, m. ... *rain*

incultus, inculta, incultum ... *untended, uncultivated*

invísus, invísa, invísum ... *hateful, hateful* to (+ dat.)

iuvencus, iuvenci, m. ... *young ox, young bull*

mitis, mite ... *mild, gentle; sweet, juicy*

mulceo, mulcére, mulsi, mulsus ... *to stroke, to caress*

necesse (indecl.) ... *necessary, essential*

*pars, partis, f. (gen. plur. **partium**) ... *part, direction;* **ex parte:** *partly, in part*

polluo, polluere, pollui, pollútus ... *to defile, to pollute, to violate;* **pollútus, pollúta, pollútum:** *defiled, polluted, violated*

pronus, prona, pronum ... *leaning forward, bending forward; down to the earth, flat on one's face*

radix, radícis, f. (gen. plur. **radicium**) ... *root* of a plant

saepio, saepíre, saepsi, saeptus ... *to surround; to enclose, to fence in*

secrétus, secréta, secrétum ... *separate; solitary, secluded*

*tenuis, tenue ... *thin, slender*

ulmus, ulmi, f. ... *elm, elm-tree*

unguis, unguis, m. (abl. sing. **ungui,** gen. plur. **unguium**) ... *finger-nail* uva, uvae, f. ... *grape*

viduus, vidua, viduum ... *deprived; unwedded, unsupported*

vitis, vitis, f. (gen. plur. vitium) ... *vine*

§B   Reading.

The Boys and Girls Sing about the Flower and the Vine.

Young Women

Ut flos in saeptis secrétus nascitur hortis,

ignótus pecori, nullo convulsus aratro,

quem mulcent aurae, firmat sol, educat imber;

multi illum pueri, multae optavére puellae—

5   idem cum tenui carptus defloruit ungui,

nulli illum pueri, nullae optavére puellae—

sic virgo, dum intacta manet, dum cara suis est;

cum castum amísit pollúto corpore florem,

nec pueris iucunda manet, nec cara puellis.

10   Hymen o Hymenaee, Hymen ades o Hymenaee!

Young Men

Ut vidua in nudo vitis quae nascitur arvo,

numquam se extollit, numquam mitem educat uvam,

sed tenerum prono deflectens pondere corpus,

iam iam contingit summum radíce flagellum;

15   hanc nulli agricolae, nulli coluére iuvenci—

at si forte eadem est ulmo coniuncta maríto,

multi illam agricolae, multi coluére iuvenci—

sic virgo, dum intacta manet, dum inculta senescit;

cum par conubium matúro tempore adepta est,

20   cara viro magis et minus est invísa parenti.

Et tu ne pugna cum tali coniuge, virgo!

Non aequum est pugnáre, pater cui tradidit ipse,

ipse pater cum matre, quibus parére necesse est.

Virginitas non tota tua est, ex parte parentum est,

25   tertia pars patrist, pars est data tertia matri,

tertia sola tua est. Noli pugnáre duóbus,

qui genero sua iura simul cum dote dedérunt!

Hymen o Hymenaee, Hymen ades o Hymenaee!

§C   **Notes and Queries.**

(1–7) **Ut flos . . . sic virgo:** An example of a *simile,* a figure of speech in which one thing is compared to another thing, usually in a phrase or clause introduced by *as* or *like.* The simile may be extended and elaborate, as here, where the fate of the blooming/withering flower is compared with that of the desirable/deflowered virgin.

(1) **secrétus:** What noun does this adjective modify?

(2) **convulsus:** Tense, voice, and mood? Subject of the verbal action?

(4) **illum:** To what does this pronoun refer?—**optavére:** An example of a gnomic perfect (see *ARA,* App. K, p. 469), which should be used first with **pueri** and then with **puellae.**

(7) **suis:** What noun should be supplied after this adjective?

(11–18) **Ut . . . vitis . . . sic virgo:** A second simile to match that offered above by the young women, where the fate of the drooping/revitalized vine is compared with that of the undesirable/newly fulfilled virgin.

(11) **nudo:** What noun does this adjective modify?

(13) **deflectens:** Tense, voice, and mood? Subject of the verbal action? Direct object of the verbal action?

(14) **summum radíce flagellum:** The equivalent of **summo radícem flagello.**

(15) **hanc:** To what does this pronoun refer?—**coluére:** Another example of the gnomic perfect (see above, note to line 4), which should be used first with **agricolae** and then with **iuvenci.**—**iuvenci:** Oxen were used to break up the ground around the vines.

(16) **ulmo ... maríto:** These two nouns stand in apposition to one another. (The elm was used to train the vine, to cause it to follow a desired course, in much the same way that a trellis is employed today.)

(19) **adepta est:** Of what verb is this a form? Why are the principal parts of this verb given in the passive?

(21) **Et tu ... virgo:** At this point the young men address the bride directly, with an injunction that has little to do with the subject of the preceding competition and that also epitomizes the male-dominator attitude associated with many civilizations, including the classical.

(22) **pugnáre:** What phrase should be supplied with this infinitive?—**tradidit:** What should be supplied as the direct object of this verb?

(24) **ex parte parentum:** Although the Latin idiom is *partly of the parents,* how would you express it in normal English?

(25) **patrist:** The equivalent of **patri est.**—**data:** This form should be taken first with the **est** in **patrist** and then with the **est** after **pars.**

(26) **Noli pugnáre:** See above, Lesson 44, Section C, First Passage, note to line 1.—**duóbus:** The equivalent of **cum duóbus.** To whom does the word **duóbus** refer?

§D   **Classical Tradition.** Catullus's poetry strongly influenced other Roman poets in classical times and other famous writers from the Renaissance through the nineteenth century. His verses became part of the language of love during the Renaissance, during which period they were translated or imitated by a number of distinguished poets.

Tributes to Catullus appear in the verses of Alfred Tennyson, the poet laureate of Victorian England, who wrote *Idylls of the King,* an epic about the legendary King Arthur. In the following poem—entitled "Hendecasyllabics"—Tennyson experiments with a meter frequently employed by his Roman predecessor (see above, Lesson 37, Section B).

O you chorus of indolent reviewers,
Irresponsible, indolent reviewers,
Look, I come to the test, a tiny poem
All composed in a metre of Catullus,
All in quantity, careful of my motion,
Like the skater on ice that hardly bears him,
Lest I fall unawares before the people,
Waking laughter in indolent reviewers.
Should I flounder awhile without a tumble
Through this metrification of Catullus,
They should speak to me not without a welcome,
All that chorus of indolent reviewers.
Hard, hard, hard is it, only not to tumble,
So fantastical is the dainty metre.
Wherefore slight me not wholly, nor believe me
Too presumptuous, indolent reviewers.
O blatant Magazines, regard me rather—
Since I blush to belaud myself a moment—
As some rare little rose, a piece of inmost
Horticultural art, or half coquette-like
Maiden, not to be greeted unbenignly.

LESSON 49

OVID. OVID: APOLLO TEASES CUPID FOR PLAYING THE ARCHER.

§A   **Ovid.** Ovid (43 B.C.–17 A.D.), Rome's most versatile poet, wrote the *Metamorphoses,* a fifteen-book epic in dactylic hexameters recounting the Greek and Roman myths. Lessons 49–60 contain two of Ovid's love stories: the first, on how the god Apollo fell in love with Daphne; the second, on how Pyramus and Thisbe pursued their love secretly.

§B   **Vocabulary.**

     addúco, adducere, adduxi, adductus ... *to lead forth; to draw back, to pull tight*

     adsero, adserere, adserui, adsertus ... *to lay hold of, to lay claim to*

     arcus, arcus, m. ... *bow*

     *****cedo, cedere, cessi** ... *to go; to withdraw; to yield* or *give way* (+ dat.)

     contentus, contenta, contentum ... *content, satisfied*

     *****cornu, cornus,** n. ... (plur. may have sing. meaning) *horn; horn-tipped bow*

     Daphne, Daphnes, f. ... the nymph *Daphne*

     Delius, Delii, m. ... the *Delian* (= Apollo)

     *****fax, facis,** f. ... *torch*

     fors, fortis, f. ... *chance*

     gestámen, gestaminis, n. ... (plur. may have sing. meaning) *armor, equipment*

     *****gloria, gloriae,** f. ... *fame, glory*

innumerus, innumera, innumerum ... *countless, innumerable*

iugerum, iugeri, n. ... *measure of land;* (in plur.) *acres, tracts*

lascívus, lascíva, lascívum ... *playful, mischievous*

nervus, nervi, m. ... *tendon; bowstring, lyrestring*

Peneius, Peneia, Peneium ... *of Peneus;* **Peneia, Peneiae,** f.: *daughter of Peneus*

Phoebus, Phoebi, m. ... *Phoebus* (= Apollo)

Python, Pythónis, m. (acc. sing. **Pythóna**) ... the snake *Python*

*****saevus, saeva, saevum** ... *cruel, fierce, savage*

serpens, serpentis, c. (gen. plur. **serpentium**) ... *snake, serpent*

*****sterno, sternere, stravi, stratus** ... *to lay out, to spread out; to knock down, to strike down*

tumidus, tumida, tumidum ... *swollen*

*****umerus, umeri,** m. ... *shoulder*

venter, ventris, m. ... *belly, stomach*

§C   **Reading.**

Apollo Teases Cupid for Playing the Archer.

Lessons 49–54 contain Ovid's story of how Apollo fell in love with Daphne, a story in which a powerful male deity desires and pursues an innocent, powerless female. Having killed the serpent Python with his bow and arrows, Apollo teases Cupid for trying to use the same weapons, only to be pierced himself by Cupid's unerring shaft.

Primus amor Phoebi Daphne Peneia; quem non

fors ignára dedit, sed saeva Cupidinis ira.

Delius hunc nuper (victo serpente superbus)

viderat adducto flectentem cornua nervo

5   "Quid" que "tibi, lascíve puer, cum fortibus armis?"

dixerat: "Ista decent umeros gestamina nostros,

qui dare certa ferae, dare vulnera possumus hosti,

qui modo pestifero tot iugera ventre prementem

stravimus innumeris tumidum Pythóna sagittis.

10   Tu face nescio quos esto contentus amóres

inritáre tua, nec laudes adsere nostras!"

Filius huic Veneris "Figat tuus omnia, Phoebe,

te meus arcus" ait; "Quantoque animalia cedunt

cuncta deo, tanto minor est tua gloria nostra."

§D   **Notes and Queries.**

(1) **Primus . . . Peneia:** What verb should be supplied in this sentence?—**Phoebi:** Another name for Apollo meaning *bright one*—applied to him in classical times because he was mistakenly confused with the sun-god Helios.—**Peneia:** Peneus himself was the god of a river that flowed through Thessaly, a region in northern Greece.—**quem:** To what does this pronoun refer?

(2) **Cupidinis:** In Roman poetry of Ovid's day, the god Cupid is usually described as a young boy with wings, carrying a bow and arrows, or a flaming torch—and generally (although not here) in the company of his mother Venus, whose orders he would continuously execute while flying from one place to another.

(3) **Delius:** Another name for Apollo meaning *the Delian*—applied to him in classical times because he was believed to have been born on the island of Delos.—**serpente:** Refers to Python, the monster with oracular powers that inhabited Delphi before the coming of Apollo.

(4) **viderat:** What is the subject? What is the direct object?—**adducto:** Tense, voice, and mood? Subject of the verbal action?—**flectentem:** Tense, voice, and mood? Subject of the verbal action?

(5) **Quid . . . tibi:** Translate *what do you want* or *what have you to do.*—**que:** Although **-que** is not attached to the end of a word in this particular instance, it still functions as a conjunction, connecting the verbs **viderat** in line 4 and **dixerat** in line 6.

(6) **Ista . . . umeros gestamina nostros:** In the dactylic hexameter, phrases consisting of nouns and adjectives may be arranged in such a way that one phrase may interlock with the other, as here, where the phrase **Ista . . . gestamina** interlocks with the phrase **umeros . . . nostros** in what may be referred to as the *interlocking word order.*—**decent:** The plural form of the impersonal verb **decet** (listed in the Cumulative Vocabulary), here meaning *are suitable for* or *are appropriate for.*

(7–9) **qui . . . possumus . . . qui . . . stravimus:** These forms are all plural, since Apollo has been speaking in the plural (beginning with **umeros . . . nostros** in line 6), with the antecedent of the relative supplied from the endings of the verbs.

(7) **dare . . . ferae, dare . . . hosti:** In the dactylic hexameter, a word (or words) needed in two or more parallel clauses may be expressed in one of them and carried over to the other(s), as here, where the words **vulnera possumus** should be carried back to the first **dare** clause and the word **certa** should be carried forward to the second **dare** clause. (In this hexameter, the nouns **ferae** and **hosti** are used in order to distinguish between wild animals and human beings, over both of whom Apollo claims to exercise unlimited power with his bow and arrows.)

(8) **modo:** The adverb, not the noun. (See above, Lesson 26, Section E, note to line 9.)

(9) **tumidum Pythóna:** Of what verb is this phrase the direct object? Of what verbal form is this phrase also the subject? (The serpent may be thought of as swollen with its own poison if **innumeris . . . sagittis** is translated directly after **stravimus,** or as swollen with Apollo's arrows if **innumeris . . . sagittis** is translated directly after **tumidum.**)

(10) **nescio quos . . . amóres:** These words should be taken together as a single phrase and translated idiomatically. (In this regard, check the Cumulative Vocabulary under **nescio** for the entry **nescio quis.**)—**esto:** The future active imperative second person singular of the verb **sum** (see *ARA,* App. J, p. 454).

(11) **tua:** What noun does this adjective modify?—**adsere:** Tense, voice, mood, person, and number?

(12) **Filius . . . Veneris:** To whom do these words refer? (Give the name of this individual.)—**Figat tuus:** That is, **Figat tuus arcus.** Tense, voice, mood, person, and number of **Figat?**

(13) **meus arcus:** That is, **figet meus arcus.** Tense, voice, mood, person, and number of **figet?** (The verb **figet,** to be supplied in line 13, should be distinguished from the verb **figat,** appearing in line 12.)

(14) **tua gloria:** In Cupid's eyes, Apollo's glory—as considerable as it is—cannot compare with his own.—**nostra:** What kind of ablative?

LESSON 50

OVID: CUPID SHOOTS HIS ARROWS INTO APOLLO AND DAPHNE.

§A Vocabulary.

acútus, acúta, acútum ... *sharp*

aemulus, aemula, aemulum ... *striving to equal, straining to excel* (+ gen.)

aer, aeris, m. (acc. sing. **aera**) ... (**ae** not pronounced as diphthong but as two separate syllables) *air*

*****amo, amáre, amávi, amátus** ... *to love; to fall in love, to fall in love with;* (pres. part. as substantive) *lover*

Apollineus, Apollinea, Apollineum ... *of Apollo*

arx, arcis, f. (gen. plur. **arcium**) ... *citadel, fortress; peak, height, summit*

aurátus, auráta, aurátum ... *golden*

aversor, aversári, aversátus sum ... *to turn away from; to spurn, to reject*

avius, avia, avium ... *pathless, untrodden*

coerceo, coercére, coercui, coercitus ... *to confine; to bind up, to keep together*

cuspis, cuspidis, f. ... *tip* or *point* of a weapon

elído, elidere, elísi, elísus ... *to strike out; to cleave, to divide*

*****laedo, laedere, laesi, laesus** ... *to hurt; to strike, to injure*

expers, expertis ... *having no part, wanting no part* (+ gen.)

exuviae, exuviárum, f. ... (plur. may have sing. meaning) *spoils; skin* or *slough* of a snake

*figo, figere, fixi, fixus ... *to fix, to place; to pierce, to impale; to drive, to shoot, to thrust*

harundo, harundinis, f. ... *reed; shaft* of an arrow

impatiens, impatientis ... *impatient, intolerant* (+ gen.)

impiger, impigra, impigrum ... *active; eager, vigorous*

latebra, latebrae, f. ... *hiding-place; den, lair*

*lex, legis, f. ... *law; order, control; term, condition*

lustro, lustráre, lustrávi, lustrátus ... *to purify; to run through, to roam through; to observe, to examine, to consider*

nemus, nemoris, n. ... *forest; glade, grove*

*nympha, nymphae, f. ... *nymph;* (as proper noun) **Nympha:** a *Nymph*

obtúsus, obtúsa, obtúsum ... *blunt*

os, ossis, n. ... *bone*

Parnásus, Parnási, m. ... the mountain *Parnasus*

Penéis, Peneidos (acc. plur. **Peneidas**) ... *of Peneus;* **Penéis, Peneidos,** f. (voc. sing. **Penéi**): *daughter of Peneus*

percutio, percutere, percussi, percussus ... *to strike; to beat, to flap*

*pharetra, pharetrae, f. ... *quiver* (= case for arrows)

Phoebe, Phoebes, f. ... *Phoebe* (= Diana)

plumbum, plumbi, n. ... *lead; leaden tip*

promo, promere, prompsi, promptus ... *to produce; to bring out, to bring forth*

*protinus ... *immediately*

sagittifer, sagittifera, sagittiferum ... *arrow-bearing* traicio, traicere, traiéci, traiectus ... *to throw across; to pierce, to transfix*

umbrósus, umbrósa, umbrósum ... *shady*

vitta, vittae, f. ... *headband*

§B   Reading.

Cupid Shoots His Arrows into Apollo and Daphne.

Dixit, et elíso percussis aere pennis,

impiger umbrósa Parnási constitit arce,

eque sagittifera prompsit duo tela pharetra

diversórum operum—fugat hoc, facit illud amórem:

5   quod facit, aurátum est et cuspide fulget acúta;

quod fugat, obtúsum est et habet sub harundine plumbum.

Hoc deus in nympha Peneide fixit; at illo

laesit Apollineas traiecta per ossa medullas.

Protinus alter amat; fugit altera nomen amantis,

10   silvárum latebris captivarumque ferárum

exuviis gaudens, innuptaeque aemula Phoebes.

Vitta coercébat positos sine lege capillos.

Multi illam petiére; illa, aversáta petentes,

impatiens expersque viri, nemora avia lustrat,

15   nec quid Hymen, quid Amor, quid sint conubia, curat.

Saepe pater dixit: "Generum mihi, filia, debes";

saepe pater dixit: "Debes mihi, nata, nepótes."

§C   **Notes and Queries.**

(1) **elíso . . . aere:** What construction? (Check the lesson vocabulary for the accentuation of **aere.**)

(2) **Parnási:** A mountain in central Greece.—**arce:** What kind of ablative?

(3) **eque:** Not from **equus.** What two elements does **eque** consist of?—**sagittifera . . . duo tela pharetra:** In the dactylic hexameter, phrases consisting of nouns and adjectives may be arranged in such a way that one phrase may contain or enclose the other, as here, where the phrase **sagittifera pharetra** contains or encloses the phrase **duo tela** in what may be referred to as the *concentric word order.*

(4) **fugat:** What should be supplied as the direct object?—**hoc . . . illud:** Here the equivalent of **alterum . . . alterum.**

(5–6) **quod facit . . . quod fugat:** What should be supplied as the antecedent of the first **quod?** What should be supplied as the antecedent of the second **quod?**

(7) **fixit:** What is the direct object of this verb?—**Hoc . . . illo:** See above, note to line 4, for a similar use of these pronouns, although when used in line 7, they appear in different cases.

(8) **traiecta:** Tense, voice, and mood? Subject of the verbal action?

(9) **nomen amantis:** That is, the very thought or mention of a lover proves unsettling for this particular victim of Cupid's arrow.

(11) **exuviis:** Refers to the skins of animals, preserved as trophies.—**Phoebes:** Another name for Diana meaning *bright one*—applied to her in classical times because she was mistakenly confused with the moon-goddess Selene (see above, Lesson 49, Section D, note to line 1).

(12) **Vitta:** The meter indicates that this noun is in the nominative.

(13) **Multi:** Refers to Daphne's suitors.—**petiére:** Tense, voice, mood, person, and number?—**petentes:** What use of the participle? Subject to be supplied here?

(15) **nec . . . curat:** What construction do these words introduce?—**quid . . . quid . . . quid sint:** Here the first **quid** and the second **quid** may mean *who* rather than *what.* What word should be supplied after the first **quid** and the second **quid?**—**Hymen . . . Amor:** These two deities are mentioned in order to emphasize Daphne's total lack of interest in love—both in the wedding-ceremony, over which Hymen presided, and in the emotional aspect, over which Amor presided.

(16–17) **pater . . . pater:** To whom does this word refer? (Give the name of this individual.)—**dixit . . . dixit:** The perfect tense normally expresses completed action in the past (see *ARA,* Lesson 31, Section A), although in these hexameters (where it is used twice with **saepe**) it expresses completed action on a number of individual occasions.

LESSON 51

OVID: APOLLO FALLS IN LOVE AND ADMIRES DAPHNE'S BEAUTY.

§A   **Vocabulary.**

abeo, abíre, abívi or **abii** ... *to go away; to turn* into, *to change* into

admoveo, admovére, admóvi, admótus ... *to move near, to place near*

adoleo, adolére ... *to burn, to kindle*

arista, aristae, f. ... (plur. may have sing. meaning) *grain*

blandus, blanda, blandum ... *coaxing; soft, smooth*

bracchium, bracchii, n. ... *lower arm;* (in general) *arm*

cervix, cervícis, f. ... (plur. may have sing. meaning) *neck*

collum, colli, n. ... *neck*

como, comere, compsi, comptus ... *to comb, to make tidy*

crimen, criminis, n. ... *charge; crime, object of reproach*

cupio, cupere, cupívi, cupítus ... *to wish, to desire*

decor, decoris, m. ... *beauty, attractiveness*

Diána, Diánae, f. ... *Diana*

digitus, digiti, m. ... *finger*

exósus, exósa, exósum ... *hating, detesting*

*genitor, genitóris, m. ... *father;* (applied to Jupiter) *father, creator*

*haereo, haerére, haesi ... *to cling* to or on; *to stick fast* to, *to become fastened* in; *to be stuck, to be at a loss, to be in difficulty*

inornátus, inornáta, inornátum ... *unkempt, disheveled*

iugális, iugále ... *yoked; nuptial, of marriage*

lacertus, lacerti, m. ... *upper arm;* (in general) *arm*

*lux, lucis, f. ... *light; day, daylight; sheen, splendor;* **sub luce:** *at daybreak*

mico, micáre, micui ... *to dart; to flash, to gleam*

nutrio, nutríre, nutrívi or **nutrii, nutrítus** ... *to nourish*

obsequor, obsequi, obsecútus sum ... *to comply, to consent*

ocior, ocius ... (only in compar.) *swifter*

oraculum, oraculi, n. ... *oracle, shrine; divine utterance, prophetic power*

*pendeo, pendére, pependi ... *to hang, to hang down; to hang* from, *to hang down* from; *to be suspended, to be discontinued*

repugno, repugnáre, repugnávi, repugnátus ... *to fight back; to be inconsistent* with, *to be incompatible* with (+ dat.)

resisto, resistere, restiti ... *to stop, to stop running; to pause, to break off speaking*

revoco, revocáre, revocávi, revocátus ... *to call back, to summon back*

rubor, rubóris, m. ... *redness; blush, flush*

saepes, saepis, f. (gen. plur. **saepium**) ... *hedge*

*sidus, sideris, n. ... *star*

*spero, speráre, sperávi, sperátus ... *to hope, to hope for*

sterilis, sterile ... *barren; futile, unproductive*

stipula, stipulae, f. ... (plur. may have sing. meaning) *stalk; straw, stubble*

suffundo, suffundere, suffúdi, suffúsus ... *to pour over; to fill, to cover*

taeda, taedae, f. ... *pine; torch* used at weddings

uro, urere, ussi, ustus ... *to burn, to be on fire; to burn with desire, to burn with passion*

*****verbum, verbi,** n. ... (plur. may have sing. meaning) *word; talk, mere talk*

veto, vetáre, vetui, vetítus ... *to forbid, to prohibit*

viátor, viatóris, m. ... *traveler, wayfarer*

votum, voti, n. ... *vow; prayer, entreaty*

§B   **Reading.**

Apollo Falls in Love and Admires Daphne's Beauty.

Illa, velut crimen taedas exósa iugáles,

pulchra verecundo suffunditur ora rubóre,

inque patris blandis haerens cervíce lacertis,

"Da mihi perpetua, genitor carissime," dixit

5   "virginitáte frui! Dedit hoc pater ante Diánae."

Ille quidem obsequitur; sed te decor iste quod optas

esse vetat, votoque tuo tua forma repugnat.

Phoebus amat, visaeque cupit conubia Daphnes;

quodque cupit, sperat; suaque illum oracula fallunt.

10   Utque leves stipulae demptis adolentur aristis,

ut facibus saepes ardent, quas forte viátor

vel nimis admóvit vel iam sub luce reliquit,

sic deus in flammas abiit, sic pectore toto

uritur et sterilem sperando nutrit amórem.

15   Spectat inornátos collo pendére capillos,

et "Quid si comantur?" ait. Videt igne micantes

sideribus similes oculos; videt oscula, quae non

est vidisse satis; laudat digitosque manusque

bracchiaque et nudos media plus parte lacertos;

20 si qua latent, melióra putat. Fugit ocior aura

illa levi, neque ad haec revocantis verba resistit:

§C   Notes and Queries.

(2) **ora:** The accusative may be used to limit an adjective or verb (see *ARA,* Appendix E, p. 424, Accusative of Respect).

(3) **inque:** What two elements does this word consist of? What noun does the preposition **in** govern?

(5) **pater:** Refers to Jupiter, who fathered Diana, Daphne's role model (see above, Lesson 50, Section B, lines 9–11).

(6–7) **te decor . . . vetat:** Occasionally Ovid pauses to address one or more of his own characters, as here, where he addresses Daphne as though she were alive and able to hear him.

(8) **visaeque:** Tense, voice, and mood of **visae?** Subject of the verbal action?—**cupit conubia Daphnes:** Although the Latin idiom is *desires marriage of Daphne,* how would you express it in normal English? (Here **conubia** is simply a euphemism—Ovid's way of saying that Apollo wants to have sex with Daphne, as he can by virtue of his divine power, with no thoughts of marriage in the traditional sense.)

(9) **quodque:** What should be supplied as the antecedent of the **quod** in **quodque?**—**oracula:** That is, the very oracles that were consecrated to Apollo in his special aspect as a god of prophecy.

(10–13) **Utque . . . stipulae . . . sic deus:** An example of a *simile,* a figure of speech in which one thing is compared to another thing, usually in a phrase or clause introduced by *as* or *like* (see above, Lesson 48, Section C, note to lines 1–7).

(10) **demptis . . . aristis:** What construction?

(11–12) **quas . . . reliquit:** That is, some nocturnal traveler has neglected to put out his campfire and before going on his way has accidentally set fire to the hedges.

(13) **in flammas abiit:** Translate *was consumed by fire.* What is the literal meaning of these words?

(14) **sperando:** What verbal form? Case and number?

(15) **Spectat:** What construction does this verb introduce? What are the elements of this construction in this sentence?—**inornátos:** See also above, Lesson 50, Section B, line 12, for the expression **positos sine lege.**—**collo:** What kind of ablative?

(16) **comantur:** Here the subjunctive shows an unreal supposition on the part of the speaker and should be translated according to sense.

(19) **media plus parte:** Translate *as far as the shoulder.* What is the literal meaning of these words?

(20) **qua:** A form of the indefinite pronoun **quis, quid.** (Check *ARA,* Appendix C, p. 413, for the declension of this pronoun and adjust its meaning to accommodate the case, number, and gender of **qua.**)—**putat:** This verb introduces an indirect statement, in which the accusative **ea** and the infinitive **esse** should be supplied from the context. (See above, Lesson 4, Section E, note to lines 2–3, for a similar use of this construction, involving the need to supply the missing elements.)

(21) **illa:** To whom does this pronoun refer?—**haec . . . verba:** Refers to the speech that Apollo is about to make—the subject of the reading in the following lesson.—**revocantis:** What use of the participle? Subject to be supplied here?

LESSON 52

OVID: APOLLO ENTREATS DAPHNE NOT TO RUN AWAY FROM HIM.

§A **Vocabulary.**

agna, agnae, f. ... *ewe* (= female lamb)

armentum, armenti, n. ... (collective sing. or plur.) *herd*

asper, aspera, asperum ... *harsh, rough, fierce*

Claros, Clari, f. ... the town *Claros*

***columba, columbae,** f. ... *dove*

concordo, concordáre, concordávi ... *to be in harmony* with

crus, cruris, n. ... *leg, shin*

Delphicus, Delphica, Delphicum ... *Delphian, of Delphi*

ei ... (interjection) *alas!;* **ei mihi:** *woe is me!*

grex, gregis, m. ... (collective sing. or plur.) *herd, flock*

***herba, herbae,** f. ... *grass; plant, herb*

hic ... (adv.) *here; in this place, at this point*

horridus, horrida, horridum ... *harsh, rough; uncouth, unkempt*

incola, incolae, m. ... *dweller, inhabitant*

inhibeo, inhibére, inhibui, inhibitus ... *to check, to restrain*

***insequor, insequi, insecútus sum** ... *to follow closely; to pursue, to attack; to follow, to come next*

inventum, inventi, n. ... *discovery, invention*

Iuppiter, Iovis, or **Iovis, Iovis,** m. ... *Jupiter, Jove*

lupus, lupi, m. ... *wolf*

medicína, medicínae, f. ... *medicine, art of healing*

moderátus, moderáta, moderátum ... *controlled, restrained;* **moderáte:** *with control, with restraint*

noto, notáre, notávi, notátus ... *to mark; to mar, to scar; to notice, to observe*

observo, observáre, observávi, observátus ... *to observe; to guard, to watch over*

opifer, opifera, opiferum ... *help-bringing;* (masc. sing. as substantive) the *help-bringer*

orbis, orbis, m. (gen. plur. **orbium**) ... *circle; earth, world*

*****pastor, pastóris,** m. ... *shepherd, herdsman*

Pataréus, Pataréa, Pataréum ... *Patarean, of Patara*

*****pateo, patére, patui** ... *to be open; to be exposed, to be revealed;* **patens, patentis:** *open, spacious*

potentia, potentiae, f. ... *power*

prosum, prodesse, profui ... *to be useful, to be helpful* (+ dat.)

qua ... (adv.) *where, by which way, in which direction*

sanabilis, sanabile ... *curable*

sentis, sentis, m. (gen. plur. **sentium**) ... *briar, bramble*

tellus, tellúris, f. ... *land, earth;* (as proper noun) **Tellus:** the goddess *Earth*

temerarius, temeraria, temerarium ... *rash, reckless, thoughtless*

Tenedos, Tenedi, f. ... the island *Tenedos*

*****trepido, trepidáre, trepidávi** ... *to be anxious, to be agitated*

*****vacuus, vacua, vacuum** ... *empty, empty of* (+ abl.); *carefree, fancy-free*

Apollo Entreats Daphne Not to Run Away from Him.

"Nympha, precor, Penéi, mane! Non insequor hostis.

Nympha, mane! Sic agna lupum, sic cerva leónem,

sic aquilam penna fugiunt trepidante columbae;

hostes quaeque suos. Amor est mihi causa sequendi.

5   Me miserum! Ne prona cadas, indignave laedi

crura notent sentes, et sim tibi causa dolóris!

Aspera, qua properas, loca sunt. Moderatius, oro,

curre fugamque inhibe, moderatius insequar ipse!

Cui placeas, inquíre tamen! Non incola montis,

10   non ego sum pastor, non hic armenta gregesque

horridus observo. Nescis, temeraria, nescis

quem fugias, ideoque fugis. Mihi Delphica tellus

et Claros et Tenedos Patareaque regia servit.

Iuppiter est genitor; per me, quod eritque fuitque

15   estque, patet; per me concordant carmina nervis.

Certa quidem nostra est, nostra tamen una sagitta

certior, in vacuo quae vulnera pectore fecit.

Inventum medicína meum est, opiferque per orbem

dicor, et herbárum subiecta potentia nobis.

20   Ei mihi, quod nullis amor est sanabilis herbis,

nec prosunt domino quae prosunt omnibus artes!"

§C   **Notes and Queries.**

(1) **insequor:** What should be supplied as the direct object?

(2–3) **Sic . . . lupum, sic . . . leónem, sic . . . columbae:** In the dactylic hexameter, a word (or words) needed in two or more parallel clauses may be expressed in one of them and carried over to the other(s) (see above, Lesson 49, Section D, note to line 7). What word should be carried back from the third **sic** clause to the first and second **sic** clauses? What adjustment must be made in the ending of that word so that it will fit in the first and second **sic** clauses?

(3) **penna . . . trepidante:** What construction?

(4) **quaeque:** Of what pronoun is this a form? What verb should be supplied after this pronoun?—**sequendi:** What verbal form? Case and number?

(5) **Me miserum:** The accusative may also be used in exclamations, where it usually consists of a noun and an adjective (see *ARA*, App. E, p. 424, Accusative of Exclamation).—**indignave laedi:** Here the adjective **indigna** is used with the infinitive **laedi** rather than (as indicated in the vocabulary entry) with the genitive or ablative of a noun.

(5–6) **Ne . . . cadas . . . notent . . . sim:** The subjunctive is used with verbs of fearing (see *ARA*, App. K, p. 474, Clauses of Fearing), with *I fear* to be supplied before the three **Ne** clauses in the subjunctive. (The **-ve** in **indignave** carries forward the **Ne** to **notent** in line 6, and the conjunction **et** carries forward the **Ne** to **sim** in line 6.)

(7) **qua:** The adverb listed in the vocabulary of this lesson.—**Moderatius:** Degree of adverb?

(9) **Cui placeas:** Translate this clause directly after **inquíre tamen.** What pronoun should be supplied as the antecedent of **Cui?**

(10) **hic:** The adverb, not the pronoun.

(12–13) **Delphica tellus . . . Claros . . . Tenedos Patareaque regia:** All locations in the Greek world famous for their oracles of Apollo—the most famous being the oracle of Apollo at Delphi, where the god revealed his prophetic powers through his priestess to those who sought his advice (see also above, Lesson 51, Section C, note to line 9).

(13) **servit:** Here the third person singular is used, since the four subjects taken separately are understood as individual locations, in this instance, oracular sites.

(14–15) **eritque fuitque estque:** Here the verb **sum** is used three times and in three different tenses. Tense, voice, mood, person, and number of each of these verb forms?

(16) **nostra . . . nostra:** What noun should be supplied after each **nostra** from elsewhere in the sentence? (Case, number, and gender of the first **nostra?** Case, number, and gender of the second **nostra?**)

(18) **medicína . . . opiferque:** Refers to Apollo in his special aspect as god of medicine.

(19) **subiecta:** The equivalent of what verb form?

(20) **Ei mihi:** See entry in the vocabulary of this lesson.

(21) **domino:** To whom does this word refer? (Give the name of this individual.)—**quae:** What is the antecedent (actually the postcedent)?

LESSON 53

OVID: APOLLO PURSUES DAPHNE UNTIL SHE BECOMES
EXHAUSTED.

§A   Vocabulary.

absúmo, absumere, absumpsi, absumptus ... *to take away; to use up,
to consume*

adflo, adfláre, adflávi, adflátus ... *to breathe on*

adiuvo, adiuváre, adiúvi, adiútus ... *to help, to assist*

ambiguus, ambigua, ambiguum ... *doubtful;* **in ambiguo:** *in doubt*

blanditia, blanditiae, f. ... *flattery;* (in plur.) *loving words, sweet talk*

citus, cita, citum ... *swift*

***corpus, corporis, n.** ... (plur. may have sing. meaning) *body*

***crinis, crinis, m.** (gen. plur. **crinium**) ... *hair; lock, tress*

decens, decentis ... *fitting; pleasing, attractive*

expallesco, expallescere, expallui ... *to turn pale*

extendo, extendere, extendi, extentus ... *to stretch out*

flamen, flaminis, n. ... *wind, blast* of wind

***flumen, fluminis, n.** ... *river;* (in plur.) *waters* of a river

fugax, fugácis ... *fleeing, running away*

Gallicus, Gallica, Gallicum ... *Gallic*

***immineo, imminére** ... *to overhang, to project over; to threaten, to be
imminent; to press closely* on, *to follow closely* on (+ dat.)

imperfectus, imperfecta, imperfectum ... *unfinished, incomplete*

inhaereo, inhaerére, inhaesi, inhaesus ... *to cling to, to grasp hold of*

lepus, leporis, m. ... *hare*

morsus, morsus, m. ... *bite; jaws, teeth*

nudo, nudáre, nudávi, nudátus ... *to lay bare; to expose, to reveal*

requies, requiétis, f. (acc. sing. **requiem**) ... *rest, respite*

rostrum, rostri, n. ... *snout, muzzle*

spargo, spargere, sparsi, sparsus ... *to scatter, to sprinkle; to stream out* or *spread out* on (+ abl.)

*stringo, stringere, strinxi, strictus ... *to draw tight; to draw out, to unsheathe; to graze, to ruffle, to almost touch*

sustineo, sustinére, sustinui, sustentus ... *to hold up, to sustain; to have the will, to have the patience*

*tergum, tergi, n. ... (plur. may have sing. meaning) *back, rear; hide, skin*

*timidus, timida, timidum ... *timid, fearful*

unda, undae, f. ... *wave* of the sea; *water* of a river or spring

§B   **Reading.**

Apollo Pursues Daphne Until She Becomes Exhausted.

Plura locutúrum timido Peneia cursu

fugit, cumque ipso verba imperfecta reliquit.

Tum quoque visa decens. Nudábant corpora venti,

obviaque adversas vibrábant flamina vestes,

5   et levis impulsos retro dàbat aura capillos,

auctaque forma fuga est. Sed enim non sustinet ultra

perdere blanditias iuvenis deus, utque movébat

ipse amor, admisso sequitur vestigia passu.

Ut canis in vacuo leporem cum Gallicus arvo

10   vidit, et hic praedam pedibus petit, ille salútem—

alter (inhaesúro similis) iam iamque tenére

sperat, et extento stringit vestigia rostro;

alter in ambiguo est an sit comprensus, et ipsis

morsibus eripitur, tangentiaque ora relinquit—

15   sic deus et virgo; est hic spe celer, illa timóre.

Qui tamen insequitur, pennis adiútus Amóris;

ocior est, requiemque negat, tergoque fugácis

imminet, et crinem sparsum cervicibus adflat.

Viribus absumptis expalluit illa, citaeque

20   victa labóre fugae, spectans Peneidas undas:

"Fer, pater," inquit, "opem, si flumina numen habétis!

Qua nimium placui, mutando perde figúram!"

§C   Notes and Queries.

(1) **Plura:** That is, more words and arguments designed to win her over.—**locutúrum:** What use of the participle? Subject to be supplied here? Direct object of the verbal action? (See above, Lesson 19, Section E, note to line 6, on **excitatúrus,** for this form of the verb.)

(2) **cumque ipso:** To whom does the pronoun **ipso** refer? (Show this along with the force of **ipso** in your translation.)

(3) **visa:** The equivalent of what verb form?

(4) **obviaque adversas . . . flamina vestes:** In the dactylic hexameter, phrases consisting of nouns and adjectives may be arranged in such a way that one phrase may interlock with the other (see above, Lesson 49, Section D, note to line 6).

(5) **retro dabat:** Translate *pushed back* or *tossed back.* What is the literal meaning of these words?

(6) **auctaque . . . est:** These two words should be taken together as a single verb form.—**Sed enim:** Between these two words supply the phrase *the end was near,* or do not translate **enim** at all, which may simply be strengthening the force of **Sed.**

(7) **blanditias:** The kind that he uttered in his twenty-one line speech, presented in the preceding lesson.

(8) **admisso . . . passu:** See also above, Lesson 21, Section E, note to lines 5–6, for a similar idiom. Translate the idiom **admisso . . . passu** first literally and then idiomatically.

(9–15) **Ut canis . . . leporem . . . sic deus et virgo:** See above, Lesson 48, Section C, note to lines 1–7.

(9) **Gallicus:** In the sense that it was originally imported from Gaul, an ancient territory corresponding roughly to present-day France and Belgium (see *ARA,* Lesson 6, Section E).

(10) **vidit:** See above, Lesson 39, Section C, note to line 26.

(11) **inhaesúro:** See above, note to line 1, for this form of the verb, here used as a substantive after the adjective **similis,** with *its prey* or *its victim* to be supplied as the direct object of its verbal action.

(13) **an sit comprensus:** What construction? Tense, voice, mood, person, and number of **sit comprensus?** (The form **comprensus** is contracted for **comprehensus.**)

(14) **morsibus:** What kind of dative?

(16) **pennis adiútus Amóris:** Although Apollo had ridiculed Cupid for trying to compete with him, Apollo is here described (somewhat ironically) as a god who actually thrives on the power that he has received from the tiny winged deity.

(17) **negat:** What should be supplied as the indirect object of this verb?—**fugácis:** What use of the adjective?

(18) **cervicibus:** For a similar use of the ablative, see above, Lesson 51, Section C, note to line 15, on **collo.**

(19) **Viribus absumptis:** What construction?

(21) **Fer:** Of what verb is this a form? Tense, voice, mood, person, and number?—**pater ... flumina:** Here Daphne addresses Peneus by referring to him in two different ways—first in the singular, by calling him her father, and then in the plural, by associating him with the element he controls (see above, Lesson 49, Section D, note to line 1).

(22) **Qua ... placui:** That is, by which she was pleasing to men and to Apollo. What is the antecedent (actually the postcedent) of **Qua?**—**mutando:** What verbal form? Case and number? (By uttering this single word, Daphne indicates that she wants her father to end all her suffering by causing her to undergo a physical metamorphosis.)

LESSON 54

OVID: DAPHNE TURNS INTO A TREE THAT APOLLO MAKES FAMOUS.

§A   Vocabulary.

adnuo, adnuere, adnui ... *to nod; to nod assent* or *agreement*

agito, agitáre, agitávi, agitátus ... *to move, to shake*

Augustus, Augusta, Augustum ... *Augustan, of Augustus*

cacúmen, cacuminis, n. ... *top; treetop*

*****cano, canere, cecini** ... *to sing, to sing of; to sound the alarm; to relate, to exclaim, to proclaim*

Capitolium, Capitolii, n. ... (plur. may have sing. meaning) *the Capitol, the Capitoline Hill*

*****coma, comae,** f. ... *hair*

cortex, corticis, m. ... *bark* of a tree

*****custos, custódis,** c. ... *guard; doorkeeper, watchman; guardian, protector*

fidus, fida, fidum ... *faithful, faithful* to (+ dat.)

*****finio, finíre, finívi** or **finii, finítus** ... *to end, to finish; to stop speaking, to draw to a close*

frons, frondis, f. (gen. plur. **frondium**) ... *leaf; leafage, foliage*

*****habeo, habére, habui, habitus** ... *to have, to hold; to bear, to carry; to beget, to give birth to; to take* or *occupy the place of; (of leaves) to be covered with* or *entwined with*

honor, honóris, m. ... (plur. may have sing. meaning) *honor; glory, beauty; gift, offering*

intonsus, intonsa, intonsum ... *unshorn, unshaven*

Latius, Latia, Latium ... *Latin, Roman*

laurea, laureae, or **laurus, lauri,** f. ... *laurel, laurel-tree*

lignum, ligni, n. ... *wood*

nitor, nitóris, m. ... *brightness; beauty, radiance*

Paean, Paeánis, m. ... *Paean* (= Apollo)

piger, pigra, pigrum ... *lazy, inactive, sluggish*

pompa, pompae, f. ... *parade, procession*

*****postis, postis,** m. (gen. plur. **postium**) ... *door, doorpost;* (sometimes in plur.) *doorway, entrance, threshold*

praecordia, praecordiórum, n. ... (plur. noun with sing. meaning) *heart; chest, breast*

quercus, quercus, f. ... *oak-tree; wreath of oak-leaves*

*****ramus, rami,** m. ... *branch*

refugio, refugere, refúgi ... *to run away from; to shrink from, to recoil from*

stipes, stipitis, m. ... *trunk* of a tree

triumphus, triumphi, m. ... *triumph, triumphal procession;* (as proper noun) **Triumphus:** the cry *Triumphus* (uttered during the triumphal procession)

tueor, tuéri, tuitus sum ... *to look at; to protect, to watch over*

velox, velócis ... *swift;* **velociter:** *swiftly*

viso, visere, visi, visus ... *to behold, to look closely at*

Daphne Turns into a Tree That Apollo Makes Famous.

Vix prece finíta, torpor gravis occupat artus;

mollia cinguntur tenui praecordia libro;

in frondem crines, in ramos bracchia crescunt;

pes, modo tam velox, pigris radicibus haeret;

5   ora cacúmen habet. Remanet nitor unus in illa.

Hanc quoque Phoebus amat, positaque in stipite dextra,

sentit adhuc trepidáre novo sub cortice pectus,

complexusque suis ramos ut membra lacertis,

oscula dat ligno. Refugit tamen oscula lignum.

10   Cui deus "At, quoniam coniunx mea non potes esse,

arbor eris certe" dixit "mea. Semper habébunt

te coma, te citharae, te nostrae—laure—pharetrae.

Tu ducibus Latiis aderis, cum laeta Triumphum

vox canet et visent longas Capitolia pompas.

15   Postibus Augustis eadem fidissima custos

ante fores stabis mediamque tuebere quercum,

utque meum intonsis caput est iuvenále capillis,

tu quoque perpetuos semper gere frondis honóres!"

Finierat Paean. Factis modo laurea ramis

20   adnuit, utque caput visa est agitasse cacúmen.

Notes and Queries.

(1) **prece finíta:** What construction?

(4) **modo:** See above, Lesson 26, Section E, note to line 9.

(5) **habet:** What is the subject of this verb? What meaning of this verb best fits the context?

(6) **Hanc quoque:** Refers to Daphne in her new form, as a laurel.

(7) **sentit:** What construction does this verb introduce? What are the elements of this construction in this sentence?

(8) **complexusque:** See above, Lesson 30, Section E, note to line 3.—**ut membra:** That is, as if they were the limbs of a woman.

(9) **Refugit . . . oscula:** Even in her arboreal form, Daphne continues to react to Apollo's amorous advances. At this point, what does Ovid imply about Daphne's attitude toward her divine pursuer?

(10) **coniunx mea:** See above, Lesson 51, Section C, note to line 8.—**potes:** Tense, voice, mood, person, and number?

(11) **arbor eris . . . mea:** That is, the laurel will become Apollo's emblem, something with which Apollo will be identified for all time.—**habébunt:** Tense, voice, mood, person, and number? What meaning of this verb best fits the context?

(12) **te coma, te citharae, te . . . pharetrae:** See above, Lesson 49, Section D, note to line 7. What word should be carried forward from the first **te** clause to the second and third **te** clauses? What word (other than **laure**) should be carried back from the third **te** clause to the first and second **te** clauses? (Apollo's three special possessions—those mentioned in the above three clauses—will somehow be associated with the laurel on every conceivable occasion; the forms **citharae** and **pharetrae** appear in the plural because these same possessions will be associated with the laurel every time that Apollo uses them.)

(13) **ducibus Latiis:** Refers to victorious Roman generals, who would wear the laurel-wreath on their heads during the triumphal procession celebrating a great military victory—something described as occurring in the Rome of the future, as foreseen by Apollo in mythical times at the instant of Daphne's metamorphosis into a laurel-tree. (Julius Caesar, for example, made continuous use of this custom, partly in order to conceal his baldness, as shown by the chanting of his own soldiers during the procession that followed his Gallic victory: **urbáni, serváte uxóres, moechum calvum adducimus!** *watch your wives, you poor civilians, here comes Baldhead Lover-Boy!*)—

Triumphum: Refers to the actual cheer—**Io Triumphe!**—shouted during the triumphal procession by all the soldiers and spectators.

(13–14) **cum . . . canet . . . visent:** What construction? Tense, voice, mood, person, and number of **canet** and **visent?**

(14) **longas . . . pompas:** In Ovid's day, the triumphal procession started at the Campus Martius (an open plain just outside Rome), continued along the Circus Maximus (Rome's largest enclosure for chariot-racing), and finished at the Capitoline Hill (the site of the temple of Jupiter Capitolinus).

(15) **Postibus Augustis:** Refers to the entrance to Augustus's palace, before which two laurel-trees presumably stood as a tribute to the emperor for his military achievements—another phenomenon occurring in the Rome of the future, as foreseen by Apollo in mythical times at the instant of Daphne's metamorphosis into a laurel-tree. (Augustus Caesar—Rome's first emperor and Ovid's own contemporary—banished Ovid in 8 A.D. to Tomi, a town in Rumania on the Black Sea, because of some scandal or indiscretion never explicitly described by the poet in his surviving verses, except for his own ambiguous references to his **ars,** his **error,** and his **carmen.**)

(16) **mediamque . . . quercum:** Over the entrance and between the two laurel-trees, there presumably hung a wreath of oak-leaves called the Civic Crown, which the Senate awarded to a Roman soldier who had saved the life of a fellow-citizen and also conferred upon Augustus himself in 27 B.C. in recognition of his military accomplishments.— **tuebere:** See above, Lesson 32, Section E, note to lines 7–8.

(17) **intonsis . . . capillis:** When described as a god of prophecy, Apollo is usually portrayed with long, flowing locks.

(18) **perpetuos . . . honóres:** Refers to the fact that the laurel-tree does not shed its leaves in the winter.— **gere:** Tense, voice, mood, person, and number?

(19) **Finierat:** Tense, voice, mood, person, and number?— **Paean:** Originally, the physician of the gods, whose name and function were transferred to Apollo (see above, Lesson 52, Section C, note to line 18).

(19–20) **laurea . . . adnuit:** The arboreal Daphne continues to react to Apollo's amorous advances by physical gesture. At this point, what does Ovid imply about Daphne's attitude toward her divine pursuer? (The true laurel—that of history and classical literature, here the object of Apollo's affection—is native to the Mediterranean area and possesses fragrant leaves and beautiful foliage, which Apollo undoubtedly smells and beholds as the tree's branches sway to and fro.)

(20) **utque caput:** The **ut** in **utque** goes only with **caput** (compare the phrase **ut membra** in line 8), and the **-que** in **utque** connects the verbs **adnuit** and **visa est.—agitasse:** What is the direct object of this verb? What is the uncontracted form of this verb?

(general) The Apollo/Daphne episode illustrates one kind of love story found in Ovid's *Metamorphoses,* the kind involving the love of a god, where a powerful male deity pursues an innocent, powerless female who wants nothing to do with him, and where he succeeds in his quest in a way that brings pleasure to himself and pain to his victim.

LESSON 55

OVID: PYRAMUS AND THISBE SPEAK THROUGH A CRACK IN THE WALL.

§A   Vocabulary.

ambo, ambae, ambo ... (declined like **duo, duae, duo;** see *ARA,* App. C, p. 416, for the declension of this numeral) *both*

coctilis, coctile ... *baked; of baked brick*

coeo, coíre, coii ... *to go together; to meet, to join, to unite*

conscius, conscia, conscium ... *aware, conscious; privy* to, *witness* to; (masc./fem. as substantive) *witness, go-between*

contiguus, contigua, contiguum ... *adjacent, adjoining*

*__cresco, crescere, crevi, cretus__ ... *to spring* from; *to grow, to increase*

findo, findere, fidi, fissus ... *to split, to cleave*

*__murmur, murmuris,__ n. ... *roar, rumble; murmur, whisper*

notitia, notitiae, f. ... *acquaintance*

nutus, nutus, m. ... a *nod,* a *nodding*

olim ... *once, at that time*

*__orior, oríri, ortus sum__ ... *to rise, to arise;* **oriens, orientis,** m.: *sunrise;* (as proper noun) **Oriens:** the *East,* the *Orient*

paries, parietis, m. ... *wall* of a house

praefero, praeferre, praetuli, praelátus ... *to carry before; to prefer* to, *to esteem more highly* than (+ dat.)

*__pulcher, pulchra, pulchrum__ ... *beautiful, lovely; excellent, splendid*

Pyramus, Pyrami, m. ... the boy *Pyramus*

rima, rimae, f. ... *crack, chink*

saeculum, saeculi, n. ... *generation; age, century*

Semiramis, Semiramidis, f. ... *Semiramis,* queen of Babylon

*****signum, signi,** n. ... *sign, mark; signal, gesture; statue, sculpture*

*****tego, tegere, texi, tectus** ... *to cover, to conceal*

Thisbe, Thisbes, f. ... the girl *Thisbe*

transeo, transíre, transii ...*to go across; to pass over, to cross over*

uterque, utraque, utrumque (gen. sing. **utriusque, utriusque, utrius-que**) ... *each* (= each of two)

*****veto, vetáre, vetui, vetítus** ... *to forbid, to prohibit*

vicinia, viciniae, f. ... *neighborhood; closeness, proximity*

vitium, vitii, n. ... *fault, defect, imperfection*

§B   **Reading.**

Pyramus and Thisbe Speak through a Crack in the Wall.

Lessons 55–60 contain Ovid's story of Pyramus and Thisbe, the star-crossed lovers of classical mythology who face terrible consequences for attempting to see each other. Having been forbidden by their parents to spend any time together, Pyramus and Thisbe speak through a crack in the wall before deciding on a more daring course of action.

Pyramus et Thisbe—iuvenum pulcherrimus alter,

altera, quas Oriens habuit praeláta puellis—

contiguas tenuére domos, ubi dicitur altam

coctilibus muris cinxisse Semiramis urbem.

5   **Notitiam primosque gradus vicinia fecit;**

tempore crevit amor; taedae quoque iure coissent,

sed vetuére patres. Quod non potuére vetáre,

ex aequo captis ardébant mentibus ambo.

Conscius omnis abest; nutu signisque loquuntur;

10   quoque magis tegitur, tectus magis aestuat ignis.

Fissus erat tenui rima, quam duxerat olim

cum fieret, paries domui commúnis utrique.

Id vitium nulli per saecula longa notátum—

quid non sentit amor?—primi vidistis amantes,

15   et vocis fecistis iter; tutaeque per illud

murmure blanditiae minimo transíre solébant.

§C   **Notes and Queries.**

(1) **pulcherrimus:** Degree of adjective?

(2) **quas:** What is the antecedent (actually the postcedent)?—**Oriens:** Refers not to the countries of eastern Asia (i.e., China and Japan) but to the eastern part of the known world in classical antiquity, embracing the lands and regions east of the Mediterranean Sea (i.e., the Middle East).

(3) **contiguas tenuére domos:** That is, they were next-door neighbors. Tense, voice, mood, person, and number of **tenuére?**

(3–4) **altam coctilibus muribus . . . urbem:** In the dactylic hexameter, phrases consisting of nouns and adjectives may be arranged in such a way that one phrase may contain or enclose the other (see above, Lesson 50, Section C, note to line 3).

(4) **Semiramis:** The mythical queen believed to have built Babylon (a city in Iraq on the Euphrates River), famous for its luxury, its hanging gardens, and its colorfully glazed brick. (Although Ovid sets the story of Pyramus and Thisbe in Babylon, it represents a common type of love story found in Greek and Roman mythology, and in life in general.)

(5) **gradus:** After this noun supply *of love.*—**vicinia:** That is, the fact that they were living in adjacent houses.

(6) **taedae . . . iure:** When a bride and groom were united *by the law of the torch,* their union was celebrated by a torchlight procession, a ritual that characterized classical wedding-ceremonies in general. (See above, Lesson 46, Section C, Lesson 47, Section B, and Lesson 48, Section B, for the wedding-song composed by Catullus, where such a torchlight procession is implied, although not directly expressed.)—**coissent:** What use of the subjunctive? (See above, Lesson 22, Section E, note to line 4.)

(7) **sed vetuére patres:** In classical antiquity, parents normally selected the spouses of their children, especially in the case of their daughters, whose futures would be arranged with absolute control. (See above, Lesson 48, Section B, lines 21–28, for the conclusion of Catullus's wedding-song, which epitomizes the male-dominator attitude associated with many civilizations such as the classical.)—**Quod:** Here the relative has its antecedent (actually its postcedent) in line 8 as a whole, in the fact that Pyramus and Thisbe were yearning to see one another.

(8) **captis . . . mentibus:** What construction?—**ardébant:** Tense, voice, mood, person, and number?

(9) **Conscius omnis abest:** That is, Pyramus and Thisbe do not have any witness (or go-between) who can report them to their parents (or help them communicate with each other). Here one cannot really tell from the context whether the person being described refers to someone who could potentially harm or help the two young lovers.

(10) **quoque:** This word consists of the elements **quo** and **-que,** where **quo** *(by which)* corresponds to an understood **eo** *(by this)* in the next clause, each going with the **magis** in its own clause *(by which . . . more, by this . . . more,* or idiomatically, *the more . . . the more . . .).* (In this regard compare the fossilized use of the definite article in such English expressions as *the more, the merrier = by which [it is] more, by this [it is] merrier,* or *the bigger they are, the harder they fall = by which they are bigger, by this they fall harder.)*—**tectus:** Tense, voice, and mood? Subject of the verbal action?—**ignis:** To what fire does this refer? (See above, Lesson 4, Section E, note to line 13.)

(11) **Fissus erat:** What is the subject of this verb? Tense, voice, mood, person, and number?

(12) **Cum fieret:** What construction? Explain the use of the mood.

(13) **nulli:** Although dative, this word is best translated as ablative.—**notátum:** Tense, voice, and mood? Subject of the verbal action?

(14) **quid non sentit amor:** An observation about the power of love, not connected to the narrative and directed specifically to the reader.—**primi vidistis amantes:** Occasionally Ovid pauses to address one or more of his own characters (see above, Lesson 51, Section C, note to lines 6–7).

(15) **vocis fecistis iter:** Although the Latin idiom is *you made a way for the voice,* how would you express it in normal English?

(16) **blanditiae . . . transíre solébant:** That is, their loving words would cross over from one side of the wall to the other side—the only means by which Pyramus and Thisbe were able to communicate.

LESSON 56

OVID: PYRAMUS AND THISBE DECIDE TO SNEAK OUT OF THEIR HOUSES.

§A   **Vocabulary.**

anhelitus, anhelitus, m. ... *breath*

arduus, ardua, arduum ... *tall, lofty, towering*

*****arvum, arvi,** n. ... *field*

Auróra, Aurórae, f. ... the goddess *Aurora;* (of Aurora's realm) the *dawn,* the *morning*

bustum, busti, n. ... (plur. may have sing. meaning) *tomb*

capto, captáre, captávi, captátus ... *to seize; to catch, to draw in*

conterminus, contermina, conterminum ... *next* to, *close* to (+ dat.)

exeo, exíre, exívi or **exii** ... *to go out; to rise up, to overflow*

gelidus, gelida, gelidum ... *cold, chilly*

illinc ... *thence, from there, on that side*

invidus, invida, invidum ... *envious, jealous*

morus, mori, f. ... *mulberry-tree*

neu, neve ... *and lest, and that . . . not*

*****nimius, nimia, nimium** ... *too much; excessive, very great;* **nimium:** (adv.) *too much; excessively, exceedingly*

Ninus, Nini, m. ... *Ninus,* king of Nineveh

niveus, nivea, niveum ... *snowy, snow-white*

*nox, noctis, f. (gen. plur. **noctium**) ... *night;* **noctu:** *at night;* **sub noctem:** *toward nightfall*

*parvus, parva, parvum ... *small, little*

*pomum, pomi, n. ... *fruit*

posterus, postera, posterum ... *next, following;* **in posterum:** *until the next day*

pruinósus, pruinósa, pruinósum ... *frosty*

*quod ... *that; since, because; inasmuch as, in view of the fact that*

radius, radii, m. ... *ray* of the sun or moon

removeo, removére, remóvi, remótus ... *to move back; to remove, to take away*

sicco, siccáre, siccávi, siccátus ... *to dry*

sileo, silére, silui ... *to be silent;* **silens, silentis:** *silent*

spatior, spatiári, spatiátus sum ... *to walk about, to roam about*

statuo, statuere, statui, statútus ... *to place, to stand; to decide, to resolve*

transitus, transitus, m. ... *passage, passageway*

uber, uberis ... *plentiful, heavily laden*

*umbra, umbrae, f. ... *shade, darkness*

vicis (= nom. sing; gen. sing. not found) f. ... *turn, change;* **in vices** or **vicissim:** *in turn*

§B   Reading.

Pyramus and Thisbe Decide to Sneak Out of Their Houses.

Saepe, ubi constiterant hinc Thisbe Pyramus illinc,

inque vices fuerat captátus anhelitus oris,

"Invide" dicébant "paries, quid amantibus obstas?

Quantum erat, ut sineres toto nos corpore iungi,

5   aut—hoc si nimium est—vel ad oscula danda patéres?

Nec sumus ingráti; tibi nos debére fatémur,

quod datus est verbis ad amícas transitus aures."

Talia diversa nequiquam sede locúti,

sub noctem dixére "Vale!" partique dedére

10   oscula quisque suae non pervenientia contra.

Postera nocturnos Auróra removerat ignes,

solque pruinósas radiis siccaverat herbas.

Ad solitum coiére locum. Tum murmure parvo

multa prius questi, statuunt ut nocte silenti

15   fallere custódes foribusque excedere temptent,

cumque domo exierint, urbis quoque tecta relinquant,

neve sit errandum lato spatiantibus arvo,

conveniant ad busta Nini lateantque sub umbra

arboris. Arbor ibi niveis uberrima pomis

20   (ardua morus) erat gelido contermina fonti.

§C   Notes and Queries.

(1) **hinc . . . illinc:** Refers to the opposite sides of the wall.

(2) **fuerat captátus:** See above, Lesson 17, Section E, note to line 15.—**anhelitus oris:** The one thing that Pyramus and Thisbe would listen for from their respective locations.

(3) **dicébant:** What is the subject of this verb? Tense, voice, mood, person, and number?—**paries:** Case and number? Function of this case?

(4) **Quantum erat:** Translate *would it be too much (to ask)*. What is the literal meaning of these words?

(4–5) **ut sineres . . . (ut) patéres:** Here the subjunctive clauses explain the interrogative **Quantum erat** (see above, Lesson 2, Section E, note to lines 11–12, and above, Lesson 7, Section E, note to line 5).

(5) **danda:** What verbal form? Case, number, and gender?

(6) **Nec sumus ingráti:** Having attacked the wall for keeping them apart, the young lovers suddenly apologize for their rash outburst.— **fatémur:** What construction does this verb introduce? What are the elements of this construction in this sentence?

(7) **quod:** What meaning of the conjunction (of the new meanings listed in the lesson vocabulary) best fits the clause **quod . . . aures?**

(8) **diversa:** The meter indicates that this adjective modifies the noun **sede.—sede:** What kind of ablative?—**locúti:** Tense, voice, and mood? Subject of the verbal action?

(9) **dixére:** Tense, voice, mood, person, and number?—**Vale:** Tense, voice, mood, person, and number?

(9–10) **partique . . . suae:** Refers to his or her own side of the wall.— **dedére . . . quisque:** See above, Lesson 25, Section F, note to line 2.

(10) **pervenientia:** Tense, voice, and mood? Subject of the verbal action?

(11) **Postera nocturnos Auróra . . . ignes:** See above, Lesson 49, Section D, note to line 6. (See also above, Lesson 46, Section D, note to line 7, for a phrase comparable to **nocturnos . . . ignes.**)

(13) **Ad solitum . . . locum:** See above, note to line 1, on **hinc . . . illinc.**

(14) **questi:** Tense, voice, and mood? Subject of the verbal action?— **statuunt:** Verbs designating something willed may introduce subjunctive clauses as their objects, which are called *substantive clauses of purpose* (see *ARA,* App. K, p. 474, Indirect Commands). Here the verb **statuunt** introduces four such subjunctive clauses, with the conjunction **ut** to be supplied with each of these clauses—**temptent** (line 15), **relinquant** (line 16), **conveniant** (line 18), and **lateantque** (line 18).

(15) **custódes:** Refers to the guardians or doorkeepers that parents employed in order to look after their children. (See above, Lesson 55, Section C, note to line 7, on how parents controlled their children in classical antiquity.)

(16) **exierint:** Either the perfect active subjunctive or the future perfect active indicative.

(17) **sit errandum ... spatiantibus:** In this use of the passive periphrastic, the dative of agent is a participle functioning as a substantive. Although the two verbal forms may seem repetitious, try to accommodate both of them in your translation.

(18) **Nini:** The mythical king believed to have founded Nineveh (a city in Iraq on the Tigris River) and believed to have been married to Semiramis (see above, Lesson 55, Section C, note to line 4, regarding the queen's architectural achievements).

LESSON 57

OVID: THISBE SEES A LIONESS AND RUNS AWAY WITHOUT HER CLOAK.

§A   Vocabulary.

adoperio, adoperíre, adoperui, adopertus ... *to cover*

amictus, amictus, m. ... (plur. may have sing. meaning) *clothing; cloak, garment*

antrum, antri, n. ... *cave, cavern*

*****aqua, aquae,** f. ... (plur. may have sing. meaning) *water; sea, ocean*

audax, audácis ... *bold*

Babylonius, Babylonia, Babylonium ... *Babylonian, of Babylon*

bos, bovis, c. (gen. plur. **bovum** or **boum**) ... *ox, cow; (in plur.) cattle*

callidus, callida, callidum ... *clever, resourceful*

cardo, cardinis, m. ... *hinge* of a door

compesco, compescere, compescui ... *to restrain; to slake or quench one's thirst*

cruento, cruentáre, cruentávi, cruentátus ... *to splatter with blood;* **cruentátus, cruentáta, cruentátum:** *bloody, blood-stained*

*****dico, dicere, dixi, dictus** ... *to say, to speak; to call, to name; to specify, to designate*

*****egredior, egredi, egressus sum** ... *to go out; to get beyond*

*****labor, labi, lapsus sum** ... *to slip, to fall; to slip or fall* from (+ abl.); *to glide, to move smoothly; to wane, to decline, to draw to a close*

lanio, laniáre, laniávi, laniátus ... *to tear, to mangle, to lacerate*

leaena, leaenae, f. ... *lioness*

*luna, lunae, f. ... *moon;* (as proper noun) **Luna:** the *moon-goddess*

oblino, oblinere, oblévi, oblitus ... *to smear, to cover*

obscúrus, obscúra, obscúrum ... *dim, dark, dusky*

paciscor, pacisci, pactus sum ... *to make an agreement;* **pactus, pacta, pactum:** *agreed upon, stipulated;* **pactum, pacti,** n.: (plur. may have sing. meaning) *agreement, arrangement*

*praecipito, praecipitáre, praecipitávi, praecipitátus ... *to cast down, to throw down;* (in pass.) *to sink* into, *to descend* into (+ dat.)

rictus, rictus, m. ... *jaw, jowl*

sitis, sitis, f. ... *thirst*

spumo, spumáre, spumávi ... *to foam, to froth*

tardus, tarda, tardum ... *slow;* **tarde:** *slowly*

tumulus, tumuli, m. ... *mound, grave*

*unda, undae, f. ... *wave* of the sea; *water* of a river or spring

velámen, velaminis, n. ... (plur. may have sing. meaning) *clothing; cloak, garment*

vicínus, vicína, vicínum ... *nearby, neighboring*

§B   **Reading.**

Thisbe Sees a Lioness and Runs Away without Her Cloak.

Pacta placent; et lux, tarde discedere visa,

praecipitátur aquis, et aquis nox exit ab isdem.

Callida per tenebras versáto cardine Thisbe

egreditur, fallitque suos, adopertaque vultum

5   pervenit ad tumulum, dictaque sub arbore sedit.

Audácem faciébat amor. Venit ecce recenti

caede leaena boum spumantes oblita rictus,

depositúra sitim vicíni fontis in unda.

Quam procul ad lunae radios Babylonia Thisbe

10 vidit et obscúrum timido pede fugit in antrum,

dumque fugit, tergo velamina lapsa reliquit.

Ut lea saeva sitim multa compescuit unda,

dum redit in silvas, inventos forte sine ipsa

ore cruentáto tenues laniávit amictus.

15 Serius egressus, vestigia vidit in alto

pulvere certa ferae totoque expalluit ore

Pyramus.

§C   Notes and Queries.

(1) **Pacta placent:** To what arrangement(s) does **pacta** refer? What
should be supplied as the indirect object of **placent?—tarde discedere
visa:** The twilight seems all too drawn out in the eyes of Ovid's impatient lovers. (Tense, voice, and mood of **visa?** Subject of the verbal action of **visa?**)

(1–2) **lux . . . nox:** According to the usual mythological tradition, a
fresh-water river called Ocean encircled the entire ancient world;
each day the 'light' (or sun) and the 'night' (or moon) were believed to
rise from and descend into this continuous stream. The sun-god was
believed to live beyond this stream, ascend in the East each morning,
and descend in the West each evening; he was also believed to return
to the East at night in a huge golden cup that floated around the
world by way of the ocean-stream.

(2) **praecipitátur:** The twilight is actually quite short in the countries
of the eastern shore of the Mediterranean Sea. (Tense, voice, mood,
person, and number of **praecipitátur?** In what voice should the verb
praecipitátur here be translated?)—**aquis . . . aquis:** Case and number of the first **aquis?** Case and number of the second **aquis?—isdem:**
Alternate for **eisdem.**

(3) **Callida . . . versáto cardine Thisbe:** See above, Lesson 50, Section C, note to line 3. What construction do the words **versáto cardine** constitute?

(4) **suos:** See above, Lesson 56, Section C, note to line 15, for the noun to be supplied here.—**vultum:** See above, Lesson 51, Section C, note to line 2, for this use of the accusative.

(5) **ad tumulum, dictaque sub arbore:** See above, Lesson 56, Section B, lines 18–20. To what tomb does the first phrase refer? To what tree does the second phrase refer?

(6) **Audácem faciébat amor:** To whom does the adjective **Audácem** refer? (Show this by supplying a suitable pronoun in your translation.) See above, Lesson 55, Section B, line 14, for another example of Ovid's assessment of love as a powerful force in the affairs of human beings.

(7) **leaena:** Not the imagined lion that Septimius offers to face to prove his love for Acme (see above, Lesson 39, Section B, line 7, and Section C, note to line 7), but a real lioness on the prowl that Thisbe happens to come upon in attempting to execute her part of the arrangement to meet Pyramus.—**rictus:** See above, note to line 4, on **vultum.**

(8) **depositúra:** Tense, voice, and mood? Subject of the verbal action? (See above, Lesson 19, Section E, note to line 6, on **excitatúrus,** for this form of the verb.)—**sitim:** See *ARA,* App. C, p. 398, notes 5 and 6.

(9) **ad:** Here the preposition may simply mean *by the light of* or *in the light of.*—**Babylonia Thisbe:** See above, Lesson 55, Section C, note to line 4, on the setting of the story of Pyramus and Thisbe.

(11) **velamina:** Ovid does not make clear the exact nature of the garment that Thisbe accidentally drops in her haste to escape the notice of the blood-stained lioness. Inasmuch as Thisbe appears to have covered up her head for the secret rendezvous, the garment in question may refer to a cloak having some sort of hood.

(12) **sitim:** See above, note to line 8.

(13) **inventos:** Tense, voice, and mood? Subject of the verbal action?—**sine ipsa:** To whom does the pronoun **ipsa** refer? (Show this along with the force of **ipsa** in your translation.)

(14) **amictus:** Another ambiguous reference to the garment left behind by the anxious Thisbe.

(15) **Serius:** Degree of adverb?

(16) **certa:** What noun does this adjective modify?

(17) **Pyramus:** Here, for dramatic purposes, the subject is delayed until the end of the sentence. (The rest of this hexameter appears as the first line of the reading in the following lesson.)

LESSON 58

OVID: PYRAMUS FINDS THISBE'S CLOAK AND DECIDES TO COMMIT SUICIDE.

§A   **Vocabulary.**

accingo, accingere, accinxi, accinctus ... *to arm, to gird, to equip*

adspergo, adsperginis, f. ... a *scattering,* a *sprinkling*

aliter ... *otherwise;* **non aliter quam cum:** *not otherwise than when (= just as when)*

*****altus, alta, altum** ... (as seen from below) *high;* (as seen from above) *deep; high-born, distinguished;* **alte:** *on high, to a great height*

arboreus, arborea, arboreum ... *of the tree*

*****color, colóris,** m. ... *color; hue, tint*

consúmo, consumere, consumpsi, consumptus ... *to destroy; to devour, to eat up*

demitto, demittere, demísi, demissus ... *to send down; to plunge, to thrust*

divello, divellere, divelli, divulsus ... *to tear apart, to tear to pieces*

eiaculor, eiaculári, eiaculátus sum ... *to shoot out, to discharge*

emico, emicáre, emicui ... *to spurt out, to gush forth*

facies, faciéi, f. ... *face; look, appearance*

ferveo, fervére, ferbui ... *to boil; to be warm, to be inflamed*

fetus, fetus, m. ... *offspring; fruit* of a plant

fistula, fistulae, f. ... *pipe* for carrying water

forámen, foraminis, n. ... *hole, opening*

haustus, haustus, m. ... (plur. may have sing. meaning) a *drawing* of water; a *shedding* or *spilling* of blood

humus, humi, f. ... *earth, ground*

*****iaceo, iacére, iacui** ... *to lie; to recline* at a table; *to lie down, to lie sick, to lie dead* or *dying*

*****ictus, ictus,** m. ... *blow, stroke; jet* or *stream* of water

ilia, ilium, n. ... (plur. noun with sing. meaning) *side, flank; groin, loins*

madefacio, madefacere, madeféci, madefactus ... *to make wet; to soak, to drench*

morum, mori, n. ... *mulberry*

noceo, nocére, nocui ... *to harm, to injure* (+ dat.); **nocens, nocentis:** *harmful, injurious*

notus, nota, notum ... *known, familiar*

perimo, perimere, perémi, peremptus ... *to destroy; to kill, to slay*

*****purpureus, purpurea, purpureum** ... *purple, dark red; gleaming, beautiful*

*****radix, radícis,** f. (gen. plur. **radicium**) ... *root* of a plant

reperio, reperíre, repperi, repertus ... *to find, to discover*

resupínus, resupína, resupínum ... *facing upwards, flat on* one's *back*

rupes, rupis, f. ... *crag, cliff*

scindo, scindere, scidi, scissus ... *to split, to cleave*

strideo, stridére ... *to shriek, to screech; to sizzle, to sputter*

*****tingo, tingere, tinxi, tinctus** ... *to moisten; to wet, to dip; to tint, to tinge*

vitio, vitiáre, vitiávi, vitiátus ... *to damage, to weaken*

Pyramus Finds Thisbe's Cloak and Decides to Commit Suicide.

Ut vero vestem quoque sanguine tinctam

repperit, "Una duos" inquit "nox perdet amantes,

e quibus illa fuit longa dignissima vita.

Nostra nocens anima est. Ego te, miseranda, perémi,

5   in loca plena metus qui iussi nocte veníres,

nec prior huc veni. Nostrum divellite corpus

et sceleráta fero consumite viscera morsu,

o quicumque sub hac habitátis rupe leónes!

Sed timidi est optáre necem." Velamina Thisbes

10   tollit et ad pactae secum fert arboris umbram.

Utque dedit notae lacrimas dedit oscula vesti,

"Accipe nunc" inquit "nostri quoque sanguinis haustus!"

Quoque erat accinctus, demísit in ilia ferrum,

nec mora, ferventi moriens e vulnere traxit.

15   Ut iacuit resupínus humo, cruor emicat alte,

non aliter quam cum vitiáto fistula plumbo

scinditur et tenui stridente foramine longas

eiaculátur aquas atque ictibus aera rumpit.

Arborei fetus adspergine caedis in atram

20   vertuntur faciem, madefactaque sanguine radix

purpureo tingit pendentia mora colóre.

(1) **vestem:** See above, Lesson 57, Section C, notes to lines 11 and 14.

(2) **perdet:** Tense, voice, mood, person, and number? Conjugate **perdo** in this tense, voice, and mood.

(3) **dignissima:** To whom does this adjective refer? What phrase does this adjective govern?

(4) **miseranda:** The gerundive of the deponent verb **miseror,** here used as a substantive in the vocative case.

(5) **iussi... veníres:** Here the verb **iubeo** takes the subjunctive rather than the infinitive (compare *ARA,* Lesson 71, Section A), with the conjunction **ut** to be supplied before the subjunctive.

(7) **sceleráta fero... viscera morsu:** What kind of word order is illustrated by these nouns and adjectives?

(9) **timidi est:** Translate *it is the sign of a coward.* What is the literal meaning of these words?—**optáre necem:** Here Pyramus realizes that he should not ask lions to do to him what he should do to himself, namely, commit suicide.

(10) **pactae... arboris:** See above, Lesson 57, Section B, line 5, for the words **dictaque sub arbore.—fert:** Tense, voice, mood, person, and number? Conjugate **fero** in this tense, voice, and mood.

(13) **Quoque:** What is the antecedent (actually the postcedent) of the **Quo** in **Quoque?**

(14) **mora:** Of what noun—**mora** or **morum**—is this a form?—**ferventi:** See *ARA,* App. C, p. 405, note 13.

(15) **humo:** What kind of ablative?

(16) **non aliter quam cum:** What figure of speech do these words introduce? What two different things are being compared in these hexameters?—**vitiáto... plumbo:** What construction?

(17–18) **longas ... aquas:** Although the Latin idiom is *long water,* how would you express it in normal English?

(18) **aera:** Check the Cumulative Vocabulary for the accentuation of this word.

(19) **adspergine caedis:** When a noun has a verbal meaning, the genitive may be used with it to denote the object of the verbal action (see above, Lesson 30, Section E, note to line 2).

(19–20) **in atram vertuntur faciem:** A metamorphosis—here not the transformation of a woman into a laurel-tree but the transformation of the color of the fruit of the mulberry-tree from white to dark red.

(20–21) **radix . . . tingit:** That is, the color spreads from the roots up to the fruit-laden branches.

(21) **mora:** Of what noun—**mora** or **morum**—is this a form?

LESSON 59

OVID: THISBE COMES OUT OF HIDING AND FINDS PYRAMUS NEAR DEATH.

§A   Vocabulary.

*attollo, attollere ... *to lift up, to raise up*

buxus, buxi, f. ... *boxwood*

clarus, clara, clarum ... *clear, bright; loud, shrill*

cruentus, cruenta, cruentum ... *bloody*

exaudio, exaudíre, exaudívi, exaudítus ... *to hear, to listen to*

exhorresco, exhorrescere, exhorrui ... *to tremble, to shudder*

*exiguus, exigua, exiguum ... *tiny, small; mild, gentle*

gestio, gestíre, gestívi or gestii ... *to yearn, to be eager*

gravo, graváre, gravávi, gravátus ... *to make heavy, to weigh down*

*incertus, incerta, incertum ... *unsure, uncertain*

instar (indecl.) ... *image, likeness* (+ gen.)

*lacertus, lacerti, m. ... *upper arm;* (in general) *arm*

pallidus, pallida, pallidum ... *pale*

plangor, plangóris, m. ... (plur. may have sing. meaning) a *wailing*, a *lamentation*

pulso, pulsáre, pulsávi, pulsátus ... *to beat on, to kick at, to strike against*

remoror, remorári, remorátus sum ... *to delay, to hesitate*

*retro ... *back, backwards, back again*

*solum, soli, n. ... *earth, ground*

suppleo, supplére, supplévi, supplétus ... *to fill, to fill up*

tremebundus, tremebunda, tremebundum ... a *trembling,* a *quivering,* a *shivering*

*tremo, tremere, tremui ... *to tremble, to quiver, to shiver*

vito, vitáre, vitávi, vitátus ... *to shun, to avoid*

§B   Reading.

Thisbe Comes out of Hiding and Finds Pyramus near Death.

Ecce metu nondum posito, ne fallat amantem

illa redit, iuvenemque oculis animoque requírit,

quantaque vitárit narráre pericula gestit.

Utque locum et visa cognoscit in arbore formam,

5   sic facit incertam pomi color; haeret an haec sit.

Dum dubitat, tremebunda videt pulsáre cruentum

membra solum, retroque pedem tulit, oraque buxo

pallidióra gerens, exhorruit aequoris instar,

quod tremit, exigua cum summum stringitur aura.

10   Sed postquam remoráta suos cognóvit amóres,

percutit indignos claro plangóre lacertos,

et laniáta comas amplexaque corpus amátum,

vulnera supplévit lacrimis fletumque cruóri

miscuit, et gelidis in vultibus oscula figens,

15   "Pyrame," clamávit, "quis te mihi casus adémit?

Pyrame, responde! Tua te carissima Thisbe

nominat. Exaudi vultusque attolle iacentes!"

Ad nomen Thisbes oculos a morte gravátos

Pyramus erexit visaque recondidit illa.

§C   **Notes and Queries.**

(1) **metu . . . posito:** What construction?

(3) **quantaque vitárit . . . pericula:** What construction? (The form **vitárit** is contracted for **vitaverit.** Tense, voice, mood, person, and number of this form?)

(4) **visa . . . in arbore:** The equivalent of **visae arboris.** (See also above, Lesson 57, Section B, line 5, for the words **dictaque sub arbore,** and Lesson 58, Section B, line 10, for the words **pactae . . . arboris.**)

(4–5) **Utque . . . sic:** Although these words frequently introduce a simile in Latin poetry (see above, for example, Lesson 48, Section C, notes to lines 1–7 and 11–18), here they do not function in that capacity but in a concessive context (see above, Lesson 29, Section E, note to line 13, for this usage, and check the Cumulative Vocabulary for the most appropriate meanings).

(5) **facit incertam pomi color:** That is, although Thisbe had actually seen the tree just a little earlier, she has a problem recognizing it this time because of the metamorphosis that took place in her absence (see above, Lesson 58, Section C, note to lines 19–20).—**an haec sit:** What construction? To what does the pronoun **haec** refer?

(6) **videt:** What construction does this verb introduce? What are the elements of this construction in this sentence?

(6–7) **pulsáre cruentum membra solum:** One of the more grisly details in Ovid's *Metamorphoses,* in which Thisbe sees someone writhing on the ground in agony, whom she does not immediately recognize as Pyramus. (Ovid occasionally employs gruesome details in his stories, as in his account of Tereus's rape of Philomela, in which the victim's severed tongue twitches on the ground, still protesting the assault.)

(7) **retroque pedem tulit:** Although the Latin idiom is *and she pulled her foot back,* how would you express it in normal English?—**buxo:** This wood has a light yellow color. What kind of ablative is used here?

(8) **aequoris instar:** What figure of speech do these words introduce? What two different things are being compared in these hexameters? (Ovid occasionally describes the way in which a character feels by associating him/her with two separate images, which may appear to clash or compete with each other, as here, where after comparing Thisbe's pallor to the color of boxwood, he associates her shuddering with a natural phenomenon that happens on the surface of the sea.)

(9) **quod:** What is the antecedent? What word picks up this antecedent in the clause **cum . . . stringitur?**

(10) **amóres:** Here Ovid uses the plural of the noun **amor** as the equivalent of the participle **amantem,** when it functions strictly as a substantive. (See above, Lesson 39, Section B, line 1, for Catullus's use of the noun **amor** in this very same sense, there with reference to Septimius's Acme.)

(11) **indignos claro plangóre lacertos:** What kind of word order is illustrated by these nouns and adjectives?

(11–12) **percutit . . . laniáta . . . amplexaque:** In certain societies, including the classical, women normally mourn the loss of a loved one by engaging in the kinds of unrestrained physical gestures mentioned in these hexameters. (One finds such behavior described in classical literature as early as Homer's *Iliad,* in which—for example—Briseis tears at her face and her breasts as she beholds the dead body of Patroclus.)

(12) **comas:** See above, Lesson 51, Section C, note to line 2, for this use of the accusative.

(13) **vulnera supplévit lacrimis:** A touching scene, in which Ovid describes the only way in which Pyramus and Thisbe are able to experience some kind of physical union during their final moments in the world of the living.

(14) **gelidis:** That is, cold with death.

(15) **quis:** The interrogative may be used as an adjective (see above, Lesson 47, Section C, note to line 1).

(17) **iacentes:** Tense, voice, and mood? Subject of the verbal action?

(18) **gravátos:** Tense, voice, and mood? Subject of the verbal action?

(18–19) **oculos . . . erexit . . . recondidit:** One of the most poignant moments in Ovid's *Metamorphoses,* in which Pyramus regains consciousness for just an instant, for one final glimpse of his beloved.

(Although Ovid displays a propensity for gaity and humor, he also demonstrates an extraordinary power to effect pathos, especially for characters thrust into a premature death.)

(19) **visaque . . . illa:** What construction? To whom does the pronoun **illa** refer?

LESSON 60

OVID: THISBE MOURNS FOR PYRAMUS AND DECIDES TO
COMMIT SUICIDE. CLASSICAL TRADITION:
SHAKESPEARE'S A MIDSUMMER NIGHT'S DREAM.

§A   Vocabulary.

aptus, apta, aptum ... *suitable, appropriate* (+ dat.)

*__comes, comitis, c.__ ... *comrade, companion*

compóno, componere, composui, compositus ... *to put together, to place together*

ebur, eboris, n. ... *ivory; ivory sheath or scabbard*

geminus, gemina, geminum ... *two, twin; double, twofold*

incumbo, incumbere, incubui ... *to fall upon; to lean upon, to bend over* (+ dat.)

*__infélix, infelícis__ ... *unhappy, unfortunate*

*__letum, leti, n.__ ... *death*

*__luctus, luctus, m.__ ... (plur. may have sing. meaning) *mourning, lamentation*

mucro, mucrónis, m. ... *sword*

*__nec, neque__ ... *and not, nor; not, not even;* **nec .. , nec .. ,** *neither .. , nor .. ;* **neque .. , neque .. ,** *neither .. , nor ..*

permaturesco, permaturescere, permaturui ... *to ripen fully*

persequor, persequi, persecútus sum ... *to follow; to pursue, to avenge*

pullus, pulla, pullum ... *dark, dark colored*

revello, revellere, revelli, revulsus ... *to tear away, to remove forcibly*

*rogo, rogáre, rogávi, rogátus ... *to ask; to entreat, to beseech*

supersum, superesse, superfui ... *to remain, to be left* (+ dat.)

tepeo, tepére ... *to be warm*

urna, urnae, f. ... *jar; funeral urn*

*votum, voti, n. ... *vow; prayer, entreaty*

§B   **Reading.**

Thisbe Mourns for Pyramus and Decides to Commit Suicide.

Quae postquam vestemque suam cognóvit et ense

vidit ebur vacuum, "Tua te manus" inquit "amorque

perdidit, infélix! Est et mihi fortis in unum

hoc manus, est et amor; dabit hic in vulnera vires.

5   Persequar exstinctum, letique miserrima dicar

causa comesque tui. Quique a me morte revelli

heu sola poteras, poteris nec morte revelli.

Hoc tamen ambórum verbis estóte rogáti,

o multum miseri meus illiusque parentes,

10   ut, quos certus amor, quos hora novissima iunxit,

compóni tumulo non invideátis eódem!

At tu, quae ramis arbor miserabile corpus

nunc tegis uníus, mox es tectúra duórum,

signa tene caedis, pullosque et luctibus aptos

15   semper habe fetus, gemini monumenta cruóris!"

Dixit, et aptáto pectus mucróne sub imum

incubuit ferro, quod adhuc a caede tepébat.

Vota tamen tetigére deos, tetigére parentes:

nam color in pomo est (ubi permaturuit) ater,

20   quodque rogis superest, una requiescit in urna.

§C   **Notes and Queries.**

(1) **Quae:** To whom does this pronoun refer?

(3–4) **in unum hoc:** Translate *for this one deed.* What is the literal meaning? To what deed do these words refer?

(4) **manus . . . amor:** Thisbe offers Pyramus the same two things that Pyramus offered Thisbe (see **manus . . . amorque** in line 2 above).—**dabit:** Tense, voice, mood, person, and number? Conjugate **do** in this tense, voice, and mood.—**hic:** To what does this pronoun refer—**manus** or **amor?** Give a grammatical explanation for your answer.

(5) **exstinctum:** Tense, voice, and mood? What should be supplied as the subject of the verbal action?—**dicar:** Tense, voice, mood, person, and number? Conjugate **dico** in this tense, voice, and mood.

(6) **tui:** What noun does this adjective modify?—**Quique:** What should be supplied as the antecedent of the **Qui** in **Quique?**

(6–7) **revelli . . . poteras, poteris nec . . . revelli:** A seeming paradox, in which Thisbe sees death as separating and yet not separating the lovers. What does Thisbe imply that she will have to do in order to overcome the obstacle of this separation? (Tense, voice, mood, person, and number of **poteras?** Tense, voice, mood, person, and number of **poteris?**)

(8) **Hoc . . . estóte rogáti:** The form **estóte** is the future active imperative second person plural of **sum** (see *ARA*, App. J, p. 454); the pronoun **Hoc**, the imperative **estóte**, and the participle **rogáti** constitute an idiom meaning *you be entreated about this* (= *we entreat you about this* or *we make this entreaty to you*).

(9) **meus illiusque:** Here, perhaps for metrical reasons, the nominative singular of the adjective **meus** is used, where one might expect the nominative plural to modify **parentes;** the genitive singular of the pronoun **ille** is also used, in keeping with the usual practice of showing possession for the third person (see *ARA*, Lesson 26, Section C).

(10) **quos . . . quos:** Supply an antecedent that points to Pyramus and Thisbe. (Keep in mind that the masculine gender may be used to refer to a set or group [two or more people] consisting of both sexes.)

(10–11) **ut . . . non invideátis:** An indirect command following the exhortation **Hoc . . . estóte rogáti.** (Here **ut . . . non** is used instead of **ne** because **non invideátis** represents the action of a positive verb.)

(11) **compóni tumulo . . . eódem:** Having been thwarted by her parents and Pyramus's parents all along, Thisbe has every reason to believe that they will refuse to grant their children this final request as well.

(12) **quae:** What is the antecedent (actually the postcedent)?

(13) **es tectúra:** The future active participle combines with the different tenses of **sum** to form the Active Periphrastic Conjugation, designating future or intended action (see above, Lesson 29, Section E, note to lines 13–14).

(14–15) **pullosque . . . semper habe fetus:** Another reference to the metamorphosis of the fruit of the mulberry-tree, recalling the death of Pyramus (see above, Lesson 58, Section C, note to lines 19–20).

(16) **aptáto . . . mucróne:** What construction?

(17) **incubuit ferro:** Like Pyramus, Babylonian Thisbe commits suicide in a very Roman way, and in much the same way as the Roman heroine Lucretia (see above, Lesson 33, Section D, lines 16–18).

(18) **tetigére deos, tetigére parentes:** The repetition of the verb **tetigére** intensifies the pathos of the tragic event, as the devoted lovers succeed in moving heaven and earth to grant their final request.

(19) **color in pomo . . . ater:** The final reference to the metamorphosis of the fruit of the mulberry-tree, which ultimately becomes a painful memorial for the blood that Pyramus and Thisbe shed for each other.

(20) **quodque:** What should be supplied as the antecedent of the **quod** in **quodque?—rogis:** Here this noun is used in the plural, because Pyramus and Thisbe were placed on separate funeral pyres even though their ashes were eventually deposited in a single funeral urn.

(general) The Pyramus/Thisbe episode illustrates one pattern of love story found in Ovid's *Metamorphoses,* the kind centering on the love of mortals, in which two young people fall in love only to face terrible consequences, sometimes resulting in the death of one or both the lovers and revealing the pathetic and transient nature of love itself.

§D **Classical Tradition.** Ovid's *Metamorphoses,* the poet's most brilliant and comprehensive work, enjoyed a distinguished reputation among many classical and post-classical authors. It has been translated into English down through the ages, during the Renaissance by Arthur Golding, whose translation became known as 'Shakespeare's Ovid.'

Shakespeare adopted the Pyramus and Thisbe theme in *Romeo and Juliet* and parodied the Pyramus and Thisbe characters themselves in *A Midsummer Night's Dream.* In the following passage (quoted from *A Midsummer Night's Dream*), the mythical king Theseus observes in his palace a performance of the Pyramus and Thisbe story.

PYRAMUS
    O grim-looked night! O night with hue so black!
        O night, which ever art when day is not!
    O night, O night! Alack, alack, alack,
        I fear my Thisby's promise is forgot!
    And thou, O wall, O sweet, O lovely wall,
    That stand'st between her father's ground and mine!
    Thou wall, O wall, O sweet and lovely wall,
        Show me thy chink, to blink through with mine eyne!
    Thanks, courteous wall. Jove shield thee well for this!
        But what see I? No Thisby do I see.
    O wicked wall, through whom I see no bliss!
        Cursed be thy stones for thus deceiving me!
THESEUS
    The wall, methinks, being sensible, should
    curse again.
PYRAMUS
    No, in truth, sir, he should not. "Deceiving
    me" is Thisby's cue. She is to enter now, and I am to
    spy her through the wall. You shall see it will fall pat
    as I told you. Yonder she comes.
THISBY
    O wall, full often hast thou heard my moans,
        For parting my fair Pyramus and me!
    My cherry lips have often kissed thy stones,
        Thy stones with lime and hair knit up in thee.
PYRAMUS
    I see a voice: now will I to the chink,
        To spy an I can hear my Thisby's face.
    Thisby!
THISBY   My love thou art, my love I think.
PYRAMUS
    Think what thou wilt, I am thy lover's grace;
    And, like Limander, am I trusty still.

THISBY

And I like Helen, till the Fates me kill.

PYRAMUS

Not Shafulus to Procrus was so true.

THISBY

As Shafulus to Procrus, I to you.

PYRAMUS

O kiss me through the hole of this vile wall!

THISBY

I kiss the wall's hole, not your lips at all.

PYRAMUS

Wilt thou at Ninny's tomb meet me straightway?

THISBY

'Tide life, 'tide death, I come without delay.

LESSON 61

VERGIL. VERGIL: AENEAS HELPS THE TROJANS DISLODGE A TOWER ONTO THE GREEKS.

§A **Vergil.** Vergil (70 B.C.–19 B.C.), Rome's most celebrated poet, wrote the *Aeneid*, a twelve-book epic in dactylic hexameters on the adventures of the Trojan warrior Aeneas. Lessons 61–72 contain two sections of this epic: the first, on how the Greeks won the Trojan War; the second, on how Dido, queen of Carthage, fell in love with Aeneas.

§B **Vocabulary.**

Achaicus, Achaica, Achaicum ... *Achaean* (= Greek)

adgredior, adgredi, adgressus sum ... *to go towards; to assail, to attack*

Andromache, Andromaches, f. ... *Andromache,* wife of Hector

astrum, astri, n. ... *star*

Astyanax, Astyanactis, m. (acc. sing. **Astyanacta**) ... *Astyanax,* son of Hector

*****at** or **ast** ... *but*

avus, avi, m. ... *grandfather*

caecus, caeca, caecum ... *blind; hidden, concealed; aimless, purposeless*

*****circum** ... *around* (+ acc.); *around* (as adv.)

*****culmen, culminis,** n. ... (plur. may have sing. meaning) *roof; top, peak*

Danaus, Danai, m. (gen. plur. **Danaum**) ... a *Danaan* (= a Greek)

edúco, educere, eduxi, eductus ... *to lead out, to draw out;* (in passive) *to rise upward* from (+ abl.), *to extend skyward* from (+ abl.)

fastigium, fastigii, n. ... (plur. may have sing. meaning) *roof; top, peak*

incomitátus, incomitáta, incomitátum ... *unescorted, unaccompanied*

inritus, inrita, inritum ... *invalid; useless, ineffectual*

iunctúra, iunctúrae, f. ... *joint, connection*

pervius, pervia, pervium ... *open; accessible, traversable*

praeceps, praecipitis ... *headlong, rushing forward;* **in praecipiti:** *on the sheer edge, over a sheer drop*

Priamus, Priami, m. ... *Priam,* king of Troy

***regnum, regni,** n. ... (plur. may have sing. meaning) *kingdom*

repente ... *suddenly*

***ruína, ruínae,** f. ... *ruin, collapse; downfall, destruction*

socer, soceri, m. ... *father-in-law;* (in plur.) *parents-in-law*

sonitus, sonitus, m. ... *sound; noise, crash*

subeo, subíre, subívi or **subii** ... *to go underneath; to come forth, to come forward; to come to* or *enter* one's *mind*

tabulátum, tabuláti, n. ... *floor* or *storey* of a building

Teucri, Teucrórum, m. ... (plur. noun with plur. meaning) the *Teucri* (= the Trojans)

***traho, trahere, traxi, tractus** ... *to drag, to pull; to drag down, to pull down; to take along, to bring along*

Troia, Troiae, f. ... the city *Troy*

***turris, turris,** f. (gen. plur. **turrium**) ... *tower*

usus, usus, m. ... *use; right-of-way, through passage*

§C   **Reading.**

Aeneas Helps the Trojans Dislodge a Tower onto the Greeks.

Lessons 61–66 contain the section of Vergil's epic in which Aeneas describes to Dido, queen of Carthage, how the Greeks invaded Troy and captured Priam's palace. At a banquet arranged by Dido for Aeneas, Aeneas recalls how he climbed to the roof of the palace, where he helped his fellow-Trojans dislodge a tower onto the Greeks.

Limen erat caecaeque fores et pervius usus

tectórum inter se Priami postesque relicti

a tergo, infélix qua se (dum regna manébant)

saepius Andromache ferre incomitáta solébat

5   ad soceros et avo puerum Astyanacta trahébat.

Evádo ad summi fastigia culminis, unde

tela manu miseri iactábant inrita Teucri.

Turrim in praecipiti stantem summisque sub astra

eductam tectis, unde omnis Troia vidéri

10   et Danaum solitae naves et Achaica castra,

adgressi ferro circum, qua summa labantis

iunctúras tabuláta dabant, convellimus altis

sedibus impulimusque. Ea lapsa repente ruínam

cum sonitu trahit et Danaum super agmina late

15   incidit. Ast alii subeunt; nec saxa nec ullum

telórum interea cessat genus.

(1–2) **Limen erat . . . postesque relicti:** A series of phrases referring to the existence of a back entrance and corridor linking the parts of Priam's palace together.

(3) **regna:** Refers to Priam's domain before the Trojan War.—**manébant:** Tense, voice, mood, person, and number?

(3–4) **infélix . . . incomitáta:** What noun do these adjectives modify?

(4) **saepius:** Degree of adverb?

(5) **soceros:** Refers to Priam and Hecuba.—**avo:** To whom does this word refer? (Give the name of this individual.)

(6) **Evádo . . . culminis:** That is, Aeneas gets to the roof by means of the back entrance and an inner stairway.

(7) **tela . . . miseri . . . inrita Teucri:** What kind of word order is illustrated by these nouns and adjectives?

(8) **Turrim:** See above, Lesson 57, Section C, note to line 8. Of what two main verbs is this noun the direct object? (Although you may find the word order in this long sentence confusing, you should not have any problem as long as you pay attention to the endings of the words.)—**stantem:** Tense, voice, and mood? Subject of the verbal action?

(9) **eductam:** Tense, voice, and mood? Subject of the verbal action?—**Troia:** See *ARA,* Lesson 57, Section G, note to line 11.

(10) **solitae:** The equivalent of **solitae sunt,** with **Danaum . . . naves** as its subject. What variation of this form should be understood with **omnis Troia?** What variation of this form should be understood with **Achaica castra?**

(11) **adgressi:** Tense, voice, and mood? Subject of the verbal action?—**labantis:** See *ARA,* App. C, p. 405, note 14.

(12–13) **convellimus . . . impulimusque:** The subject is Aeneas and the other Trojans.

(13) **Ea:** To what does this pronoun refer?

(15) **alii:** Refers to other Greeks uninjured and undaunted by the sudden Trojan maneuver.—**subeunt:** Tense, voice, mood, person, and number?

(15–16) **nec . . . nec . . . cessat:** That is, the volleying of Trojan missiles does not let up in spite of the growing number of Greek soldiers who come on the scene in order to replace their fallen comrades.

(16) **telórum interea cessat genus:** An example of an incomplete hexameter, of which more than fifty are found throughout the *Aeneid,* commonly referred to as 'half-lines.' Vergil very likely intended to finish these half-lines but died before completing his epic, which was published posthumously by his literary executors Varius and Tucca.

LESSON 62

VERGIL: PYRRHUS STANDS AT THE GATE AND BREAKS THROUGH THE ENTRANCE.

§A   **Vocabulary.**

Achilles, Achillis, m. ... *Achilles,* the Greek warrior

aénus, aéna, aénum ... (**ae** not pronounced as diphthong but as two separate syllables) *brazen, of bronze*

aerátus, aeráta, aerátum ... *brazen, of bronze*

agitátor, agitatóris, m. ... *driver*

*__appareo, apparére, apparui__ ... *to appear; to become clear or evident*

armiger, armigeri, m. ... *armorbearer*

atrium, atrii, n. ... (plur. may have sing. meaning) *court; hall, room*

Automedon, Automedontis, m. ... *Automedon,* the Greek warrior

bipennis, bipennis, f. (abl. sing. **bipenni**) ... *ax*

bruma, brumae, f. ... *winter*

*__cardo, cardinis__,** m. ... *hinge* of a door

cavo, caváre, cavávi, cavátus ... *to hollow out, to cut through*

coluber, colubri, m. ... *snake, serpent*

convolvo, convolvere, convolvi, convolútus ... *to roll, to coil;* (of a snake) *to move* the back *in a winding path*

coruscus, corusca, coruscum ... *gleaming, glittering*

*__do, dare, dedi, datus__ ... *to give, to grant, to furnish; to make, to cause, to produce*

durus, dura, durum ... *hard, solid*

excído, excidere, excídi, excísus ... *to cut out, to hew out*

exsulto, exsultáre, exsultávi ... *to spring up; to exult, to rejoice*

fenestra, fenestrae, f. ... *window; hole, breach*

firmus, firma, firmum ... *firm, solid*

*flamma, flammae, f. ... *fire, flame; firebrand*

*frigidus, frigida, frigidum ... *cold;* (fem. sing. as substantive) *cold water*

gramen, graminis, n. ... *grass; plant, herb*

intus ... (adv.) *inside, within*

*lingua, linguae, f. ... (plur. may have sing. meaning) *tongue*

lubricus, lubrica, lubricum ... *slippery; sinuous, wriggling*

nitidus, nitida, nitidum ... *bright; shining, gleaming*

pasco, pascere, pavi, pastus ... (perf. part. may have act. meaning) *to feed, to feed on*

patesco, patescere, patui ... *to be open; to be revealed, to become visible*

penetrále, penetrális, n. (gen. plur. **penetralium**) ... *inner part* or *inner chamber* of a house

Periphas, Periphantis, m. ... *Periphas,* the Greek warrior

perrumpo, perrumpere, perrúpi, perruptus ... *to break through, to burst through*

*primus, prima, primum ... *first, foremost; nearest, closest; primal, primordial;* (masc. plur. as substantive) *chiefs, leaders, princes;* **primo** or **primum:** *first, at first, for the first time*

pubes, pubis, f. ... the *youth* (= young men)

Pyrrhus, Pyrrhi, m. ... *Pyrrhus,* son of Achilles (= Neoptolemus)

robur, roboris, n. ... (plur. may have sing. meaning) *oak tree, oak wood*

Scyrius, Scyria, Scyrium ... *Scyrian, of Scyros*

succédo, succedere, successi ... *to go under; to come up* or *come close* (+ dat.)

trabs, trabis, f. ... *beam* of wood

trisulcus, trisulca, trisulcum ... *three-forked*

vello, vellere, velli, vulsus ... *to tear, to pluck; to wrench, to dislodge*

vestibulum, vestibuli, n. ... *forecourt, entrance hall*

§B   Reading.

Pyrrhus Stands at the Gate and Breaks through the Entrance.

Vestibulum ante ipsum primoque in limine Pyrrhus

exsultat, telis et luce coruscus aéna—

qualis ubi in lucem coluber mala gramina pastus,

frigida sub terra tumidum quem bruma tegébat,

5   nunc, positis novus exuviis nitidusque iuventa,

lubrica convolvit subláto pectore terga,

arduus ad solem, et linguis micat ore trisulcis.

Una ingens Periphas et equórum agitátor Achillis,

armiger Automedon, una omnis Scyria pubes

10   succédunt tecto et flammas ad culmina iactant.

Ipse inter primos correpta dura bipenni

limina perrumpit, postisque a cardine vellit

aerátos; iamque, excísa trabe, firma cavávit

robora et ingentem lato dedit ore fenestram.

15   Appáret domus intus et atria longa patescunt;

apparent Priami et veterum penetralia regum,

armatosque vident stantis in limine primo.

§C   **Notes and Queries.**

(1) **primoque:** That is, *nearest* or *closest,* in the sense of being the first to be reached. (Here **primus** may also be regarded as the equivalent of **ipse** and may thus be translated with the usual meanings of **ipse.**)—**Pyrrhus:** This name, meaning *red-haired,* was given to Pyrrhus because he had red hair like Achilles or because Achilles was called Pyrrha when he disguised himself as girl in the court of Lycomedes (see *ARA,* Lesson 62, Section E, and Section F, note to lines 5–7). While he was hiding in Scyros, Achilles impregnated the king's daughter Deidamia, who gave birth to Pyrrhus, brought him up to adulthood, and handed him over to the Greeks when they needed him to fight in the Trojan War after Achilles himself was killed.

(2) **aéna:** Check the lesson vocabulary for the accentuation.

(3) **qualis ubi:** What figure of speech do these words introduce? What two different things are being compared in these hexameters?—**coluber:** After this noun supply the verb **exsultat.**

(4) **frigida:** The meter indicates that this adjective modifies the noun **bruma.**—**quem:** What is the antecedent?—**tegébat:** Tense, voice, mood, person, and number?

(5) **positis . . . exuviis:** What construction?

(6) **subláto:** Of what verb is this a form?

(8) **Periphas:** An obscure Greek warrior, whose name Vergil borrowed from Homer's *Iliad.*

(9) **Automedon:** This person came to Troy with Achilles and served as his charioteer.—**Scyria:** Why is this adjective used to describe the followers of Pyrrhus?

(11) **Ipse:** To whom does this pronoun refer?—**primos:** That is, the first of the Greeks prepared to break through the entrance.—**correpta . . . bipenni:** What construction?—**dura:** The meter indicates that this adjective modifies the noun **limina.**

(12) **postisque:** See above, Lesson 57, Section C, note to line 8, on **sitim.**

(13) **aerátos:** What noun does this adjective modify?

(14) **ingentem lato . . . ore fenestram:** What kind of word order is illustrated by these nouns and adjectives?

(15–16) **Appáret . . . appárent:** The repetition of the verb at the beginning of these hexameters calls attention to the violent military profanation of a peaceful domestic scene.

(17) **armatosque vident:** The subject of **vident** is either the Greeks (standing outside and looking inside) or the Trojans (standing inside and looking outside). If the subject is the Greeks, to whom does the word **armátos** refer? If the subject is the Trojans, to whom does the word **armátos** refer?—**stantis:** See above, Lesson 61, Section D, note to line 11.—**primo:** What meaning(s) of the adjective best fit(s) this context? (See above, note to line 1, for a similar use of this adjective.)

LESSON 63

VERGIL: THE GREEKS INVADE THE PALACE AND SLAUGHTER THE TROJANS.

§A   Vocabulary.

aditus, aditus, m. ... (plur. may have sing. meaning) *entry, approach; entrance, passageway*

agger, aggeris, m. ... (plur. may have sing. meaning) *heap, pile; dam, dike*

amnis, amnis, c. (gen. plur. **amnium**) ... *river, torrent*

*****ara, arae,** f. ... *altar*

aries, arietis, m. ... *ram; battering-ram;* (of the action of a battering-ram) a *pounding,* a *battering*

Atrídes, Atrídae, m. ... *son of Atreus;* (in plur.) *sons of Atreus* (= Agamemnon and Menelaus)

barbaricus, barbarica, barbaricum ... *foreign*

*****campus, campi,** m. ... *field, plain, ground*

cavus, cava, cavum ... *hollow, echoing*

claustrum, claustri, n. ... *bar, bolt*

compleo, complére, complévi, complétus ... *to fill; to fill* something (acc.) *with* something (abl.)

cumulus, cumuli, m. ... *heap, mass*

evinco, evincere, evíci, evictus ... *to conquer entirely; to win a way past, to overcome the resistance of*

femineus, feminea, femineum ... *womanly; of a woman, of the women*

ferio, feríre ... *to strike*

foedo, foedáre, foedávi, foedátus ... *to befoul; to defile, to pollute*

*furo, furere ... *to rage, to rush; to be frantic* or *frenzied*

*gemitus, gemitus, m. ... a *sigh,* a *groan;* a *sighing,* a *groaning*

gurges, gurgitis, m. ... *eddy, torrent;* a *flooding,* a *swirling*

Hecuba, Hecubae, f. ... *Hecuba,* queen of Troy

immitto, immittere, immísi, immissus ... *to let go, to urge on; to let in, to grant entry*

insto, instáre, institi ... *to press on, to pursue eagerly*

interior, interius ... (compar. adj.) *inner, inner part of*

*miles, militis, m. ... *soldier;* (collective sing.) *army, soldiers*

moles, molis, f. (gen. plur. **molium**) ... *mass, rock; breakwater, embankment*

Neoptolemus, Neoptolemi, m. ... *Neoptolemus,* son of Achilles (= Pyrrhus)

*nepos, nepótis, m. ... *grandchild; grandson*

oppóno, opponere, opposui, oppositus ... *to place before* or *against*

patrius, patria, patrium ... *of a father, of* one's *father*

procumbo, procumbere, procubui ... *to fall forward*

quinquaginta (indecl.) ... *fifty*

sacro, sacráre, sacrávi, sacrátus ... *to dedicate, to consecrate*

spolium, spolii, n. ... *booty, spoils*

spumeus, spumea, spumeum ... *foaming, frothing*

stabulum, stabuli, n. ... *shed, stable*

suffero, sufferre, sustuli, sublátus ... *to endure; to sustain, to withstand*

thalamus, thalami, m. ... (plur. may have sing. meaning) *bedroom, bedchamber*

trucído, trucidáre, trucidávi, trucidátus ... *to slaughter, to massacre*

*tumultus, tumultus, m. ... *confusion, disturbance*

ululo, ululáre, ululávi ... *to ring, to resound; to howl, to scream, to shriek*

§B   **Reading.**

The Greeks Invade the Palace and Slaughter the Trojans.

At domus interior gemitu miseroque tumultu

miscétur, penitusque cavae plangoribus aedes

femineis ululant. Ferit aurea sidera clamor.

Tum pavidae tectis matres ingentibus errant,

5   amplexaeque tenent postis atque oscula figunt.

Instat vi patria Pyrrhus; nec claustra nec ipsi

custódes sufferre valent; labat ariete crebro

ianua, et emóti procumbunt cardine postes.

Fit via vi; rumpunt aditus primosque trucídant

10   immissi Danai et late loca milite complent.

Non sic, aggeribus ruptis cum spumeus amnis

exiit oppositasque evícit gurgite moles,

fertur in arva furens cumulo camposque per omnis

cum stabulis armenta trahit. Vidi ipse furentem

15   caede Neoptolemum geminosque in limine Atrídas;

vidi Hecubam centumque nurus Priamumque per aras

sanguine foedantem quos ipse sacraverat ignis.

Quinquaginta illi thalami, spes tanta nepótum,

barbarico postes auro spoliisque superbi

20   procubuére. Tenent Danai, qua deficit ignis.

§C   **Notes and Queries.**

(3) **Ferit aurea sidera clamor:** This short poignant statement calls attention to the violent military profanation of the tranquil celestial order (compare above, Lesson 62, Section B, lines 15–16, and Section C, note to lines 15–16).

(4) **pavidae tectis matres ingentibus:** What kind of word order is illustrated by these nouns and adjectives?

(5) **amplexaeque tenent . . . figunt:** Here the women engage in these unrestrained physical gestures because they realize that as slaves of the Greeks they will never see their homeland again (compare above, Lesson 59, Section B, lines 11–12, and Section C, note to lines 11–12).—**postis:** See above, Lesson 57, Section C, note to line 8, on **sitim.**

(6) **vi:** Of what noun is this a form?

(8) **emóti:** Tense, voice, and mood? Subject of the verbal action?

(9) **Fit:** Of what verb is this a form? Tense, voice, mood, person, and number?—**primosque:** That is, the first men whom the Greeks see as soon as they break through the entrance.

(10) **immissi:** Tense, voice, and mood? Subject of the verbal action?

(11) **Non sic . . . cum:** What figure of speech do these words introduce? What two different things are being compared in these hexameters?—**aggeribus ruptis:** What construction?

(13) **furens:** Tense, voice, and mood? Subject of the verbal action?—**omnis:** See above, Lesson 46, Section D, note to line 3.

(14) **furentem:** Tense, voice, and mood? Subject of the verbal action?

(15) **Neoptolemum:** Pyrrhus's other name, meaning *new to the war* (see also above, Lesson 62, Section C, note to line 1, on his name).—**geminosque . . . Atrídas:** Refers to Agamemnon, who led the Greek forces in the Trojan War, and Menelaus, who sailed to Troy in order to reclaim his wife Helen.

(16) **centumque nurus:** Actually refers to Priam's fifty daughters and fifty daughters-in-law. (Priam is believed to have fathered fifty sons and fifty daughters by Hecuba and other women in the palace.)

(17) **quos:** What is the antecedent (actually the postcedent)? Why does the postcedent have the ending that it does?

(19) **barbarico:** That is, Trojan, from the point of view of Vergil's audience. (Vergil may not have noticed the oddity of having this word spoken by Aeneas, himself a Trojan.)—**superbi:** What noun does this adjective modify?

(20) **procubuére:** Tense, voice, mood, person, and number?

LESSON 64

VERGIL: PRIAM PUTS ON HIS ARMOR BUT IS RESTRAINED BY HECUBA.

§A   Vocabulary.

aether, aetheris, m. ... *sky, heaven*

aevum, aevi, n. ... *time, life; old age, length of years*

altaria, altarium, n. ... (plur. may have sing. meaning) *high altar; altar stones, altar shrines*

axis, axis, m. (gen. plur. **axium**) ... *axis; arch, vault*

ceu ... *as, like*

circumdo, circumdáre, circumdedi, circumdátus ... (perf. part. may have act. meaning) *to surround; to put on, to wear; to put or place* something (acc.) *around* something (dat.)

concédo, concedere, concessi ... *to withdraw, to come over*

condensus, condensa, condensum ... *crowded together, huddled together*

defensor, defensóris, m. ... *defender, protector;* (in plur.) *defense, protection*

***densus, densa, densum** ... *thick, thick of; crowding, thronging*

desuesco, desuescere, desuévi, desuétus ... *to become unaccustomed;* **desuétus, desuéta, desuétum:** *unaccustomed to being used*

***dirus, dira, dirum** ... *dreadful, frightful*

effor, effári, effátus sum ... *to speak*

egeo, egére, egui ... *to need, to require* (+ abl.)

*fatum, fati, n. ... (plur. may have sing. meaning) *fate, fortune, destiny*

Hector, Hectoris, m. ... *Hector,* the Trojan warrior

inutilis, inutile ... *useless, unfit for action*

*iuxta ... *next to, close to* (+ acc.); *near by, close by* (as adv.)

loco, locáre, locávi, locátus ... *to put, to place*

longaevus, longaeva, longaevum ... *old, aged*

senior, senióris, m. ... *older man;* (in plur.) *older men* (= the seniors)

*simulacrum, simulacri, n. ... *likeness; image, statue*

*sumo, sumere, sumpsi, sumptus ... *to take, to choose; to take up* or *strap on* arms

*tueor, tuéri, tuitus or tutus sum ... *to look at, to look after; to protect, to watch over*

§B   Reading.

Priam Puts On His Armor but Is Restrained by Hecuba.

Forsitan et, Priami fuerint quae fata, requíras.

Urbis uti captae casum convulsaque vidit

limina tectórum et medium in penetralibus hostem,

arma diu senior desuéta trementibus aevo

5   circumdat nequiquam umeris et inutile ferrum

cingitur, ac densos fertur moritúrus in hostis.

Aedibus in mediis nudoque sub aetheris axe

ingens ara fuit iuxtaque veterrima laurus,

incumbens arae atque umbra complexa penátis.

10   Hic Hecuba et natae nequiquam altaria circum,

praecipites atra ceu tempestáte columbae,

condensae et divum amplexae simulacra sedébant.

Ipsum autem sumptis Priamum iuvenalibus armis

ut vidit, "Quae mens tam dira, miserrime coniunx,

15   impulit his cingi telis? Aut quo ruis?" inquit.

"Non tali auxilio nec defensoribus istis

tempus eget; non, si ipse meus nunc adforet Hector.

Huc tandem concéde! Haec ara tuebitur omnis,

aut moriére simul." Sic, ore effáta, recépit

20   ad sese et sacra longaevum in sede locávit.

§C   **Notes and Queries.**

(1) **requíras:** What is the subject? (See above, Lesson 61, Section C.) What use of the subjunctive? What construction does it introduce? (The fact that the main verb is itself a subjunctive has no bearing on the rule for sequence of tenses or on the time designated by the subjunctive in the subordinate clause relative to that of the main verb.)

(2) **uti:** A variant of the conjunction **ut,** as listed in the Cumulative Vocabulary.

(3) **medium:** The accusative singular masculine, where one might expect the ablative plural neuter **mediis** modifying **penetralibus** (**mediis** appears in some manuscripts). Since **mediis** is metrically inadmissible, **medium** is the form usually printed, which modifies **hostem** by grammatical rule and **penetralibus** according to the sense.

(4) **senior:** Although this form is clearly comparative, here it may be translated simply as *old man,* as indeed Priam was at the time that the Greeks conquered the Trojans. (In ancient Rome, the **senióres**—men over the age of forty-five—were regarded as unsuitable for military service [compare above, Lesson 36, Section E, note to line 5].)—**desuéta:** Tense, voice, and mood? Subject of the verbal action?—**trementibus:** Tense, voice, and mood? Subject of the verbal action?

(5) **nequiquam . . . inutile:** These words call attention to the futility of Priam's gesture, to his pathetic attempt to assume a valiant stance in the face of a hopeless situation.

(6) **cingitur:** Here the passive should be translated in the active.— **moritúrus:** Tense, voice, and mood? Subject of the verbal action?

(8) **ara:** Refers to the altar of Zeus (= Jupiter) located in the courtyard of Priam's palace.—**laurus:** Here the laurel stands in a quasi-Roman setting because of its association with the penates (see above, Lesson 29, Section E, note to line 9).

(9) **umbra:** The meter indicates that this noun is in the ablative.

(10) **Hic:** The adverb, not the pronoun.—**natae:** See above, Lesson 63, Section C, note to line 16.

(11) **praecipites atra . . . tempestáte columbae:** What kind of word order is illustrated by these nouns and adjectives?

(12) **amplexae simulacra:** Here Vergil associates the women with the same activity that he had attributed a little earlier to the laurel-tree (see above, Section B, line 9; for the phrase **complexa penátis**).

(13) **sumptis . . . armis:** What construction?

(14) **Quae:** The interrogative may be used as an adjective (see above, Lesson 47, Section C, note to line 1).

(15) **impulit:** What should be supplied as the direct object?

(17) **si . . . adforet Hector:** The protasis of a present contrary to fact conditional sentence (see above, Lesson 23, Section A), where the apodosis is understood with the **non** and may be rendered by a clause such as *he would not be able to save Troy*. (Hector, Troy's greatest warrior during the Trojan War, had already been killed by Achilles at this point in time; for **adforet**, see *ARA*, App. J, p. 453, on **foret** as the alternate imperfect subjunctive third person singular of **esset**.)

(18) **tuebitur:** Tense, voice, mood, person, and number?—**omnis:** See above, Lesson 46, Section D, note to line 3.

(19) **moriére:** See above, Lesson 32, Section E, note to lines 7–8.— **simul:** What phrase should be supplied after this adverb?—**ore effáta:** Although the Latin idiom is *having spoken with her mouth*, how would you express it in normal English?—**recépit:** What should be supplied as the direct object?

(20) **sese:** See above, Lesson 37, Section E, note to line 8.—**sacra:** The meter indicates that this adjective modifies the noun **sede.**—**sede:** Refers to some sort of chair of throne in the vicinity of the altar.—**longaevum:** What use of the adjective?

(19–20) **Sic . . . recépit . . . locávit:** One of the most poignant moments in Vergil's *Aeneid,* where the helpless old king, wearing the armor of his youth, is assisted to his seat by the equally defenseless queen, who realizes that Troy is about to fall.

LESSON 65

VERGIL: PYRRHUS MURDERS POLITES AND IS REBUKED BY PRIAM.

§A   **Vocabulary.**

abstineo, abstinére, abstinui, abstentus ... *to hold back; to restrain* oneself

aes, aeris, n. ... *bronze*

ausum, ausi, n. ... *bold deed; crime, outrage*

clipeus, clipei, m. ... *shield*

conicio, conicere, coniéci, coniectus ... *to throw, to shoot; to throw* or *place* something (acc.) *in / into* something (acc.)

coram ... (adv.) *in* one's *presence, before* one's *own eyes*

*****curo, curáre, curávi, curátus** ... *to care; to care for, to look after*

elábor, elábi, elapsus sum ... *to slip away; to escape* from or *make* one's *escape* from (+ abl.)

erubesco, erubescere, erubui ... *to grow red; to feel shame for, to show respect for*

exclámo, exclamáre, exclamávi ... *to cry out, to utter aloud*

exsanguis, exsangue ... *bloodless*

for, fari, fatus sum ... *to speak*

fundo, fundere, fudi, fusus ... *to pour, to pour out*

*****funus, funeris,** n. ... *funeral; death, dead body*

grates, gratium, f. ... (plur. noun with sing. meaning) *thanks; gratitude, appreciation*

hasta, hastae, f. ... *spear*

Hectoreus, Hectorea, Hectoreum ... *of Hector*

imbellis, imbelle ... *unwarlike; not ready for war, not suited for war*

*****lustro, lustráre, lustrávi, lustrátus** ... *to purify; to run through, to roam through; to observe, to examine, to consider*

*****natus, nati,** m. ... *son*

*****parco, parcere, peperci** ... *to spare, to refrain from using* (+ dat.)

persolvo, persolvere, persolvi, persolútus ... *to pay back, to pay in full*

Polítes, Polítae, m. ... *Polites,* the Trojan warrior

porticus, porticus, f. ... *portico, colonnade*

*****praemium, praemii,** n. ... *reward, payment*

raucus, rauca, raucum ... *harsh-sounding; clanging, clashing*

remitto, remittere, remísi, remissus ... *to send back*

*****sero, serere, sevi, satus** ... *to plant; to arise* or *spring* from (+ abl.); **satus, sata, satum:** *born* from, *sprung* from (+ abl.)

umbo, umbónis, m. ... *boss* of a shield

§B   **Reading.**

Pyrrhus Murders Polites and Is Rebuked by Priam.

Ecce autem elapsus Pyrrhi de caede Polítes,

unus natórum Priami, per tela per hostis

porticibus longis fugit et vacua atria lustrat

saucius. Illum ardens infesto vulnere Pyrrhus

5   insequitur, iam iamque manu tenet et premit hasta.

Ut tandem ante oculos evásit et ora parentum,

concidit ac multo vitam cum sanguine fudit.

Hic Priamus, quamquam in media iam morte tenétur,

non tamen abstinuit nec voci iraeque pepercit:

10 "At tibi pro scelere," exclámat, "pro talibus ausis

di—si qua est caelo pietas, quae talia curet—

persolvant grates dignas et praemia reddant

debita, qui nati coram me cernere letum

fecisti et patrios foedasti funere vultus.

15 At non ille, satum quo te mentíris, Achilles

talis in hoste fuit Priamo; sed iura fidemque

supplicis erubuit, corpusque exsangue sepulchro

reddidit Hectoreum, meque in mea regna remísit."

Sic fatus senior, telumque imbelle sine ictu

20 coniécit, rauco quod protinus aere repulsum,

et summo clipei nequiquam umbóne pependit.

§C   **Notes and Queries.**

(1) **Pyrrhi de caede:** That is, from being murdered by Pyrrhus.—
Polítes: The last of Priam's sons to be killed during the Trojan War.

(2) **per tela per hostis:** Here the prepositional phrases are not joined
by any conjunction—a stylistic means of demonstrating how rapidly
Polites is running.

(3) **porticibus longis:** Very possibly an ablative of means rather than
place where.—**vacua atria:** That is, a part of the palace not yet filled
with Greek soldiers.

(4) **infesto vulnere:** What does this phrase suggest that Pyrrhus is
straining to do? (Here the noun **vulnus** does not mean *wound* but indicates the prospective source of the wound.)

(5) **iam iamque . . . tenet:** See above, Lesson 53, Section B, lines 11–12, where Ovid uses the same words in the simile about the hound chasing the hare. Ovid may well have borrowed this turn of phrase from Vergil, whose *Aeneid* was published prior to the *Metamorphoses.*—**premit hasta:** These words indicate either that Pyrrhus is running after Polites with the fervent intention of stabbing him with his spear or that he is already stabbing him, until he inflicts on the Trojan the death-dealing blow (a blow usually referred to as the coup de grâce).

(6–7) **evásit . . . concidit . . . fudit:** Having been stabbed by Pyrrhus, Polites has just enough strength to stagger to his father's feet, where he collapses and dies.

(8) **Hic:** The adverb, not the pronoun.

(9) **voci iraeque:** Although the Latin idiom is *voice and anger,* how would you express it in normal English?—**pepercit:** Of what verb is this a form? Tense, voice, mood, person, and number of this form?

(11) **si qua:** See above, Lesson 45, Section C, note to line 1.—**caelo:** What kind of ablative?—**quae . . . curet:** What construction? Tense, voice, mood, person, and number of **curet?**

(12) **persolvant . . . reddant:** See above, Lesson 39, Section C, note to line 7. Tense, voice, mood, person, and number of these two verbs?

(14) **foedasti:** What is the uncontracted form?

(15) **satum:** Of what verb is this a form? Tense, voice, and mood of this form? (Here **satum** is the equivalent of **satum esse.**)—**quo:** Translate the relative after **ille . . . Achilles** (a combined antecedent/postcedent) and remember to adjust the meaning of the relative to fit the clause in which it appears.—**mentíris:** What construction does this verb introduce? What are the elements of this construction in this sentence?

(15–16) **non . . . talis . . . fuit:** Translate *did not behave in such a way.* What is the literal meaning of these words?

(17–18) **erubuit . . . reddidit . . . remísit:** A reference to the meeting between Achilles and Priam—fully described in Homer's *Iliad,* Book 24—in which (after murdering Priam's son Hector) Achilles received Priam in his own tent, allowed the king to recover the body of Hector, and then enabled him to return safely to Troy in order to bury his son.

(19) **fatus:** The equivalent of what verb form?—**senior:** See above, Lesson 64, Section C, note to line 4.

(20) **repulsum:** The equivalent of what verb form?

(21) **umbóne:** A raised ornamentation on the shield, shaped (either by carving or hammering) from the material of the shield and intended to deflect a weapon thrown at the shield by one's adversary.

(20–21) **coniécit . . . pependit:** The final pathetic gesture of the old king, who (as he faces imminent death) throws the spear in vain, only to see it pierce the boss of the shield and hang there by its point.

LESSON 66

VERGIL: PYRRHUS MURDERS PRIAM AS AENEAS LOOKS ON IN HORROR.

§A   Vocabulary.

aequaevus, aequaeva, aequaevum ... *equal in age, of the same age*

Asia, Asiae, f. ... *Asia*

capulus, capuli, m. ... *hilt* of a sword

circumsto, circumstáre, circumsteti ... *to stand around; to surround, to encompass*

*****copia, copiae,** f. ... *plenty, abundance; force of men, supply of men;*
copiam facere: *to give* someone (dat.) *the chance or opportunity*

Creúsa, Creúsae, f. ... *Creusa,* wife of Aeneas

defetiscor, defetisci, defessus sum ... *to become tired, to become weary;* **defessus, defessa, defessum:** *tired, weary*

degener, degeneris ... *of inferior stock; unworthy, degenerate*

*****desero, deserere, deserui, desertus** ... *to desert, to abandon*

diripio, diripere, diripui, direptus ... *to snatch apart; to pillage, to plunder*

exhálo, exhaláre, exhalávi ... *to breathe out*

horror, horróris, m. ... a *bristling; fright, horror*

*****imágo, imaginis,** f. ... *image; form, likeness*

implico, implicáre, implicui, implicitus ... *to enfold, to entwine*

Iulus, Iuli, m. ... *Iulus,* son of Aeneas (= Ascanius)

laevus, laeva, laevum ... *left;* (fem. sing. as substantive): *left hand*

lapso, lapsáre ... *to slip*

*latus, lateris, n. ... *side, flank*

*mitto, mittere, misi, missus ... *to send, to let go; to bring, to place; to throw, to let fly; to throw down, to fling down*

*narro, narráre, narrávi, narrátus ... *to tell, to speak, to relate; to tell someone (dat.) about something (acc.)*

Pelídes, Pelídae, m. ... *Pelides* (= son of Peleus, i.e., Achilles)

Pergama, Pergamórum, n. ... (plur. noun with sing. meaning) *Pergamum,* citadel of Troy

regnátor, regnatóris, m. ... *king, ruler*

*respicio, respicere, respexi ... *to look back, to look around; to look at, to take notice of, to turn* one's *thoughts to*

tenus ... *up to, as far as* (+ abl.)

§B   **Reading.**

Pyrrhus Murders Priam As Aeneas Looks On in Horror.

Cui Pyrrhus: "Referes ergo haec et nuntius ibis

Pelídae genitóri. Illi mea tristia facta

degeneremque Neoptolemum narráre memento!

Nunc morere!" Hoc dicens, altaria ad ipsa trementem

5   traxit et in multo lapsantem sanguine nati,

implicuitque comam laeva, dextraque coruscum

extulit ac lateri capulo tenus abdidit ensem.

Haec finis Priami fatórum; hic exitus illum

sorte tulit, Troiam incensam et prolapsa videntem

10   Pergama, tot quondam populis terrisque superbum

regnatórem Asiae. Iacet ingens litore truncus,

avulsumque umeris caput et sine nomine corpus.

At me tum primum saevus circumstetit horror.

Obstipui; subiit cari genitóris imágo,

15   ut regem aequaevum crudéli vulnere vidi

vitam exhalantem; subiit deserta Creúsa

et direpta domus et parvi casus Iuli.

Respicio et, quae sit me circum copia, lustro.

Deseruére omnes defessi, et corpora saltu

20   ad terram misére aut ignibus aegra dedére.

§C   Notes and Queries.

(1) **Cui Pyrrhus:** What verb should be supplied with these words?—
Referes: Tense, voice, mood, person, and number?—**nuntius:**
Priam's final demeaning role, assigned to him by Pyrrhus with con-
siderable sarcasm.—**ibis:** Tense, voice, mood, person, and number?
Conjugate **eo** in the present tense of this voice and mood.

(2) **Pelídae genitóri:** These two nouns stand in apposition. Case and
number of these two nouns?

(2–3) **Illi . . . narráre memento:** A sarcastic reference to Priam's ac-
cusation that Pyrrhus lacks the compassion that Achilles had ultimately extended to him (see above, Lesson 65, Section B, lines 15–18).
(The form **memento** is the future active imperative second person
singular of the verb **memini**, listed in the Cumulative Vocabulary.)—
mea tristia facta degeneremque Neoptolemum: Here the direct objects consist of two different things—Pyrrhus's deeds and Pyrrhus
himself (that is, how degenerate Pyrrhus has become)—a seeming
disparity that one may alleviate in translation by balancing *my* in
mea tristia facta with *his* applied to **degeneremque Neoptolemum.**

(4) **morere:** See above, Lesson 8, Section E, note to line 7, on the deponent **Miserére.**—**trementem:** Tense, voice, and mood? Subject of the
verbal action?

(5) **nati:** To whom does this word refer? (Give the name of this individual.)

(6–7) **implicuitque . . . extulit . . . abdidit:** The murder is accomplished through a series of three specific actions, all of them performed rapidly and ruthlessly.

(6) **laeva, dextraque:** The meter indicates that these words are in the ablative.—**coruscum:** What noun does this adjective modify?

(7) **lateri:** The equivalent of **in latus.**—**capulo tenus:** The preposition **tenus** (*up to, as far as*) is used with the ablative of the word that precedes it, as here, where it is used with the ablative **capulo** (compare *ARA,* Lesson 68, Section F, note to line 9, on **deridendi gratia**).

(8) **Haec finis:** What verb should be supplied with these words?

(9) **tulit:** Tense, voice, mood, person, and number? Write out the conjugation of **fero** in the present tense of this voice and mood.

(10) **Pergama:** The Trojan citadel—a military stronghold serving as Troy's principal defense against any attack by an external enemy.—**populis terrisque:** Either dative, designating the peoples and places for whom the **regnatórem Asiae** was ruler, or ablative, designating the peoples and places in whom the **regnatórem Asiae** was glorying.

(11) **regnatórem Asiae:** Either in apposition with **illum,** referring to Priam, or in apposition with **Pergama,** referring to the Trojan citadel—a reference that Vergil may have deliberately left ambiguous in order to emphasize that the monarch who ruled for so many years and the city that stood for so many years fell at exactly the same time.

(11–12) **truncus . . . caput . . . corpus:** Here Vergil switches from the scene at the altar to a scene on the shore, where the subject is described as a nameless, headless corpse—a transition that provides a poignant picture of the horror of immediate destruction followed by the permanent desolation ultimately resulting from this destruction. Some scholars think that in this passage Vergil may be adapting another version of Priam's death, in which Pyrrhus murdered him at the shore near Achilles' tomb—a theory that may reflect badly on the poet, by implying that he is juxtaposing in the same passage two different versions of the murder, associated with two different places. Yet one may resolve this problem by identifying the corpse either with Priam, whom Pyrrhus could have killed at the altar and dragged to the shore, or with the Trojan citadel, which the Greek invaders left burning in ashes and crumbling in the dust, or (as with the phrase **regnatórem Asiae**) with the fallen monarch and his fallen kingdom.

(13) **primum saevus . . . horror:** Until the moment that Aeneas witnessed the murder of Priam, he had not shown any fear of the Greek soldiers, some of whom he and his comrades cut down on his way to Priam's palace.

(14) **genitóris:** Refers to Anchises, whom Aeneas had left at home while he himself went out to help his fellow-Trojans. (Aeneas was not one of the fifty sons of Priam, but the son of Anchises and the goddess Venus.)

(15–16) **regem . . . exhalantem:** The third and final reference to the murder of Priam—the event that shocks Aeneas into accepting the fact that Troy has finally and irrevocably fallen (see also above, Lesson 63, Section B, lines 16–17, and Lesson 66, Section B, lines 4–7).

(16) **Creúsa:** Aeneas's wife, one of the daughters of Priam and Hecuba, whom Aeneas had also left at home during the turmoil.

(17) **direpta domus:** Although Aeneas's house has not yet been plundered by the Greeks, Aeneas imagines that it has in fact been plundered because of the horror that has gripped hold of his mind.—**Iuli:** Aeneas's son, only a child at the time of the fall of Troy.

(18) **lustro:** This verb introduces the construction **quae sit . . . copia.** What construction do you think this is and what noun does the adjective **quae** modify?

(19–20) **Deseruére . . . misére . . . dedére:** Tense, voice, mood, person, and number of these three verbs? What did the soldiers on the roof eventually decide to do, as indicated by the verbs **misére** and **dedére?** (These two hexameters convey the despair and hopelessness of the situation in the citadel faced by the single surviving Trojan prince, who can no longer do anything to save his besieged homeland but must now concentrate on escaping from the flames with his followers and the members of his family who have managed to stay alive.)

(20) **aegra:** What noun does this adjective modify?

(general) Although one cannot know whether King Priam's Troy ever really existed or whether the Trojan War was actually fought, archaeologists believe that if Troy did exist, it must have stood in northwest Turkey near the city of Istanbul, on a site occupied by nine successive cities piled up one on top of the other over the centuries. As the result of numerous excavations conducted at this location in modern times in conjunction with comparative dating techniques, archaeologists associate the Troy of the Trojan War with the city of the seventh layer—that is, Troy 7A (counting from bottom to top)—a city once destroyed by a great fire and under violent circumstances.

(general) Of all the archaeologists associated with the excavations conducted in Turkey, the nineteenth-century German entrepreneur Heinrich Schliemann continues to receive the greatest attention, partly because of the buried treasure (vases, rings, crowns, daggers) he smuggled from Turkey to Greece and from Greece to Germany. Although the disputed treasure remained in Berlin from 1881 to 1945, the Russian troops discovered it at the end of World War II and sent it back through their lines to Moscow, where it remained out of sight for almost fifty years, until the Russians finally admitted its whereabouts and (in 1996) proceeded to display it at the Pushkin Museum.

LESSON 67

VERGIL: DIDO FALLS IN LOVE WITH AENEAS AND NEGLECTS HER DUTIES.

§A   Vocabulary.

*absens, absentis ... *away, absent*

Aenéas, Aenéae, m. (acc. sing. Aenéan) ... *Aeneas,* the Trojan warrior

aequo, aequáre, aequávi, aequátus ... *to make equal; to raise* to, *to lift up* to (+ dat.)

Ascanius, Ascanii, m. ... *Ascanius,* son of Aeneas (= Iulus)

*convivium, convivii, n. ... (plur. may have sing. meaning) *feast, banquet*

Cresius, Cresia, Cresium ... *Cretan, of Crete*

*demens, dementis ... *out of* one's *mind; frantic, frenzied*

Dictaeus, Dictaea, Dictaeum ... *of Mt. Dicte* (= Cretan, of Crete)

Dido, Didónis, f. ... *Dido,* queen of Carthage

exerceo, exercére, exercui, exercitus ... *to busy* or *occupy* oneself *with; to train* or *exercise* oneself *with*

exposco, exposcere, expoposci ... *to demand; to entreat earnestly*

Iliacus, Iliaca, Iliacum ... *of Ilium* (= Trojan, of Troy)

incautus, incauta, incautum ... *unwary, not alert*

incubo, incubáre, incubui ... *to lie on, to fall upon* (+ dat.)

interrumpo, interrumpere, interrúpi, interruptus ... *to break off, to interrupt* *iterum ... *again, a second time*

iuventus, iuventútis, f. ... *youth,* the *youth*

letális, letále ... *deadly*

machina, machinae, f. ... *machine; machinery, equipment*

maereo, maerére ... *to mourn, to grieve*

*nescius, nescia, nescium ... *not knowing, not realizing*

ostento, ostentáre, ostentávi, ostentátus ... *to display, to exhibit*

peragro, peragráre, peragrávi, peragrátus ... *to travel through; to traverse, to range over*

portus, portus, m. ... *port, harbor; haven, refuge*

propugnaculum, propugnaculi, n. ... *bulwark, rampart*

saltus, saltus, m. ... *pass, glade, ravine*

Sidonius, Sidonia, Sidonium ... *Sidonian, of Sidon*

stratum, strati, n. ... (plur. may have sing. meaning) *covering; bed, couch*

suadeo, suadére, suasi ... *to urge, to advise; to induce, to invite*

*uro, urere, ussi, ustus ... *to burn, to be on fire; to burn with desire, to burn with passion*

volatilis, volatile ... *able to fly; swift, rapid*

§B   Reading.

Dido Falls in Love with Aeneas and Neglects Her Duties.

Lessons 67–72 contain the section of Vergil's epic in which Dido, queen of Carthage, falls in love with Aeneas—one of the most memorable sections of this Latin classic. Having listened to Aeneas's tales of the Trojans at the banquet held in his honor, Dido becomes distracted in the extreme, to the point of neglecting her royal obligations.

Uritur infélix Dido totaque vagátur

urbe furens, qualis coniecta cerva sagitta,

quam procul incautam nemora inter Cresia fixit

pastor agens telis liquitque volatile ferrum

5   nescius; illa fuga silvas saltusque peragrat

Dictaeos; haeret lateri letális harundo.

Nunc media Aenéan secum per moenia ducit,

Sidoniasque ostentat opes urbemque parátam;

incipit effári, mediaque in voce resistit.

10   Nunc eadem labente die convivia quaerit,

Iliacosque iterum demens audíre labóres

exposcit, pendetque iterum narrantis ab ore.

Post ubi digressi, lumenque obscúra vicissim

luna premit suadentque cadentia sidera somnos,

15   sola domo maeret vacua, stratisque relictis

incubat. Illum absens absentem auditque videtque,

aut gremio Ascanium (genitóris imagine capta)

detinet, infandum si fallere possit amórem.

Non coeptae adsurgunt turres, non arma iuventus

20   exercet, portusve aut propugnacula bello

tuta parant; pendent opera interrupta, minaeque

murórum ingentes, aequataque machina caelo.

(general) This episode takes place the morning after the banquet in Aeneas's honor, shortly after Dido's sister Anna encourages her to seek a lasting union with Aeneas.

(2) **urbe:** What kind of ablative?—**qualis:** What figure of speech does this word introduce? What two different things are being compared in these hexameters?—**coniecta . . . sagitta:** What construction?

(3) **quam:** What is the antecedent?—**Cresia:** Crete is the largest of the Greek islands in the Mediterranean Sea.

(4) **liquitque:** After the verb **liquit** supply *in his prey* or *in his victim.*

(5) **illa:** To what does this pronoun refer?

(8) **Sidoniasque:** Refers to Tyre, Dido's original home in Phoenicia, on the coast of present-day Lebanon, from which she fled with her sister immediately after her brother murdered her husband.—**urbemque parátam:** Refers to Carthage, Dido's city under construction in northern Africa, in the vicinity of present-day Libya, which she has been building with the help of her Phoenician companions.

(9) **mediaque in voce resistit:** That is, she is overcome with emotion.

(10) **eadem:** The meter indicates that this adjective modifies the noun **convivia.**

(11) **Iliacosque . . . labóres:** Refers to the hardships that the Trojans suffered during the fall of Troy and during their wanderings after the Trojan War.

(12) **pendetque . . . ab ore:** Translate *and she hangs on the words.* What is the literal meaning of these words?—**narrantis:** Tense, voice, and mood? What should be supplied as subject of the verbal action?

(13) **digressi:** What is the subject of this verb? Explain the gender of this verb form.

(15) **vacua:** The meter indicates that this adjective modifies the noun **domo.**—**stratisque relictis:** Refers to the couch on which Aeneas had reclined at the banquet.

(16) **absens absentem:** That is, each is absent from the other—Dido from Aeneas, and Aeneas from Dido—although Dido imagines that Aeneas is present.

(17) **gremio Ascanium:** Here Dido imagines that she is again holding in her lap (as she did at the banquet) Aeneas's son Iulus, now seven years older than he was at the time of the fall of Troy (compare above, Lesson 66, Section C, note to line 17). At the banquet, Dido actually had fondled not Aeneas's son but Cupid disguised as Aeneas's son—the culmination of Venus's plan to cause Dido to fall in love with Aeneas in order to prevent her from doing anything to harm him.—**capta:** Tense, voice, and mood? Subject of the verbal action?

(18) **infandum:** That is, unable to be expressed in words.—**si fallere possit amórem:** A special kind of protasis, which does not set up the condition for the apodosis but conveys the idea of hope or purpose, in which instance **si** has the meaning *in the hope that.* (Tense, voice, mood, person, and number of **possit?**)

(20) **portusve:** Here the **-ve** in **portusve** has a negative force, since it introduces a third activity abandoned by the young Carthaginians.—**bello:** Either dative or ablative, both of which fit the context. If ablative, what kind of ablative do you think this is? (See above, Lesson 18, Section E, note to line 7, on **clade.**)

(21) **parant; pendent:** Whereas the verb **parant** has as its subject the young Carthaginians, the verb **pendent** has its subjects the three phrases that appear in succession after it.

(21–22) **minaeque murórum ingentes:** Although the Latin idiom is *huge threats of walls,* how would you express it in normal English?

(22) **machina:** Refers to the machinery/equipment used in the construction (such as a crane or scaffold) or to the brickwork/stonework resulting from the construction (such as a tower or rampart).

LESSON 68

VERGIL: DIDO AND AENEAS GO HUNTING, DRESSED IN MAGNIFICENT ATTIRE.

§A **Vocabulary.**

Agathyrsi, Agathyrsórum, m. ... (plur. noun with plur. meaning) the *Agathyrsi*

caterva, catervae, f. ... *crowd, throng*

chlamys, chlamydis, f. ... *cape, cloak*

chorus, chori, m. ... (plur. may have sing. meaning) the *festive dancing,* the *singing and dancing*

Cres, Cretis, m. ... a *Cretan*

Cynthus, Cynthi, m. ... the mountain *Cynthus*

deligo, deligere, delégi, delectus ... *to choose, to select*

Delos, Deli, f. ... the island *Delos*

Dryopes, Dryopum, m. ... (plur. noun with plur. meaning) the *Dryopes*

egregius, egregia, egregium ... *excellent, outstanding, illustrious*

eniteo, enitére ... *to shine forth* from (+ abl.)

eques, equitis, m. ... *horseman*

exorior, exoríri, exortus sum ... *to appear; to rise, to arise*

fibula, fibulae, f. ... *clasp, brooch*

fluentum, fluenti, n. ... *stream*

*fremo, fremere, fremui ... *to roar; to clamor, to raise* one's *voice*

frenum, freni, n. ... (plur. may have sing. meaning) *bridle; bit, rein*

gradior, gradi, gressus sum ... *to step, to walk*

*haud ... *not, not at all*

hibernus, hiberna, hibernum ... *wintry, of the winter*

*incédo, incedere, incessi ... *to go; to advance, to proceed*

infero, inferre, intuli, illátus ... *to carry in;* (with reflexive) *to advance* or *proceed* as someone (acc.)

instauro, instauráre, instaurávi, instaurátus ... *to renew, to restore*

iubar, iubaris, n. ... *sunlight, sunshine*

iugum, iugi, n. ... *yoke; ridge, slope*

limbus, limbi, m. ... *border* of a cloak

Lycia, Lyciae, f. ... the country *Lycia*

mando, mandere, mandi, mansus ... *to chew, to champ*

Massýlus, Massýla, Massýlum ... *Massylian* (= African)

maternus, materna, maternum ... *maternal, of one's mother*

nodo, nodáre, nodávi, nodátus ... *to knot, to fasten*

Oceanus, Oceani, m. ... the god *Ocean;* (of Ocean's realm) the *sea* or the *ocean*

odórus, odóra, odórum ... *keen-scented, strong-smelling*

ostrum, ostri, n. ... *purple*

Phrygius, Phrygia, Phrygium ... *Phrygian* (= Trojan)

*pingo, pingere, pinxi, pictus ... *to paint; to embroider*

plaga, plagae, f. ... (plur. may have sing. meaning) *net, snare*

Poenus, Poena, Poenum ... *Phoenician, Carthaginian;* (masc. sing. as substantive) a *Phoenician,* a *Carthaginian*

progredior, progredi, progressus sum ... *to go forth, to come forth* *rarus, rara, rarum ... *thin, loose; sparse, scattered; unusual, exquisite*

rete, retis, n. ... *net*

sonipes, sonipedis, m. ... *horse* (= one 'sounding with the feet')

*sono, sonáre, sonui ... *to sound, to shout; to rattle, to clatter;* **sonans, sonantis:** *loud, noisy*

*spumo, spumáre, spumávi ... *to foam, to froth*

stipo, stipáre, stipávi, stipátus ... *to crowd, to throng; to attend, to surround*

subnecto, subnectere, subnexi, subnexus ... *to bind, to bind up*

venabulum, venabuli, n. ... *hunting-spear*

Xanthus, Xanthi, m. ... the river *Xanthus*

§B   Reading.

Dido and Aeneas Go Hunting, Dressed in Magnificent Attire.

Oceanum interea surgens Auróra reliquit.

It portis iubare exorto delecta iuventus;

retia rara, plagae, lato venabula ferro;

Massylique ruunt equites et odóra canum vis.

5   Regínam thalamo cunctantem ad limina primi

Poenórum exspectant, ostroque insignis et auro

stat sonipes ac frena ferox spumantia mandit.

Tandem progreditur magna stipante caterva

Sidoniam picto chlamydem circumdata limbo.

10   Cui pharetra ex auro; crines nodantur in aurum;

aurea purpuream subnectit fibula vestem.

Nec non et Phrygii comites et laetus Iulus

incédunt. Ipse ante alios pulcherrimus omnis

infert se socium Aenéas atque agmina iungit.

15 Qualis ubi hibernam Lyciam Xanthique fluenta

deserit ac Delum maternam invísit Apollo

instauratque choros, mixtique altaria circum

Cretesque Dryopesque fremunt pictique Agathyrsi—

ipse iugis Cynthi graditur mollique fluentem

20 fronde premit crinem fingens atque implicat auro;

tela sonant umeris—haud illo segnior ibat

Aenéas; tantum egregio decus enitet ore.

§C **Notes and Queries.**

(general) This episode takes place shortly after a conversation between Juno and Venus, in which the two goddesses plot to unite Dido and Aeneas in a cave during a hunting-party.

(1) **Oceanum . . . reliquit:** See above, Lesson 57, Section C, note to lines 1–2.

(2) **It:** Tense, voice, mood, person, and number? Write out the conjugation of **eo** in this tense, voice, and mood.—**portis:** *Place from which* is occasionally expressed by the ablative without a preposition.—**iubare exorto:** What construction?—**delecta iuventus:** A collective singular, referring to the Carthaginians.

(3) **retia . . . plagae . . . venabula:** What verb should be supplied with these three subjects?

(4) **Massylique:** The Massylians were a people who lived in northern Africa.—**odóra:** Modifies what noun grammatically? Modifies what noun according to sense? (Translate the words involved according to sense.)

(5) **thalamo:** What kind of ablative?

(8) **progreditur:** What is the subject of this verb?—**magna:** The meter indicates that this adjective modifies the noun **caterva.**

(9) **Sidoniam picto chlamydem ... limbo:** What kind of word order is illustrated by these nouns and adjectives?

(10) **in aurum:** Refers to golden clasps or hairpins.

(11) **fibula:** The meter indicates that this noun is in the nominative.

(12) **Nec non:** See *ARA,* Lesson 66, Section H, note to line 4.—**Phrygii:** See *ARA,* Lesson 57, Section G, note to line 11.

(13) **omnis:** What word does this adjective modify?

(14) **agmina:** Refers to the two royal processions.

(15) **Qualis ubi:** What figure of speech do these words introduce? What two different things are being compared in these hexameters?

(15–16) **hibernam Lyciam ... deserit:** During the winter Apollo gave oracles in Lycia (a country in present-day Turkey), through which the river Xanthus flowed.

(16) **Delum maternam invísit:** During the summer Apollo gave oracles in Delos (an island in the Aegean Sea), where his mother Latona had given birth to him and his sister Diana.

(17) **instauratque choros:** Refers to a festival that took place in Delos in honor of Apollo, to which people traveled from the islands and coastal-cities of the Aegean Sea.

(18) **Cretesque:** See above, Lesson 67, Section C, note to line 3.—**Dryopesque:** The Dryopes were a people who lived in northern Greece.—**Agathyrsi:** The Agathyrsi were a people who lived in Scythia (see *ARA,* Lesson 16, Section H, note to line 7) and who apparently painted or tattooed their skin.

(19) **Cynthi:** A mountain on the island of Delos.

(19–20) **mollique ... fronde:** See above, Lesson 54, Section C, note to line 12.—**fluentem ... crinem:** See above, Lesson 54, Section C, note to line 17.

(21) **haud illo segnior:** That is, as dignified as Apollo. What kind of ablative is **illo?**—**ibat:** Tense, voice, mood, person, and number?

(22) **tantum:** What noun does this adjective modify?

LESSON 69

VERGIL: DIDO AND AENEAS SEEK SHELTER FROM A STORM IN THE SAME CAVE.

§A **Vocabulary.**

*acer, acris, acre ... *keen, sharp; wild, fierce; excited, spirited;* **acriter:** *keenly, sharply; wildly, fiercely; excitedly, spiritedly*

aper, apri, m. ... *boar*

capra, caprae, f. ... *she-goat*

commisceo, commiscére, commiscui, commixtus ... *to mix in, to mix together*

*culpa, culpae,** f. ... *fault, blame; sin, wrongdoing*

Dardanius, Dardania, Dardanium ... *Dardanian* (= Trojan)

decurro, decurrere, decurri ... *to run down* from, *to hurry down* from (+ abl.)

deicio, deicere, deiéci, deiectus ... *to throw down; to drive* from, *to dislodge* from (+ abl.)

devenio, deveníre, devéni ... *to come to, to arrive at*

*diversus, diversa, diversum** ... *different; opposite, separate*

*fama, famae,** f. ... *talk, rumor; fame, glory; reputation, respectability;* (as proper noun) **Fama:** the goddess *Rumor*

fulvus, fulva, fulvum ... *brown, tawny*

furtívus, furtíva, furtívum ... *stolen; secret, clandestine*

glomero, glomeráre, glomerávi, glomerátus ... *to mass* or *gather together* something (acc.)

grando, grandinis, f. ... *hail* (= pellets of ice)

invius, invia, invium ... *pathless, impassable*

Iuno, Iunónis, f. ... *Juno*

lustrum, lustri, n. ... *woodland; den* or *lair* of a wild animal

nimbus, nimbi, m. ... *cloud; rain, storm*

passim ... *far and wide, here and there*

praetereo, praeteríre, praeterívi or **praeterii** ... *to go past; to ride past, to gallop past*

praetexo, praetexere, praetexui, praetectus ... *to border; to cloak, to conceal*

pronuba, pronubae, f. ... *bride-attendant, bride-conductor*

pulverulentus, pulverulenta, pulverulentum ... *dusty, covered with dust*

*__saxum, saxi,__ n. ... *rock, stone; crag, cliff*

*__spelunca, speluncae,__ f. ... *cave*

transmitto, transmittere, transmísi, transmissus ... *to send across; to cross, to cross over*

Troiánus, Troiána, Troiánum ... *Trojan;* (masc. sing. as substantive) a *Trojan*

Tyrius, Tyria, Tyrium ... *Tyrian, of Tyre*

*__vertex, verticis,__ m. ... *whirlpool, whirlwind; top, peak, summit* of a cliff or mountain

§B   **Reading.**

Dido and Aeneas Seek Shelter from a Storm in the Same Cave.

Postquam altos ventum in montis atque invia lustra,

ecce ferae (saxi deiectae vertice) caprae

decurrére iugis; alia de parte patentis

transmittunt cursu campos atque agmina cervi

5   pulverulenta fuga glomerant montisque relinquunt.

At puer Ascanius mediis in vallibus acri

gaudet equo, iamque hos cursu iam praeterit illos,

spumantemque dari pecora inter inertia votis

optat aprum aut fulvum descendere monte leónem.

10   Interea magno miscéri murmure caelum

incipit; insequitur commixta grandine nimbus.

Et Tyrii comites passim et Troiána iuventus

Dardaniusque nepos Veneris diversa per agros

tecta metu petiére; ruunt de montibus amnes.

15   Speluncam Dido dux et Troiánus eandem

deveniunt. Prima et Tellus et pronuba Iuno

dant signum; fulsére ignes et conscius aether

conubiis, summoque ululárunt vertice Nymphae.

Ille dies primus leti primusque malórum

20   causa fuit; neque enim specie famáve movétur

nec iam furtívum Dido meditátur amórem;

coniugium vocat; hoc praetexit nomine culpam.

§C   Notes and Queries.

(1) **altos:** What noun does this adjective modify?—**ventum:** The equivalent of **ventum est.** How should this verb form be translated? (See above, Lesson 28, Section E, note to line 7.)

(2) **deiectae:** Tense, voice, and mood? Subject of the verbal action? (Here Vergil implies that the hunters have frightened the animals out of their dwellings.)

(3) **decurrére:** Tense, voice, mood, person, and number?—**patentis:** See above, Lesson 61, Section D, note to line 11.

(4) **cervi:** Of what three verbs is this noun the subject?

(5) **pulverulenta:** The meter indicates that this adjective modifies the noun **agmina.**

(7) **hos . . . illos:** These two pronouns probably refer to the **caprae** and the **cervi** as groups of animals in a general sense, despite their differences in gender.

(8) **spumantemque:** Tense, voice, and mood of **spumantem?** Subject of the verbal action of **spumantem?**

(9) **optat:** What construction does this verb introduce two times? What are the elements of this construction in this sentence? (See *ARA,* Lesson 61, Section F, note to line 15, on the translation of the present infinitive after verbs meaning *to hope/to pray/to promise.*)

(10–11) **Interea . . . nimbus:** The storm sent by Juno as part of the plot to unite Dido and Aeneas in a cave (see above, Lesson 68, Section C, general note).

(11) **commixta grandine:** What construction?

(12) **Tyrii:** See above, Lesson 67, Section C, note to line 8.

(13) **Dardaniusque nepos Veneris:** To whom do these words refer? (Give the name of this individual.) See above, Lesson 66, Section C, notes to lines 14 and 17, for a clue to the identity of this character.

(14) **metu:** What kind of ablative?

(15) **Dido dux et Troiánus:** That is, **Dido et dux Troiánus.** By postponing the conjunction, perhaps for metrical reasons, Vergil links Dido and Aeneas more closely—a connection strengthened by the repetition of the d's at the beginning of the words.

(16) **Prima . . . Tellus:** Here Earth is described as *primal* or *primordial,* because she is regarded as the oldest of divinities, the most elemental power and producer of living things.—**pronuba Iuno:** Here Juno, the patron goddess of marriage, is described as performing the function of the married woman who would normally conduct the bride to the bridal chamber.

(17–18) **ignes . . . aether . . . Nymphae:** A travesty of a traditional marriage-ceremony, in which nature and the supernatural take the parts normally performed by human beings: the lightning replaces the wedding-torches; the heaven replaces the human witnesses; the shrieking of the Nymphs replaces the singing of the wedding-song.

(18) **ululárunt:** What is the uncontracted form?—**vertice:** What kind of ablative?

(19) **primus:** Translate this adjective after rather than before the noun that it modifies.—**leti . . . malórum:** Alludes to the future suicide of Dido and possibly to the future conflict between the Romans (Aeneas's descendants) and the Carthaginians (Dido's descendants).

(22) **coniugium vocat:** The noun **coniugium** is in apposition with the direct object of the verb **vocat,** to be supplied from the overall context. (See above, Lesson 19, Section E, note to line 8, for the similar phrase **constantiam vocáre,** with the same kind of understood direct object.) Misled by the primal and elemental forces that seem to perform the ritual of a marriage-ceremony, Dido deludes herself into thinking that she is actually married to Aeneas and accordingly justifies to herself that she may now consummate her relationship with him.— **hoc . . . nomine:** That is, on the assumption that she is married.— **praetexit . . . culpam:** In many civilizations, including the classical, society has generally regarded sex outside of marriage as morally wrong, especially for women.

LESSON 70

VERGIL: RUMOR, A FOUL GODDESS, SPREADS THE TALE OF DIDO AND AENEAS.

§A   Vocabulary.

adquíro, adquirere, adquisívi, adquisítus ... *to acquire, to obtain*

Coeus, Coei, m. ... the Titan *Coeus*

***condo, condere, condidi, conditus** ... *to found; to put away, to preserve; to bury, to hide, to conceal*

declíno, declináre, declinávi, declinátus ... *to turn away; to shut or close one's eyes*

dignor, dignári, dignátus sum ... *to consider worthy; to deign, to condescend* (+ inf.)

Enceladus, Enceladi, m. ... the Giant *Enceladus*

extemplo ... *immediately*

***foedus, foeda, foedum** ... *foul; horrible, shameful*

***foveo, fovére, fovi, fotus** ... *to keep warm; to fondle, to caress; to coddle, to pamper, to indulge*

hiems, hiemis, f. ... *winter*

immemor, immemoris ... *unmindful* (+ gen.)

infectus, infecta, infectum ... *not done*

***ingredior, ingredi, ingressus sum** ... *to enter; to step on, to walk on* (+ abl.); *to begin, to begin to deal with*

luxus, luxus, m. ... *indulgence, extravagance*

mobilitas, mobilitátis, f. ... *speed*

monstrum, monstri, n. ... *omen; monster*

multiplex, multiplicis ... *manifold, multifarious*

nuntius, nuntia, nuntium ... *bringing word* or *news of* (+ gen.)

perhibeo, perhibére, perhibui, perhibitus ... *to assert, to maintain*

pluma, plumae, f. ... *feather*

pravus, prava, pravum ... *crooked, distorted*

progigno, progignere, progenui, progenitus ... *to beget, to give birth to*

***quot** . . . *as many;* **quot** . . , **tot** . . , *as many . . , so many . .*

repleo, replére, replévi, replétus ... *to fill again; to fill, to fill up*

subrigo, subrigere, subrexi, subrectus ... *to raise; to prick up* one's ears

subter ... (adv.) *below, beneath*

tenax, tenácis ... *tenacious* or *possessive of* (+ gen.)

***terra, terrae,** f. ... (plur. may have sing. meaning) *land, earth;* (as proper noun) **Terra:** the goddess *Earth*

territo, territáre, territávi, territátus ... *to terrify, to frighten*

***velox, velócis** ... *swift;* **velociter:** *swiftly*

vigeo, vigére, vigui ... *to thrive, to flourish*

vigil, vigilis ... *wakeful, watchful*

§B   Reading.

Rumor, A Foul Goddess, Spreads the Tale of Dido and Aeneas.

Extemplo Libyae magnas it Fama per urbes,

Fama, malum qua non aliud velocius ullum.

Mobilitáte viget, virisque adquírit eundo;

parva metu primo, mox sese attollit in auras,

5   ingrediturque solo, et caput inter nubila condit.

Illam Terra parens, ira inritáta deórum,

extrémam (ut perhibent) Coeo Enceladoque sorórem

progenuit, pedibus celerem et pernicibus alis,

monstrum horrendum, ingens, cui quot sunt corpore plumae,

10   tot vigiles oculi subter (mirabile dictu),

tot linguae, totidem ora sonant, tot subrigit auris.

Nocte volat caeli medio terraeque per umbram

stridens, nec dulci declínat lumina somno;

luce sedet custos aut summi culmine tecti

15   turribus aut altis, et magnas territat urbes,

tam ficti pravique tenax quam nuntia veri.

Haec tum multiplici populos sermóne replébat

gaudens, et pariter facta atque infecta canébat:

venisse Aenéan, Troiáno sanguine cretum,

20   cui se pulchra viro dignétur iungere Dido;

nunc hiemem inter se luxu (quam longa) fovére,

regnórum immemores turpique cupidine captos.

Haec passim dea foeda virum diffundit in ora.

§C   **Notes and Queries.**

(1) **Libyae:** See above, Lesson 67, Section C, note to line 8.—**it:** Tense, voice, mood, person, and number?

(2) **qua:** What kind of ablative is illustrated by the relative? What verb should be supplied in the clause introduced by the relative?

(3) **Mobilitáte viget:** Although other creatures grow weaker the faster they travel, Rumor becomes stronger the faster she travels.—**virisque:** The form **viris** is the alternate accusative plural for **vires.**—**eundo:** The gerund of the verb **eo.** (The four forms of the gerund of this verb are **eundi, eundo, eundum, eundo.**)

(4) **metu:** See above, Lesson 69, Section C, note to line 14.—**sese:** See above, Lesson 37, Section E, note to line 8.

(5) **solo:** What kind of ablative?

(6) **inritáta:** The meter indicates that this word is in the nominative—a form of the participle that introduces the phrase **ira . . . deórum.** (Regarding the translation of **ira . . . deórum,** see above, Lesson 30, Section E, note to line 2, and *ARA*, App. E, p. 423, Objective Genitive.) Earth was angry at Jupiter for killing her children, the Titans and the Giants, in the power struggle between Jupiter and her offspring.

(7) **extrémam . . . sorórem:** Rumor was Earth's youngest child, who would avenge the death of her siblings by punishing both gods and mortals with her malicious tongue.—**ut perhibent:** Refers to people in general, perhaps classical mythographers.—**Coeo Enceladoque:** The Titan Coeus and the Giant Enceladus were the children destroyed in the power struggle between Jupiter and Earth's offspring.

(10) **dictu:** What verbal form? Case and number?

(11) **tot:** What noun does the final **tot** in this hexameter modify?—**subrigit:** What is the subject of this verb?

(12) **caeli medio terraeque:** Translate *midway between heaven and earth.* What is the literal meaning of these words?

(16) **tenax . . . nuntia:** These adjectives refer to the same subject and introduce the same case.—**ficti pravique . . . veri:** Here the participle and the adjectives are used as substantives. How should these forms be translated in order to reflect this usage?

(18) **facta atque infecta:** Translate *fact and fiction* or *truths and lies.* Identify the forms joined by **atque** and give their literal meaning.—**canébat:** What construction does this verb introduce? What are the elements of this construction in this sentence? (This construction occurs two times in this sentence—the first time in lines 19–20, and the second time in lines 21–22, where one element needs to be supplied.)

(20) **cui . . . dignétur:** What construction? (See above, Lesson 18, Section A.) What noun does the adjective **cui** modify? Tense, voice, mood, person, and number of **dignétur?**

(21) **hiemem inter se . . . fovére:** Translate *keep warm the winter between them* or *fondle one another during the winter.* How does the accusative **hiemem** function grammatically in each of these translations?—**quam longa:** Translate *as long (as it lasts).*

(22) **regnórum immemores:** This phrase clearly applies to both Dido and Aeneas—Dido, who has neglected her royal responsibilities (see above, Lesson 67, Section B, lines 19–22), and Aeneas, who has postponed his mission to found a city in Italy, as prophesied to him on several occasions, during the fall of Troy and after the Trojan War.

(23) **virum:** The alternate genitive plural of **virórum.**—**diffundit:** What is the direct object of this verb?

LESSON 71

VERGIL: IARBAS INVOKES JUPITER ABOUT THE AFFAIR OF DIDO AND AENEAS.

§A   Vocabulary.

aggero, aggeráre, aggerávi, aggerátus ... *to heap up; to increase, to intensify*

amárus, amára, amárum ... *bitter*

*__aro, aráre, arávi, arátus__ ... *to plow, to cultivate*

comitátus, comitátus, m. ... *retinue, company, following*

detorqueo, detorquére, detorsi, detortus ... *to bend, to turn, to direct one's course*

*__dictum, dicti,__ n. ... *word*

excubiae, excubiárum, f. ... (plur. noun with sing. meaning) *vigil; sentry, sentinel*

*__floreo, florére, florui__ ... *to bloom, to flourish; to be decked* with, *to be covered* with (+ abl.)

*__fulmen, fulminis,__ n. ... *thunderbolt*

Garamantis, Garamantidis ... *Garamantian* (= African)

Hammon, Hammónis, m. ... the god *Hammon*

*__horreo, horrére, horrui__ ... *to bristle; to shudder, to tremble; to shudder at, to tremble at*

Iarbas, Iarbae, m. (acc. sing. **Iarban**) ... the king *Iarbas*

immánis, immáne ... *huge, enormous*

*__inánis, ináne__ ... *empty, hollow*

Lenaeus, Lenaea, Lenaeum ... *Lenaean* (= Bacchic, of Bacchus)

libo, libáre, libávi, libátus ... *to pour as a libation; to pour* something (acc.) *as a libation* for someone (dat.)

madeo, madére ... *to be wet; to be wet with perfume*

Maeonius, Maeonia, Maeonium ... *Maeonian* (= Phrygian)

Maurusius, Maurusia, Maurusium ... *Maurusian* (= African)

mentum, menti, n. ... *chin*

mitra, mitrae, f. ... *turban, bonnet*

omnipotens, omnipotentis ... *almighty, all-powerful;* (as proper noun) **Omnipotens:** the *Almighty,* the *All-Powerful* (= Jupiter)

Paris, Paridis, m. ... *Paris* (= the Trojan Alexander)

pecus, pecudis, f. ... *beast, animal*

*****pretium, pretii,** n. ... *price*

quippe ... *indeed, of course, to be sure*

raptum, rapti, n. ... *booty, spoils*

semivir, semiviri, m. ... (noun with adj. force) *half-man; castrated, emasculated*

serta, sertórum, n. ... (plur. noun with plur. meaning) *wreaths, garlands*

supínus, supína, supínum ... *lying face upwards;* (of the hands) *upturned, turned upwards*

terrifico, terrificáre ... *to terrify, to frighten*

torus, tori, m. ... *bed, couch*

§B   Reading.

Iarbas Invokes Jupiter about the Affair of Dido and Aeneas.

Protinus ad regem cursus detorquet Iarban,

incenditque animum dictis atque aggerat iras.

Hic, Hammóne satus (rapta Garamantide nympha)

templa Iovi centum latis immania regnis,

5   centum aras posuit, vigilemque sacraverat ignem,

excubias divum aeternas; pecudumque cruóre

pingue solum et variis florentia limina sertis.

Isque, amens animi et rumóre accensus amáro,

dicitur ante aras media inter numina divum

10   multa Iovem manibus supplex orasse supínis:

"Iuppiter omnipotens, cui nunc Maurusia pictis

gens epuláta toris Lenaeum libat honórem,

aspicis haec? An te, genitor, cum fulmina torques,

nequiquam horrémus, caecique in nubibus ignes

15   terrificant animos et inania murmura miscent?

Femina, quae nostris errans in finibus urbem

exiguam pretio posuit, cui litus arandum

cuique loci leges dedimus, conubia nostra

reppulit ac dominum Aenéan in regna recépit.

20   At nunc ille Paris cum semiviro comitátu,

Maeonia mentum mitra crinemque madentem

subnexus, rapto potitur. Nos munera templis

quippe tuis ferimus famamque fovémus inánem."

§C   **Notes and Queries.**

(1) **detorquet:** What is the subject of this verb?—**Iarban:** An African king, who helped Dido get settled after she arrived in his country.

(3) **Hammóne:** A Libyan deity with a ram's head or horns, usually identified by the Romans with their own Jupiter (Jupiter Hammon = the cult-title of Jupiter in Africa).—**satus:** Of what verb is this a form? (See above, Lesson 65, Section B, line 15, and Section C, note to line 15, concerning this verb.)—**rapta . . . nympha:** What construction?—**Garamantide:** The Garamantes were a people who lived in the Eastern Sahara Desert, the home of the nymph ravished by Jupiter.

(7) **solum:** What verb should be supplied after this subject?

(8) **amens animi:** Although the Latin idiom is *crazed of mind,* how would you express it in normal English?

(9) **media inter numina:** Translate *amid the majesty.* What is the literal meaning?

(10) **orasse:** What is the uncontracted form? What meaning of this verb best accommodates the accusatives **multa** and **Iovem?**

(11–12) **Maurusia . . . gens:** Maurusia (or Mauretania) was a country in northern Africa, corresponding to parts of present-day Algeria and Morocco.

(12) **toris:** What kind of ablative?—**Lenaeum . . . honórem:** That is, the offering of wine, which the Maurusians poured as a libation to Bacchus, who was also known as Lenaeus (god of the wine-press).

(15) **inania murmura:** Of what verb is this the direct object?

(16) **Femina:** At this point Iarbas begins to speak about Dido in a way that exemplifies the male-dominator attitude of a primitive barbarian despot, who conceives of the queen as a mere possession, as someone whom he wanted to control as soon as she had arrived in his country.

(16–17) **urbem exiguam . . . posuit:** Here Iarbas refers to how Dido tricked him into giving her a large tract of land, first by getting him to agree to give her as much land as she could cover with a bull's hide, and then by cutting up the bull's hide into strips with which she proceeded to enclose enough land on which to build her new citadel.

(17) **pretio:** See above, Lesson 7, Section E, note to line 15.—**arandum:** What verbal form? Case, number, and gender? (Here translate this form not literally but according to sense.)

(18) **loci leges:** Refers to the conditions of tenancy imposed by Iarbas on the land that had been acquired by Dido.—**dedimus:** See above, Lesson 49, Section D, note to lines 7–9.—**conubia nostra:** Apparently Iarbas had made some kind of futile overture to Dido about marriage.

(20) **ille Paris:** Here Iarbas sarcastically refers to Aeneas as another Paris, inasmuch as he sees each of them as the abductor of another man's woman—Paris, as having taken away Helen from Menelaus, and Aeneas, as having taken away Dido from himself (Iarbas).—**semiviro comitátu:** Here Iarbas sarcastically compares Aeneas's companions to the eunuch-priests of the Phrygian goddess Cybele, who would work themselves into a frenzy during her ritual and castrate themselves as the culmination of their fanatical devotion to her.

(21) **Maeonia . . . mitra:** A kind of headdress fastened with ribbons under the chin, which was normally worn by Phrygian women.—**crinemque madentem:** That is, hair wet with myrrh or some similar perfume. (See *ARA*, Lesson 25, Section G, note to line 10, on the origin of the name of this arboreal substance.) Elsewhere in the *Aeneid,* the Italian warrior Turnus delivers a speech filled with sarcasm, in which he accuses Aeneas of heating his hair with a curling-iron.

(22) **subnexus:** Tense, voice, and mood? Subject of the verbal action?—**rapto:** To whom does this word refer?

(23) **famamque fovémus inánem:** A derogatory statement directed at Jupiter's character, in which Iarbas focuses on the god's inability to help him in spite of the fact that he has worshiped the god faithfully.

LESSON 72

VERGIL: JUPITER ASKS MERCURY TO ORDER AENEAS TO LEAVE CARTHAGE. CLASSICAL TRADITION: CHRISTOPHER MARLOWE'S DIDO, QUEEN OF CARTHAGE.

§A   Vocabulary.

*arx, arcis, f. (gen. plur. arcium) ... *citadel, fortress; peak, height, summit*

Ausonius, Ausonia, Ausonium ... *Ausonian* (= Italian)

bis ... *twice, on two occasions*

genetrix, genetrícis, f. ... *mother*

Graius, Graii, m. (gen. plur. Graiórum or Graium) ... a *Greek*

gravidus, gravida, gravidum ... *pregnant; swollen, teeming*

*inimícus, inimíca, inimícum ... *unfriendly*

Italia, Italiae, f. ... *Italy*

Karthágo, Karthaginis, f. ... the city *Carthage*

Lavinius, Lavinia, Lavinium ... *Lavinian, of Lavinium*

mando, mandáre, mandávi, mandátus ... *to entrust; to order, to command*

Mercurius, Mercurii, m. ... *Mercury*

molior, molíri, molítus sum ... *to work at, to build up; to take on, to shoulder*

*moror, morári, morátus sum ... *to delay, to tarry; to detain, to hold back*

*obliviscor, oblivisci, oblítus sum ... *to forget; to lose sight* of, *to put aside thoughts* of (+ gen.)

*orbis, orbis, m. (gen. plur. **orbium**) ... *circle; earth, world*

proles, prolis, f. ... *offspring*

struo, struere, struxi, structus ... *to arrange; to plan, to intend*

*super ... *over* (root meaning); *over, above* (+ acc.); *on, upon, on top of* (+ acc.); *regarding, concerning, in the matter of* (+ abl.)

Teucer, Teucri, m. ... *Teucer,* king of Troy

*vado, vadere, vasi ... *to go, to go forth*

vindico, vindicáre, vindicávi, vindicátus ... *to avenge; to claim, to claim* something (acc.) *for oneself* (dat.); *to rescue* or *protect* someone (acc.) *from something* (abl.)

Zephyrus, Zephyri, m. ... a *Zephyr* (= a west wind)

§B   **Reading.**

Jupiter Asks Mercury to Order Aeneas to Leave Carthage.

Talibus orantem dictis arasque tenentem

audiit Omnipotens, oculosque ad moenia torsit

regia et oblítos famae melióris amantis.

Tum sic Mercurium adloquitur ac talia mandat:

5   "Vade age, nate, voca Zephyros et labere pennis,

Dardaniumque ducem (Tyria Karthagine qui nunc

exspectat fatisque datas non respicit urbes)

adloquere, et celeris defer mea dicta per auras!

Non illum nobis genetrix pulcherrima talem

10   promísit (Graiumque ideo bis vindicat armis)

sed fore, qui gravidam imperiis belloque frementem

Italiam regeret, genus alto a sanguine Teucri

proderet, ac totum sub leges mitteret orbem.

Si nulla accendit tantárum gloria rerum,

15   nec super ipse sua molítur laude labórem,

Ascanióne pater Románas invidet arces?

Quid struit? Aut qua spe inimíca in gente morátur,

nec prolem Ausoniam et Lavinia respicit arva?

Naviget! Haec summa est, hic nostri nuntius esto!"

§C   **Notes and Queries.**

(1) **orantem . . . tenentem:** Tense, voice, and mood? Subject of the verbal action?

(3) **regia:** What noun does this adjective modify?—**oblítos famae melióris:** See above, Lesson 70, Section C, note to line 22.—**amantis:** To whom does this word refer? (Give the names of these individuals.)

(5) **Vade age:** These two imperatives combine to form an idiom meaning *go now* or *come now*.—**nate:** Mercury was the son of Jupiter and Maia, and is summoned in his capacity as messenger of the gods.—**labere:** See above, Lesson 8, Section E, note to line 7.—**pennis:** Refers to Mercury's winged sandals.

(6) **Dardaniumque ducem:** To whom do these words refer? (Give the name of this individual.)—**Tyria Karthagine:** See above, Lesson 67, Section C, note to line 8.

(7) **fatisque datas . . . urbes:** Refers to the cities that Aeneas and his descendants were destined to found, beginning with Aeneas's founding of Lavinium and culminating in the establishment of Rome.

(8) **adloquere:** Tense, voice, mood, person, and number?—**defer:** Tense, voice, mood, person, and number?

(9) **genetrix pulcherrima:** To whom do these words refer? (Give the name of this individual.) See also above, Lesson 66, Section C, note to line 14.

(10) **promísit:** This verb is used twice—first with a direct object in line 9 (**illum . . . talem,** referring to Aeneas as a man who has put off his mission for the sake of a love affair), then with an indirect statement in line 11 (with Aeneas to be supplied as the subject of **fore,** the future active infinitive of **sum** [see *ARA,* Appendix J, p. 454, note 2]).— **Graiumque . . . vindicat armis:** Refers to Venus's rescue of Aeneas during the Trojan War—first from the Greek warrior Diomedes and later from the flames of burning Troy. How can you explain Vergil's use of the present tense in this sentence, apart from the notion that he may be trying to depict the effects of Venus's actions as ongoing?

(12) **genus . . . Teucri:** In Vergil's day, the Romans claimed that they had achieved supremacy by fate and divine will—something that they attempted to prove by tracing their genealogy all the way back to Troy, in accordance with a prophecy in Homer's *Iliad* that Aeneas would survive the Trojan War and help perpetuate the race sprung from Teucer (Teucer was the first king of Troy, who ruled before Priam).

(12–13) **regeret . . . proderet . . . mitteret:** Tense, voice, mood, person, and number? Give two possible explanations for the use of the mood.

(15) **super:** What words does this preposition govern?

(16) **Ascanióne:** What two elements does this word consist of?— **Románas . . . arces:** Ascanius was destined to shift the seat of power from Lavinium to Alba Longa—another step in the direction of the eventual founding of Rome.

(17) **inimíca in gente:** Earlier in the *Aeneid,* in preparation for the arrival of Aeneas and the Trojans in Carthage, Jupiter had ordered Mercury to soften the militaristic attitude of the Carthaginians.

(19) **Naviget:** What use of the subjunctive?—**hic nostri nuntius esto:** This clause follows the structure and meaning of **Haec summa est,** with the unexpected change of mood from **est** to **esto.** (In this clause **nostri** is the alternate genitive plural of the pronoun **ego** [see *ARA,* App. C, p. 408, note 16], and **esto** is the future active imperative third person singular of the verb **sum** [see *ARA,* App. J, p. 454].)

(general) Jupiter's speech contains one of the finest statements in the *Aeneid* about Rome's mission to conquer and civilize other nations— a mission that Rome succeeded in accomplishing over the course of a millennium, during five hundred years in which she ruled as a Republic and five hundred years in which she ruled as an Empire. Rome indeed became the supreme power in the Mediterranean, rising from an insignificant pastoral settlement in central Italy to the most successful lawgiver and organizer in classical antiquity—a phenomenon foreseen by the king of the gods at a moment in time when Aeneas cannot fully understand the significance of his destiny.

(general) Although Vergil composed the *Aeneid* at the request of the emperor Augustus, partly to give the Romans a sense of their destiny through the experiences of Aeneas, he also conceived of his epic as a means of teaching the Romans a moral lesson about the horrors of war, at a time when they had just emerged from a period of anarchy. Under the reign of Augustus, who had transformed the Republic into an Empire and who would rule the Roman people and the Roman provinces with supreme authority, Vergil presented his country with an epic poem in which he not only glorified her magnificent heritage but also described the terrible penalty exacted on the road to conquest.

§D **Classical Tradition.** Vergil's *Aeneid* became Rome's great national epic, a work admired by the poet's own contemporaries and classical authors of subsequent generations. Its influence continued through the Middle Ages and the Renaissance, inspiring such poetic master-pieces as Dante's *Divine Comedy* and Milton's *Paradise Lost*.

The Dido and Aeneas story captured the imagination of Christopher Marlowe, regarded by some literary critics as the greatest English dramatist before Shakespeare. In the following selection (quoted from his *Dido, Queen of Carthage*), an interesting dialogue takes place between Dido and Aeneas during their rendezvous in the cave.

DIDO
  Aeneas!
AENEAS
  Dido!
DIDO
  Tell me, dear love, how found you out this cave?
AENEAS
  By chance, sweet Queen, as Mars and Venus met.
DIDO
  Why, that was in a net, where we are loose;
  And yet I am not free—O would I were!
AENEAS
  Why, what is it that Dido may desire
  And not obtain, be it in human power?
DIDO
  The thing that I will die before I ask,
  And yet desire to have before I die.
AENEAS
  It is not aught Aeneas may achieve?
DIDO
  Aeneas? No, although his eyes do pierce.

AENEAS
    What, hath Iarbas anger'd her in aught?
    And will she be avenged on his life?
DIDO
    Not anger'd me, except in ang'ring thee.
AENEAS
    Who, then, of all so cruel may he be
    That should detain thy eye in his defects?
DIDO
    The man that I do eye where'er I am,
    Whose amorous face, like Paean, sparkles fire,
    When as he butts his beams on Flora's bed.
    Prometheus hath put on Cupid's shape,
    And I must perish in his burning arms.
    Aeneas, O Aeneas, quench these flames!
AENEAS
    What ails my Queen, if she fall'n sick of late?
DIDO
    Not sick, my love, but sick I must conceal
    The torment that it boots me not reveal.
    And yet I'll speak, and yet I'll hold my peace.
    Do shame her worst, I will disclose my grief.
    Aeneas, thou art he—what did I say?
    Something it was that now I have forgot.
AENEAS
    What means fair Dido by this doubtful speech?
DIDO
    Nay, nothing, but Aeneas loves me not.
AENEAS
    Aeneas' thoughts dare not ascend so high
    As Dido's heart, which monarchs might not scale.

APPENDIX A

MODELS

This appendix includes all the new models that were presented in this text. The numbers in parentheses refer to the lessons in which these new models were first presented.

1. **amábo** (13)

2. **traham** (14)

3. **amavero** (15)

4. **amábor** (19)

5. **trahar** (20)

6. **amátus ero** (21)

	1.		2.		3.
	amábo		traham		amavero
	amábis		trahes		amaveris
	amábit		trahet		amaverit
	amabimus		trahémus		amaverimus
	amabitis		trahétis		amaveritis
	amábunt		trahent		amaverint

	4.		5.		6.
	amábor		trahar		amátus, -a, -um ero
	amaberis		trahéris		amátus, -a, -um eris
	amabitur		trahétur		amátus, -a, -um erit
	amabimur		trahémur		amáti, -ae, -a erimus
	amabimini		trahemini		amáti, -ae, -a eritis
	amabuntur		trahentur		amáti, -ae, -a erunt

1. **amábo** ⇒ Fut. act. ind.:

    amo (13)

    moneo (13)

2. **traham** ⇒ Fut. act. ind.:

    traho (14)

    audio (14)

    capio (14)

3. **amavero** ⇒ Fut. perf. act. ind.:

    amo (15)

    moneo (15)

    traho (15)

    audio (15)

    capio (15)

4. **amábor** ⇒ Fut. pass. ind.:

    amo (19)

    moneo (19)

5. **trahar** ⇒ Fut. pass. ind.:

    traho (20)

    audio (20)

    capio (20)

6. **amátus ero** ⇒ Fut. perf. pass. ind.:

    amo (21)

    moneo (21)

    traho (21)

    audio (21)

    capio (21)

APPENDIX B

IRREGULAR VERB FORMS

This appendix includes all the irregular verb forms required for memorization. The numbers in parentheses refer to the lessons in which these irregular verb forms were first presented.

1. **sum** (25)
2. **eram** (25)
3. **ero** (25)
4. **sim** (26)

5. **volo** (28)
6. **velim** (29)
7. **fero** (31)
8. **eo** (34)

1.	2.	3.	4.
sum	eram	ero	sim
es	eras	eris	sis
est	erat	erit	sit
sumus	erámus	erimus	simus
estis	erátis	eritis	sitis
sunt	erant	erunt	sint

5.	6.	7.	8.
volo	velim	fero	eo
vis	velis	fers	is
vult	velit	fert	it
volumus	velímus	ferimus	imus
vultis	velítis	fertis	itis
volunt	velint	ferunt	eunt

VERBS CONJUGATED LIKE IRREGULAR VERB FORMS

1. **sum** ⇒ Pres. act. ind.:

    sum (25)

    possum (25)

2. **eram** ⇒ Imperf. act. ind.:

    sum (25)

    possum (25)

3. **ero** ⇒ Fut. act. ind.:

    sum (25)

    possum (25)

4. **sim** ⇒ Pres. act. subj.:

    sum (26)

    possum (26)

5. **volo** ⇒ Pres. act. ind.:

    volo (28)

    nolo (28)

    malo (28)

6. **velim** ⇒ Pres. act. subj.:

    volo (29)

    nolo (29)

    malo (29)

7. **fero** ⇒ Pres. act. ind.:

    fero, act. (31)

    fero, pass. (31)

8. **eo** ⇒ Pres. act. ind.:

    eo (34)

APPENDIX C

VOCABULARY TO MEMORIZE

Lesson 1

amícus, aut, iuvenis, mihi, scio, osculum, te

Lesson 2

ago, casus, meus, nata, noster, tibi, tuus

Lesson 3

ante, iste, melior, misceo, plus, tu, vox

Lesson 4

animus, ignis, opto, sic, studium, tamen, unus

Lesson 5

bonus, dignus, domina, laudo, miser, quoque, torqueo

Lesson 6

ego, rumpo, me, membrum, per, quisquis, vultus

Lesson 7

amplus, civitas, emo, leno, princeps, prior, virginitas

Lesson 8

oro, dominus, populus, quis, turpis, valeo, villicus

Lesson 9

duco, ecce, libído, maximus, pietas, quam, similis

Lesson 10

verto, claudo, exitus, foris, modo, quantus, sto

Lesson 11

alter, ergo, eripio, exspecto, latus, pecunia, quicumque

Lesson 12

adhuc, ars, dein, liberális, lyra, maneo, universus

Lesson 13

gusto, magis, posco, rego, sol, studeo, -ve

Lesson 14

domus, fuga, malus, metus, nam, teneo, video

Lesson 15

an, avunculus, certus, inquit, lavo, magnus, quamquam

Lesson 16

levis, limen, nego, reddo, relinquo, surgo, tectum

Lesson 17

adversus, apud, cado, litus, lumen, novus, operio

Lesson 18

bellum, gero, liber, opera, otium, summus, vel

Lesson 19

coepi, debeo, divido, dubito, ideo, lego, somnus

Lesson 20

hora, ingens, ne, nubes, premo, quasi, vestigium

Lesson 21

bene, cingo, cinis, contra, cursus, modus, salvus

Lesson 22

augeo, fingo, liberi, qualis, quidem, ruo, via

Lesson 23

mox, nuntius, soleo, spes, tamquam, tandem, tenebrae

Lesson 24

ops, opus, parens, quisque, sors, tristis, urbs

Lesson 25

de, dux, fallo, plenus, recipio, res, sum

Lesson 26

ager, convenio, ferox, iungo, pater, plebs, pono

Lesson 27

accipio, flecto, frango, locus, pax, possum, trado

Lesson 28

adsum, agmen, cognosco, consilium, in, invenio, prex

Lesson 29

felix, -ne, obvius, pugno, sedes, ut, vita

Lesson 30

amplector, atrox, fletus, fortúna, invideo, laus, saepe

Lesson 31

adventus, cum, forte, muliebris, paucus, regius, specto

Lesson 32

circa, cum, ferrum, morior, satis, sinister, velut

Lesson 33

fero, ceterus, cubiculum, dexter, minimus, quaero, ullus

Lesson 34

cruor, fio, moveo, quisquam, superbus, voco, vulnus

Lesson 35

eo, caedes, celer, curro, facio, labor, simul

Lesson 36

armo, comprimo, imperium, incendo, inter, laetus, vetus

Lesson 37

bellus, cupído, deliciae, fleo, gremium, passer, puella

Lesson 38

amor, basium, candidus, cena, ceno, centum, mille

Lesson 39

beátus, malo, mollis, ni, os, paro, perdo

Lesson 40

desino, doleo, fulgeo, nolo, nullus, obdúro, volo

Lesson 41

barba, dens, fugio, indignus, praeter, puto, scribo

Lesson 42

ater, tango, excito, morbus, pinguis, quare, vester

Lesson 43

crux, demo, dulcis, excrucio, ludo, numquam, verus

Lesson 44

dono, gens, interea, lapis, mirus, multus, nequiquam

Lesson 45

credo, deus, difficilis, divus, mens, numen, potis

Lesson 46

cura, igitur, incipio, innuptus, ius, par, requíro

Lesson 47

ardeo, caelum, carpo, conubium, crudélis, lateo, vigilo

Lesson 48

aura, carus, dum, flos, iam, pars, tenuis

Lesson 49

cedo, cornu, fax, gloria, saevus, sterno, umerus

Lesson 50

amo, laedo, figo, lex, nympha, pharetra, protinus

Lesson 51

genitor, haereo, lux, pendeo, sidus, spero, verbum

Lesson 52

columba, herba, insequor, pastor, pateo, trepido, vacuus

Lesson 53

corpus, crinis, flumen, immineo, stringo, tergum, timidus

Lesson 54

cano, coma, custos, finio, habeo, postis, ramus

Lesson 55

cresco, murmur, orior, pulcher, signum, tego, veto

Lesson 56

arvum, nimius, nox, parvus, pomum, quod, umbra

Lesson 57

aqua, dico, egredior, labor, luna, praecipito, unda

Lesson 58

altus, color, iaceo, ictus, purpureus, radix, tingo

Lesson 59

attollo, exiguus, incertus, lacertus, retro, solum, tremo

Lesson 60

comes, infélix, letum, luctus, nec, rogo, votum

Lesson 61

at, circum, culmen, regnum, ruína, traho, turris

Lesson 62

appareo, cardo, do, flamma, frigidus, lingua, primus

Lesson 63

ara, campus, furo, gemitus, miles, nepos, tumultus

Lesson 64

densus, dirus, fatum, iuxta, simulacrum, sumo, tueor

Lesson 65

curo, funus, lustro, natus, parco, praemium, sero

Lesson 66

copia, desero, imágo, latus, mitto, narro, respicio

Lesson 67

absens, convivium, demens, iterum, iuventus, nescius, uro

Lesson 68

fremo, haud, incédo, pingo, rarus, sono, spumo

Lesson 69

acer, culpa, diversus, fama, saxum, spelunca, vertex

Lesson 70

condo, foedus, foveo, ingredior, quot, terra, velox

Lesson 71

aro, dictum, floreo, fulmen, horreo, inánis, pretium

Lesson 72

arx, inimícus, moror, obliviscor, orbis, super, vado

.

.

CUMULATIVE VOCABULARY

The Cumulative Vocabulary contains all the words that appear in the lesson vocabularies, as well as words marked for memorization in *ARA*. Words marked with an asterisk in this text are indicated by the number of the lesson enclosed in brackets following the vocabulary entry, e.g., [*1]. Words marked with an asterisk in *ARA* are indicated by the abbreviation *ARA* enclosed in brackets following the vocabulary entry, e.g., [*ARA]. Words marked with an asterisk in *ARA* that are updated are indicated by *ARA* and the number of the lesson in which they are updated, e.g., [*ARA, *1].

A

a, ab (**a** before a consonant, **ab** before a vowel or consonant) ... *from* (root meaning); *from, away from* (+ abl.); *by, at the hands of* (+ abl.) *[*ARA]*

abdo, abdere, abdidi, abditus ... *to hide, to conceal; to bury, to plunge*

abdúco, abducere, abduxi, abductus ... *to lead away*

abeo, abíre, abívi or **abii** ... *to go away; to turn* into, *to change* into

abicio, abicere, abiéci, abiectus ... *to throw from; to throw down*

ablátus ... see **aufero**

abrogo, abrogáre, abrogávi, abrogátus ... *to take away* from; *to revoke, to rescind*

abscédo, abscedere, abscessi ... *to depart, to go away*

abscondo, abscondere, abscondi, absconditus ... *to hide, to conceal*

absens, absentis ... *away, absent* [*67]

absolvo, absolvere, absolvi, absolútus ... *to free* someone (acc.) *from* something (abl.); *to finish, to complete* a project such as a book

abstergeo, abstergére, abstersi, abstersus ... *to wipe off, to wipe clean*

abstineo, abstinére, abstinui, abstentus ... *to hold back; to restrain* oneself

abstuli ... see **aufero**

absum, abesse, afui ... *to be absent, to be away*

absúmo, absumere, absumpsi, absumptus ... *to take away; to use up, to consume*

abútor, abúti, abúsus sum ... *to use up; to abuse, to exploit* (+ abl.)

ac, atque ... *and* [*ARA]

accédo, accedere, accessi ... *to approach, to come near*

accendo, accendere, accendi, accensus ... *to set on fire; to heat up, to intensify; to stir up, to instigate*

accido, accidere, accidi ... *to occur, to happen*

accingo, accingere, accinxi, accinctus ... *to arm, to gird, to equip*

accipio, accipere, accépi, acceptus ... *to obtain, to receive; to agree to, to consent to* [*ARA, *27]

acclamatio, acclamatiónis, f. ... *shout, shout of approval*

accommodo, accommodáre, accommodávi, accommodátus ... *to fit, to put on*

accubo, accubáre ... *to recline* at a table

acer, acris, acre ... *keen, sharp; wild, fierce; excited, spirited;* **acriter:** *keenly, sharply; wildly, fiercely; excitedly, spiritedly* [*69]

Achaicus, Achaica, Achaicum ... *Achaean* (= Greek)

Achilles, Achillis, m. ... *Achilles,* the Greek warrior

Acme, Acmes, f. (acc. sing. **Acmen**) ... the girl *Acme*

actio, actiónis, f. ... *deed, action*

acútus, acúta, acútum ... *sharp*

ad ... *to* (root meaning); *to, toward* (+ acc.); *upon, against* (+ acc.); *at, near, among* (+ acc.); *in response to* (+ acc.); *at the house of* (+ acc.); *for, for the purpose of* (+ acc.) *[*ARA]*

addíco, addicere, addixi, addictus ... *to give over; to sell, to assign*

addo, addere, addidi, additus ... *to add; to increase, to quicken* one's *step* or *pace*

addúco, adducere, adduxi, adductus ... *to lead forth; to draw back, to pull tight*

adeo ... *to the point, to such a degree, to such an extent [*ARA]*

adeo, adíre, adii ... *to go near, to approach*

adfero, adferre, attuli, adlátus ... *to bring to, to bring along*

adflo, adfláre, adflávi, adflátus ... *to breathe on*

adgredior, adgredi, adgressus sum ... *to go towards; to assail, to attack*

adhibeo, adhibére, adhibui, adhibitus ... *to hold out to; to summon, to call upon*

adhuc ... *still* [*12]

adimo, adimere, adémi, ademptus ... *to take away; to take* something (acc.) *from* someone (dat.)

adipiscor, adipisci, adeptus sum ... *to obtain, to acquire*

aditus, aditus, m. ... (plur. may have sing. meaning) *entry, approach; entrance, passageway*

adiungo, adiungere, adiunxi, adiunctus ... *to join to, to attach to;* (of an army) *to join* or *attach* oneself as an ally

adiúro, adiuráre, adiurávi, adiurátus ... *to swear to, to pledge to*

adiuvo, adiuváre, adiúvi, adiútus ... *to help, to assist*

adlátus ... see **adfero**

adloquor, adloqui, adlocútus sum ... *to speak to, to address*

administro, administráre, administrávi, administrátus ... *to assist; to manage, to administer*

admirabilis, admirabile ... *wonderful, remarkable;* **admirabiliter:** *wonderfully, remarkably*

admíror, admirári, admirátus sum ... *to wonder, to be amazed*

admitto, admittere, admísi, admissus ... *to send to; to admit, to let go; to allow* or *permit* a course of action

admoveo, admovére, admóvi, admótus ... *to move near, to place near*

adnítor, adníti, adnísus sum ... *to lean on; to strive, to exert effort*

adnuo, adnuere, adnui ... *to nod; to nod assent* or *agreement*

adoleo, adolére ... *to burn, to kindle*

adoperio, adoperíre, adoperui, adopertus ... *to cover*

adóro, adoráre, adorávi, adorátus ... *to beg, to entreat; to worship, to pay homage to*

adquíro, adquirere, adquisívi, adquisítus ... *to acquire, to obtain*

adsero, adserere, adserui, adsertus ... *to lay hold of, to lay claim to*

adspergo, adsperginis, f. ... *a scattering, a sprinkling*

adsum, adesse, adfui ... *to be present, to be present* for (+ dat.) [*28]

adsurgo, adsurgere, adsurrexi, adsurrectus ... *to rise, to rise up, to rise to* one's *feet*

adulescens, adulescentis, m. ... *young man*

adulter, adulteri, m. ... *adulterer; lecher, debaucher*

adulterium, adulterii, n. ... *adultery*

adultus, adulta, adultum ... *mature, grown-up*

advenio, adveníre, advéni ... *to come to; to arrive, to return* [*ARA]

advento, adventáre, adventávi, adventátus ... *to come toward; to approach, to draw near*

adventus, adventus, m. ... *arrival* [*31]

adversor, adversári, adversátus sum ... *to oppose, to be contrary*

adversus, adversa, adversum ... *facing, exposed; opposed, unfavorable;* (neut. as substantive) *disaster, catastrophe;* **adversus:** (prep.) *against, to ward off* (+ acc.) [*17]

advoco, advocáre, advocávi, advocátus ... *to summon*

aedes, aedis, f. (gen. plur. **aedium**) ... (plur. may have sing. meaning) *house; room, hall*

aedifico, aedificáre, aedificávi, aedificátus ... *to build*

aeger, aegra, aegrum ... *ill, sick; weary, exhausted;* **aegre:** *painfully, grudgingly, reluctantly*

aegritúdo, aegritudinis, f. ... *illness, sickness*

aemulus, aemula, aemulum ... *striving to equal, straining to excel* (+ gen.)

Aenéas, Aenéae, m. (acc. sing. **Aenéan**) ... *Aeneas,* the Trojan warrior

aénus, aéna, aénum ... (ae not pronounced as diphthong but as two separate syllables) *brazen, of bronze*

aequaevus, aequaeva, aequaevum ... *equal in age, of the same age*

aequális, aequális, c. ... *peer, companion*

Aequus, Aequa, Aequum ... *Aequian;* **Aequus, Aequi,** m.: an *Aequian*

aequo, aequáre, aequávi, aequátus ... *to make equal; to raise* to, *to lift up* to (+ dat.)

aequor, aequoris, n. ... *level surface; sea* (as level and smooth)

aequus, aequa, aequum ... *equal; just, right;* **aeque:** *equally; justly, rightly;* **ex aequo:** *equally, on equal terms*

aer, aeris, m. (acc. sing. **aera**) ... (ae not pronounced as diphthong but as two separate syllables) *air*

aerátus, aeráta, aerátum ... *brazen, of bronze*

aes, aeris, n. ... *bronze*

aestimo, aestimáre, aestimávi, aestimátus ... *to think, to realize; to value* or *assess* something (acc.) at something (gen.)

aestuo, aestuáre, aestuávi ... *to be hot, to be inflamed; to blaze, to burn fiercely*

aestus, aestus, m. ... *heat, blaze*

aetas, aetátis, f. ... *age; life, lifetime* [*ARA]

aeternus, aeterna, aeternum ... *eternal, everlasting*

aether, aetheris, m. ... *sky, heaven*

aevum, aevi, n. ... *time, life; old age, length of years*

affectus, affectus, m. ... *feeling; love, devotion*

afflictus, afflicta, afflictum ... *damaged, destroyed*

Agathyrsi, Agathyrsórum, m. ... (plur. noun with plur. meaning) the *Agathyrsi*

ager, agri, m. ... *land, field; territory, countryside* [*26]

agger, aggeris, m. ... (plur. may have sing. meaning) *heap, pile; dam, dike*

aggero, aggeráre, aggerávi, aggerátus ... *to heap up; to increase, to intensify*

agitátor, agitatóris, m. ... *driver*

agito, agitáre, agitávi, agitátus ... *to move, to shake*

agmen, agminis, n. ... (plur. may have sing. meaning) *band, mass; army, host; crowd, throng* [*28]

agna, agnae, f. ... *ewe* (= female lamb)

agnosco, agnoscere, agnóvi, agnitus ... *to find out, to get to know*

ago, agere, egi, actus ... *to do, to drive; to act, to perform; to discuss, to consider; to give* thanks, *to live* life, *to hunt* animals [*2]

agrestis, agrestis, m. (gen. plur. **agrestium**) ... *rustic, peasant*

agricola, agricolae, m. ... *farmer*

ait ... *he, she, it says* or *said* [*ARA]

ala, alae, f. ... *wing; arm, arm-pit*

alias ... *otherwise, at another time*

alibi ... *else, elsewhere*

aliénus, aliéna, aliénum ... *another's; hostile, unfriendly*

alioqui ... *otherwise*

aliquanto ... *somewhat, considerably*

aliquis, aliquid (gen. sing. **alicuius, alicuius**) ... (formed from **ali-** and the indefinite pronoun **quis, quid**; see *ARA,* App. C, for the declension of the indefinite pronouns) *someone, something* [*ARA]

aliter ... *otherwise;* **non aliter quam cum:** *not otherwise than when (= just as when)*

alius, alia, aliud (gen. sing. **alíus, alíus, alíus**) ... *other, another;* **alius . . , alius . . ,** *one . . , another . . ;* **alii . . , alii . . ,** *some . . , others . .* [*ARA]

allevo, alleváre, allevávi, allevátus ... *to lift up;* (used with the reflexive **se,** which is not translated in this idiom) *to arise, to get up*

alo, alere, alui, altus ... *to rear, to nourish*

altaria, altarium, n. ... (plur. may have sing. meaning) *high altar; altar stones, altar shrines*

alter, altera, alterum (gen. sing. **alteríus, alteríus, alteríus**) *the other, another; the second, the next (best);* **alter . . , alter . . ,** *the one . . , the other . .* [*ARA, *11]

altus, alta, altum ... (as seen from below) *high;* (as seen from above) *deep; high-born, distinguished;* **alte:** *on high, to a great height* [*ARA, *58]

amárus, amára, amárum ... *bitter*

amatrix, amatrícis, f. ... (applied to a woman) *lover*

ambiguus, ambigua, ambiguum ... *doubtful;* **in ambiguo:** *in doubt*

ambo, ambae, ambo ... (declined like **duo, duae, duo;** see *ARA*, App. C, p. 416, for the declension of this numeral) *both*

ambrosia, ambrosiae, f. ... *ambrosia*

ambúro, amburere, ambussi, ambustus ... *to burn up, to scorch*

amens, amentis ... *crazed, frantic, frenzied*

amictus, amictus, m. ... (plur. may have sing. meaning) *clothing; cloak, garment*

amícus, amíca, amícum ... *friendly, loving;* (masc. sing. as substantive) *friend* [*1]

amitto, amittere, amísi, amissus ... *to send away; to let go, to lose*

amnis, amnis, c. (gen. plur. **amnium**) ... *river, torrent*

amo, amáre, amávi, amátus ... *to love; to fall in love, to fall in love with;* (pres. part. as substantive) *lover* [*ARA, *50]

amoenitas, amoenitátis, f. ... *pleasantness; pleasant area* or *stretch*

amor, amóris, m. ... (plur. may have sing. meaning) *love, desire; lover,* one's *beloved;* (as proper noun) **Amor:** the god *Love* [*ARA, *38]

amplector, amplecti, amplexus sum ... *to clasp, to embrace; to take hold of, to seize hold of* [*30]

amplio, ampliáre, ampliávi, ampliátus ... *to enlarge, to increase*

amplitúdo, amplitudinis, f. ... *size, greatness*

amplus, ampla, amplum ... *large; a lot, much;* **amplius** (neut. compar.) *more, any more, for more* than [*7]

an ... (in direct question) *or;* (in indirect question) *whether, if;* (in double indirect question, appearing once but translated twice) *whether . . , or . .* [*15]

ancilla, ancillae, f. ... *maidservant*

Andromache, Andromaches, f. ... *Andromache,* wife of Hector

angustus, angusta, angustum ... *narrow, constricted*

anhelitus, anhelitus, m. ... *breath*

anima, animae, f. ... *life, soul; breath, breathing*

animal, animális, n. (gen. plur. **animalium**) ... *animal, living creature*

animus, animi, m. ... (plur. may have sing. meaning) *mind, heart; spirit, courage* [*4]

annus, anni, m. ... *year* [*ARA]

ante ... *before* (+ acc.); *previously* (as adv.) [*3]

antecédo, antecedere, antecessi ... *to go before; to precede, to lead the way*

anteeo, anteíre, anteívi or **anteii** ... *to go before; to take the lead, to march at the head of* a procession

antiquus, antiqua, antiquum ... *ancient*

antrum, antri, n. ... *cave, cavern*

aper, apri, m. ... *boar*

apertus, aperta, apertum ... *open, clear;* **aperte:** *openly, clearly*

Apollineus, Apollinea, Apollineum ... *of Apollo*

Apollo, Apollinis, m. ... *Apollo*

Apollonius, Apollonii, m. ... *Apollonius,* king of Tyre

appareo, apparére, apparui ... *to appear; to become clear* or *evident* [*62]

approbatio, approbatiónis, f. ... *assent, approval*

appropinquo, appropinquáre, appropinquávi ... *to approach*

apto, aptáre, aptávi, aptátus ... *to fit; to make ready, to put in position*

aptus, apta, aptum ... *suitable, appropriate* (+ dat.)

apud ... *near, with, among* (+ acc.); *as for, in the case of* (+ acc.); *in the works of, in the writings of* (+ acc.); *at the house of, in the quarters of* (+ acc.) [*ARA, *17]

aqua, aquae, f. ... (plur. may have sing. meaning) *water; sea, ocean* [*ARA, *57]

aquila, aquilae, f. ... *eagle* [*ARA]

ara, arae, f. ... *altar* [*63]

aranea, araneae, f. ... *spider; cobweb*

aratrum, aratri, n. ... *plow*

arbitror, arbitrári, arbitrátus sum ... *to think* [*ARA]

arbor, arboris, f. ... *tree; mast* of a ship [*ARA]

arboreus, arborea, arboreum ... *of the tree*

Archistrátes, Archistrátis, m. ... *Archistrates,* king of Cyrene

arcus, arcus, m. ... *bow*

Ardea, Ardeae, f. ... the town *Ardea*

ardeo, ardére, arsi ... *to burn, to be on fire; to burn with anger, to burn with desire* [*ARA, *47]

ardor, ardóris, m. ... *fire, flame; flash, gleam*

arduus, ardua, arduum ... *tall, lofty, towering*

area, areae, f. ... *space; court, courtyard*

argentum, argenti, n. ... *silver* [*ARA]

aries, arietis, m. ... *ram; battering-ram;* (of the action of a battering-ram) a *pounding,* a *battering*

arista, aristae, f. ... (plur. may have sing. meaning) *grain*

arma, armórum, n. ... (plur. noun with plur. meaning) *arms* (= weapons) [*ARA]

armentum, armenti, n. ... (collective sing. or plur.) *herd*

armiger, armigeri, m. ... *armorbearer*

armo, armáre, armávi, armátus ... *to arm, to provide with weapons;* **armátus, armáta, armátum:** *armed, provided with weapons* [*36]

aro, aráre, arávi, arátus ... *to plow, to cultivate* [*71]

arripio, arripere, arripui, arreptus ... *to seize, to grab hold of*

ars, artis, f. (gen. plur. **artium**) ... *art, craft, skill* [*12]

articulus, articuli, m. ... *joint; finger*

artus, artus, m. ... *limb* of the body

arvum, arvi, n. ... *field* [*56]

arx, arcis, f. (gen. plur. **arcium**) ... *citadel, fortress; peak, height, summit* [*72]

as, assis, m. ... *coin; cent, penny*

Ascanius, Ascanii, m. ... *Ascanius,* son of Aeneas (= Iulus)

ascendo, ascendere, ascendi ... *to climb, to ascend; to climb* or *ascend* to a place; *to go on board* a ship, *to embark* on a journey

Asia, Asiae, f. ... *Asia*

aspectus, aspectus, m. ... *look, sight; watching-place, vantage-point*

asper, aspera, asperum ... *harsh, rough, fierce*

aspicio, aspicere, aspexi, aspectus ... *to see, to observe, to look at*

assiduus, assidua, assiduum ... *constant, continuous;* **assidue:** *constantly, continuously*

astrum, astri, n. ... *star*

Astyanax, Astyanactis, m. (acc. sing. **Astyanacta**) ... *Astyanax,* son of Hector

at or **ast** ... *but* [*ARA, *61]

ater, atra, atrum ... *dark, black* [*42]

Athenagora, Athenagorae, m. ... *Athenagora,* prince of Mytilene

atque ... see **ac**

atqui ... *and yet, nevertheless*

Atrídes, Atrídae, m. ... *son of Atreus;* (in plur.) *sons of Atreus* (= Agamemnon and Menelaus)

atrium, atrii, n. ... (plur. may have sing. meaning) *court; hall, room*

atrox, atrócis ... *cruel, harsh; terrible, horrible* [*30]

attingo, attingere, attigi, attactus ... *to touch; to touch on, to mention briefly*

Attius, Attii, m. ... *Attius* (= Attius Tullius)

attollo, attollere ... *to lift up, to raise up* [*59]

attonitus, attonita, attonitum ... *struck by lightning; thunderstruck, panic-stricken*

attribuo, attribuere, attribui, attribútus ... *to apply, to assign*

attuli ... see **adfero**

auctor, auctóris, m. ... *author, authority; advocate, instigator, perpetrator*

audax, audácis ... *bold*

audeo, audére, ausus sum ... (semi-deponent verb) *to dare* (+ acc. or inf.)

audio, audíre, audívi or **audii, audítus** ... *to hear, to listen to* [*ARA]

aufero, auferre, abstuli, ablátus ... *to carry off, to take away; to take away* something (acc.) *from* someone (dat.)

augeo, augére, auxi, auctus ... *to increase; to enhance, to strengthen* [*22]

Augustus, Augusta, Augustum ... *Augustan, of Augustus*

aura, aurae, f. ... *wind, breeze;* (in plur.) *sky, heaven* [*48]

aurátus, auráta, aurátum ... *golden*

aureus, aurea, aureum ... *golden* [*ARA]

auris, auris, f. (gen. plur. **aurium**) ... *ear* [*ARA]

Auróra, Aurórae, f. ... the goddess *Aurora;* (of Aurora's realm) the *dawn,* the *morning*

aurum, auri, n. ... *gold* [*ARA]

Ausonius, Ausonia, Ausonium ... *Ausonian* (= Italian)

auspicátus, auspicáta, auspicátum ... *auspicious, favorable*

auspicium, auspicii, n. ... *augury; omen, portent*

ausum, ausi, n. ... *bold deed; crime, outrage*

aut ... *or;* **aut .. , aut .. ,** *either .. , or .. * [*1]

autem ... *however, moreover* [*ARA]

Automedon, Automedontis, m. ... *Automedon,* the Greek warrior

auxilium, auxilii, n. ... *aid, help* [*ARA]

avárus, avára, avárum ... *greedy*

avello, avellere, avelli, avulsus ... *to tear away; to tear away* from; *to tear away* something (acc.) from something (abl.)

aveo, avére ... *to be well;* **ave:** (imperative sing.) *hail!*

aversor, aversári, aversátus sum ... *to turn away from; to spurn, to reject*

averto, avertere, averti, aversus ... *to turn away; to turn away* some-one (acc.) *from* something (abl.)

avius, avia, avium ... *pathless, untrodden*

avolo, avoláre, avolávi ... *to fly away; to rush off*

avunculus, avunculi, m. ... *uncle* [*15]

avus, avi, m. ... *grandfather*

axis, axis, m. (gen. plur. **axium**) ... *axis; arch, vault*

B

Babylonius, Babylonia, Babylonium ... *Babylonian, of Babylon*

balineum, balinei, n. ... *bath, bathroom*

barba, barbae, f. ... *beard* [*41]

barbaricus, barbarica, barbaricum ... *foreign*

basio, basiáre, basiávi, basiátus ... *to kiss*

basium, basii, n. ... *kiss* [*38]

beátus, beáta, beátum ... *happy, blessed, fortunate* [*39]

bellátor, bellatóris, m. ... *warrior*

bellum, belli, n. ... *war* [*18]

bellus, bella, bellum ... *pretty, charming, attractive* [*37]

bene ... *well, kindly; at peace, contentedly* [*21]

benefactum, benefacti, n. ... *service, good deed*

beneficium, beneficii, n. ... *favor, kindness [*ARA]*

benignus, benigna, benignum ... *kind, generous;* **benigne:** *kindly, generously*

bestia, bestiae, f. ... *beast*

bibo, bibere, bibi ... *to drink*

bipennis, bipennis, f. (abl. sing. **bipenni**) ... *ax*

bis ... *twice, on two occasions*

blanditia, blanditiae, f. ... *flattery;* (in plur.) *loving words, sweet talk*

blandus, blanda, blandum ... *coaxing; soft, smooth*

bonitas, bonitátis, f. ... *goodness, kindness*

bonus, bona, bonum ... *good; presentable, respectable;* (neut. plur. as substantive) *goods, property* [*5]

bos, bovis, c. (gen. plur. **bovum** or **boum**) ... *ox, cow;* (in plur.) *cattle*

bracchium, bracchii, n. ... *lower arm;* (in general) *arm*

brevis, breve ... *brief, short*

Britannia, Britanniae, f. ... *Britain*

bruma, brumae, f. ... *winter*

Brutus, Bruti, m. ... *Brutus,* Lucius Tarquinius's nephew

bustum, busti, n. ... (plur. may have sing. meaning) *tomb*

buxus, buxi, f. ... *boxwood*

C

cachinnus, cachinni, m. ... (plur. may have sing. meaning) *laugh, laughter*

cacúmen, cacuminis, n. ... *top; treetop*

cado, cadere, cecidi ... *to fall; to set, to sink; to abate, to lessen, to subside* (+ dat.) [*17]

caecus, caeca, caecum ... *blind; hidden, concealed; aimless, purposeless*

caedes, caedis, f. (gen. plur. **caedium**) ... (plur. may have sing. meaning) *murder, slaughter; blood* (shed in killing) [*35]

caelum, caeli, n. ... *sky, heaven* [*47]

Caere, Caeritis, n. ... the town *Caere*

caesius, caesia, caesium ... *gray-eyed*

calidus, calida, calidum ... *hot*

calígo, caliginis, f. ... *darkness; fog, mist; smoke, vapor*

callidus, callida, callidum ... *clever, resourceful*

Campania, Campaniae, f. ... the region *Campania*

campus, campi, m. ... *field, plain, ground* [*63]

candidus, candida, candidum ... *white, bright; fair, lovely, beautiful* [*ARA, *38]

canis, canis, c. ... *dog, hound* [*ARA]

cano, canere, cecini ... *to sing, to sing of; to sound the alarm; to relate, to exclaim, to proclaim* [*ARA, *54]

cantus, cantus, m. ... *song* [*ARA]

caper, capri, m. ... *goat; goatish-smell*

capillátus, capilláta, capillátum ... *long-haired*

capillus, capilli, m. ... *hair* [*ARA]

capio, capere, cepi, captus ... *to take, to seize; to form, to adopt; to charm, to captivate* [*ARA]

Capitolium, Capitolii, n. ... (plur. may have sing. meaning) the *Capitol,* the *Capitoline Hill*

capra, caprae, f. ... *she-goat*

Capreae, Capreárum, f. ... (plur. noun with sing. meaning) *Capri*

captívus, captíva, captívum ... *captured;* (masc./fem. as substantive) a *captive* [*ARA]

capto, captáre, captávi, captátus ... *to seize; to catch, to draw in*

capulus, capuli, m. ... *hilt* of a sword

caput, capitis, n. ... *head* [*ARA]

cardo, cardinis, m. ... *hinge* of a door [*62]

carmen, carminis, n. ... *song; riddle* [*ARA]

carpo, carpere, carpsi, carptus ... *to pluck, to seize; to carp at, to criticize* [*47]

carus, cara, carum ... *dear, dear* to (+ dat.) [*48]

castigátor, castigatóris, m. ... *chider, scolder*

castitas, castitátis, f. ... *purity, chastity, fidelity*

castra, castrórum, n. ... (plur. noun with sing. meaning) *camp* [*ARA]

castus, casta, castum ... *pure, chaste, untouched*

casus, casus, m. ... (plur. may have sing. meaning) *fall, falling; fate, fortune; peril, dilemma, predicament* [*2]

caterva, catervae, f. ... *crowd, throng*

Catullus, Catulli, m. ... *Catullus,* the Roman poet

causa, causae, f. ... *cause, reason* [*ARA]

cavo, caváre, cavávi, cavátus ... *to hollow out, to cut through*

cavus, cava, cavum ... *hollow, echoing*

cedo, cedere, cessi ... *to go; to withdraw; to yield* or *give way* (+ dat.) [*49]

celer, celeris, celere ... *swift, speedy;* (masc. plur. as substantive) *the celeres* (= the cavalry) [*35]

cella, cellae, f. ... *room, chamber*

Celtiber, Celtibri, m. ... a *Celtiberian*

Celtiberia, Celtiberiae, f. ... the region *Celtiberia*

cena, cenae, f. ... *dinner* [*38]

ceno, cenáre, cenávi ... *to eat, to dine* [*38]

centum (indecl.) ... a *hundred* [*38]

cerno, cernere, crevi, cretus ... *to sift; to see, to observe*

certámen, certaminis, n. ... *dispute, rivalry; contest, struggle*

certus, certa, certum ... *sure, certain; unerring, sure of aim; resolved* on, *determined* on (+ gen.); **certe:** *surely, certainly* [*ARA, *15]

cerva, cervae, f. ... *deer* [*ARA]

cervícal, cervicális, n. ... *pillow, cushion*

cervix, cervícis, f. ... (plur. may have sing. meaning) *neck*

cervus, cervi, m. ... *stag* [*ARA]

cesso, cessáre, cessávi ... *to stop, to cease; to delay, to hesitate*

ceterus, cetera, ceterum ... *other,* the *rest;* **ceterum:** (adv.) *but, however, moreover* [*ARA, *33]

ceu ... *as, like*

chlamys, chlamydis, f. ... *cape, cloak*

chorda, chordae, f. ... *string* of a lyre

chorus, chori, m. ... (plur. may have sing. meaning) the *festive dancing,* the *singing and dancing*

cingo, cingere, cinxi, cinctus ... *to encircle, to surround; to fasten, to gird up, to strap on* [*21]

cinis, cineris, c. ... *ashes* [*21]

circa ... *around* (+ acc.); *around* (as adv.) [*ARA, *32]

Circeii, Circeiórum, m. ... (plur. noun with sing. meaning) the town *Circeii*

circum ... *around* (+ acc.); *around* (as adv.) [*ARA, *61]

circumágo, circumagere, circumégi, circumactus ... *to bend around, to curve around*

circumdo, circumdáre, circumdedi, circumdátus ... (perf. part. may have act. meaning) *to surround; to put on, to wear; to put* or *place* something (acc.) *around* something (dat.)

circumiaceo, circumiacére, circumiacui ... *to lie around, to lie in the neighborhood*

circumsilio, circumsilíre ... *to hop around, to jump around*

circumsto, circumstáre, circumsteti ... *to stand around; to surround, to encompass*

cithara, citharae, f. ... *lyre* [*ARA]

cito, citáre, citávi, citátus ... *to excite, to arouse*

citus, cita, citum ... *swift*

civis, civis, c. (gen. plur. **civium**) ... *citizen*

civitas, civitátis, f. (gen. plur. **civitátum** or **civitatium**) ... *state; city, town* [*7]

clades, cladis, f. (gen. plur. **cladium**) ... *disaster, destruction*

clamo, clamáre, clamávi ... *to call, to shout*

clamor, clamóris, m. ... a *shout, a shouting* [*ARA]

claritas, claritátis, f. ... *clearness, brightness*

Claros, Clari, f. ... the town *Claros*

clarus, clara, clarum ... *clear, bright; loud, shrill*

classis, classis, f. (gen. plur. **classium**) ... *fleet, naval force*

claudo, claudere, clausi, clausus ... *to shut, to close, to block* [*10]

claustrum, claustri, n. ... *bar, bolt*

clipeus, clipei, m. ... *shield*

cloáca, cloácae, f. ... *sewer*

Cluilius, Cluilia, Cluilium ... *Cluilian*

coctilis, coctile ... *baked; of baked brick*

codicilli, codicillórum, m. ... (plur. noun with sing. meaning) *letter, petition*

coeo, coíre, coii ... *to go together; to meet, to join, to unite*

coepi, coepisti, coepit, etc. ... (perf. ind. of **coepi,** found only in the perf., plup., and fut. perf. tenses) *I began, you began, he/she/it began, etc.;* **coeptus, coepta, coeptum:** *having been begun* [*ARA, *19]

coerceo, coercére, coercui, coercitus ... *to confine; to bind up, to keep together*

Coeus, Coei, m. ... the Titan *Coeus*

cogito, cogitáre, cogitávi, cogitátus ... *to think, to consider*

cognosco, cognoscere, cognóvi, cognitus ... *to learn, to find out, to discover; to recognize* a person whom one already knows [*ARA, *28]

cogo, cogere, coégi, coactus ... *to force, to drive*

Collatia, Collatiae, f. ... the town *Collatia*

Collatínus, Collatíni, m. ... *Collatinus,* husband of Lucretia

collatio, collatiónis, f. ... *comparison*

colléga, collégae, m. ... *colleague, associate*

colligo, colligere, collégi, collectus ... *to pick up, to gather together; to infer, to deduce, to conclude*

collum, colli, n. ... *neck*

colo, colere, colui, cultus ... *to inhabit; to tend, to cultivate*

colónus, colóni, m. ... *farmer; settler, colonist*

color, colóris, m. ... *color; hue, tint* [*58]

coluber, colubri, m. ... *snake, serpent*

columba, columbae, f. ... *dove* [*52]

coma, comae, f. ... *hair* [*54]

comes, comitis, c. ... *comrade, companion* [*60]

comicus, comica, comicum ... *comic*

comis, come ... *kind, courteous;* **comiter:** *kindly, courteously*

comitátus, comitátus, m. ... *retinue, company, following*

comitor, comitári, comitátus sum ... *to accompany*

commeio, commeiere, comminxi, commictus ... *to defile with urine;* **commictus, commicta, commictum:** *defiled, polluted*

commendo, commendáre, commendávi, commendátus ... *to commit, to entrust*

commisceo, commiscére, commiscui, commixtus ... *to mix in, to mix together*

committo, committere, commísi, commissus ... *to send together; to bring about, to allow to happen*

commúnis, commúne ... *common* to, *shared* by (+ dat.); **in commúne:** *together, with one another*

como, comere, compsi, comptus ... *to comb, to make tidy*

compesco, compescere, compescui ... *to restrain; to slake* or *quench* one's thirst

complaceo, complacére, complacui ... *to please greatly* (+ dat.); (impersonal use) *to seem very pleasing*

complector, complecti, complexus sum ... *to clasp, to embrace*

compleo, complére, complévi, complétus ... *to fill; to fill* something (acc.) *with* something (abl.)

complexus, complexus, m. ... an *embrace*

comploratio, comploratiónis, f. ... *mourning, lamentation*

complúres, complurium ... (plur. adj. used as substantive) *several*

compóno, componere, composui, compositus ... *to put together, to place together*

comprehendo, comprehendere, comprehendi, comprehensus ... *to grasp firmly; to seize, to capture; to include* in, *to deal with* in

comprimo, comprimere, compressi, compressus ... *to rape, to ravage, to violate; to crush, to subdue, to suppress* [*ARA, *36]

concédo, concedere, concessi ... *to withdraw, to come over*

concido, concidere, concidi ... *to fall; to fall down, to collapse*

concieo, conciére, concívi, concítus ... *to collect, to attract; to incite, to provoke*

concito, concitáre, concitávi, concitátus ... *to incite, to stir up*

conclámo, conclamáre, conclamávi ... *to shout loudly, to scream in horror*

concordia, concordiae, f. ... *peace, harmony*

concordo, concordáre, concordávi ... *to be in harmony* with

concupisco, concupiscere, concupívi, concupítus ... *to conceive a desire; to desire greatly* or *ardently*

condensus, condensa, condensum ... *crowded together, huddled together*

condo, condere, condidi, conditus ... *to found; to put away, to preserve; to bury, to hide, to conceal* [*ARA, *70]

conficio, conficere, conféci, confectus ... *to make together; to defeat, to destroy*

conflagratio, conflagratiónis, f. ... *eruption*

confundo, confundere, confúdi, confúsus ... *to pour together; to confuse, to disturb, to embarrass*

confutuo, confutuere, confutui ... *to have sex with*

conicio, conicere, coniéci, coniectus ... *to throw, to shoot; to throw or place* something (acc.) *in/into* something (acc.)

coniugium, coniugii, n. ... *marriage* [*ARA]

coniungo, coniungere, coniunxi, coniunctus ... *to join to, to attach to;* (of an army) *to join or combine* into a single force

coniunx, coniugis, c. ... *husband, wife* [*ARA]

conscendo, conscendere, conscendi ... *to climb, to mount, to ascend*

conscius, conscia, conscium ... *aware, conscious; privy to, witness to;* (masc./fem. as substantive) *witness, go-between*

considero, consideráre, considerávi, considerátus ... *to examine, to consider*

consído, considere, consédi ... *to sit down; to take* one's *seat; to set up quarters*

consilium, consilii, n. ... (plur. may have sing. meaning) *plan, advice; policy, decision; purpose, intention* [*ARA, *28]

consisto, consistere, constiti ... *to stop moving, to come to a halt; to set foot, to take* one's *place or position*

consolátor, consolatóris, m. ... *consoler, comforter*

consólor, consolári, consolátus sum ... *to console, to comfort*

conspectus, conspectus, m. ... *view, sight* [*ARA]

conspicio, conspicere, conspexi, conspectus ... *to look at, to watch*

conspicuus, conspicua, conspicuum ... *visible, in full view*

constantia, constantiae, f. ... *steadiness; courage, fearlessness*

consterno, consternáre, consternávi, consternátus ... *to alarm, to shock;* (in passive) *to be driven, to be startled*

constituo, constituere, constitui, constitútus ... *to place, to set up; to arrange, to establish* [*ARA]

constringo, constringere, constrinxi, constrictus ... *to tie up; to bind, to fasten*

consuetúdo, consuetudinis, f. ... *habit, custom*

consul, consulis, m. ... *consul*

consuláris, consuláris, m. (gen. plur. **consularium**) ... *ex-consul*

consulo, consulere, consului, consultus ... *to consult* (+ acc.); *to look after the interests of* (+ dat.)

consulto, consultáre, consultávi, consultátus ... *to consult, to discuss*

consúmo, consumere, consumpsi, consumptus ... *to destroy; to devour, to eat up*

consurgo, consurgere, consurrexi, consurrectus ... *to rise up, to stand up*

contendo, contendere, contendi, contentus ... *to hasten; to compete* [*ARA]

contentus, contenta, contentum ... *content, satisfied*

conterminus, contermina, conterminum ... *next to, close to* (+ dat.)

conterreo, conterrére, conterrui, conterritus ... *to terrify* or *frighten thoroughly*

contiguus, contigua, contiguum ... *adjacent, adjoining*

continens, continentis ... *unbroken, continuous;* **continenter:** *in a row, in close succession*

contineo, continére, continui, contentus ... *to hold together; to control, to restrain*

contingo, contingere, contigi, contactus ... *to touch, to come into contact with*

continuus, continua, continuum ... *continuous, uninterrupted*

contra ... *against, opposite* (+ acc.); (adv.) *in reply, in return; on the other hand, on the other side* [*ARA, *21]

contraho, contrahere, contraxi, contractus ... *to draw together; to catch, to contract*

contrarius, contraria, contrarium ... *opposite, unfavorable*

contremesco, contremescere, contremui ... *to tremble, to tremble with fear*

contubernális, contubernális, c. ... *tent-mate; fellow-barfly, fellow-drinker*

conturbo, conturbáre, conturbávi, conturbátus ... *to mix up, to confound, to throw into disorder*

conubium, conubii, n. ... (plur. may have sing. meaning) *marriage, marriage-proposal* [*47]

convello, convellere, convelli, convulsus ... *to pull up, to uproot; to wrench* from, *to dislodge* from

convenio, convenire, convéni, conventus ... *to come together, to make an agreement;* (impersonal use) *to be agreed upon;* (use in passive) *to be approached* or *confronted* by someone or something [*26]

converto, convertere, converti, conversus ... *to turn, to change; to direct* one's *mind* toward an activity

convíva, convívae, c. ... *guest*

convivium, convivii, n. ... (plur. may have sing. meaning) *feast, banquet* [*67]

convolvo, convolvere, convolvi, convolútus ... *to roll, to coil;* (of a snake) *to move* the back *in a winding path*

copia, copiae, f. ... *plenty, abundance; force of men, supply of men;* **copiam facere:** *to give* someone (dat.) *the chance or opportunity* [*66]

copiósus, copiósa, copiósum ... *rich, opulent*

cor, cordis, n. ... *heart*

coram ... (adv.) *in* one's *presence, before* one's *own eyes*

Corbio, Corbiónis, f. ... the town *Corbio*

Coriolánus, Coriolání, m. ... *Coriolanus*

Corioli, Coriolórum, m. ... (plur. noun with sing. meaning) the town *Corioli*

cornu, cornus, n. ... (plur. may have sing. meaning) *horn; horn-tipped bow* [*ARA, *49]

coróna, corónae, f. ... *crown, wreath*

coróno, coronáre, coronávi, coronátus ... *to crown, to wreathe*

corpus, corporis, n. ... (plur. may have sing. meaning) *body* [*ARA, *53]

corpusculum, corpusculi, n. ... *small body*

corripio, corripere, corripui, correptus ... *to seize, to snatch; to criticize, to find fault with*

cortex, corticis, m. ... *bark* of a tree

coruscus, corusca, coruscum ... *gleaming, glittering*

cotidie ... *daily, every day*

crassus, crassa, crassum ... *thick, dense, heavy*

crastinus, crastina, crastinum ... *of tomorrow*

creber, crebra, crebrum ... *frequent, repeated*

credo, credere, credidi, creditus ... *to believe; to entrust* (+ dat.) [*ARA, *45]

Cres, Cretis, m. ... a *Cretan*

cresco, crescere, crevi, cretus ... *to spring* from; *to grow, to increase* [*55]

Cresius, Cresia, Cresium ... *Cretan, of Crete*

Creúsa, Creúsae, f. ... *Creusa,* wife of Aeneas

crimen, criminis, n. ... *charge; crime, object of reproach*

criminor, criminári, criminátus sum ... *to make charges* or *accusations* against

crinis, crinis, m. (gen. plur. **crinium**) ... *hair; lock, tress* [*53]

crudélis, crudéle ... *cruel, fierce, savage* [*47]

cruento, cruentáre, cruentávi, cruentátus ... *to splatter with blood;* **cruentátus, cruentáta, cruentátum:** *bloody, blood-stained*

cruentus, cruenta, cruentum ... *bloody*

cruor, cruóris, m. ... *blood; murder, slaughter* [*34]

crus, cruris, n. ... *leg, shin*

crux, crucis, f. ... *cross* [*43]

cubiculum, cubiculi, n. ... *bedroom* [*33]

cubo, cubáre, cubui ... *to lie down* with; *to have sex* with

culmen, culminis, n. ... (plur. may have sing. meaning) *roof; top, peak* [*61]

culpa, culpae, f. ... *fault, blame; sin, wrongdoing* [*69]

culter, cultri, m. ... *knife*

cum ... (conj.) *when, since, although;* **cum . . , tum . . ,** *both . . , and . . or not only . . , but also . .* or *while . . , at the same time . .* [*ARA, *31]

cum ... (prep.) *with* (+ abl.); *next to, at the side of* (+ abl.) [*ARA, *32]

cumulo, cumuláre, cumulávi, cumulátus ... *to heap, to pile up;* (in pass.) *to be gifted in, to be endowed with* (+ gen.)

cumulus, cumuli, m. ... *heap, mass*

cunctor, cunctári, cunctátus sum ... *to delay, to linger, to hesitate*

cunctus, cuncta, cunctum ... *all*

cuniculósus, cuniculósa, cuniculósum ... *rabbit-filled*

cupído, cupidinis, m. ... *desire, carnal desire;* (as proper noun)
    Cupído: the god *Cupid* [*37]

cupio, cupere, cupívi, cupítus ... *to wish, to desire*

cur ... *why?*

cura, curae, f. ... *care; anxiety, concern; heartache, lovesickness*
    [*46]

curátor, curatóris, m. ... *supervisor, commissioner*

curo, curáre, curávi, curátus ... *to care; to care for, to look after* [*65]

curro, currere, cucurri ... *to run; to hurry, to hasten* [*35]

cursus, cursus, m. ... (plur. may have sing. meaning) a *running;*
    voyage, journey; **cursu:** (of animals) *at a run, at a gallop* [*21]

curvo, curváre, curvávi, curvátus ... *to form* or *extend in a curve*

cuspis, cuspidis, f. ... *tip* or *point* of a weapon

custodia, custodiae, f. ... *guard*

custodio, custodíre, custodívi, custodítus ... *to guard; to keep, to save*

custos, custódis, c. ... *guard; doorkeeper, watchman; guardian, pro-*
    tector [*ARA, *54]

Cynthus, Cynthi, m. ... the mountain *Cynthus*

D

Danaus, Danai, m. (gen. plur. **Danaum**) ... a *Danaan* (= a Greek)

Daphne, Daphnes, f. ... the nymph *Daphne*

Dardanius, Dardania, Dardanium ... *Dardanian* (= Trojan)

de ... *from* (root meaning); *from, down from* (+ abl.); *about, concerning* (+ abl.); *according to, in keeping with* (+ abl.) [*ARA, *25]

dea, deae, f. ... *goddess* [*ARA]

debeo, debére, debui, debitus ... *to owe; to be indebted* or *beholden* to someone (dat.) for something (acc.) [*19]

decédo, decedere, decessi ... *to go away; to fade away, to drift away*

decem (indecl.) ... *ten*

decens, decentis ... *fitting; pleasing, attractive*

decet, decére, decuit ... (impersonal verb) **decet** = *it is fitting,* **decére** = *to be fitting,* **decuit** = *it was fitting*

declíno, declináre, declinávi, declinátus ... *to turn away; to shut* or *close* one's eyes

decor, decoris, m. ... *beauty, attractiveness*

decurro, decurrere, decurri ... *to run down* from, *to hurry down* from (+ abl.)

decus, decoris, n. ... *honor, dignity; beauty, splendor*

dedecus, dedecoris, n. ... *dishonor, disgrace*

dedico, dedicáre, dedicávi, dedicátus ... *to dedicate*

deditus, dedita, deditum ... *devoted* to, *attentive* to (+ dat.)

dedúco, deducere, deduxi, deductus ... *to lead down; to launch* a ship; *to escort, to conduct*

defendo, defendere, defendi, defensus ... *to defend, to protect*

defensor, defensóris, m. ... *defender, protector;* (in plur.) *defense, protection*

defero, deferre, detuli, delátus ... *to carry* to, *to bring* to; *to carry down, to bring down*

defetiscor, defetisci, defessus sum ... *to become tired, to become weary;* **defessus, defessa, defessum:** *tired, weary*

deficio, deficere, deféci, defectus ... *to let down; to subside, to become weak;* (of the sun) *to undergo an eclipse;* (of soldiers) *to become disaffected* or *discontented*

defígo, defigere, defixi, defixus ... *to thrust, to plunge*

deflecto, deflectere, deflexi, deflexus ... *to bend* something *down; to turn aside, to change* one's *direction*

defloresco, deflorescere, deflorui ... *to shed blossom; to fade, to wither*

defrico, defricáre, defricui, defricátus ... *to rub* or *brush thoroughly*

defunctus, defuncta, defunctum ... *dead, deceased*

degener, degeneris ... *of inferior stock; unworthy, degenerate*

dehinc ... *from here; after this, from now on*

dehisco, dehiscere ... *to gape, to yawn; to burst open, to split open*

deicio, deicere, deiéci, deiectus ... *to throw down; to drive* from, *to dislodge* from (+ abl.)

dein or **deinde** ... *then, next; afterwards, henceforth* [*12]

deinceps ... *in succession, one after another*

delátus ... see **defero**

deliciae, deliciárum, f. ... (plur. noun with sing. meaning) *darling, delight; allurement, enticement* [*37]

delictum, delicti, n. ... *crime, outrage*

deligo, deligere, delégi, delectus ... *to choose, to select*

Delius, Delii, m. ... the *Delian* (= Apollo)

Delos, Deli, f. ... the island *Delos*

Delphicus, Delphica, Delphicum ... *Delphian, of Delphi*

demens, dementis ... *out of* one's *mind; frantic, frenzied* [*67]

demergo, demergere, demersi, demersus ... *to plunge, to submerge; to send below* or *underground*

demitto, demittere, demísi, demissus ... *to send down; to plunge, to thrust*

demo, demere, dempsi, demptus ... *to remove, to take away* [*43]

demum ... *at last, finally*

denego, denegáre, denegávi, denegátus ... *to deny*

deni, denae, dena ... (plur. adj. with plur. meaning) *ten each, ten together*

denique ... *finally; in short, to sum up*

dens, dentis, m. (gen. plur. **dentium**) ... *tooth;* (collective sing.) *teeth* [*41]

densus, densa, densum ... *thick, thick of; crowding, thronging*

dentátus, dentáta, dentátum ... *toothy*

depóno, deponere, deposui, depositus ... *to put down, to put aside; to slake* or *quench* one's thirst

deprecor, deprecári, deprecátus sum ... *to entreat, to implore*

deprehendo, deprehendere, deprehendi, deprehensus ... *to grasp; to observe, to examine*

descendo, descendere, descendi ... *to go down, to come down, to descend* to or from *[*ARA]*

desero, deserere, deserui, desertus ... *to desert, to abandon* [*66]

desiderium, desiderii, n. ... *desire, longing [*ARA]*

desino, desinere, desii ... *to stop, to cease* [*40]

despondeo, despondére, despondi, desponsus ... *to pledge, to promise*

destino, destináre, destinávi, destinátus ... *to fix; to put* or *set aside* something (acc.) for something (dat.); **destinátus, destináta, destinátum:** *fixed; stubborn, obstinate*

destituo, destituere, destitui, destitútus ... *to set down; to desert, to forsake; to leave unsupported*

desuesco, desuescere, desuévi, desuétus ... *to become unaccustomed;* **desuétus, desuéta, desuétum:** *unaccustomed to being used*

detineo, detinére, detinui, detentus ... *to hold, to hold back; to hold captive, to cause to remain*

detorqueo, detorquére, detorsi, detortus ... *to bend, to turn, to direct* one's course

detuli ... see **defero**

deus, dei, m. (nom. plur. **dei, dii, di;** dat./abl. plur. **deis, diis, dis**) ... *god* [*ARA, *45]

devenio, deveníre, devéni ... *to come to, to arrive at*

devoro, devoráre, devorávi, devorátus ... *to eat, to swallow*

dexter, dextra, dextrum ... *right;* (fem. sing. as substantive) *right hand;* **dextra:** (adv.) *on the right* [*33]

diaeta, diaetae, f. ... *room, apartment*

Diána, Diánae, f. ... *Diana*

dico, dicere, dixi, dictus ... *to say, to speak; to call, to name; to specify, to designate* [*ARA, *57]

Dictaeus, Dictaea, Dictaeum ... *of Mt. Dicte* (= Cretan, of Crete)

dictito, dictitáre, dictitávi, dictitátus ... *to keep saying*

dicto, dictáre, dictávi, dictátus ... *to recite, to dictate*

dictum, dicti, n. ... *word* [*71]

Dido, Didónis, f. ... *Dido,* queen of Carthage

dies, diéi, c. ... *day;* **in dies:** *daily, each day* [*ARA]

difficilis, difficile ... *difficult;* **difficiliter:** *with difficulty* [*45]

diffundo, diffundere, diffúdi, diffúsus ... *to spread, to spread out*

digitus, digiti, m. ... *finger*

dignor, dignári, dignátus sum ... *to consider worthy; to deign, to condescend* (+ inf.)

dignus, digna, dignum ... *worthy, deserving; worthy* of, *deserving* of (+ gen. or abl.); *fitting, suitable, appropriate;* **digne:** *worthily, as is fitting, in a suitable manner* [*5]

digredior, digredi, digressus sum ... *to go off, to go away;* (with plur. subject) *to go separate ways*

diligens, diligentis ... *careful;* **diligenter:** *carefully*

diligo, diligere, dilexi, dilectus ... *to love, to cherish*

dilútus, dilúta, dilútum ... *diluted, cleaned*

dimidius, dimidia, dimidium ... *half*

dimitto, dimittere, dimísi, dimissus ... *to send away*

dirimo, dirimere, dirémi, diremptus ... *to separate*

diripio, diripere, diripui, direptus ... *to snatch apart; to pillage, to plunder*

dirus, dira, dirum ... *dreadful, frightful* [*64]

discédo, discedere, discessi ... *to depart, to go away*

disco, discere, didici ... *to learn; to master, to acquire skill in*

discordia, discordiae, f. ... *discord, dissension*

discrímen, discriminis, n. ... *dividing line; critical point, dangerous situation*

discumbo, discumbere, discubui ... *to recline* at a table

discursus, discursus, m. ... a *running about; discharge, explosion*

distribuo, distribuere, distribui, distribútus ... *to distribute; to station, to position*

diu ... *long, for a long time* [*ARA]

dium, dii, or **divum, divi,** n. ... *open sky, open air*

divello, divellere, divelli, divulsus ... *to tear apart, to tear to pieces*

diversus, diversa, diversum ... *different; opposite, separate* [*69]

dives, divitis ... *rich, wealthy*

divido, dividere, divísi, divísus ... *to divide, to separate* [*19]

divínus, divína, divínum ... *divine*

divus, divi, m. (gen. plur. **divórum** or **divum**) ... *god* [*45]

do, dare, dedi, datus ... *to give, to grant, to furnish; to make, to cause, to produce* [*ARA, *62]

doceo, docére, docui, doctus ... *to teach, to instruct*

doleo, dolére, dolui ... *to grieve* [*40]

dolor, dolóris, m. ... (plur. may have sing. meaning) *pain, distress*

domina, dominae, f. ... *lady* or *mistress* of a household [*5]

dominus, domini, m. ... *lord* or *master* of a household [*8]

domus, domus, f. ... (see *ARA*, App. C, p. 400, for the declension of this noun) *house, home* [*ARA, *14]

donec ... *until*

dono, donáre, donávi, donátus ... *to give, to present, to provide* [*ARA, *44]

dormio, dormíre, dormívi ... *to sleep* [*ARA]

dos, dotis, f. ... *dowry*

Dryopes, Dryopum, m. ... (plur. noun with plur. meaning) the *Dryopes*

dubito, dubitáre, dubitávi, dubitátus ... *to doubt, to hesitate, to be uncertain* [*19]

dubius, dubia, dubium ... *doubtful, uncertain*

ducenti, ducentae, ducenta ... *two hundred*

duco, ducere, duxi, ductus ... *to lead; to lead into marriage; to induce, to influence; to think, to regard, to consider; to acquire, to develop, to receive* [*ARA, *9]

dulcédo, dulcedinis, f. ... *sweetness*

dulcis, dulce ... *sweet; delightful* [*43]

dum ... *while, until, as long as;* **dum . . , dum . . ,** *as long as . . , so long . .* [*ARA, *48]

duo, duae, duo ... (see *ARA*, App. C, p. 416, for the declension of this numeral) *two, both* [*ARA]

duodevicesimus, duodevicesima, duodevicesimum ... *eighteenth*

durus, dura, durum ... *hard, solid*

dux, ducis, m. ... *leader, guide; general, commander* [*ARA, *25]

E

e, ex (**e** before a consonant, **ex** before a vowel or consonant) ... *from* (root meaning); *from, out of* (+ abl.); *with, by means of* (+ abl.); *because of, on account of* (+ abl.) [*ARA]

ebrius, ebria, ebrium ... *drunk; drunk with love*

ebur, eboris, n. ... *ivory; ivory sheath* or *scabbard*

ecce ... (interjection) *see! look! behold!* [*9]

ecquid ... *whether*

edictum, edicti, n. ... *edict, decree*

educo, educáre, educávi, educátus ... *to rear, to bring up; to produce, to bring forth*

edúco, educere, eduxi, eductus ... *to lead out, to draw out;* (in passive) *to rise upward* from (+ abl.), *to extend skyward* from (+ abl.)

effero, efferre, extuli, elátus ... *to carry out, to bring out; to lift up, to raise high;* (used with the reflexive pronoun **se**, which is not translated in this idiom) *to rise* or *appear* or *move up* in the sky

efficio, efficere, efféci, effectus ... *to accomplish, to bring about*

effor, effári, effátus sum ... *to speak*

effulgeo, effulgére, effulsi ... *to shine, to come out*

effundo, effundere, effúdi, effúsus ... *to pour out; to shed* tears

egeo, egére, egui ... *to need, to require* (+ abl.)

Egerius, Egerii, m. ... *Egerius,* father of Collatinus

Egnatius, Egnatii, m. ... the Spaniard *Egnatius*

ego ... (first person sing. pronoun) *I* [*6]

egredior, egredi, egressus sum ... *to go out; to get beyond* [*57]

egregius, egregia, egregium ... *excellent, outstanding, illustrious*

ei ... (interjection) *alas!;* **ei mihi:** *woe is me!*

eiaculor, eiaculári, eiaculátus sum ... *to shoot out, to discharge*

elábor, elábi, elapsus sum ... *to slip away; to escape* from or *make* one's *escape* from (+ abl.)

elátus ... see **effero**

elegans, elegantis ... *elegant, graceful, tasteful*

elído, elidere, elísi, elísus ... *to strike out; to cleave, to divide*

eligo, eligere, elégi, electus ... *to choose; to lead* someone *to choose*

elleborum, ellebori, n. ... the plant *hellebore*

emico, emicáre, emicui ... *to spurt out, to gush forth*

emitto, emittere, emísi, emissus ... *to send out; to discharge; to speak* a word, *to utter* a sound

emo, emere, emi, emptus ... *to buy, to purchase* [*7]

emoveo, emovére, emóvi, emótus ... *to move out; to dislodge from*

Enceladus, Enceladi, m. ... the Giant *Enceladus*

enim ... (conj. introducing an explanation) *for* [*ARA]

eniteo, enitére ... *to shine forth* from (+ abl.)

enoto, enotáre, enotávi, enotátus ... *to note down, to write down*

ensis, ensis, m. (gen. plur. **ensium**) ... *sword* [*ARA]

eo ... (adv.) *there, to that place, for that reason*

eo, ire, ivi or **ii** ... *to go, to proceed* [*35]

Eóus, Eói, m. ... *Dawn* (= the Morning-Star)

epulor, epulári, epulátus sum ... *to feast, to feast on* [*ARA]

eques, equitis, m. ... *horseman*

equester, equestris, equestre ... *equestrian; proper to* or *required of an equestrian*

equus, equi, m. ... *horse* [*ARA]

erat ... *he, she, it was; there was* [*ARA]

ergo ... *therefore* [*11]

erigo, erigere, erexi, erectus ... *to lift up; to open* one's eyes; (with the reflexive **se**, which is not translated in this idiom) *to arise, to get up*

eripio, eripere, eripui, ereptus ... *to snatch from* (+ dat.); *to untie* or *loosen* a knot; *to rescue* someone (acc.) *from* something (dat.); *to take away* something (acc.) *from* someone (dat.) [*11]

erro, erráre, errávi, errátus ... *to wander* [*ARA]

erubesco, erubescere, erubui ... *to grow red; to feel shame for, to show respect for*

erudio, erudíre, erudívi or **erudii, erudítus** ... *to educate, to instruct;* **erudítus, erudíta, erudítum:** *educated; learned, scholarly*

esse ... (pres. inf. of **sum**) *to be* [*ARA]

est ... *he, she, it is; there is* [*ARA]

et ... *and; also, even;* **et . . , et . . ,** *both . . , and . .* [*ARA]

etiam ... *also, even* [*ARA]

Etruscus, Etrusci, m. ... *an Etruscan*

etsi ... *even if, although*

evádo, evadere, evási ... *to go out; to escape, to get away; to go upward, to come upward*

eveho, evehere, evexi, evectus ... *to carry out, to carry up*

evinco, evincere, evíci, evictus ... *to conquer entirely; to win a way past, to overcome the resistance of*

ex ... see **e**

exaudio, exaudíre, exaudívi, exaudítus ... *to hear, to listen to*

excédo, excedere, excessi ... *to leave, to go out* from, *to depart* from

excerpo, excerpere, excerpsi, excerptus ... *to pick out; to make excerpts* or *extracts* of a literary text

excido, excidere, excidi ... *to fall out; to fall* or *escape* or *slip away from* (+ dat.)

excído, excidere, excídi, excísus ... *to cut out, to hew out*

excipio, excipere, excépi, exceptus ... *to take out; to gather, to pick up; to except, to exclude; to receive, to welcome*

excito, excitáre, excitávi, excitátus ... *to cause to move; to excite, to stir up; to arouse, to awaken; to heighten, to intensify* [*42]

exclámo, exclamáre, exclamávi ... *to cry out, to utter aloud*

excrebresco, excrebrescere, excrebui ... *to grow thick; to spring forth*

excrucio, excruciáre, excruciávi, excruciátus ... *to torment, to torture* [*43]

excubiae, excubiárum, f. ... (plur. noun with sing. meaning) *vigil; sentry, sentinel*

excutio, excutere, excussi, excussus ... *to shake out, to shake off*

exedo, exedere, exédi, exésus ... *to eat up; to make porous*

exemplum, exempli, n. ... *example*

exeo, exíre, exívi or **exii** ... *to go out; to rise up, to overflow*

exerceo, exercére, exercui, exercitus ... *to busy* or *occupy* oneself *with; to train* or *exercise* oneself *with*

exercitus, exercitus, m. ... *army* [*ARA]

exhálo, exhaláre, exhalávi ... *to breathe out*

exhaurio, exhauríre, exhausi, exhaustus ... *to draw out; to drain out, to clean out*

exhorresco, exhorrescere, exhorrui ... *to tremble, to shudder*

exigo, exigere, exégi, exactus ... *to drive out; to spend* one's time or life

exiguus, exigua, exiguum ... *tiny, small; mild, gentle* [*59]

existimo, existimáre, existimávi, existimátus ... *to judge, to think*

exitus, exitus, m. ... (plur. may have sing. meaning) *exit, way out; fate, death, outcome* [*10]

exorior, exoríri, exortus sum ... *to appear; to rise, to arise*

exósus, exósa, exósum ... *hating, detesting*

expallesco, expallescere, expallui ... *to turn pale*

expello, expellere, expuli, expulsus ... *to drive out*

experior, experíri, expertus sum ... *to try out; to undergo, to experience*

expers, expertis ... *having no part, wanting no part* (+ gen.)

explóro, exploráre, explorávi, explorátus ... *to ascertain, to investigate*

expolítus, expolíta, expolítum ... *smooth, polished*

expóno, exponere, exposui, expositus ... *to put out, to display; to explain, to set forth*

exposco, exposcere, expoposci ... *to demand; to entreat earnestly*

expostulo, expostuláre, expostulávi, expostulátus ... *to demand*

exprimo, exprimere, expressi, expressus ... *to press out; to convey, to express; to bear a resemblance to*

expugno, expugnáre, expugnávi, expugnátus ... *to capture, to conquer* [*ARA]

exsanguis, exsangue ... *bloodless*

exsecror, exsecrári, exsecrátus sum ... *to curse*

exsequor, exsequi, exsecútus sum ... *to pursue, to punish*

exsilio, exsilíre, exsilui ... *to leap up, to spring up*

exsilium, exsilii, n. ... *exile, banishment*

exspecto, exspectáre, exspectávi, exspectátus ... *to await, to wait for; to wait in expectation; to delay, to waste time* [*11]

exstinguo, exstinguere, exstinxi, exstinctus ... *to put out;* (in passive) *to die, to perish*

exsto, exstáre, exstiti ... *to stand out; to exist, to be found*

exsul, exsulis, c. ... an *exile*

exsulo, exsuláre, exsulávi, exsulátus ... *to be an exile, to live in exile*

exsulto, exsultáre, exsultávi ... *to spring up; to exult, to rejoice*

extemplo ... *immediately*

extendo, extendere, extendi, extentus ... *to stretch out*

externus, externa, externum ... *outside, external; of something outside, of something external*

exterreo, exterrére, exterrui, exterritus ... *to scare, to terrify, to frighten*

extollo, extollere ... *to lift up, to raise up*

extraho, extrahere, extraxi, extractus ... *to drag out, to draw out*

extrémus, extréma, extrémum ... *outermost; last, last of all; extremely urgent* or *desperate*

extuli ... see **effero**

exuviae, exuviárum, f. ... (plur. may have sing. meaning) *spoils; skin* or *slough* of a snake

F

Fabius, Fabii, m. ... *Fabius,* the Roman historian

fabula, fabulae, f. ... *story; rumor, gossip*

Fabullus, Fabulli, m. ... *Fabullus,* friend of Catullus

facies, faciéi, f. ... *face; look, appearance*

facilis, facile ... *easy;* **facile:** *easily* [*ARA]

facio, facere, feci, factus ... *to do, to make; to cause, to produce, to bring about* [*ARA, *35]

factum, facti, n. ... *deed* [*ARA]

facultas, facultátis, f. ... *power; means, resources*

facundia, facundiae, f. ... *eloquence*

fallo, fallere, fefelli, falsus ... *to deceive, to mislead; to appease, to satisfy; to disappoint, to fail to measure up to* [*25]

falsus, falsa, falsum ... *false, deceptive;* **falso:** *falsely, mistakenly*

fama, famae, f. ... *talk, rumor; fame, glory; reputation, respectability;* (as proper noun) **Fama:** the goddess *Rumor* [*69]

familiáris, familiáre ... *of the household;* (masc. as substantive) *member of the household*

famulus, famuli, m. ... *slave, attendant*

fastigium, fastigii, n. ... (plur. may have sing. meaning) *roof; top, peak*

fateor, fatéri, fassus sum ... *to admit, to confess; to declare, to profess*

fatum, fati, n. ... (plur. may have sing. meaning) *fate, fortune, destiny* [*64]

faveo, favére, favi ... *to favor, to be favorable* to (+ dat.)

favilla, favillae, f. ... *ashes*

fax, facis, f. ... *torch* [*49]

felicitas, felicitátis, f. ... *happiness; enjoyable exercise, delightful practice*

felix, felícis ... *happy, fortunate* [*29]

femina, feminae, f. ... *woman; wife* [*ARA]

femineus, feminea, femineum ... *womanly; of a woman, of the women*

femur, femoris, n. ... *thigh*

fenestra, fenestrae, f. ... *window; hole, breach*

fera, ferae, f. ... *beast, wild animal* [*ARA]

fere ... *almost, approximately; generally, for the most part*

ferio, feríre ... *to strike*

fero, ferre, tuli, latus ... *to carry; to bear, to bring; to bear away* or *off* or *along; to say, to relate, to report;* (in passive or with reflexive) *to move, to proceed, to make* one's *way* [*33]

ferox, ferócis ... *angry, cruel, fierce* [*26]

ferrum, ferri, n. ... *iron, steel; sword, weapon* [*32]

ferus, fera, ferum ... *wild, savage* [*ARA]

ferveo, fervére, ferbui ... *to boil; to be warm, to be inflamed*

fetus, fetus, m. ... *offspring; fruit* of a plant

fibula, fibulae, f. ... *clasp, brooch*

fidélis, fidéle ... *faithful, trustworthy*

fides, fidei, f. ... *faith, trust; help, promise* [*ARA]

fidus, fida, fidum ... *faithful, faithful* to (+ dat.)

figo, figere, fixi, fixus ... *to fix, to place; to pierce, to impale; to drive, to shoot, to thrust* [*ARA, *50]

figúra, figúrae, f. ... *form, shape; beauty, good looks* [*ARA]

filia, filiae, f. ... *daughter* [*ARA]

filius, filii, m. ... *son* [*ARA]

findo, findere, fidi, fissus ... *to split, to cleave*

fingo, fingere, finxi, fictus ... *to form, to shape; to feign, to invent, to contrive* [*22]

finio, finíre, finívi or **finii, finítus** ... *to end, to finish; to stop speaking, to draw to a close* [*54]

finis, finis, c. (gen. plur. **finium**) ... *end, limit;* (in plur.) *territory* [*ARA]

fio, fieri, factus sum ... (see *ARA*, App. J, pp. 466–68, for the conjugation of this irregular verb) *to become, to happen; to be made, to be built* [*34]

firmo, firmáre, firmávi, firmátus ... *to strengthen; to confirm, to make good*

firmus, firma, firmum ... *firm, solid*

fistula, fistulae, f. ... *pipe* for carrying water

flagellum, flagelli, n. ... *lash, whip; shoot* of a vine

flagro, flagráre, falgrávi ... *to be ablaze, to be on fire*

flamen, flaminis, n. ... *wind, blast* of wind

flamma, flammae, f. ... *fire, flame; firebrand* [*ARA, *62]

flebilis, flebile ... *tearful, weeping*

flecto, flectere, flexi, flexus ... *to bend; to turn* back, *to change* one's course; *to influence* or *prevail upon* one's mind [*27]

fleo, flere, flevi ... *to cry, to weep; to cry for, to weep for* [*37]

fletus, fletus, m. ... *crying, weeping;* (as the result of the crying or weeping) *tears* [*30]

floreo, florére, florui ... *to bloom, to flourish; to be decked* with, *to be covered* with (+ abl.) [*71]

flos, floris, m. ... *flower; chastity, virginity* [*ARA, *48]

fluentum, fluenti, n. ... *stream*

flumen, fluminis, n. ... *river;* (in plur.) *waters* of a river [*ARA, *53]

fluo, fluere, fluxi ... *to flow* [*ARA]

fluxus, fluxa, fluxum ... *flowing; weak, sick*

foedo, foedáre, foedávi, foedátus ... *to befoul; to defile, to pollute*

foedus, foeda, foedum ... *foul; horrible, shameful* [*70]

foedus, foederis, n. ... *compact, covenant*

fons, fontis, m. (gen. plur. **fontium**) ... *spring, fountain* [*ARA]

for, fari, fatus sum ... *to speak*

forámen, foraminis, n. ... *hole, opening*

foris, foris, f. (gen. plur. **forium**) ... *door;* **foras** or **foris:** (adv.) *outside, out of doors* [*10]

forma, formae, f. ... *form, shape; beauty, good looks* [*ARA]

formído, formidinis, f. ... *fear, alarm; dreadful* or *frightful thing*

formidolósus, formidolósa, formidolósum ... *alarming, frightful*

fors, fortis, f. ... *chance*

forsitan ... *perhaps*

forte ... *by chance, as it happened* [*31]

fortis, forte ... *brave, strong* [*ARA]

fortuitus, fortuita, fortuitum ... *disastrous, unfortunate*

fortúna, fortúnae, f. ... *fortune;* (as proper noun) **Fortúna:** the goddess *Fortune* [*30]

forum, fori, n. ... *forum* (= public square or market place)

fossa, fossae, f. ... *ditch, trench*

foveo, fovére, fovi, fotus ... *to keep warm; to fondle, to caress; to coddle, to pamper, to indulge* [*70]

frango, frangere, fregi, fractus ... *to break, to smash, to crush; to humble, to soften, to weaken* [*ARA, *27]

frater, fratris, m. ... *brother* [*ARA]

fraternus, fraterna, fraternum ... *brotherly, of a brother*

fremo, fremere, fremui ... *to roar; to clamor, to raise* one's *voice* [*68]

frenum, freni, n. ... (plur. may have sing. meaning) *bridle; bit, rein*

frequens, frequentis ... *crowded, frequented; in a crowd, in large numbers; densely* or *thickly populated;* **frequenter:** *often, frequently*

frigidus, frigida, frigidum ... *cold;* (fem. sing. as substantive) *cold water* [*62]

frons, frondis, f. (gen. plur. **frondium**) ... *leaf; leafage, foliage*

frons, frontis, f. (gen. plur. **frontium**) ... *brow, forehead; front, facade*

fruor, frui, fructus sum ... *to enjoy* (+ abl.)

frustra ... *in vain*

frustror, frustrári, frustrátus sum ... *to deceive, to mislead*

fuga, fugae, f. ... *flight, escape* [*14]

fugax, fugácis ... *fleeing, running away*

fugio, fugere, fugi ... *to flee, to run away; to flee* from, *to run away* from [*ARA, *41]

fugo, fugáre, fugávi, fugátus ... *to rout, to drive away* [*ARA]

fuit ... *he, she, it was; there was* [*ARA]

fulcio, fulcíre, fulsi, fultus ... *to prop up, to support*

fulgeo, fulgére, fulsi ... *to flash, to gleam, to shine* [*40]

fulgor, fulgóris, m. ... *brightness; lightning, flash of lightning*

fulgur, fulguris, n. ... *flash of lightning*

fulmen, fulminis, n. ... *thunderbolt* [*71]

fulvus, fulva, fulvum ... *brown, tawny*

fumus, fumi, m. ... *smoke*

fundo, fundere, fudi, fusus ... *to pour, to pour out*

fungor, fungi, functus sum ... *to perform, to execute* (+ abl.)

funus, funeris, n. ... *funeral; death, dead body* [*65]

fur, furis, c. ... *thief*

furia, furiae, f. ... *frenzy, madness;* (in plur.) the *Furies*

Furius, Furii, m. ... *Furius,* the Roman consul

furo, furere ... *to rage, to rush; to be frantic* or *frenzied* [*63]

furtívus, furtíva, furtívum ... *stolen; secret, clandestine*

G

Gabii, Gabiórum, m. ... (plur. noun with sing. meaning) the town *Gabii*

Gallicus, Gallica, Gallicum ... *Gallic*

Garamantis, Garamantidis ... *Garamantian* (= African)

gaudeo, gaudére, gavísus sum ... (semi-deponent verb) *to rejoice; to delight* in (+ abl.)

gaudium, gaudii, n. ... *joy, delight, gladness*

gelidus, gelida, gelidum ... *cold, chilly*

geminus, gemina, geminum ... *two, twin; double, twofold*

gemitus, gemitus, m. ... a *sigh,* a *groan;* a *sighing,* a *groaning* [*63]

gemma, gemmae, f. ... *jewel*

gener, generi, m. ... *son-in-law*

generositas, generositátis, f. ... *manner, noble bearing*

genetrix, genetrícis, f. ... *mother*

genitor, genitóris, m. ... *father;* (applied to Jupiter) *father, creator* [*51]

gens, gentis, f. (gen. plur. **gentium**) ... *race, stock; nation, people* [*ARA, *44]

genus, generis, n. ... *race, offspring; kind, variety* [*ARA]

Germánus, Germáni, m. ... a *German*

gero, gerere, gessi, gestus ... *to bear, to carry; to wage, to conduct; to display, to exhibit* [*18]

gestámen, gestaminis, n. ... (plur. may have sing. meaning) *armor, equipment*

gestio, gestíre, gestívi or **gestii** ... *to yearn, to be eager*

gigno, gignere, genui, genitus ... *to beget, to give birth to*

gingíva, gingívae, f. ... (collective sing.) *gums*

gladius, gladii, m. ... *sword* [*ARA]

glomero, glomeráre, glomerávi, glomerátus ... *to mass* or *gather together* something (acc.)

gloria, gloriae, f. ... *fame, glory* [*49]

glorior, gloriári, gloriátus sum ... *to brag, to boast*

gradior, gradi, gressus sum ... *to step, to walk*

gradus, gradus, m. ... *step, pace; stage, phase*

Graius, Graii, m. (gen. plur. **Graiórum** or **Graium**) ... a *Greek*

gramen, graminis, n. ... *grass; plant, herb*

grando, grandinis, f. ... *hail* (= pellets of ice)

grates, gratium, f. ... (plur. noun with sing. meaning) *thanks; gratitude, appreciation*

gratia, gratiae, f. ... *thanks; favor, friendship* [*ARA]

gratus, grata, gratum ... *pleasing; grateful, thankful;* **grate:** *willingly, obligingly*

gravidus, gravida, gravidum ... *pregnant; swollen, teeming*

gravis, grave ... *heavy, painful;* **graviter:** *heavily, painfully* [*ARA]

gravo, graváre, gravávi, gravátus ... *to make heavy, to weigh down*

gremium, gremii, n. ... *lap, bosom* [*37]

grex, gregis, m. ... (collective sing. or plur.) *herd, flock*

gubernaculum, gubernaculi, n. ... (plur. may have sing. meaning) *oar; helm*

gubernátor, gubernatóris, m. ... *helmsman*

gurges, gurgitis, m. ... *eddy, torrent;* a *flooding,* a *swirling*

gusto, gustáre, gustávi, gustátus ... *to taste; to eat, to have lunch* [*ARA, *13]

gutta, guttae, f. ... *drop* of water

gymnasium, gymnasii, n. ... *gymnasium*

H

habeo, habére, habui, habitus ... *to have, to hold; to bear, to carry; to beget, to give birth to; to take* or *occupy the place of;* (of leaves) *to be covered with* or *entwined with* [*ARA, *54]

habito, habitáre, habitávi, habitátus ... *to inhabit; to live, to dwell*

habitus, habitus, m. ... *manner, posture; costume, clothing*

haereo, haerére, haesi ... *to cling* to or on; *to stick fast* to, *to become fastened* in; *to be stuck, to be at a loss, to be in difficulty* [*51]

Hammon, Hammónis, m. ... the god *Hammon*

haréna, harénae, f. ... (plur. may have sing. meaning) *sand*

harundo, harundinis, f. ... *reed; shaft* of an arrow

hasta, hastae, f. ... *spear*

haud ... *not, not at all* [*68]

haudquaquam ... *not at all, by no means*

haurio, hauríre, hausi, haustus ... *to draw* water; *to drink* water

haustus, haustus, m. ... (plur. may have sing. meaning) a *drawing* of water; a *shedding* or *spilling* of blood

Hector, Hectoris, m. ... *Hector,* the Trojan warrior

Hectoreus, Hectorea, Hectoreum ... *of Hector*

Hecuba, Hecubae, f. ... *Hecuba,* queen of Troy

herba, herbae, f. ... *grass; plant, herb* [*52]

heres, herédis, c. ... *heir*

Hesperus, Hesperi, m. ... the *Evening-Star*

hesternus, hesterna, hesternum ... *yesterday's, of yesterday*

heu ... (interjection) *alas!*

hibernus, hiberna, hibernum ... *wintry, of the winter*

Hibérus, Hibéra, Hibérum ... *Spanish*

hic ... (adv.) *here; in this place, at this point*

hic, haec, hoc (gen. sing. **huius, huius, huius**) ... *this man, this woman, this thing* (as a pronoun); *this* (as an adjective) [*ARA]

hiems, hiemis, f. ... *winter*

hilaris, hilare ... *cheerful*

hinc ... *hence, from here, on this side*

hircus, hirci, m. ... *goat*

Hispania, Hispaniae, f. ... *Spain*

historia, historiae, f. ... *history*

hodie ... *today*

homo, hominis, m. ... *man; human being* [*ARA]

honor, honóris, m. ... (plur. may have sing. meaning) *honor; glory, beauty; gift, offering*

honorátus, honoráta, honorátum ... *honored, respected*

hora, horae, f. ... *hour* [*20]

horrendus, horrenda, horrendum ... *terrible, dreadful*

horreo, horrére, horrui ... *to bristle; to shudder, to tremble; to shudder at, to tremble at* [*71]

horridus, horrida, horridum ... *harsh, rough; uncouth, unkempt*

horror, horróris, m. ... a *bristling; fright, horror*

hortor, hortári, hortátus sum ... *to urge, to exhort*

hortus, horti, m. ... (plur. may have sing. meaning) *garden*

hospes, hospitis, m. ... *host; guest; stranger* [*ARA]

hospitális, hospitále ... *hospitable, used for a guest;* (neut. plur. as substantive) *guest-accommodations*

hostílis, hostíle ... *hostile, unfriendly*

hostis, hostis, c. (gen. plur. **hostium**) ... (plur. may have sing. meaning) *enemy* [*ARA]

huc ... *this way, to this place*

humánus, humána, humánum ... *human; of a human being, involving a human being* [*ARA]

humus, humi, f. ... *earth, ground*

Hymen, Hymenis, or **Hymenaeus, Hymenaei, m.** ... the god *Hymen* or *Hymenaeus* (= god of marriage)

I

iaceo, iacére, iacui ... *to lie; to recline* at a table; *to lie down, to lie sick, to lie dead* or *dying* [*58]

iacto, iactáre, iactávi, iactátus ... *to throw; to toss about* or *around; to utter forcefully* or *vehemently* [*ARA]

iam ... *now, already; soon, presently;* **iam iam:** *now indeed;* **iam iamque:** *now at any moment;* **iam . . , iam . . ,** *now . . , now . . * or *first . . , then . .* [*ARA, *48]

iamdúdum ... *now for a long time*

ianua, ianuae, f. ... *door, entrance* [*ARA]

Iarbas, Iarbae, m. (acc. sing. **Iarban**) ... the king *Iarbas*

ibi ... *there, in that place* [*ARA]

ictus, ictus, m. ... *blow, stroke; jet* or *stream* of water [*58]

idem, eadem, idem (gen. sing. **eiusdem, eiusdem, eiusdem**) ... (formed from **is, ea, id** and the suffix **-dem**) *same man, same woman, same thing* (as a pronoun); *same* (as an adjective) [*ARA]

identidem ... *repeatedly*

ideo ... *on that account, for that reason* [*19]

igitur ... *then, therefore* [*46]

ignárus, ignára, ignárum ... *ignorant, not knowing; blind, casual, accidental*

igneus, ignea, igneum ... *fiery*

ignis, ignis, m. (abl. sing. **igne** or **igni**, gen. plur. **ignium**) ... *fire, flame; lightning, thunderbolt* [*4]

ignóro, ignoráre, ignorávi, ignorátus ... *to not know, to not recognize*

ignótus, ignóta, ignótum ... *unknown*

ilia, ilium, n. ... (plur. noun with sing. meaning) *side, flank; groin, loins*

Iliacus, Iliaca, Iliacum ... *of Ilium* (= Trojan, of Troy)

illaesus, illaesa, illaesum ... *unharmed, uninjured*

illátus ... see **infero**

ille, illa, illud (gen. sing. **illíus, illíus, illíus**) ... *that man, that woman, that thing* (as a pronoun); *that* (as an adjective) [*ARA]

illic ... *there, in that place*

illído, illidere, illísi, illísus ... *to drive into; to strike, to beat on* (+ dat.)

illinc ... *thence, from there, on that side*

illuc ... *that way, to that place*

illúnis, illúne ... *moonless*

imágo, imaginis, f. ... *image; form, likeness* [*66]

imbecillis, imbecille ... *weak, sick*

imbellis, imbelle ... *unwarlike; not ready for war, not suited for war*

imber, imbris, m. ... *rain*

immánis, immáne ... *huge, enormous*

immatúrus, immatúra, immatúrum ... *unripe, immature; untimely, premature*

immemor, immemoris ... *unmindful* (+ gen.)

immineo, imminére ... *to overhang, to project over; to threaten, to be imminent; to press closely on, to follow closely on* (+ dat.) [*53]

immitto, immittere, immísi, immissus ... *to let go, to urge on; to let in, to grant entry*

impatiens, impatientis ... *impatient, intolerant* (+ gen.)

impello, impellere, impuli, impulsus ... *to drive, to drive forward; (of the wind) to blow on, to caress roughly*

impendo, impendere, impendi, impensus ... *to weigh out; to devote, to set aside*

imperátor, imperatóris, m. ... *ruler; general, commander*

imperfectus, imperfecta, imperfectum ... *unfinished, incomplete*

imperium, imperii, n. ... (plur. may have sing. meaning) *order, command; power, authority; empire, dominion* [*36]

impiger, impigra, impigrum ... *active; eager, vigorous*

implico, implicáre, implicui, implicitus ... *to enfold, to entwine*

impóno, imponere, imposui, impositus ... *to put on, to place on*

impotens, impotentis ... *powerless; out of control, lacking in control*

imprudentia, imprudentiae, f. ... *ignorance, inexperience*

impudícus, impudíca, impudícum ... *brazen, shameless; impure, unchaste, unfaithful*

impúne ... *without punishment;* **impúne ferre:** *to do something without punishment*

imus, ima, imum ... (alternate superl. of **inferus;** see *ARA,* App. D, p. 419) *lowest, very low; bottom of, bottommost part of*

in ... *in, into* (root meanings); *into, to, against* (+ acc.); *in order to cause* or *produce* (+ acc.); *in, on, among* (+ abl.); *at, during, in the course of* (+ abl.); *in respect to, when dealing with* (+ abl.); *as embodied in, as represented by* (+ abl.) [*ARA, *28]

inánis, ináne ... *empty, hollow* [*71]

inaudítus, inaudíta, inaudítum ... *unheard; unheard of, remarkable*

incalesco, incalescere, incalui ... *to grow hot, to become heated*

incautus, incauta, incautum ... *unwary, not alert*

incédo, incedere, incessi ... *to go; to advance, to proceed* [*68]

incendium, incendii, n. ... *fire, flame*

incendo, incendere, incendi, incensus ... *to set on fire; to inflame, to provoke* [*36]

incertus, incerta, incertum ... *unsure, uncertain* [*59]

incido, incidere, incidi ... *to occur, to happen; to fall* or *stumble in, on, into* (followed by dat. or prep. + acc.); *to come up in conversation, to present itself in conversation*

incipio, incipere, incépi, inceptus ... *to begin* [*46]

incito, incitáre, incitávi, incitátus ... *to excite, to arouse*

inclino, inclináre, inclinávi, inclinátus ... *to bend, to turn; to incline to change, to persuade to give in*

incoho, incoháre, incohávi, incohátus ... *to begin, to start*

incola, incolae, m. ... *dweller, inhabitant*

incomitátus, incomitáta, incomitátum ... *unescorted, unaccompanied*

incubo, incubáre, incubui ... *to lie on, to fall upon* (+ dat.)

incultus, inculta, incultum ... *untended, uncultivated*

incumbo, incumbere, incubui ... *to fall upon; to lean upon, to bend over* (+ dat.)

incurro, incurrere, incurri ... *to run* or *come* into; *to acquire, to contract*

incúso, incusáre, incusávi, incusátus ... *to blame, to criticize, to find fault with*

inde ... *then; from there, for that reason* [*ARA]

India, Indiae, f. ... *India*

indicium, indicii, n. ... *disclosure; proof, evidence*

indico, indicáre, indicávi, indicátus ... *to show, to reveal, to disclose*

indíco, indicere, indixi, indictus ... *to proclaim, to declare*

indignitas, indignitátis, f. ... *outrage, heinousness*

indignus, indigna, indignum ... *unworthy, undeserving; unworthy of, undeserving of* (+ gen. or abl.); *shameful, shocking, outrageous;* **indigne:** *unworthily, undeservedly, outrageously* [*41]

indulgentia, indulgentiae, f. ... *kindness, indulgence*

induo, induere, indui, indútus ... *to put on; to clothe, to dress*

industrius, industria, industrium ... *careful, diligent;* **industrie:** *carefully, diligently*

ineptio, ineptíre ... *to be silly, to act foolishly*

ineptus, inepta, ineptum ... *silly, foolish*

iners, inertis ... *useless, spiritless; lazy, inactive, slow-moving*

infandus, infanda, infandum ... *unspeakable; unnatural, disgraceful* [*ARA]

infans, infantis, c. ... *baby; child*

infaustus, infausta, infaustum ... *unlucky; hateful, sinister*

infectus, infecta, infectum ... *not done*

infelicitas, infelicitátis, f. ... *unhappiness; deplorable condition, unfortunate situation*

infélix, infelícis ... *unhappy, unfortunate* [*60]

infensus, infensa, infensum ... *hostile, hostile* to (+ dat.)

inferiae, inferiárum, f. ... (plur. noun with plur. meaning) *rites for the dead*

infero, inferre, intuli, illátus ... *to carry in;* (with reflexive) *to advance* or *proceed* as someone (acc.)

infestus, infesta, infestum ... *hostile, hostile* to (+ dat.)

infirmitas, infirmitátis, f. ... *weakness, sickness*

infundo, infundere, infundi, infúsus ... *to pour in* or *into* (+ dat.)

ingenium, ingenii, n. ... (plur. may have sing. meaning) *talent; character, disposition*

ingens, ingentis ... *huge, enormous* [*20]

ingrátus, ingráta, ingrátum ... *thankless, ungrateful;* **ingráte:** *unwillingly, ungratefully*

ingredior, ingredi, ingressus sum ... *to enter; to step on, to walk on* (+ abl.); *to begin, to begin to deal with* [*70]

inhaereo, inhaerére, inhaesi, inhaesus ... *to cling to, to grasp hold of*

inhibeo, inhibére, inhibui, inhibitus ... *to check, to restrain*

inimícus, inimíca, inimícum ... *unfriendly* [*72]

iniuria, iniuriae, f. ... *wrong, injustice*

innítor, inníti, innixus sum ... *to lean on, to support* oneself *on* (+ dat.)

innumerus, innumera, innumerum ... *countless, innumerable*

innuptus, innupta, innuptum ... *unmarried;* (fem. plur. as substantive) *unmarried women* (= maidens) [*46]

inornátus, inornáta, inornátum ... *unkempt, disheveled*

inquam ... *I say* or *said*

inquiétus, inquiéta, inquiétum ... *unquiet, restless*

inquíro, inquirere, inquisii, inquisítus ... *to ask about, to inquire about*

inquit ... *he, she, it says* or *said* [*15]

inríto, inritáre, inritávi, inritátus ... *to incite, to stir up, to inflame*

inritus, inrita, inritum ... *invalid; useless, ineffectual*

inscius, inscia, inscium ... *not knowing; unknowing, unwitting*

insequor, insequi, insecútus sum ... *to follow closely; to pursue, to attack; to follow, to come next* [*52]

insidior, insidiári, insidiátus sum ... *to lie in wait, to wait and watch*

insignis, insigne ... *conspicuous, standing out;* (neut. plur. as substantive) *attire, costume, regalia*

insons, insontis ... *innocent, guiltless*

instans, instantis ... *urgent, pressing, insistent;* **instanter:** *urgently, pressingly, insistently*

instar (indecl.) ... *image, likeness* (+ gen.)

instauro, instauráre, instaurávi, instaurátus ... *to renew, to restore*

instígo, instigáre, instigávi, instigátus ... *to incite, to provoke*

instituo, instituere, institui, institútus ... *to arrange, to establish; to appoint, to designate*

insto, instáre, institi ... *to press on, to pursue eagerly*

insulsus, insulsa, insulsum ... *unsalted; dull, boring, stupid*

insum, inesse, infui ... *to be in; to be present, to be at hand*

intactus, intacta, intactum ... *untouched, undamaged*

integer, integra, integrum ... *whole, intact, untouched*

integritas integritátis, f. ... *wholeness; integrity, uprightness*

intellego, intellegere, intellexi, intellectus ... *to perceive, to recognize, to understand* [*ARA]

intendo, intendere, intendi, intentus ... *to stretch out, to spread out;* **intentus, intenta, intentum:** *intent; exerting* oneself; *keenly focused* on, *intensely interested* in (+ acc.)

inter ... *among, between* (+ acc.); *amid, in the midst of* (+ acc.); *in between, in their midst* (as adv.) [*ARA, *36]

interdum ... *at times, sometimes*

interea ... *meanwhile; anyhow, at any rate* [*44]

interficio, interficere, interféci, interfectus ... *to kill* [*ARA]

intericio, intericere, interiéci, interiectus ... *to throw between;* (in passive) *to pass, to intervene*

interim ... *meanwhile, in the meantime* [*ARA]

interior, interius ... (compar. adj.) *inner, inner part of*

interpóno, interponere, interposui, interpositus ... *to place* someone or something *between;* (in pass.) *to pass, to elapse, to intervene*

interpretor, interpretári, interpretátus sum ... *to interpret; to take the view* or *position*

interrogo, interrogáre, interrogávi, interrogátus ... *to ask, to question* [*ARA]

interrumpo, interrumpere, interrúpi, interruptus ... *to break off, to interrupt*

intonsus, intonsa, intonsum ... *unshorn, unshaven*

intra ... *within, inside* (+ acc.) [*ARA]

intro, intráre, intrávi, intrátus ... *to enter, to go in*

introdúco, introducere, introduxi, introductus ... *to lead in, to bring in*

intueor, intuéri, intuitus sum ... *to watch, to gaze at, to look at*

intuli ... see **infero**

intus ... (adv.) *inside, within*

inusitátus, inusitáta, inusitátum ... *strange, unusual*

inutilis, inutile ... *useless, unfit for action*

invalesco, invalescere, invalui ... *to become strong, to become violent*

invalidus, invalida, invalidum ... *weak, powerless*

inveho, invehere, invexi, invectus ... *to carry in;* (in passive) *to sail, to sail to* (+ acc.); *to run over, to drive over* (+ dat.)

invenio, inveníre, invéni, inventus ... *to come upon; to find, to discover;* **parum inveníre:** *to be at a loss to know, to be unable to find out* [*ARA, *28]

inventum, inventi, n. ... *discovery, invention*

invicem ... *in turn, each in turn*

invideo, invidére, invídi, invísus ... *to cast a spell* or *evil eye on; to begrudge* someone (dat.) something (acc. or abl.); *to begrudge* someone (acc.) to do something (inf.) [*30]

invidia, invidiae, f. ... *envy, jealousy; resentment, indignation*

invidus, invida, invidum ... *envious, jealous*

invíso, invisere, invísi, invísus ... *to visit; to look at, to observe*

invísus, invísa, invísum ... *hateful, hateful* to (+ dat.)

invíto, invitáre, invitávi, invitátus ... *to invite; to entertain*

invítus, invíta, invítum ... *unwilling, not wishing, against* one's *will*

invius, invia, invium ... *pathless, impassable*

invoco, invocáre, invocávi, invocátus ... *to invoke*

iocósus, iocósa, iocósum ... *funny, humorous; joyous, pleasurable*

ipse, ipsa, ipsum (gen. sing. **ipsíus, ipsíus, ipsíus**) ... (intensive pronoun: appearing after the word it intensifies) *self* (e.g., **deus ipse**, *the god himself*); (appearing before the word it intensifies) *very* (e.g., **ipse deus**, *the very god*) [*ARA]

ira, irae, f. ... (plur. may have sing. meaning) *anger* [*ARA]

irátus, iráta, irátum ... *angry* [*ARA]

irrumo, irrumáre, irrumávi ... *to perform oral sex on*

irrumpo, irrumpere, irrúpi, irruptus ... *to break in* or *into, to burst in* or *into*

is, ea, id (gen. sing. **eius, eius, eius**) ... *he, she, it* (as a pronoun); *this, that* (as an adjective) [*ARA]

iste, ista, istud (gen. sing. **istíus, istíus, istíus**) ... *that man, that woman, that thing* (as a pronoun); *that, that of yours, such as you offer* (as an adjective) [*3]

istic ... *there, there by you*

istinc ... *from there; from the situation* one is *in*

ita ... *thus, in this way, in such a way* [*ARA]

Italia, Italiae, f. ... *Italy*

itaque ... *and so, therefore* [*ARA]

item ... *also* [*ARA]

iter, itineris, n. ... *way, road, journey* [*ARA]

iterum ... *again, a second time* [*67]

iubar, iubaris, n. ... *sunlight, sunshine*

iubeo, iubére, iussi, iussus ... *to order, to command* [*ARA]

iucundus, iucunda, iucundum ... *pleasant, delightful*

iugális, iugále ... *yoked; nuptial, of marriage*

iugerum, iugeri, n. ... *measure of land;* (in plur.) *acres, tracts*

iugulo, iuguláre, iugulávi, iugulátus ... *to cut the throat of; to kill, to murder*

iugum, iugi, n. ... *yoke; ridge, slope*

Iulus, Iuli, m. ... *Iulus,* son of Aeneas (= Ascanius)

iunctúra, iunctúrae, f. ... *joint, connection*

iungo, iungere, iunxi, iunctus ... *to join, to yoke; to unite, to bring together; to join* someone (acc.) *in marriage* to someone (dat.) [*26]

iunior, iunióris, m. ... *younger man;* (in plur.) *younger men* (= the juniors)

Iunius, Iunii, m. ... *Iunius* (= Brutus's clan-name)

Iuno, Iunónis, f. ... *Juno*

Iuppiter, Iovis, or **Iovis, Iovis,** m. ... *Jupiter, Jove*

iuro, iuráre, iurávi, iurátus ... *to swear*

ius, iuris, n. ... *law, right;* **iure:** *justly, rightly* [*46]

iustus, iusta, iustum ... *just, proper*

iuvenális, iuvenále ... *youthful, of* one's *youth*

iuvencus, iuvenci, m. ... *young ox, young bull*

iuvenis, iuvene ... *young;* (masc. sing. as substantive) *young man* [*1]

iuventa, iuventae, f. ... *youth*

Iuventius, Iuventii, m. ... the boy *Juventius*

iuventus, iuventútis, f. ... *youth, the youth* [*67]

iuvo, iuváre, iuvi, iutus ... *to help, to assist*

iuxta ... *next to, close to* (+ acc.); *near by, close by* (as adv.) [*64]

K

Kalendae, Kalendárum, f. (abbreviated **Kal.**) ... the *Calends*

Karthágo, Karthaginis, f. ... the city *Carthage*

L

labefacto, labefactáre, labefactávi, labefactátus ... *to weaken, to make unsteady; to corrupt, to cause to waver*

labellum, labelli, n. ... *lip*

Labíci, Labicórum, m. ... (plur. noun with sing. meaning) the town *Labici*

labo, labáre, labávi ... *to totter; to waver, to become weak*

labor, labi, lapsus sum ... *to slip, to fall; to slip or fall* from (+ abl.); *to glide, to move smoothly; to wane, to decline, to draw to a close* [*57]

labor, labóris, m. ... *work, toil; struggle, hardship* [*35]

labóro, laboráre, laborávi, laborátus ... *to work; to toil, to struggle*

lacertus, lacerti, m. ... *upper arm;* (in general) *arm* [*59]

lacrima, lacrimae, f. ... *tear* [*ARA]

laedo, laedere, laesi, laesus ... *to hurt; to strike, to injure* [*50]

laetitia, laetitiae, f. ... (plur. may have sing. meaning) *happiness*

laetus, laeta, laetum ... *happy, joyful* [*36]

laevus, laeva, laevum ... *left;* (fem. sing. as substantive): *left hand*

Lampsacénus, Lampsacéna, Lampsacénum ... *of Lampsacus* or *from Lampsacus*

lana, lanae, f. ... *wool; spinning*

languidus, languida, languidum ... *weak, faint*

lanio, laniáre, laniávi, laniátus ... *to tear, to mangle, to lacerate*

Lanuvínus, Lanuvíni, m. ... a *Lanuvinian*

lapicída, lapicídae, m. ... *stone-cutter*

lapis, lapidis, m. ... *stone; precious stone* (= gem or jewel) [*ARA, *44]

lapso, lapsáre ... *to slip*

lascívus, lascíva, lascívum ... *playful, mischievous*

latebra, latebrae, f. ... *hiding-place; den, lair*

lateo, latére, latui ... *to hide; to lie hidden, to be concealed; to escape notice* or *detection* [*47]

Latínus, Latína, Latínum ... *Latin*

latitúdo, latitudinis, f. ... *width, breadth;* **in latitudinem:** *horizontally*

Latius, Latia, Latium ... *Latin, Roman*

latus ... see **fero**

latus, lata, latum ... *wide, broad;* **late:** *widely, over a large area* [*11]

latus, lateris, n. ... *side, flank* [*66]

laudo, laudáre, laudávi, laudátus ... *to praise* [*5]

laurea, laureae, or **laurus, lauri,** f. ... *laurel, laurel-tree*

laus, laudis, f. ... *praise; award, prize; honor, renown* [*30]

Lavinium, Lavinii, n. ... the town *Lavinium*

Lavínius, Lavinia, Lavinium ... *Lavinian, of Lavinium*

lavo, laváre, lavi, lautus or **lotus** ... *to wash, to bathe; to clean, to brush* [*ARA, *15]

lea, leae, f. ... *lioness* [*ARA]

leaena, leaenae, f. ... *lioness*

lectus, lecti, m. ... *bed, couch* [*ARA]

legátus, legáti, m. ... *envoy, ambassador*

legio, legiónis, f. ... *legion*

lego, legere, legi, lectus ... *to gather; to read, to recite; to choose, to select* [*19]

Lenaeus, Lenaea, Lenaeum ... *Lenaean* (= Bacchic, of Bacchus)

lenio, leníre, lenívi, lenítus ... *to calm, to appease, to alleviate*

leno, lenónis, m. ... *procurer, brothel-keeper* [*7]

leo, leónis, m. ... *lion* [*ARA]

lepus, leporis, m. ... *hare*

Lesbia, Lesbiae, f. ... *Lesbia,* mistress of Catullus

letális, letále ... *deadly*

letum, leti, n. ... *death* [*60]

levis, leve ... *light, gentle;* **leviter:** *lightly, gently* [*16]

levo, leváre, leávi, levátus ... *to lift up;* (used with the reflexive **se,** which is not translated in this idiom) *to arise, to get up*

lex, legis, f. ... *law; order, control; term, condition* [*50]

liber, libera, liberum ... *free;* **libere:** *freely* [*ARA]

liber, libri, m. ... *book, volume; bark* of a tree [*18]

liberális, liberále ... *kind, generous;* (referring to studies, education, etc.) *artistic, liberal, humane;* **liberaliter:** *kindly, generously* [*ARA, *12]

liberalitas, liberalitátis, f. ... *kindness, generosity*

liberátor, liberatóris, m. ... *liberator*

liberi, liberórum, m. ... (plur. noun with plur. meaning) *children; sons* [*22]

libero, liberáre, liberávi, liberátus ... *to free; to free* someone (acc.) *from* something (abl.) [*ARA]

libet, libére, libuit ... (impersonal verb) **libet** = *it is pleasing,* **libére** = *to be pleasing,* **libuit** = *it was pleasing*

libído, libidinis, f. ... (plur. may have sing. meaning) *pleasure; lust, passion* [*9]

libo, libáre, libávi, libátus ... *to pour as a libation; to pour* something (acc.) *as a libation* for someone (dat.)

libra, librae, f. ... *pound* (= unit of weight)

Liburnica, Liburnicae, f. ... *Liburnian galley*

Libya, Libyae, f. ... *Libya*

licet ... (conj.) *although*

licet, licére, licuit ... (impersonal verb) **licet** = *it is allowed,* **licére** = *to be allowed,* **licuit** = *it was allowed*

lignum, ligni, n. ... *wood*

limbus, limbi, m. ... *border* of a cloak

limen, liminis, n. ... (plur. may have sing. meaning) *doorway, entrance, threshold* [*16]

lingua, linguae, f. ... (plur. may have sing. meaning) *tongue* [*62]

linquo, linquere, liqui ... *to leave*

linteum, lintei, n. ... (plur. may have sing. meaning) *linen, linen-cloth*

litus, litoris, n. ... *beach, shore* [*17]

Livius, Livii, m. ... *Livy,* the Roman historian

loco, locáre, locávi, locátus ... *to put, to place*

locuples, locuplétis ... *rich; richly endowed*

locupléto, locupletáre, locupletávi, locupletátus ... *to enrich, to make wealthy*

locus, loci, m. (in plur.: **loci, locórum,** m., or **loca, locórum,** n.) ... (plur. may have sing. meaning) *place; area, region* [*ARA, *27]

longaevus, longaeva, longaevum ... *old, aged*

Longula, Longulae, f. ... the town *Longula*

longus, longa, longum ... *long, tall;* **longe:** *far, by far; far off, far away* [*ARA]

loquor, loqui, locútus sum ... *to speak; to say, to tell* [*ARA]

lotium, lotii or **loti,** n. ... *urine*

lubricus, lubrica, lubricum ... *slippery; sinuous, wriggling*

luceo, lucére, luxi ... *to shine*

Lucretia, Lucretiae, f. ... *Lucretia,* wife of Collatinus

Lucretius, Lucretii, m. ... *Lucretius,* father of Lucretia

luctus, luctus, m. ... (plur. may have sing. meaning) *mourning, lamentation* [*60]

lucubro, lucubráre, lucubrávi ... *to work by lamplight*

ludificor, ludificári, ludificátus sum ... *to make* something *seem ludicrous* or *ridiculous*

ludo, ludere, lusi ... *to play, to have fun; to tease, to trifle with* [*43]

ludus, ludi, m. ... *play; game, prank*

lugeo, lugére, luxi ... *to mourn, to lament* [*ARA]

lumen, luminis, n. ... (plur. may have sing. meaning) *light, source of light;* (of the light in one's head) *eye* [*17]

luna, lunae, f. ... *moon;* (as proper noun) **Luna:** the *moon-goddess* [*57]

lupa, lupae, f. ... *she-wolf; whore, prostitute*

lupánar, lupanáris, n. ... *brothel, house of prostitution*

lupus, lupi, m. ... *wolf*

luridus, lurida, luridum ... *murky, sickly, ghastly*

lustro, lustráre, lustrávi, lustrátus ... *to purify; to run through, to roam through; to observe, to examine, to consider* [*65]

lustrum, lustri, n. ... *woodland; den* or *lair* of a wild animal

lusus, lusus, m. ... *play; amusement, entertainment*

lux, lucis, f. ... *light; day, daylight; sheen, splendor;* **sub luce:** *at daybreak* [*51]

luxus, luxus, m. ... *indulgence, extravagance*

Lycia, Lyciae, f. ... the country *Lycia*

lymphátus, lympháta, lymphátum ... *crazed, frantic, frenzied*

lyra, lyrae, f. ... *lyre* [*12]

M

machina, machinae, f. ... *machine; machinery, equipment*

maculósus, maculósa, maculósum ... *spotted, blotched*

madefacio, madefacere, madeféci, madefactus ... *to make wet; to soak, to drench*

madeo, madére ... *to be wet; to be wet with perfume*

Maeonius, Maeonia, Maeonium ... *Maeonian* (= Phrygian)

maereo, maerére ... *to mourn, to grieve*

maeror, maeróris, m. ... *grief, sorrow*

maestitia, maestitiae, f. ... *sadness, sorrow*

maestus, maesta, maestum ... *sad, sorrowful; distressed, disturbed*

magis ... (compar. of **magnopere;** see *ARA,* App. D, p. 421) *more, rather;* **magis .., quam ..,** *more .., than ..* [*ARA, *13]

magister, magistri, m. ... *master, teacher*

magistrátus, magistrátus, m. ... *office, official position*

magnitúdo, magnitudinis, f. ... *size, magnitude*

magnus, magna, magnum ... *great; brave, heroic* [*ARA, *15]

maiestas, maiestátis, f. ... *dignity, majesty*

maior, maius ... (compar. of **magnus;** see *ARA,* App. D, p. 419) *greater*

malo, malle, malui ... *to prefer* [*39]

malus, mala, malum ... *bad, evil; harmful, poisonous;* (neut. sing. as substantive) *bad thing, evil thing;* **male:** *badly, unfavorably* [*ARA, *14]

mancipium, mancipii, n. ... *property; slave, chattel*

mando, mandáre, mandávi, mandátus ... *to entrust; to order, to command*

mando, mandere, mandi, mansus ... *to chew, to champ*

mane ... (adv.) *in the morning, early in the morning;* **primo mane:** *at the crack of dawn*

maneo, manére, mansi ... *to stay, to remain; to await, to be in store for* [*12]

mano, manáre, manávi ... *to flow* [*ARA]

mansio, mansiónis, f. ... *lodging, dwelling*

manus, manus, f. ... *hand* [*ARA]

Marcius, Marcii, m. ... *Marcius* (= Coriolanus's clan-name)

mare, maris, n. (gen. plur. **marium**) ... *sea* [*ARA]

marítus, maríti, m. ... *husband; partner, helpmate*

Massýlus, Massýla, Massýlum ... *Massylian* (= African)

mater, matris, f. ... *mother* [*ARA]

maternus, materna, maternum ... *maternal, of* one's *mother*

matróna, matrónae, f. ... *matron, married woman*

matúro, maturáre, maturávi, maturátus ... *to ripen, to mature; to hasten, to advance in time*

matúrus, matúra, matúrum ... *ripe, mature;* **matúre:** *quickly, expeditiously*

Maurusius, Maurusia, Maurusium ... *Maurusian* (= African)

maximus, maxima, maximum ... (superl. of **magnus**; see *ARA,* App. D, p. 419) *greatest, very great; very brave, very heroic;* **maxime:** *very greatly, most of all* [*9]

me ... (acc. or abl. sing. of **ego**) *me* or *by/with me* [*6]

meátus, meátus, m. ... *way, path, passage*

medeor, medéri ... *to cure*

medicína, medicínae, f. ... *medicine, art of healing*

medicus, medici, m. ... *doctor, physician*

meditor, meditári, meditátus sum ... (perf. participle may have pass. meaning) *to think over; to ponder, to consider; to practice, to rehearse*

medius, media, medium ... *midmost, middle of, in the middle;* **in medium:** *into everyone's midst* or *sight* [*ARA]

medulla, medullae, f. ... (plur. may have sing. meaning) *marrow, inmost part*

mei ... (gen. sing. of **ego**) *of me*

meio, meiere, minxi ... *to urinate; to excrete* something (acc.) during urination

melior, melius ... (compar. of **bonus**; see *ARA,* App. D, p. 419) *better* [*3]

mellítus, mellíta, mellítum ... *honey-sweet*

melos, meleos, n. (Greek word with gen. sing. **meleos** and acc. sing. **melos**) ... *song, tune*

membrum, membri, n. ... *limb* of the body [*6]

memini, meminisse ... (perf. act. ind. first pers. sing. and perf. act. inf. of the defective verb **memini**, translated with pres. force) **memini** = *I remember;* **meminisse** = *to remember*

memor, memoris ... *mindful* (+ gen.) [*ARA]

memorabilis, memorabile ... *memorable, worthy of memory*

memoro, memoráre, memorávi, memorátus ... *to speak, to mention, to call to mind;* **memorátus, memoráta, memorátum:** *famous for, celebrated for* (+ gen.)

mens, mentis, f. (gen. plur. **mentium**) ... *mind, heart; frame of mind; purpose, intention* [*ARA, *45]

mensa, mensae, f. ... *table*

mentio, mentiónis, f. ... *mention*

mentior, mentíri, mentítus sum ... *to lie; to invent, to make up*

mentula, mentulae, f. ... *penis, phallus*

mentum, menti, n. ... *chin*

Mercurius, Mercurii, m. ... *Mercury*

merus, mera, merum ... *pure, sheer*

metuo, metuere, metui ... *to fear, to be afraid of*

metus, metus, m. ... *fear* [*14]

meus, mea, meum ... (possessive adj. related to **ego**) *my* [*2]

mico, micáre, micui ... *to dart; to flash, to gleam*

mihi or **mi** ... (dat. sing. of **ego**) *to/for me* [*1]

miles, militis, m. ... *soldier;* (collective sing.) *army, soldiers* [*ARA, *63]

militia, militiae, f. ... (plur. may have sing. meaning) *military duty* or *service*

mille (indecl.) ... a *thousand;* **milia, milium,** n.: *thousands* [*38]

minae, minárum, f. ... (plur. noun with plur. meaning) *threats*

minax, minácis ... *threatening*

minimus, minima, minimum ... (superl. of **parvus;** see *ARA,* App. D, p. 419) *smallest;* **minime:** *very little; not at all, not in the least* [*33]

minor, minus ... (compar. of **parvus;** see *ARA,* App. D, p. 419) *smaller*

minus ... (compar. of **parum;** see *ARA,* App. D, p. 421) *less*

mirabilis, mirabile ... *wonderful, remarkable*

miraculum, miraculi, n. ... *wonder, marvel*

miror, mirári, mirátus sum ... *to wonder, to be amazed;* (gerundive) **mirandus, miranda, mirandum:** *amazing, astonishing*

mirus, mira, mirum ... *amazing, astonishing;* (in negative context) not *surprising,* not *unexpected* [*ARA, *44]

misceo, miscére, miscui, mixtus ... *to mix, to mingle; to stir up, to throw into confusion; to mix* or *mingle* something (acc.) with something (dat. or abl.) [*3]

misellus, misella, misellum ... *sad little, poor little, wretched little*

Misenensis, Misenense ... *of Misenum, stationed at Misenum*

Misénum, Miséni, n. ... the town *Misenum*

miser, misera, miserum ... *sad, poor, wretched* [*5]

miserabilis, miserabile ... *pitiable, deplorable*

misereor, miseréri, miseritus or **misertus sum** ... *to have pity, to show compassion; to have pity for, to show compassion for* (+ gen. or dat.)

miseria, miseriae, f. ... *trouble, distress*

misericordia, misericordiae, f. ... *pity, compassion* [*ARA]

misericors, misericordis ... *having pity* or *compassion for* (+ gen.)

miseror, miserári, miserátus sum ... *to bewail; to pity, to have pity for;* (gerundive) **miserandus, miseranda, miserandum:** *to be pitied, to be lamented*

mitis, mite ... *mild, gentle; sweet, juicy*

mitra, mitrae, f. ... *turban, bonnet*

mitto, mittere, misi, missus ... *to send, to let go; to bring, to place; to throw, to let fly; to throw down, to fling down* [*ARA, *66]

mobilitas, mobilitátis, f. ... *speed*

moderátus, moderáta, moderátum ... *controlled, restrained;* **moderáte:** *with control, with restraint*

modicus, modica, modicum ... *modest, moderate*

modo ... *just, only; just now, recently;* **modo . . , modo . . ,** *now . . , now . . ;* **non modo . . , sed (etiam) . . ,** *not only . . , but (also) . .* [*10]

modulátus, moduláta, modulátum ... *rhythmical, modulated;* **modulanter:** *rhythmically, melodiously*

modulor, modulári, modulátus sum ... *to attune, to modulate; to play* or *sing to the accompaniment of* an instrument (+ abl.)

modus, modi, m. ... *way, manner;* (abl. sing. + gen.) *in the way* of; (abl. sing. + adj.) *in . . . way;* (abl. plur. + adj.) *in . . . ways* [*ARA, *21]

moechus, moechi, m. ... *adulterer; lecher, debaucher*

moenia, moenium, n. ... (plur. noun with plur. meaning) *city-walls*

moles, molis, f. (gen. plur. **molium**) ... *mass, rock; breakwater, embankment*

molestus, molesta, molestum ... *annoying, troublesome*

molior, molíri, molítus sum ... *to work at, to build up; to take on, to shoulder*

mollis, molle ... *soft, gentle* [*39]

moneo, monére, monui, monitus ... *to warn, to advise* [*ARA]

mons, montis, m. (gen. plur. **montium**) ... *mountain* [*ARA]

monstrum, monstri, n. ... *omen; monster*

monumentum, monumenti, n. ... *memorial, monument*

mora, morae, f. ... *delay*

morbus, morbi, m. ... *disease, sickness* [*42]

mordeo, mordére, momordi, morsus ... *to bite*

moribundus, moribunda, moribundum ... *dying*

morior, mori, mortuus sum (fut. act. part. **moritúrus**) ... *to die;* **mortuus, mortua, mortuum:** *dead* [*ARA, *32]

moror, morári, morátus sum ... *to delay, to tarry; to detain, to hold back* [*72]

mors, mortis, f. (gen. plur. **mortium**) ... *death* [*ARA]

morsus, morsus, m. ... *bite; jaws, teeth*

mortalitas, mortalitátis, f. ... *mortality; humanity, human condition*

morum, mori, n. ... *mulberry*

morus, mori, f. ... *mulberry-tree*

mos, moris, m. ... *way, custom, manner*

motus, motus, m. ... (plur. may have sing. meaning) *motion, movement; outbreak, uprising*

moveo, movére, movi, motus ... *to move; to incite, to provoke* [*ARA, *34]

mox ... *then, soon, presently* [*23]

mucro, mucrónis, m. ... *sword*

Mugilla, Mugillae, f. ... the town *Mugilla*

mulceo, mulcére, mulsi, mulsus ... *to stroke, to caress*

muliebris, muliebre ... *womanly; of a woman, of the women; involving the women, concerning the women* [*ARA, *31]

mulier, mulieris, f. ... *woman* [*ARA]

multiplex, multiplicis ... *manifold, multifarious*

multitúdo, multitudinis, f. ... *multitude*

multus, multa, multum ... (sing.) *much,* (plur.) *many;* **multo** or **multum:** *much, by much, greatly* [*ARA, *44]

mundus, mundi, m. ... *world, universe*

munimentum, munimenti, n. ... *defense, protection*

munus, muneris, n. ... *duty; gift, present* [*ARA]

murmur, murmuris, n. ... *roar, rumble; murmur, whisper* [*55]

murus, muri, m. ... *wall* [*ARA]

musicus, musica, musicum ... *musical*

muto, mutáre, mutávi, mutátus ... *to change* [*ARA]

mutus, muta, mutum ... *silent*

mutuus, mutua, mutuum ... *mutual;* **mutuo:** *mutually, in turn*

Mytiléna, Mytilénae, f. ... the city *Mytilene*

N

nam or **namque** ... (conj. introducing an explanation) *for* [*14]

narro, narráre, narrávi, narrátus ... *to tell, to speak, to relate; to tell someone* (dat.) *about something* (acc.) [*ARA, *66]

nascor, nasci, natus sum ... *to be born, to be formed; to spring up, to spring* from (+ abl.) [*ARA]

nasus, nasi, m. ... *nose*

nata, natae, f. ... *daughter* [*2]

natúra, natúrae, f. ... *nature* [*ARA]

naturális, naturále ... *natural*

natus, nati, m. ... *son* [*65]

naufrágus, naufrága, naufrágum ... *shipwrecked*

Nautius, Nautii, m. ... *Nautius,* the Roman consul

navigo, navigáre, navigávi, navigátus ... *to sail* [*ARA]

navis, navis, f. (gen. plur. **navium**) ... *ship* [*ARA]

ne ... *lest, that not, in order that not;* **ne . . . quidem:** (emphasizing the intervening word) *not even* (e.g., **ne aurum quidem,** *not even gold*) [*ARA, *20]

-ne ... (in direct question, attached to the first word of the question but itself not translated) e.g., **amasne puellam?** *do you love the girl?* (in indirect question) *whether, if;* (in double indirect question, appearing once but translated twice) *whether . . , or . .* [*29]

nebula, nebulae, f. ... *mist, cloud*

nec, neque ... *and not, nor; not, not even;* **nec . . , nec . . ,** *neither . . , nor . . ;* **neque . . , neque . . ,** *neither . . , nor . .* [*ARA, *60]

necesse (indecl.) ... *necessary, essential*

neco, necáre, necávi, necátus ... *to kill* [*ARA]

necopinátus, necopináta, necopinátum ... *unexpected*

nefandus, nefanda, nefandum ... *unspeakable; abominable, despicable*

neglegens, neglegentis ... *careless* [*ARA]

nego, negáre, negávi, negátus ... *to deny, to say no; to deny* that; *to say* that . . . *not; to block, to prevent, to prohibit* [*ARA, *16]

nemus, nemoris, n. ... *forest; glade, grove*

Neoptolemus, Neoptolemi, m. ... *Neoptolemus,* son of Achilles (= Pyrrhus)

nepos, nepótis, m. ... *grandchild; grandson* [*63]

nequaquam ... *not at all, by no means*

neque ... see **nec**

nequiquam ... *in vain* [*44]

nervus, nervi, m. ... *tendon; bowstring, lyrestring*

nescio, nescíre, nescívi or **nescii** ... *to not know, not to know;* **nescio quis, nescio quid:** (masc./fem.) *someone or other, suitable for someone or other,* (neut.) *something or other, for some unexplained reason*

nescius, nescia, nescium ... *not knowing, not realizing* [*67]

neu, neve ... *and lest, and that . . . not*

nex, necis, f. ... *death*

ni or **nisi** ... *if not, unless; except* [*ARA, *39]

niger, nigra, nigrum ... *black*

nihil or **nil** (indecl.) ... *nothing;* (used with adv. force) *not at all, in no respect* [*ARA]

nihilominus ... *nevertheless, none the less*

nihilum, nihili, n. ... *nothing;* (abl. with compar. word) *not at all, by no degree*

nimbus, nimbi, m. ... *cloud; rain, storm*

nimírum ... *indeed, certainly*

nimis ... *too much; excessively, exceedingly*

nimius, nimia, nimium ... *too much; excessive, very great;* **nimium:** (adv.) *too much; excessively, exceedingly* [*56]

Ninus, Nini, m. ... *Ninus,* king of Nineveh

nisi ... see **ni**

nitidus, nitida, nitidum ... *bright; shining, gleaming*

nitor, nitóris, m. ... *brightness; beauty, radiance*

niveus, nivea, niveum ... *snowy, snow-white*

nix, nivis, f. ... *snow*

nobilis, nobile ... *noble, well-born*

nobilitas, nobilitátis, f. ... *high birth, nobility of birth*

nobis ... (dat. or abl. plur. of **ego**) *to/for us* or *by/with us*

noceo, nocére, nocui ... *to harm, to injure* (+ dat.); **nocens, nocentis:** *harmful, injurious*

Noctifer, Noctiferi, m. ... the *Evening-Star*

nocturnus, nocturna, nocturnum ... *nocturnal*

nodo, nodáre, nodávi, nodátus ... *to knot, to fasten*

nodus, nodi, m. ... *knot, bond*

nolo, nolle, nolui ... *to not wish, to be unwilling* [*40]

nomen, nominis, n. ... *name* [*ARA]

nomino, nomináre, nominávi, nominátus ... *to call, to name* [*ARA]

non ... *not* [*ARA]

nondum ... *not yet*

nonus, nona, nonum ... *ninth*

nos ... (nom. or acc. plur. of **ego**) *we* or *us*

noscito, noscitáre, noscitávi, noscitátus ... *to try to recognize*

nosco, noscere, novi, notus ... (perf. may have pres. meaning) *to know; to get to know, to investigate*

noster, nostra, nostrum ... (possessive adj. related to **nos**) *our* [*2]

notitia, notitiae, f. ... *acquaintance*

noto, notáre, notávi, notátus ... *to mark; to mar, to scar; to notice, to observe*

notus, nota, notum ... *known, familiar*

novicius, novicia, novicium ... *new, newly purchased;* (fem. sing. as substantive) *new girl*

Novocomensis, Novocomense ... *of Novum Comum*

novus, nova, novum ... *new, fresh; strange, unusual;* **novissime:** *last, last in time, for the last time* [*17]

nox, noctis, f. (gen. plur. **noctium**) ... *night;* **noctu:** *at night;* **sub noctem:** *toward nightfall* [*ARA, *56]

noxa, noxae, f. ... *guilt, wrongdoing*

nubes, nubis, f. (gen. plur. **nubium**) ... *cloud* [*20]

nubilus, nubila, nubilum ... *cloudy;* (neut. plur. as substantive) *clouds*

nudo, nudáre, nudávi, nudátus ... *to lay bare; to expose, to reveal*

nudus, nuda, nudum ... *bare, naked; stripped, despoiled* [*ARA]

nullus, nulla, nullum (gen. sing. **nullíus, nullíus, nullíus**) ... *no, not any;* (used with adv. force) *not at all, in no respect;* (masc./fem. as substantive) *no man, no woman* [*ARA, *40]

numen, numinis, n. ... (plur. may have sing. meaning) *majesty, divinity, divine power* [*45]

numerus, numeri, m. ... *number*

numquam ... *never* [*43]

numquid ... (interrogative adverb introducing a question that expects a negative answer) *surely it cannot be that . . .* or *it is not possible, is it, that . . .*

nunc ... *now* [*ARA]

nuntio, nuntiáre, nuntiávi, nuntiátus ... *to report* [*ARA]

nuntius, nuntia, nuntium ... *bringing word* or *news of* (+ gen.)

nuntius, nuntii, m. ... *messenger; message, report* [*23]

nuper ... *recently, not long ago*

nurus, nurus, f. ... *daughter-in-law*

nusquam ... *nowhere*

nuto, nutáre, nutávi ... *to nod; to rock, to sway*

nutrio, nutríre, nutrívi or **nutrii, nutrítus** ... *to nourish*

nutus, nutus, m. ... a *nod,* a *nodding*

nympha, nymphae, f. ... *nymph;* (as proper noun) **Nympha:** a *Nymph* [*50]

O

o ... (interjection) *oh!*

obdúco, obducere, obduxi, obductus ... *to lead to; to cover up, to cover over*

obdúro, obduráre, obdurávi, obdurátus ... *to be hard; to hold out, to stand firm* [*40]

obésus, obésa, obésum ... *fat, plump*

oblído, oblidere, oblísi, oblísus ... *to crush*

oblino, oblinere, oblévi, oblitus ... *to smear, to cover*

obliviscor, oblivisci, oblítus sum ... *to forget; to lose sight of, to put aside thoughts of* (+ gen.) [*ARA, *72]

oborior, oboríri, obortus sum ... *to rise up, to well up*

obscúrus, obscúra, obscúrum ... *dim, dark, dusky*

obsequor, obsequi, obsecútus sum ... *to comply, to consent*

observo, observáre, observávi, observátus ... *to observe; to guard, to watch over*

obstinátus, obstináta, obstinátum ... *stubborn, obstinate*

obstipesco, obstipescere, obstipui ... *to be dazed, to be astonished, to be dumbfounded*

obsto, obstáre, obstiti ... *to block the way; to stand in the way of* (+ dat.)

obstruo, obstruere, obstruxi, obstructus ... *to build against; to block, to stifle, to obstruct*

obtero, obterere, obtrívi, obtrítus ... *to crush, to trample*

obtrectatio, obtrectatiónis, f. ... *detraction, disparagement*

obtúsus, obtúsa, obtúsum ... *blunt*

obversor, obversári, obversátus sum ... *to go to and fro; to walk before or in front of* (+ dat.)

obvius, obvia, obvium ... *opposing; toward, up against* (+ dat.); *standing in* one's *way or path* [*29]

occido, occidere, occidi ... *to die, to perish;* (of the sun) *to set, to go down*

occído, occídere, occídi, occísus ... *to kill* *[*ARA]*

occultus, occulta, occultum ... *hidden, secret;* **in occulto:** *in hiding, in a secret place*

occupo, occupáre, occupávi, occupátus ... *to seize, to occupy*

occurro, occurrere, occurri ... *to run; to become visible* to the eyes

occurso, occursáre, occursávi ... *to keep running; to become visible* to the eyes

Oceanus, Oceani, m. ... the god *Ocean;* (of Ocean's realm) the *sea* or the *ocean*

ocellus, ocelli, m. ... *little eye*

ocior, ocius ... (only in compar.) *swifter*

oculus, oculi, m. ... *eye* *[*ARA]*

odor, odóris, m. ... *smell*

odórus, odóra, odórum ... *keen-scented, strong-smelling*

Oetaeus, Oetaea, Oetaeum ... *Oetaean* (= of Mount Oeta)

offirmo, offirmáre, offirmávi, offirmátus ... *to become firm, to become resolute*

offundo, offundere, offúdi, offúsus ... *to pour over; to convey* to, *to communicate* to

olfacio, olfacere, olféci, olfactus ... *to smell, to sniff*

olim ... *once, at that time*

Olympus, Olympi, m. ... the mountain *Olympus;* (in general) *sky, heaven*

omníno ... *altogether; at all, in any degree*

omnipotens, omnipotentis ... *almighty, all-powerful;* (as proper noun) **Omnipotens:** the *Almighty,* the *All-Powerful* (= Jupiter)

omnis, omne ... *all, every, whole* *[*ARA]*

opácus, opáca, opácum ... *shady; thick, bushy*

opera, operae, f. ... *work, effort, service;* **operam dare:** *to give or de-vote attention to* (+ dat.) [*ARA, *18]

operio, operíre, operui, opertus ... *to cover; to clothe, to dress* [*ARA, *17]

opifer, opifera, opiferum ... *help-bringing;* (masc. sing. as substan-tive) the *help-bringer*

opifex, opificis, m. ... *artisan, workman*

opitulor, opitulári, opitulátus sum ... *to provide help or assistance*

oppidum, oppidi, n. ... *town* [*ARA]

oppleo, opplére, opplévi, opplétus ... *to fill up, to fill completely*

oppóno, opponere, opposui, oppositus ... *to place before or against*

opprimo, opprimere, oppressi, oppressus ... *to press down; to crush, to destroy; to suffocate, to asphyxiate*

oppugno, oppugnáre, oppugnávi, oppugnátus ... *to attack, to assault*

ops, opis, f. ... *aid, help, assistance;* (in plur.) *wealth, property, re-sources* [*ARA, *24]

optimus, optima, optimum ... (superl. of **bonus;** see *ARA,* App. D, p. 419) *best; excellent, exceptional*

opto, optáre, optávi, optátus ... *to desire; to wish, to pray; to wish for, to pray for* [*4]

opus, operis, n. ... *work, labor; effect, function; public works or build-ings;* **opus est:** *there is need for* (+ abl.) [*ARA, *24]

ora, orae, f. ... *coast, shore*

oraculum, oraculi, n. ... *oracle, shrine; divine utterance, prophetic power*

oratio, oratiónis, f. ... *speech;* **oratiónem habére:** *to make a speech*

orátor, oratóris, m. ... *speaker; envoy, ambassador*

orbis, orbis, m. (gen. plur. **orbium**) ... *circle; earth, world* [*72]

orbitas, orbitátis, f. ... *bereavement*

orbus, orba, orbum ... *deprived; bereft, bereaved*

Orcus, Orci, m. ... the god *Orcus*

ordo, ordinis, m. ... *rank, order, succession*

origo, originis, f. ... *origin, source*

orior, oríri, ortus sum ... *to rise, to arise;* **oriens, orientis,** m.: *sunrise;* (as proper noun) **Oriens:** the *East,* the *Orient* [*ARA, *55]

ornamentum, ornamenti, n. ... *ornament, adornment*

orno, ornáre, ornávi, ornátus ... *to furnish, to decorate*

oro, oráre, orávi, orátus ... *to beg, to entreat, to implore; to pray to* someone (acc.) for something (acc.) [*8]

os, oris, n. ... (plur. may have sing. meaning) *mouth; face, head; opening, aperture* [*39]

os, ossis, n. ... *bone*

osculor, osculári, osculátus sum ... *to kiss*

osculum, osculi, n. ... (plur. may have sing. meaning) *kiss; mouth, lips* [*1]

ostendo, ostendere, ostendi, ostentus ... *to show, to reveal* [*ARA]

ostento, ostentáre, ostentávi, ostentátus ... *to display, to exhibit*

ostium, ostii, n. ... *door*

ostrum, ostri, n. ... *purple*

otium, otii, n. ... *leisure* [*18]

P

paciscor, pacisci, pactus sum ... *to make an agreement;* **pactus, pacta, pactum:** *agreed upon, stipulated;* **pactum, pacti,** n.: (plur. may have sing. meaning) *agreement, arrangement*

Paean, Paeánis, m. ... *Paean* (= Apollo)

pallidus, pallida, pallidum ... *pale*

palma, palmae, f. ... *palm-tree, palm-branch; glory, honor, victory*

pango, pangere, pepigi, pactus ... *to fix, to fasten; to arrange, to agree upon*

par, paris ... *equal, similar; suitable, appropriate;* **pariter:** *equally, similarly; together, at the same time* [*ARA, *46]

parco, parcere, peperci ... *to spare, to refrain from using* (+ dat.) [*65]

parens, parentis, c. ... *parent; father, mother; ancestor, forefather* [*ARA, *24]

pareo, parére, parui ... *to obey* (+ dat.)

paries, parietis, m. ... *wall* of a house

pario, parere, peperi, partus ... *to beget, to give birth to* [*ARA]

Paris, Paridis, m. ... *Paris* (= the Trojan Alexander)

Parnásus, Parnási, m. ... the mountain *Parnasus*

paro, paráre, parávi, parátus ... *to prepare; to furnish, to provide* [*39]

pars, partis, f. (gen. plur. **partium**) ... *part, direction;* **ex parte:** *partly, in part* [*ARA, *48]

parum ... *not, not at all; too little, not enough*

parvus, parva, parvum ... *small, little* [*56]

pasco, pascere, pavi, pastus ... (perf. part. may have act. meaning) *to feed, to feed on*

passer, passeris, m. ... *sparrow* [*37]

passim ... *far and wide, here and there*

passus, passus, m. ... *step, pace*

pastor, pastóris, m. ... *shepherd, herdsman* [*52]

Pataréus, Pataréa, Pataréum ... *Patarean, of Patara*

pateo, patére, patui ... *to be open; to be exposed, to be revealed;* **patens, patentis:** *open, spacious* [*52]

pater, patris, m. ... *father;* (sometimes in plur.) *parents; patricians* [*ARA, *26]

patesco, patescere, patui ... *to be open; to be revealed, to become visible*

patientia, patientiae, f. ... *patience; apathy, passivity*

patior, pati, passus sum ... *to experience; to allow, to permit; to suffer, to endure*

patria, patriae, f. ... *country; fatherland, native land* [*ARA]

patricius, patricii, m. ... *patrician*

patrius, patria, patrium ... *of a father, of* one's *father*

paucus, pauca, paucum ... (adj. usually found in plur.) *few* [*31]

paulum, pauli, n. ... *little, little bit;* **paulum:** (adv.) *a little bit, for a little while;* **paulo ante:** *a little while ago, a little while earlier*

pavidus, pavida, pavidum ... *alarmed, startled, frightened*

pavor, pavóris, m. ... *fear; panic, terrifying situation*

pax, pacis, f. ... *peace* [*27]

peccátum, peccáti, n. ... *sin, crime*

pecco, peccáre, peccávi ... *to sin, to do wrong, to make a mistake*

pectus, pectoris, n. ... *chest, breast; heart, spirit* [*ARA]

pecunia, pecuniae, f. ... (plur. may have sing. meaning) *money* [*11]

pecus, pecoris, n. ... *herd, flock; sheep, cattle* [*ARA]

pecus, pecudis, f. ... *beast, animal*

Pedum, Pedi, n. ... the town *Pedum*

Pelídes, Pelídae, m. ... *Pelides* (= son of Peleus, i.e., Achilles)

pello, pellere, pepuli, pulsus ... *to drive; to strike, to beat upon*

penátes, penatium, m. ... (plur. noun with plur. meaning) the *penates* (= Roman household gods)

pendeo, pendére, pependi ... *to hang, to hang down; to hang* from, *to hang down* from; *to be suspended, to be discontinued* [*51]

Penéis, Peneidos (acc. plur. **Peneidas**) ... *of Peneus;* **Penéis, Peneidos,** f. (voc. sing. **Penéi**): *daughter of Peneus*

Peneius, Peneia, Peneium ... *of Peneus;* **Peneia, Peneiae,** f.: *daughter of Peneus*

penes ... *worthy of bestowment on, worthy of conferment on* (+ acc.)

penetrále, penetrális, n. (gen. plur. **penetralium**) ... *inner part* or *inner chamber* of a house

penitus ... *deeply, deep inside*

penna, pennae, f. ... *wing; feather* [*ARA]

per ... *through* (root meaning); *through, because of, by means of* (+ acc.); *along, among, in the midst of* (+ acc.); *for, during, during the course of* (+ acc.); *by, by the power of, in the name of* (+ acc.) [*ARA, *6]

perago, peragere, perégi, peractus ... *to drive through; to finish, to complete*

peragro, peragráre, peragrávi, peragrátus ... *to travel through; to traverse, to range over*

percipio, percipere, percépi, perceptus ... *to lay hold of; to learn, to take lessons in*

percutio, percutere, percussi, percussus ... *to strike; to beat, to flap*

perdo, perdere, perdidi, perditus ... *to lose, to ruin, to destroy; to use without purpose, to waste* one's *time on;* **perditus, perdita, perditum:** *lost, ruined, destroyed;* **perdite:** *desperately, without restraint* [*39]

pereo, períre, perívi or **perii** ... *to die, to perish; to be ruined, to be destroyed*

perfectus, perfecta, perfectum ... *perfect, complete, flawless;* **perfecte:** *perfectly, completely, flawlessly*

perfero, perferre, pertuli, perlátus ... *to carry through; to convey, to deliver; to endure, to suffer, to withstand*

Pergama, Pergamórum, n. ... (plur. noun with sing. meaning) *Pergamum,* citadel of Troy

pergo, pergere, perrexi ... *to proceed, to continue*

perhibeo, perhibére, perhibui, perhibitus ... *to assert, to maintain*

periculum, periculi, n. ... *danger* [*ARA]

perimo, perimere, perémi, peremptus ... *to destroy; to kill, to slay*

Periphas, Periphantis, m. ... *Periphas,* the Greek warrior

perlátus ... see **perfero**

perlucidulus, perlucidula, perlucidulum ... *translucent, transparent*

permaneo, permanére, permansi ... *to stay, to remain*

permaturesco, permaturescere, permaturui ... *to ripen fully*

permitto, permittere, permísi, permissus ... *to allow, to permit*

pernicies, perniciéi, f. ... *ruin, destruction*

perniciósus, perniciósa, perniciósum ... *ruinous, destructive*

pernix, pernícis ... *swift, quick;* **perniciter:** *swiftly, quickly*

perpello, perpellere, perpuli, perpulsus ... *to drive; to urge, to incite*

perpetuus, perpetua, perpetuum ... *continuous, everlasting;* **in perpetuum:** *forever, for all time*

perrumpo, perrumpere, perrúpi, perruptus ... *to break through, to burst through*

persequor, persequi, persecútus sum ... *to follow; to pursue, to avenge*

persevéro, perseveráre, perseverávi ... *to persist, to continue*

persolvo, persolvere, persolvi, persolútus ... *to pay back, to pay in full*

pertendo, pertendere, pertendi, pertensus ... *to persist, to push on; to continue on* one's *way*

pertinax, pertinácis ... *stubborn, obstinate*

pertuli ... see **perfero**

pervenio, pervenire, pervéni ... *to come* to, *to arrive* at; *to come through, to pass through*

pervigilo, pervigiláre, pervigilávi, pervigilátus ... *to stay awake all night*

pervinco, pervincere, pervíci, pervictus ... *to overcome completely; to persuade* or *prevail upon* someone to do something

pervius, pervia, pervium ... *open; accessible, traversable*

pes, pedis, m. ... *foot* [*ARA]

pestifer, pestifera, pestiferum ... *destructive, destructive* to (+ dat.)

pestilentia, pestilentiae, f. ... *plague*

pestis, pestis, f. (gen. plur. **pestium**) ... *plague, disease*

peto, petere, petii or **peti, petítus** ... *to ask, to seek* [*ARA]

pharetra, pharetrae, f. ... *quiver* (= case for arrows) [*50]

Phoebe, Phoebes, f. ... *Phoebe* (= Diana)

Phoebus, Phoebi, m. ... *Phoebus* (= Apollo)

Phrygius, Phrygia, Phrygium ... *Phrygian* (= Trojan)

pietas, pietátis, f. ... *piety; duty, devotion; respect, sympathy* [*9]

piger, pigra, pigrum ... *lazy, inactive, sluggish*

pila, pilae, f. ... *pillar, column*

pilleátus, pilleáta, pilleátum ... *wearing a felt cap*

pingo, pingere, pinxi, pictus ... *to paint; to embroider* [*68]

pinguis, pingue ... *fat; covered* with; *well-laden, sumptuous* [*42]

pinus, pini, f. ... *pine*

pipio, pipiáre ... *to chirp*

pius, pia, pium ... *pious; dutiful, devoted*

placeo, placére, placui ... *to please* (+ dat.); (impersonal use) *to seem good* (+ dat. sometimes) [e.g., **placet ei** = *it seems good to him*]

plaga, plagae, f. ... (plur. may have sing. meaning) *net, snare*

plangor, plangóris, m. ... (plur. may have sing. meaning) a *wailing,* a *lamentation*

planus, plana, planum ... *even, flat, level*

plebs, plebis, or **plebes, plebéi,** f. ... (collective sing.) *plebeians* [*26]

plectrum, plectri, n. ... *plectrum*

plenus, plena, plenum ... *full, full of* (+ gen. or abl.) [*25]

plerique, pleraeque, pleraque ... (plur. adjective used as substantive) *very many*

Plinius, Plinii, m. ... *Pliny* (= Pliny the Elder)

ploro, ploráre, plorávi ... *to weep; to lament*

pluma, plumae, f. ... *feather*

plumbum, plumbi, n. ... *lead; leaden tip*

plurimum ... (superl. of **multum;** see *ARA,* App. D, p. 421) *very much, most of all*

plus, pluris ... (compar. of **multus;** see *ARA,* App. D, p. 419) *more, several* [*3]

poena, poenae, f. ... (plur. may have sing. meaning) *penalty, punishment* [*ARA]

Poenus, Poena, Poenum ... *Phoenician, Carthaginian;* (masc. sing. as substantive) a *Phoenician,* a *Carthaginian*

Polítes, Polítae, m. ... *Polites,* the Trojan warrior

polluo, polluere, pollui, pollútus ... *to defile, to pollute, to violate;* **pollútus, pollúta, pollútum:** *defiled, polluted, violated*

Polusca, Poluscae, f. ... the town *Polusca*

pompa, pompae, f. ... *parade, procession*

Pomponiánus, Pomponiáni, m. ... *Pomponianus,* friend of Pliny

pomum, pomi, n. ... *fruit* [*56]

pondus, ponderis, n. ... *weight; pound*

pono, ponere, posui, positus ... *to put, to place; to put* or *place aside; to build, to erect; to pitch* a camp; *to arrange* one's hair [*ARA, *26]

populátor, populatóris, m. ... *ravager, plunderer*

populor, populári, populátus sum ... *to ravage, to plunder*

populus, populi, m. ... *people;* (in plur.) *peoples, nations* [*8]

porro ... *in the future, in time to come*

porta, portae, f. ... *gate*

porticus, porticus, f. ... *portico, colonnade*

portus, portus, m. ... *port, harbor; haven, refuge*

posco, poscere, poposci ... *to demand* [*13]

possum, posse, potui ... *to be able; to bring* oneself or *have the heart* to do something [*27]

post ... *after, behind* (+ acc.); *later, afterward* (as adv.) [*ARA]

postea ... *afterward* [*ARA]

posterus, postera, posterum ... *next, following;* **in posterum:** *until the next day*

posthac ... *hereafter, from now on*

postis, postis, m. (gen. plur. **postium**) ... *door, doorpost;* (sometimes in plur.) *doorway, entrance, threshold* [*54]

postquam or **posteaquam** ... (conj.) *after* [*ARA]

postrémus, postréma, postrémum ... *last, final;* **postrémum:** *finally, last of all*

potentia, potentiae, f. ... *power*

potior, potíri, potítus sum ... *to get possession of; to seize, to capture* (+ abl.) *[*ARA]*

potis or **pote** (indecl.) ... *able, possible* [*45]

poto, potáre, potávi, potátus ... *to drink*

prae ... *before, in front of* (+ abl.); *because of, on account of* (+ abl.)

praebeo, praebére, praebui, praebitus ... *to offer, to furnish, to provide*

praecédo, praecedere, praecessi ... *to go before, to occur earlier*

praeceps, praecipitis ... *headlong, rushing forward;* **in praecipiti:** *on the sheer edge, over a sheer drop*

praecipio, praecipere, praecépi, praeceptus ... *to advise, to instruct*

praecipito, praecipitáre, praecipitávi, praecipitátus ... *to cast down, to throw down;* (in pass.) *to sink* into, *to descend* into (+ dat.) *[*ARA, *57]*

praeco, praecónis, m. ... *crier, herald*

praecordia, praecordiórum, n. ... (plur. noun with sing. meaning) *heart; chest, breast*

praeda, praedae, f. ... *booty, spoils [*ARA]*

praedico, praedicáre, praedicávi, praedicátus ... *to declare, to proclaim*

praefectus, praefecti, m. ... *prefect*

praefero, praeferre, praetuli, praelátus ... *to carry before; to prefer* to, *to esteem more highly* than (+ dat.)

praemium, praemii, n. ... *reward, payment* [*65]

praenuntius, praenuntii, m. ... *harbinger, forerunner* (= something that announces in advance what is coming)

praepóno, praeponere, praeposui, praepositus ... *to put before; to put in charge*

praesens, praesentis ... *present, in person; pressing, immediate; favorable, well-disposed;* **in praesenti:** *instantly, immediately*

praesidium, praesidii, n. ... *defense, protection; garrison, detachment*

praesto, praestáre, praestiti, praestátus ... *to stand out, to be superior to; to furnish, to present, to provide*

praeter ... *beyond; except, except for; more than, apart from* (+ acc.) [*ARA, *41]

praeterea ... *besides, further*

praetereo, praeteríre, praeterívi or **praeterii** ... *to go past; to ride past, to gallop past*

praetexo, praetexere, praetexui, praetectus ... *to border; to cloak, to conceal*

praetorium, praetorii, n. ... *palace, mansion*

praevaleo, praevalére, praevalui ... *to be very strong; to prevail, to predominate*

pravus, prava, pravum ... *crooked, distorted*

precor, precári, precátus sum ... *to pray for; to beseech, to implore; (pres. ind. first pers. sing.) I beseech you*

premo, premere, pressi, pressus ... *to press; to push, to pursue; to bind, to secure; to cover, to conceal* [*20]

pretium, pretii, n. ... *price* [*71]

prex, precis, f. ... *prayer, entreaty* [*28]

Priamus, Priami, m. ... *Priam,* king of Troy

Priápus, Priápi, m. ... *Priápus*

primóris, primóre ... *first, foremost; (masc. plur. as substantive) leaders*

primus, prima, primum ... *first, foremost; nearest, closest; primal, primordial; (masc. plur. as substantive) chiefs, leaders, princes;* **primo** or **primum:** *first, at first, for the first time* [*ARA, *62]

princeps, principis, m. ... *first man; chief, prince; (of the ruler of the Roman Empire) emperor* [*7]

prior, prius ... (compar. adj.: see *ARA*, App. D, p. 419) *first, former, earlier;* **prius:** (adv.) *first, in advance, beforehand* [*7]

priscus, prisca, priscum ... *ancient*

priusquam ... (conj.) *before*

pro ... *in place of, in behalf of, in return for* (+ abl.) [*ARA]

procédo, procedere, processi ... *to go forth, to come out; to advance, to increase in extent*

procido, procidere, procidi ... *to fall down, to fall forward*

procul ... *from afar, from a distance*

procumbo, procumbere, procubui ... *to fall forward*

procuratio, procuratiónis, f. ... *procuratorship*

procurro, procurrere, procurri ... *to run forward; to extend, to project*

prodo, prodere, prodidi, proditus ... *to put forth, to bring forth; to betray* someone (acc.) *to someone* (dat.)

prodúco, producere, produxi, productus ... *to lead out, to bring forth*

proelium, proelii, n. ... *battle* [*ARA]

profecto ... *indeed, assuredly, undoubtedly*

proficiscor, proficisci, profectus sum ... *to depart, to set out; to proceed, to journey* [*ARA]

profugio, profugere, profúgi ... *to flee* from, *to run away* from

profundo, profundere, profúdi, profúsus ... *to pour forth; to shed* tears

progigno, progignere, progenui, progenitus ... *to beget, to give birth to*

progredior, progredi, progressus sum ... *to go forth, to come forth*

proinde ... *therefore, accordingly*

prolábor, prolábi, prolapsus sum ...*to fall forward; to give way, to collapse*

proles, prolis, f. ... *offspring*

promitto, promittere, promísi, promissus ... *to promise; to promise* someone (dat.) something (acc.); *to promise* someone *that* (+ indirect statement)

promo, promere, prompsi, promptus ... *to produce; to bring out, to bring forth*

pronuba, pronubae, f. ... *bride-attendant, bride-conductor*

pronus, prona, pronum ... *leaning forward, bending forward; down to the earth, flat on* one's *face*

prope ... *near, at hand; only, almost*

propero, properáre, properávi, properátus ... *to hurry, to hasten*

propíno, propináre, propinávi, propinátus ... *to drink* a toast; *to pass along, to make a present of*

propius ... (compar. of **prope**; see *ARA*, App. D, p. 421) *nearer, more closely*

propóno, proponere, proposui, propositus ... *to put out, to display; to hold out, to propose*

propter ... *because of, on account of* (+ acc.)

propugnaculum, propugnaculi, n. ... *bulwark, rampart*

proripio, proripere, proripui, proreptus ... *to seize, to snatch;* (used with the reflexive **se**, which is not translated in this idiom) *to rush off, to hurry off*

prosterno, prosternere, prostrávi, prostrátus ... *to cast down, to stretch out*

prostibulum, prostibuli, n. ... *brothel, house of prostitution*

prosum, prodesse, profui ... *to be useful, to be helpful* (+ dat.)

protinus ... *immediately* [*50]

prout ... *as if, just as if*

proximus, proxima, proximum ... (superl. related to **prope**: see *ARA*, App. D, p. 419) *nearest, very near;* **ex proximo:** *close at hand*

prudentia, prudentiae, f. ... *intelligence; good judgment, rational thinking*

pruinósus, pruinósa, pruinósum ... *frosty*

pubes, pubis, f. ... the *youth* (= young men)

publicus, publica, publicum ... *public;* **publice:** *publicly, in public*

pudicitia, pudicitiae, f. ... *purity, chastity, fidelity*

pudícus, pudíca, pudícum ... *pure, chaste, faithful*

puella, puellae, f. ... *girl; mistress, sweetheart* [*ARA, *37]

puer, pueri, m. ... *boy* [*ARA]

pugno, pugnáre, pugnávi, pugnátus ... *to fight* [*29]

pulcher, pulchra, pulchrum ... *beautiful, lovely; excellent, splendid* [*ARA, *55]

pullus, pulla, pullum ... *dark, dark colored*

pulso, pulsáre, pulsávi, pulsátus ... *to beat on, to kick at, to strike against*

pulverulentus, pulverulenta, pulverulentum ... *dusty, covered with dust*

pulvis, pulveris, m. ... *dust*

pumex, pumicis, m. ... *pumice-stone*

purgo, purgáre, purgávi, purgátus ... *to clean, to clear away; to excuse* oneself; *to apologize for* oneself

purpureus, purpurea, purpureum ... *purple, dark red; gleaming, beautiful* [*58]

purus, pura, purum ... *pure, clean;* **puriter:** *in a pure or clean manner*

pusillus, pusilla, pusillum ... *very small; unimportant, insignificant*

puto, putáre, putávi, putátus ... *to think, to believe; to regard* as, *to consider* to be [*ARA, *41]

Pyramus, Pyrami, m. ... the boy *Pyramus*

Pyrrhus, Pyrrhi, m. ... *Pyrrhus,* son of Achilles (= Neoptolemus)

Python, Pythónis, m. (acc. sing. **Pythóna**) ... the snake *Python*

Q

qua ... (adv.) *where, by which way, in which direction*

quacumque ... *whenever, wherever*

quadrirémis, quadrirémis, f. ... *quadrireme*

quaero, quaerere, quaesii, quaesítus ... *to seek, to search for; to seek to know, to ask a question* [*ARA, *33]

qualis, quale ... *as, just as, such as* [*22]

qualubet ... *no matter how, somehow or other*

quam ... (conj.) *as;* (after compar. word) *than, rather than* [*9]

quamdiu ... *as long as, for how long*

quamquam ... *although* [*15]

quamvis ... *although, even though, however much*

quandoquidem ... *since, because*

quantum ... (adv.) *as much as; how much, to what extent*

quantus, quanta, quantum ... *how great, how much, of what size;* **quanto . . , tanto . . ,** *by how much . . , by so much . .* [*10]

quare ... (relative adv.) *why, wherefore, for which reason;* (interrogative adv.) *why? wherefore? for which reason?* [*42]

quasi ... *as if, just as; as it were, so to speak* [*20]

quasso, quassáre, quassávi, quassátus ... *to shake repeatedly, to cause* something *to shake violently*

quatenus ... *as far as, to what extent*

quater (indecl.) ... *four times*

-que ... (attached to the word it connects) *and* (e.g., **filius filiaque,** *son and daughter*) [ARA]

quercus, quercus, f. ... *oak-tree; wreath of oak-leaves*

querella, querellae, f. ... *lament, protest, complaint*

queror, queri, questus sum ... *to lament, to protest, to complain about*

questus, questus, m. ... *protest, complaint*

qui, quae, quod (gen. sing. **cuius, cuius, cuius**) ... (relative pronoun) *who, which, that* [*ARA]

qui, quae, quod (gen. sing. **cuius, cuius, cuius**) ... (interrogative adjective) *which? what? what kind of?* [*ARA]

quia ... *that; since, because*

quicumque, quaecumque, quodcumque ... (indefinite relative pronoun; formed from **qui, quae, quod** and the suffix **-cumque**) *whoever, whatever* [*11]

quidam, quaedam, quiddam (gen. sing. **cuiusdam, cuiusdam, cuiusdam**) ... (formed from **qui, quae, quod** and the suffix **-dam**) *certain man, certain woman, certain thing* (as a pronoun); *certain* (as an adjective) [*ARA]

quidem ... *indeed, certainly* [*22]

quies, quiétis, f. ... *rest, peace, sleep*

quiesco, quiescere, quiévi ... *to rest, to sleep; to remain still* or *steady*

quilubet, quaelubet, quidlubet ... (indefinite relative pronoun) *anyone at all, anything at all; whoever you please, whatever you please*

quin ... *why not?* (= *why don't? why doesn't?*)

quinquaginta (indecl.) ... *fifty*

quinque (indecl.) ... *five*

quippe ... *indeed, of course, to be sure*

quiritátus, quiritátus, m. ... (plur. may have sing. meaning) *crying, screaming*

quis, quid (gen. sing. **cuius, cuius**) ... (indefinite pronoun formed from **qui, quae, quod**; see *ARA*, App. C, for the declension of this pronoun) *anyone, anything* [*ARA]

quis, quid (gen. sing. **cuius, cuius**) ... (interrogative pronoun) *who? which? what?;* **quid:** (interrogative adverb) *why?* [*ARA, *8]

quisquam, quicquam (gen. sing. **cuiusquam, cuiusquam**) ... (indefinite pronoun) *anyone, anything* [*34]

quisque, quidque (gen. sing. **cuiusque, cuiusque**) ... (see *ARA*, App. C, p. 414, for the declension of this pronoun) *each person, each thing;* (in plur.) *all persons, all things* [*ARA, *24]

quisquis, quaequae, quicquid or **quidquid** ... (indefinite relative pronoun; only **quisquis** and **quicquid/quidquid** are regularly used) *whoever, whatever* [*ARA, *6]

quo ... (adv.) *where, to which place (= there, to that place)*

quod ... *that; since, because; inasmuch as, in view of the fact that* [*ARA, *56]

quomodo ... *as; in what way, in what manner* [*ARA]

quondam ... *once, formerly*

quoniam ... *since, because* [*ARA]

quoque ... (placed after the word it emphasizes) *also* [*5]

quot ... *as many;* **quot .., tot ..,** *as many .., so many ..* [*70]

quousque ... *until*

R

radius, radii, m. ... *ray* of the sun or moon

radix, radícis, f. (gen. plur. **radicium**) ... *root* of a plant [*58]

ramus, rami, m. ... *branch* [*54]

rapína, rapínae, f. ... (plur. may have sing. meaning) *pillage, plunder*

rapio, rapere, rapui, raptus ... *to seize, to snatch* [*ARA]

raptum, rapti, n. ... *booty, spoils*

rarus, rara, rarum ... *thin, loose; sparse, scattered; unusual, exquisite* [*68]

ratio, rationis, f. ... *reason, method, manner*

raucus, rauca, raucum ... *harsh-sounding; clanging, clashing*

recens, recentis ... *fresh, recent*

recenseo, recensére, recensui, recensus ... *to review, to inspect*

recipio, recipere, recépi, receptus ... *to admit, to receive; to recover, to recapture; to take* or *draw* someone (acc.) *to oneself* (acc.) [*ARA, *25]

recondo, recondere, recondidi, reconditus ... *to put away; to set, to cover; to close* the eyes *again*

recordor, recordári, recordátus sum ... *to recall, to recollect*

Rectina, Rectinae, f. ... *Rectina,* wife of Tascius

recubo, recubáre ... *to lie back, to lie down*

reddo, reddere, reddidi, redditus ... *to give back; to return, to deliver;* (used with the reflexive **se,** which is not translated in this idiom) *to return* or *go back* to someone (dat.) [*ARA, *16]

redeo, redíre, redívi or **redii** ... *to go back, to return;* (of the sun) *to rise again*

redúco, reducere, reduxi, reductus ... *to lead back; to draw back, to pull back*

refero, referre, rettuli, relátus ... *to carry back; to relate, to report*

reflecto, reflectere, reflexi, reflexus ... *to bend back; to turn back, to turn around*

refugio, refugere, refúgi ... *to run away from; to shrink from, to recoil from*

regia, regiae, f. ... *palace* [*ARA]

regína, regínae, f. ... *queen* [*ARA]

regius, regia, regium ... *royal* [*31]

regnátor, regnatóris, m. ... *king, ruler*

regno, regnáre, regnávi, regnátus ... *to rule* [*ARA]

regnum, regni, n. ... (plur. may have sing. meaning) *kingdom* [*ARA, *61]

rego, regere, rexi, rectus ... *to rule; to command, to be in charge of;* **rectus, recta, rectum:** *direct; straight, straight ahead* [*13]

regredior, regredi, regressus sum ... *to return, to go back*

relatio, relatiónis, f. ... *proposal, petition*

relátus ... see **refero**

religio, religiónis, f. ... *religion*

relinquo, relinquere, reliqui, relictus ... *to leave, to leave behind* [*ARA, *16]

reliquus, reliqua, reliquum ... *rest, remaining*

reluceo, relucére, reluxi ... *to shine out, to blaze forth*

relucesco, relucescere, reluxi ... *to grow bright again*

remaneo, remanére, remansi ... *to stay, to remain*

remedium, remedii, n. ... *remedy; drug, antidote*

remeo, remeáre, remeávi ... *to return, to go back*

remitto, remittere, remísi, remissus ... *to send back*

remoror, remorári, remorátus sum ... *to delay, to hesitate*

removeo, removére, remóvi, remótus ... *to move back; to remove, to take away*

renideo, renidére ... *to shine; to grin, to smile*

renovo, renováre, renovávi, renovátus ... *to renew, to revive*

reor, reri, ratus sum ... *to think, to believe*

repello, repellere, reppuli, repulsus ... *to drive back* or *away; to drive back* or *away* from; *to spurn, to reject, to rebuff*

repente ... *suddenly*

reperio, reperíre, repperi, repertus ... *to find, to discover*

repleo, replére, replévi, replétus ... *to fill again; to fill, to fill up*

repóno, reponere, reposui, repositus ... *to put back; to place* in

repugno, repugnáre, repugnávi, repugnátus ... *to fight back; to be inconsistent* with, *to be incompatible* with (+ dat.)

requies, requiétis, f. (acc. sing. **requiem**) ... *rest, respite*

requiesco, requiescere, requiévi ... *to rest, to repose*

requíro, requirere, requisii, requisítus ... *to seek, to desire; to look for, to try to find; to ask about, to inquire about;* (of verses) *to examine carefully, to commit to memory* [*46]

res, rei, f. ... *thing; matter, affair; situation, circumstance; affairs of state, political structure* [*ARA, *25]

resído, residere, resédi ... *to sit down; to subside, to die down*

resisto, resistere, restiti ... *to stop, to stop running; to pause, to break off speaking*

resorbeo, resorbére, resorbui ... *to swallow again; to suck back* or *away*

respicio, respicere, respexi ... *to look back, to look around; to look at, to take notice of, to turn* one's *thoughts to*

respondeo, respondére, respondi, responsus ... *to answer, to reply to* [*ARA]

responsum, responsi, n. ... *answer; divine utterance* [*ARA]

restituo, restituere, restitui, restitútus ... *to restore, to rebuild*

restitutio, restitutiónis, f. ... *restoration*

resupínus, resupína, resupínum ... *facing upwards, flat on* one's *back*

rete, retis, n. ... *net*

retineo, retinére, retinui, retentus ... *to hold back; to hold fast, to cling tightly*

retro ... *back, backwards, back again* [*59]

retrorsum ... *back, backwards, back again*

rettuli ... see **refero**

reus, rei, m. ... *culprit;* the *accused,* the *defendant*

revello, revellere, revelli, revulsus ... *to tear away, to remove forcibly*

revertor, reverti, reversus sum ... *to return, to go back* [*ARA]

revoco, revocáre, revocávi, revocátus ... *to call back, to summon back*

rex, regis, m. ... *king* [*ARA]

rictus, rictus, m. ... *jaw, jowl*

rideo, ridére, risi, risus ... *to laugh, to laugh at*

rima, rimae, f. ... *crack, chink*

risus, risus, m. ... *laughter;* a *grin,* a *smile*

robur, roboris, n. ... (plur. may have sing. meaning) *oak tree, oak wood*

rogo, rogáre, rogávi, rogátus ... *to ask; to entreat, to beseech* [*ARA, *60]

rogus, rogi, m. ... *funeral pyre*

Roma, Romae, f. ... *Rome*

Románus, Romána, Románum ... *Roman;* **Románus, Románi,** m.: a *Roman*

rostrum, rostri, n. ... *snout, muzzle*

rubeo, rubére ... *to be red*

rubor, rubóris, m. ... *redness; blush, flush*

Rufus, Rufi, m. ... *Rufus* (perhaps Caelius Rufus)

ruína, ruínae, f. ... a *falling down; ruin, collapse, destruction*

rumor, rumóris, m. ... (plur. may have sing. meaning) *talk, rumor, gossip*

rumpo, rumpere, rupi, ruptus ... *to break* in, into, or open, *to burst* in, into, or open [*6]

ruo, ruere, rui ... *to rush, to move swiftly; to fall, to collapse, to be destroyed* [*22]

rupes, rupis, f. ... *crag, cliff*

rursus or **rursum** ... *again, back again; on the other hand*

russus, russa, russum ... *red*

S

Sabínus, Sabíni, m. ... a *Sabine*

sacculus, sacculi, m. ... *small bag; purse, money-bag*

sacer, sacra, sacrum ... *holy, sacred;* **sacrum, sacri,** n.: (plur. may have sing. meaning) *ritual, sacrifice* [*ARA]

sacerdos, sacerdótis, c. ... *priest, priestess* [*ARA]

sacrificium, sacrificii, n. ... *sacrifice*

sacro, sacráre, sacrávi, sacrátus ... *to dedicate, to consecrate*

saeculum, saeculi, n. ... *generation; age, century*

saepe ... *often* [*30]

saepes, saepis, f. (gen. plur. **saepium**) ... *hedge*

saepio, saepíre, saepsi, saeptus ... *to surround; to enclose, to fence in*

saevitia, saevitiae, f. ... *cruelty, fierceness, savageness*

saevus, saeva, saevum ... *cruel, fierce, savage* [*49]

sagitta, sagittae, f. ... *arrow* [*ARA]

sagittifer, sagittifera, sagittiferum ... *arrow-bearing*

sal, salis, m. ... *salt; wit, humor*

salax, salácis ... *lusty, lecherous*

salíva, salívae, f. ... *saliva, spittle*

saltem ... *at least, in any case*

saltus, saltus, m. ... *jump, leap, bound*

saltus, saltus, m. ... *pass, glade, ravine*

salus, salútis, f. ... *health, safety; salvation, deliverance*

salutatorium, salutatorii, n. ... *reception-room*

salvus, salva, salvum ... *safe, well;* **salve:** *safe, well* [*21]

sanabilis, sanabile ... *curable*

sanctus, sancta, sanctum ... *holy, sacred, blessed*

sanguis, sanguinis, m. ... *blood* [*ARA]

sanus, sana, sanum ... *well, healthy;* **sane:** *certainly, by all means*

sapiens, sapientis ... *wise, intelligent*

sarcina, sarcinae, f. ... *bundle;* (in plur.) *belongings, possessions*

satis ... *enough* [*32]

Satricum, Satrici, n. ... the town *Satricum*

saucius, saucia, saucium ... *wounded; smitten* or *afflicted* with

saxum, saxi, n. ... *rock, stone; crag, cliff* [*ARA, *69]

scamnum, scamni, n. ... *bench, stool*

scelerátus, sceleráta, scelerátum ... *wicked, accursed*

scelestus, scelesta, scelestum ... *wicked, accursed*

scelus, sceleris, n. ... *crime, impiety* [*ARA]

scindo, scindere, scidi, scissus ... *to split, to cleave*

scio, scire, scivi or **scii** ... *to know, to understand* [*1]

scribo, scribere, scripsi, scriptus ... *to write; to write on* something (acc.) to someone (dat.); *to write on* something (acc.) to someone (dat.) with something (abl.) [*ARA, *41]

scriptor, scriptóris, m. ... *writer; author, authority*

Scyrius, Scyria, Scyrium ... *Scyrian, of Scyros*

secrétus, secréta, secrétum ... *separate; solitary, secluded*

sector, sectári, sectátus sum ... *to follow eagerly; to chase, to pursue, to run after*

secundus, secunda, secundum ... *second; following, favorable*

Secundus, Secundi, m. ... *Secundus* (= Pliny's family name)

securitas, securitátis, f. ... *unconcern; composure, complacence*

sed ... *but* [*ARA]

sedeo, sedére, sedi ... *to sit, to sit down* [*ARA]

sedes, sedis, f. (gen. plur. **sedium**) ... (plur. may have sing. meaning) *seat, place; base, foundation* [*29]

seditio, seditiónis, f. ... *mutiny, rebellion*

seditiósus, seditiósa, seditiósum ... *mutinous, rebellious*

segnis, segne ... *slow, sluggish, inactive;* **segniter:** *halfheartedly, unenthusiastically*

semel ... *once, a single time; once and no more, once and for all*

Semiramis, Semiramidis, f. ... *Semiramis,* queen of Babylon

semitarius, semitaria, semitarium ... *back-alley, back-street*

semivir, semiviri, m. ... (noun with adj. force) *half-man; castrated, emasculated*

semper ... *always* [*ARA]

senátus, senátus, m. ... *senate*

senecta, senectae, f. ... *old age*

senectus, senectútis, f. ... *old age*

senesco, senescere, senui ... *to grow old; to subside, to die down*

senex, senis ... *old;* (masc. sing. as substantive) *old man*

senior, senióris, m. ... *older man;* (in plur.) *older men* (= the seniors)

sensim ... *slowly, gradually*

sententia, sententiae, f. ... *opinion; decision, judgment*

sentio, sentíre, sensi, sensus ... *to feel, to perceive, to realize* [*ARA]

sentis, sentis, m. (gen. plur. **sentium**) ... *briar, bramble*

September, Septembris, Septembre ... *of September*

Septimius, Septimii, m. ... the boy *Septimius;* **Septimillus, Septimilli,**
m.: *little Septimius*

septimus, septima, septimum ... *seventh*

sepulchrum, sepulchri, n. ... *grave, tomb* [*ARA]

sequor, sequi, secútus sum ... *to follow* [*ARA]

sermo, sermónis, m. ... *talk, speech; rumor, gossip*

sero, serere, sevi, satus ... *to plant; to arise* or *spring* from (+ abl.);
satus, sata, satum: *born* from, *sprung* from (+ abl.) [*65]

serpens, serpentis, c. (gen. plur. **serpentium**) ... *snake, serpent*

serta, sertórum, n. ... (plur. noun with plur. meaning) *wreaths, garlands*

serus, sera, serum ... *late*

servio, servíre, servívi ... *to serve, to be a slave* to (+ dat.)

servitium, servitii, n. ... *slavery; duty, service*

servitus, servitútis, f. ... *slavery* [*ARA]

servo, serváre, servávi, servátus ... *to keep, to save, to protect* [*ARA]

servolus, servoli, m. ... *young slave*

servus, servi, m. ... *slave* [*ARA]

sessor, sessóris, m. ... *sitter* (= one sitting or seated)

sestertium, sestertii, n. ... *sesterce* (= unit of money)

seu ... *or if*

sevérus, sevéra, sevérum ... *stern, strict, severe*

si ... *if* [*ARA]

sic ... *so, thus, in such a way* [*4]

sicco, siccáre, siccávi, siccátus ... *to dry*

siccus, sicca, siccum ... *dry*

sicut or **sicuti** ... *as, just as*

Sidonius, Sidonia, Sidonium ... *Sidonian, of Sidon*

sidus, sideris, n. ... *star* [*51]

signum, signi, n. ... *sign, mark; signal, gesture; statue, sculpture* [*ARA, *55]

silentium, silentii, n. ... *silence*

sileo, siláre, silui ... *to be silent;* **silens, silentis:** *silent*

silva, silvae, f. ... (plur. may have sing. meaning) *forest* [*ARA]

similis, simile ... *similar, similar to* (+ dat.); **similiter:** *similarly, in a similar manner* [*9]

similitúdo, similitudinis, f. ... *likeness, appearance*

simul ... (conj.) *as soon as, at the same time as;* (as adv.) *along, together, at the same time* [*35]

simulacrum, simulacri, n. ... *likeness; image, statue* [*64]

simulo, simuláre, simulávi, simulátus ... *to pretend; to feign, to simulate;* (used with the reflexive **se,** which is not translated in this idiom) *to take the form of, to assume the guise of* [*ARA]

simultas, simultátis, f. (gen. plur. **simultatium**) ... *labor, contest; dispute, quarrel*

sine ... *without* (+ abl.) *[*ARA]*

singuli, singulae, singula ... (plur. adj. with sing. meaning) *single, separate, individual*

sinister, sinistra, sinistrum ... *left;* (fem. sing. as substantive) *left hand;* **sinistra:** (adv.) *on the left* *[*32]*

sino, sinere, sivi, situs ... *to allow, to permit*

sinus, sinus, m. ... *curve; embrace; bay, gulf*

sitis, sitis, f. ... *thirst*

sive ... *or if;* **sive . . , sive . . ,** *whether . . , or . .* (e.g., **sive dicit sive audit,** *whether he speaks or listens*)

socer, soceri, m. ... *father-in-law;* (in plur.) *parents-in-law*

socius, socii, m. ... *ally, comrade, companion* *[*ARA]*

sol, solis, m. ... *sun* *[*13]*

solacium, solacii, n. ... *comfort, consolation*

solea, soleae, f. ... *sandal*

soleo, solére, solitus sum ... (semi-deponent verb) *to be accustomed* (+ inf.); **solitus, solita, solitum:** *usual, normal, customary* *[*23]*

solitúdo, solitudinis, f. ... *solitude; solitary* or *desolate area(s)*

sollicitúdo, sollicitudinis, f. ... *care, concern*

sollicitus, sollicita, sollicitum ... *anxious, concerned*

solum, soli, n. ... *earth, ground* *[*59]*

solus, sola, solum (gen. sing. **solíus, solíus, solíus**) ... *alone, only* *[*ARA]*

solvo, solvere, solvi, solútus ... *to loosen; to untie, to release* *[*ARA]*

somnus, somni, m. ... (plur. may have sing. meaning) *sleep* *[*19]*

sonipes, sonipedis, m. ... *horse* (= one 'sounding with the feet')

sonitus, sonitus, m. ... *sound; noise, crash*

sono, sonáre, sonui ... *to sound, to shout; to rattle, to clatter;* **sonans, sonantis:** *loud, noisy* [*68]

sonus, soni, m. ... *sound*

sopio, sopiónis, m. ... (plur. may have sing. meaning) *penis, phallus*

sopio, sopíre, sopívi, sopítus ... *to be asleep*

sordidus, sordida, sordidum ... *dark, dirty; base, shabby*

soror, soróris, f. ... *sister* [*ARA]

sors, sortis, f. (gen. plur. **sortium**) ... (plur. may have sing. meaning) *oracle, prophecy; fate, fortune, destiny;* **sorte ducere:** *to choose at random, to select at random* [*ARA, *24]

spargo, spargere, sparsi, sparsus ... *to scatter, to sprinkle; to stream out* or *spread out* on (+ abl.)

spatior, spatiári, spatiátus sum ... *to walk about, to roam about*

spatium, spatii, n. ... *space, period, interval*

species, speciéi, f. ... *sight, appearance; form, shape, beauty* [*ARA]

speciósus, speciósa, speciósum ... *good-looking, outwardly splendid* [*ARA]

spectaculum, spectaculi, n. ... (plur. may have sing. meaning) *show, sight, spectacle*

specto, spectáre, spectávi, spectátus ... *to look at, to observe;* **spectátus, spectáta, spectátum:** *proven, tested; reliable, believable* [*31]

spelunca, speluncae, f. ... *cave* [*69]

spero, speráre, sperávi, sperátus ... *to hope, to hope for* [*51]

spes, spei, f. ... *hope* [*23]

spiritus, spiritus, m. ... *breath, breathing; blast, blast of air*

splendidus, splendida, splendidum ... *bright, shining; distinguished, outstanding*

spolium, spolii, n. ... *booty, spoils*

spons, spontis, f. ... (found only in abl. sing.) *will;* **sua sponte:** *of one's own will; voluntarily, spontaneously*

spumeus, spumea, spumeum ... *foaming, frothing*

spumo, spumáre, spumávi ... *to foam, to froth* [*68]

spurcus, spurca, spurcum ... *dirty, filthy*

Stabiae, Stabiárum, f. ... (plur. noun with sing. meaning) *Stabiae*

stabulum, stabuli, n. ... *shed, stable*

statim ... *immediately* [*ARA]

statio, statiónis, f. ... *guard, picket*

statuo, statuere, statui, statútus ... *to place, to stand; to decide, to resolve*

status, status, m. ... *state, stance; costume, clothing*

stemma, stemmátis, n. ... (plur. may have sing. meaning) *descent, lineage, pedigree*

sterilis, sterile ... *barren; futile, unproductive*

sterno, sternere, stravi, stratus ... *to lay out, to spread out; to knock down, to strike down* [*49]

sternuo, sternuere, sternui ... *to sneeze*

stipes, stipitis, m. ... *trunk of a tree*

stipo, stipáre, stipávi, stipátus ... *to crowd, to throng; to attend, to surround*

stipula, stipulae, f. ... (plur. may have sing. meaning) *stalk; straw, stubble*

stirps, stirpis, f. ... *root, stock, offspring*

sto, stare, steti ... *to stand* [*10]

stomachus, stomachi, m. ... *esophagus; belly, stomach*

stratum, strati, n. ... (plur. may have sing. meaning) *covering; bed, couch*

strideo, stridére ... *to shriek, to screech; to sizzle, to sputter*

stringo, stringere, strinxi, strictus ... *to draw tight; to draw out, to unsheathe; to graze, to ruffle, to almost touch* [*ARA, *53]

struo, struere, struxi, structus ... *to arrange; to plan, to intend*

studeo, studére, studui ... *to be eager, to be zealous; to study, to apply* oneself *to* one's *books* [*ARA, *13]

studiósus, studiósa, studiósum ... *eager, zealous; studious, scholarly*

studium, studii, n. ... *zeal, eagerness; study, skill, pursuit; artistic* or *literary skill; artistic* or *literary pursuit* [*ARA, *4]

stupeo, stupére, stupui ... *to be stunned, to be astounded* (+ abl.)

stupro, stuprére, stuprávi, stuprátus ... *to rape, to ravish, to violate*

stuprum, stupri, n. ... *violation, defilement*

suadeo, suadére, suasi ... *to urge, to advise; to induce, to invite*

suaviolum, suavioli, n. ... *little kiss*

suavior, suaviári, suaviátus sum ... *to kiss*

suavis, suave ... *sweet, pleasant*

sub ... *under* (root meaning); *under, down under* (+ acc.); *under, under the power of* (+ abl.) [*ARA]

subeo, subíre, subívi or **subii** ... *to go underneath; to come forth, to come forward; to come to* or *enter* one's *mind*

subiaceo, subiacére, subiacui ... *to lie below* or *at the foot of; to lie exposed* to, *to be subject* to (+ dat.)

subicio, subicere, subiéci, subiectus ... *to place under, to put under* one's *control; to bring to the fore, to cause to come forward*

subitaneus, subitanea, subitaneum ... *sudden*

subitus, subita, subitum ... *sudden;* **subito:** *suddenly*

sublátus ... see **tollo**

subnecto, subnectere, subnexi, subnexus ... *to bind, to bind up*

subrépo, subrepere, subrepsi, subreptus ... *to creep* into or under; *to crawl* into or under

subrigo, subrigere, subrexi, subrectus ... *to raise; to prick up* one's ears

subsellium, subsellii, n. ... *seat, bench*

subsequor, subsequi, subsecútus sum ... *to follow closely, to follow secretly*

subsisto, subsistere, substiti ... *to stand firm; to stop, to subside; to remain, to stay behind*

subter ... (adv.) *below, beneath*

subvenio, subveníre, subvéni ... *to come under; to come to the aid* of, *to bring help* or *relief* to (+ dat.)

succédo, succedere, successi ... *to go under; to come up* or *come close* (+ dat.)

succurro, succurrere, succurri ... *to run under; to help save* or *preserve* (+ dat.); *to come to* or *occur in* one's *mind*

suffero, sufferre, sustuli, sublátus ... *to endure; to sustain, to withstand*

suffígo, suffigere, suffixi, suffixus ... *to fix up, to fasten, to attach*

suffundo, suffundere, suffúdi, suffúsus ... *to pour over; to fill, to cover*

sui (gen.), **sibi** (dat.), **se** (acc.), **se** (abl.) ... (reflexive pronoun, serving all genders sing. and plur. and referring back to the subject) *of himself, herself, itself, themselves,* etc. *[*ARA]*

sulpur, sulpuris, n. ... *sulphur*

sum, esse, fui ... *to be* [*25]

summus, summa, summum ... (alternate superl. of **superus;** see *ARA,* App. D, p. 419) *highest, very great; top of, surface of; topmost, uppermost;* (fem. sing. as substantive) *sum total, central point;* (neut. sing. as substantive) *surface, topmost layer, uppermost layer* [*18]

sumo, sumere, sumpsi, sumptus ... *to take, to choose; to take up* or *strap on* arms [*ARA, *64]

super ... *over* (root meaning); *over, above* (+ acc.); *on, upon, on top of* (+ acc.); *regarding, concerning, in the matter of* (+ abl.) [*ARA, *72]

superbia, superbiae, f. ... *pride, arrogance*

superbus, superba, superbum ... *proud, arrogant; exultant* in, *glorying* in [*34]

superstes, superstitis ... *standing over; surviving* or *remaining alive* after someone's death

supersum, superesse, superfui ... *to remain, to be left* (+ dat.)

supínus, supína, supínum ... *lying face upwards;* (of the hands) *upturned, turned upwards*

suppeto, suppetere, suppetívi ... *to allow, to permit*

suppleo, supplére, supplévi, supplétus ... *to fill, to fill up*

supplex, supplicis ... *suppliant;* (masc. as substantive) a *suppliant,* a *supplicant*

supplicium, supplicii, n. ... *entreaty; punishment*

suppóno, supponere, supposui, suppositus ... *to place under; to place* something (acc.) *under* someone (dat.)

supra ... (adv.) *more, in addition*

surgo, surgere, surrexi, surrectus ... *to rise, to arise; to rise to a higher level* [*16]

surripio, surripere, surripui, surreptus ... *to steal; to steal* something (acc.) *from* someone (dat.)

suspensus, suspensa, suspensum ... *anxious, uncertain*

suspicio, suspicere, suspexi, suspectus ... *to suspect, to distrust;* **suspectus, suspecta, suspectum:** *suspected, distrusted*

sustineo, sustinére, sustinui, sustentus ... *to hold up, to sustain; to have the will, to have the patience*

sustuli ... see **tollo**

suus, sua, suum ... (reflexive adjective, agreeing with the noun it modifies and referring back to the subject) *his own, her own, its own, their own* [*ARA]

symphoniacus, symphoniaca, symphoniacum ... *singing* or *playing in a band;* (masc. as substantive) *singer, musician*

Syria, Syriae, f. ... *Syria*

T

taberna, tabernae, f. ... *inn, tavern*

tabulátum, tabuláti, n. ... *floor* or *storey* of a building

taceo, tacére, tacui ... *to be silent*

taciturnitas, taciturnitátis, f. ... *silence*

tacitus, tacita, tacitum ... *silent*

taeda, taedae, f. ... *pine; torch* used at weddings

taeter, taetra, taetrum ... *foul, horrible*

talentum, talenti, n. ... *talent* (= unit of weight)

talis, tale ... *such, such a, of such a kind;* **talis . . , qualis . . ,** *of such a kind . . , as . .* (e.g., **talis filius est qualis pater,** *the son is of such a kind as the father*) [*ARA]

tam ... *so, such a;* **tam . . , quam . . ,** *as . . , as . .* (e.g., **tam ferus est quam lupus,** *he is as wild as a wolf*) [*ARA]

tamen ... *yet, however, nevertheless* [*4]

tamquam ... *as if, just as if* [*23]

tandem ... *at last, at length;* (as emphatic affirmation) *I ask you, I beg you* [*23]

tango, tangere, tetigi, tactus ... *to touch; to examine, to explore* [*42]

tantillus, tantilla, tantillum ... *so small;* (neut. sing. as substantive) *so small a quantity*

tantum ... (adv.) *just, only; so much, to such an extent*

tantus, tanta, tantum ... *so great, such great;* **tantus . . , quantus . . ,** *as great . . , as . .* or *as much . . , as . .* (e.g., **tantus filius est quantus pater,** *the son is as great as the father*) [*ARA]

tardus, tarda, tardum ... *slow;* **tarde:** *slowly*

Tarquinius, Tarquinii, m. ... (1) *Tarquinius* (= Lucius Tarquinius), (2) *Tarquinius* (= Sextus Tarquinius)

Tascius, Tascii or **Tasci,** m. ... *Tascius,* husband of Rectina

te ... (acc. or abl. sing. of **tu**) *you* or *by / with you* [*1]

tectum, tecti, n. ... (plur. may have sing. meaning) *roof, hall; house, dwelling, shelter* [*16]

tego, tegere, texi, tectus ... *to cover, to conceal* [*55]

tellus, tellúris, f. ... *land, earth;* (as proper noun) **Tellus:** the goddess *Earth*

telum, teli, n. ... *weapon; spear, javelin* [*ARA]

temerarius, temeraria, temerarium ... *rash, reckless, thoughtless*

temere ... *rashly, blindly, recklessly;* **non temere** or **haud temere:** *not easily, not readily, not without care*

tempestas, tempestátis, f. ... *storm* [*ARA]

templum, templi, n. ... *temple* [*ARA]

tempto, temptáre, temptávi, temptátus ... *to try, to test*

tempus, temporis, n. ... *time, season* [*ARA]

tenax, tenácis ... *tenacious* or *possessive* of (+ gen.)

tenebrae, tenebrárum, f. ... (plur. may have sing. meaning) *darkness, shadows* [*23]

tenebricósus, tenebricósa, tenebricósum ... *dark, gloomy*

Tenedos, Tenedi, f. ... the island *Tenedos*

teneo, tenére, tenui, tentus ... *to hold, to possess; to keep, to retain; to clasp, to grasp; to live in, to dwell in; to hold to, to continue on; to hold sway, to be in control* [*14]

tener, tenera, tenerum ... *tender, delicate*

tenuis, tenue ... *thin, slender* [*48]

tenuo, tenuáre, tenuávi, tenuátus ... *to make thin; to weaken, to diminish*

tenus ... *up to, as far as* (+ abl.)

tepeo, tepére ... *to be warm*

tergum, tergi, n. ... (plur. may have sing. meaning) *back, rear; hide, skin* [*53]

tero, terere, trivi, tritus ... *to rub; to wear out; to while away* time

terra, terrae, f. ... (plur. may have sing. meaning) *land, earth;* (as proper noun) **Terra:** the goddess *Earth* [*ARA, *70]

terrifico, terrificáre ... *to terrify, to frighten*

terrificus, terrifica, terrificum ... *terrifying, frightening*

territo, territáre, territávi, territátus ... *to terrify, to frighten*

terror, terróris, m. ... *terror, fright*

tertius, tertia, tertium ... *third*

testis, testis, c. (gen. plur. **testium**) ... *witness*

testor, testári, testátus sum ... *to assert* or *declare solemnly*

Teucer, Teucri, m. ... *Teucer,* king of Troy

Teucri, Teucrórum, m. ... (plur. noun with plur. meaning) the *Teucri* (= the Trojans)

thalamus, thalami, m. ... (plur. may have sing. meaning) *bedroom, bedchamber*

Tharsia, Tharsiae, f. ... *Tharsia,* daughter of Apollonius

thesaurus, thesauri, m. ... *treasure*

Thisbe, Thisbes, f. ... the girl *Thisbe*

thorus, thori, m. ... *bed*

tibi ... (dat. sing. of **tu**) *to/for you* [*2]

Tiburs, Tiburtis, m. ... a *Tiburtine*

timeo, timére, timui ... *to fear, to be afraid* [*ARA]

timidus, timida, timidum ... *timid, fearful* [*53]

timor, timóris, m. ... *fear*

tingo, tingere, tinxi, tinctus ... *to moisten; to wet, to dip; to tint, to tinge* [*ARA, *58]

titulus, tituli, m. ... *sign, placard*

Titus, Titi, m. ... *Titus* (= Livy's given name)

Tolerium, Tolerii, n. ... the town *Tolerium*

tolero, toleráre, tolerávi, tolerátus ... *to endure, to sustain*

tollo, tollere, sustuli, sublátus ... *to lift up; to take away; to take, to accept* [*ARA]

torpor, torpóris, m. ... *numbness, paralysis*

torqueo, torquére, torsi, tortus ... *to turn, to twist; to torment, to torture; to hurl, to throw, to fling* [*5]

torrens, torrentis, m. ... *torrent*

torreo, torrére, torrui, tostus ... *to burn, to parch, to roast*

tortor, tortóris, m. ... *tormentor, torturer*

torus, tori, m. ... *bed, couch*

tot ... *so many* [*ARA]

totidem ... *just as many*

totus, tota, totum (gen. sing. **totíus, totíus, totíus**) ... *all, whole, entire* [*ARA]

trabs, trabis, f. ... *beam* of wood

trado, tradere, tradidi, traditus ... *to hand over; to deliver, to entrust; to say, to relate, to report* [*ARA, *27]

tragicus, tragica, tragicum ... *tragic*

traho, trahere, traxi, tractus ... *to drag, to pull; to drag down, to pull down; to take along, to bring along* [*ARA, *61]

traicio, traicere, traiéci, traiectus ... *to throw across; to pierce, to transfix*

trames, tramitis, m. ... *path, road*

transeo, transíre, transii ...*to go across; to pass over, to cross over*

transgredior, transgredi, transgressus sum ... *to go across*

transitus, transitus, m. ... *passage, passageway*

transmitto, transmittere, transmísi, transmissus ... *to send across; to cross, to cross over*

Transpadánus, Transpadáni, m. ... a *Transpadine*

transversus, transversa, transversum ... *running crosswise*

tremebundus, tremebunda, tremebundum ... a *trembling,* a *quivering,* a *shivering*

tremo, tremere, tremui ... *to tremble, to quiver, to shiver* [*59]

tremor, tremóris, m. ... *tremor, quake*

trepidatio, trepidatiónis, f. ... *anxiety, agitation*

trepido, trepidáre, trepidávi ... *to be anxious, to be agitated* [*52]

trepidus, trepida, trepidum ... *alarmed, agitated*

tribúnus, tribúni, m. ... *tribune*

Tricipitinus, Tricipitini, m. ... *Tricipitinus* (= Lucretius's family name)

triclinium, triclinii, n. ... *dining-room*

triduum, tridui, n. ... period of *three days*

tristis, triste ... *bitter; sad, gloomy* [*24]

trisulcus, trisulca, trisulcum ... *three-forked*

triumphus, triumphi, m. ... *triumph, triumphal procession;* (as proper noun) **Triumphus:** the cry *Triumphus* (uttered during the triumphal procession)

Troia, Troiae, f. ... the city *Troy*

Troiánus, Troiána, Troiánum ... *Trojan;* **Troiánus, Troiáni,** m.: a *Trojan*

trucído, trucidáre, trucidávi, trucidátus ... *to slaughter, to massacre*

truncus, trunci, m. ... *trunk* of a tree; *body* of a man

trux, trucis ... *cruel, fierce, savage*

tu ... (second person sing. pronoun) *you* [*3]

tueor, tuéri, tuitus or **tutus sum** ... *to look at, to look after; to protect, to watch over* [*64]

tuli ... see **fero**

Tullia, Tulliae, f. ... *Tullia,* Lucius Tarquinius's wife

Tullius, Tullii, m. ... (1) *Tullius* (= Attius Tullius), (2) *Tullius* (= Servius Tullius)

tum ... *then* [*ARA]

tumidus, tumida, tumidum ... *swollen*

tumultus, tumultus, m. ... *confusion, disturbance* [*63]

tumulus, tumuli, m. ... *mound, grave*

tunc ... *then, at that time* [*ARA]

turba, turbae, f. ... *tumult; crowd, crowd of people*

turgidulus, turgidula, turgidulum ... *tiny swollen*

turpis, turpe ... *foul, horrible, shameful* [*8]

turris, turris, f. (gen. plur. **turrium**) ... *tower* [*61]

tutus, tuta, tutum ... *safe, secure; affording protection*

tuus, tua, tuum ... (possessive adj. related to **tu**) *your* [*2]

Tyrius, Tyria, Tyrium ... *Tyrian, of Tyre*

U

uber, uberis ... *plentiful, heavily laden*

ubi ... *when, where* [*ARA]

ubicumque ... *wherever, in whatever place*

ullus, ulla, ullum (gen. sing. **ullíus, ullíus, ullíus**) ... *any;* (as substantive) *anyone, anything* [*33]

ulmus, ulmi, f. ... *elm, elm-tree*

ultor, ultóris, m. ... *avenger*

ultra ... *beyond, further; any more, any longer*

ultro ... *of* one's *own accord, on* one's *own initiative*

ululátus, ululátus, m. ... (plur. may have sing. meaning) *screaming, shrieking*

ululo, ululáre, ululávi ... *to ring, to resound; to howl, to scream, to shriek*

Umber, Umbri, m. ... an *Umbrian*

umbo, umbónis, m. ... *boss of a shield*

umbra, umbrae, f. ... *shade, darkness* [*56]

umbrósus, umbrósa, umbrósum ... *shady*

umerus, umeri, m. ... *shoulder* [*49]

umquam ... *ever*

unda, undae, f. ... *wave of the sea; water of a river or spring* [*57]

unde ... *from where, for which reason* [*ARA]

unguentum, unguenti, n. ... *perfume; scent, essence*

unguis, unguis, m. (abl. sing. **ungui,** gen. plur. **unguium**) ... *finger-nail*

unicus, unica, unicum ... *only, sole; unique, special*

universus, universa, universum ... *all, whole, entire* [*12]

unus, una, unum ... (see *ARA,* App. C, p. 416, for the declension of this numeral) *one, only, alone;* **una:** (adv.) *along, together, at the same time* [*ARA, *4]

urbánus, urbána, urbánum ... *of the city, from the city; refined, sensitive, sophisticated*

urbs, urbis, f. (gen. plur. **urbium**) ... *city* [*24]

urína, urínae, f. ... *urine*

urna, urnae, f. ... *jar; funeral urn*

uro, urere, ussi, ustus ... *to burn, to be on fire; to burn with desire, to burn with passion* [*67]

usque ... *all the way, continuously*

usquequaque ... *all over the place, in every possible situation*

usurpo, usurpáre, usurpávi, usurpátus ... *to use, to usurp; to utter, to mention*

usus, usus, m. ... *use; right-of-way, through passage*

ut or **uti** ... *as, when, how, as if, although* (+ ind.); *that, so that, in order that, to the extent that* (+ subj.); **ut .. , sic .. ,** *just as .. , so .. or although .. , nevertheless ..* (+ ind. in both clauses) [*ARA, *29]

utcumque ... *in whatever manner, by whatever means possible*

uterque, utraque, utrumque (gen. sing. **utriusque, utriusque, utriusque**) ... *each* (= each of two)

utor, uti, usus sum ... *to use* (+ abl.)

uva, uvae, f. ... *grape*

uxor, uxóris, f. ... *wife* [*ARA]

V

vacuus, vacua, vacuum ... *empty, empty of* (+ abl.); *carefree, fancy-free* [*52]

vado, vadere, vasi ... *to go, to go forth* [*72]

vadum, vadi, n. ... *ford, shoal* (= shallow part of the water)

vae ... (interjection) *woe!*

vagor, vagári, vagátus sum ... *to wander*

valeo, valére, valui ... *to be well; to have strength* or *influence;* **vale:** (imperative sing.) *goodbye! farewell!* [*8]

Valerius, Valerii, m. ... *Valerius,* son of Volesus

valetúdo, valetudinis, f. ... *health; illness, sickness*

validus, valida, validum ... *strong, powerful;* **valide** or **valde:** *greatly, very much, exceedingly*

valles, vallis, f. (gen. plur. **vallium**) ... (plur. may have sing. meaning) *valley; hollow, cavity*

vanesco, vanescere ... *to disperse; to break up, to spread out*

varius, varia, varium ... *various, different*

vastus, vasta, vastum ... *enormous, turbulent*

vaticinatio, vaticinatiónis, f. ... *prophecy, prediction*

-ve ... (attached to the word it connects) *or* (e.g., **filius filiave,** *son or daughter*); **-ve . . , -ve . . ,** *either . . , or . .* [*13]

vehemens, vehementis ... *violent, vehement;* **vehementer:** *exceedingly, tremendously*

vehiculum, vehiculi, n. ... *vehicle; cart, wagon; chariot, carriage*

veho, vehere, vexi, vectus ... *to carry;* (in passive) *to travel, to journey*

vel ... *or; even, at least;* **vel . . , vel . . ,** *either . . , or . .* [*18]

velámen, velaminis, n. ... (plur. may have sing. meaning) *clothing; cloak, garment*

vello, vellere, velli, vulsus ... *to tear, to pluck; to wrench, to dislodge*

velo, veláre, velávi, velátus ... *to cover, to clothe*

velox, velócis ... *swift;* **velociter:** *swiftly* [*70]

velut ... *as if, just as; as it were, so to speak* [*32]

vena, venae, f. ... *vein, artery;* (sometimes in plur.) *pulse*

venabulum, venabuli, n. ... *hunting-spear*

venális, venále ... *on sale, for sale*

venditor, venditóris, m. ... *seller, vendor*

venio, veníre, veni ... *to come* [*ARA]

venter, ventris, m. ... *belly, stomach*

ventito, ventitáre, ventitávi ... *to keep coming, to come frequently* or *repeatedly*

ventus, venti, m. ... (plur. may have sing. meaning) *wind* [*ARA]

Venus, Veneris, f. ... *Venus*

venustus, venusta, venustum ... *pretty, charming, attractive*

verbum, verbi, n. ... (plur. may have sing. meaning) *word; talk, mere talk* [*51]

verecundus, verecunda, verecundum ... *modest, restrained*

veritas, veritátis, f. ... *truth*

verso, versáre, versávi, versátus ... *to turn, to open; to keep turning, to keep pressuring*

vertex, verticis, m. ... *whirlpool, whirlwind; top, peak, summit* of a cliff or mountain [*69]

verto, vertere, verti, versus ... *to turn, to drive; to change, to reverse, to overturn* [*10]

verus, vera, verum ... *true;* **verum, veri,** n.: *truth;* **vere** or **vero:** *truly, in truth;* **verum** (conj.): *but, but at the same time* [*ARA, *43]

Vesper, Vesperi, m. ... the *Evening-Star*

vester, vestra, vestrum ... (possessive adj. related to **vos**) *your* [*42]

vestibulum, vestibuli, n. ... *forecourt, entrance hall*

vestigium, vestigii, n. ... *footstep, footprint; trace, track, position* [*20]

vestis, vestis, f. (gen. plur. **vestium**) ... *clothing; cloak, garment* [*ARA]

vestrum ... (gen. plur. of **tu**) *of you*

Vesuvius, Vesuvii, m. ... the volcano *Vesuvius*

Vetelia, Veteliae, f. ... the town *Vetelia*

veto, vetáre, vetui, vetítus ... *to forbid, to prohibit* [*55]

Veturia, Veturiae, f. ... *Veturia,* mother of Coriolanus

vetus, veteris ... *old, ancient* [*36]

via, viae, f. ... *way, road, path* [*22]

viátor, viatóris, m. ... *traveler, wayfarer*

vibro, vibráre, vibrávi, vibrátus ... *to flash; to hurl out, to shoot out; to cause* something *to flap* or *flutter*

vicinia, viciniae, f. ... *neighborhood; closeness, proximity*

vicínus, vicína, vicínum ... *nearby, neighboring*

vicis (= nom. sing; gen. sing. not found) f. ... *turn, change;* **in vices** or **vicissim:** *in turn*

victor, victóris, m. ... *conqueror* [*ARA]

victoria, victoriae, f. ... *victory* [*ARA]

victrix, victrícis ... *victorious, triumphant*

video, vidére, vidi, visus ... *to see;* (in passive) *to be seen; to seem, to appear;* (impersonal use) *to seem, to appear* (+ dat. sometimes) [e.g., **visum est ei** = *it seemed to him* or *it appeared to him*] [*ARA, *14]

viduus, vidua, viduum ... *deprived; unwedded, unsupported*

vigeo, vigére, vigui ... *to thrive, to flourish*

vigil, vigilis ... *wakeful, watchful*

vigilia, vigiliae, f. ... *patrol, sentry*

vigilo, vigiláre, vigilávi, vigilátus ... *to be awake, to stay awake* [*47]

vigor, vigóris, m. ... *vigor, energy*

vilis, vile ... *cheap*

villa, villae, f. ... *villa, estate*

villicus, villici, m. ... *overseer, supervisor* [*8]

vinco, vincere, vici, victus ... *to conquer, to defeat* [*ARA]

vinculum, vinculi, n. ... *bond, link* (= a force or impulse joining people together)

vindico, vindicáre, vindicávi, vindicátus ... *to avenge; to claim, to claim* something (acc.) *for oneself* (dat.); *to rescue* or *protect* someone (acc.) *from something* (abl.)

vinum, vini, n. ... *wine* [*ARA]

violo, violáre, violávi, violátus ... *to injure, to violate* [*ARA]

vir, viri, m. ... *man; husband* [*ARA]

virginitas, virginitátis, f. ... *virginity* [*7]

virgo, virginis, f. ... *maiden, virgin* [*ARA]

vis, vis, f. (sing. decl. = **vis, vis, vi, vim, vi;** plur. decl. = **vires, virium, viribus, vires, viribus**) ... (plur. may have sing. meaning) *force, power, strength* [*ARA]

viscus, visceris, n. ... *flesh, entrails* [*ARA]

viso, visere, visi, visus ... *to behold, to look closely at*

vita, vitae, f. ... *life* [*29]

vitio, vitiáre, vitiávi, vitiátus ... *to damage, to weaken*

vitis, vitis, f. (gen. plur. **vitium**) ... *vine*

vitium, vitii, n. ... *fault, defect, imperfection*

vito, vitáre, vitávi, vitátus ... *to shun, to avoid*

vitta, vittae, f. ... *headband*

vitupero, vituperáre, vituperávi, vituperátus ... *to criticize, to find fault with*

vivo, vivere, vixi ... *to live* [*ARA]

vix ... *hardly, scarcely;* **vix tandem:** *only just after all this time*

vobis ... (dat. or abl. plur. of **tu**) *to/for you* or *by/with you*

voco, vocáre, vocávi, vocátus ... *to call, to call upon* [*ARA, *34]

volatilis, volatile ... *able to fly; swift, rapid*

Volesus, Volesus, m. ... *Volesus,* father of Valerius

volo, velle, volui ... *to wish, to be willing* [*40]

volo, voláre, volávi ... *to fly* [*ARA]

Volscus, Volsca, Volscum ... *Volscian;* **Volscus, Volsci,** m.: a *Volscian*

volúmen, voluminis, n. ... *book, volume*

Volumnia, Volumniae, f. ... *Volumnia,* wife of Coriolanus

voluntarius, voluntaria, voluntarium ... *voluntary;* (masc. sing. as substantive) *volunteer*

voluptas, voluptátis, f. ... *pleasure, enjoyment*

vos ... (nom. or acc. plur. of **tu**) *you*

votum, voti, n. ... *vow; prayer, entreaty* [*60]

vox, vocis, f. ... *voice; word, sound; saying, expression; sentence, utterance* [*3]

vulgus, vulgi, n. ... *people; crowd, throng*

vulnus, vulneris, n. ... *wound, injury;* (as the prospective source of a wound) *weapon* [*34]

vultus, vultus, m. ... (plur. may have sing. meaning) *head, face; appearance* [*6]

X

Xanthus, Xanthi, m. ... the river *Xanthus*

Z

zaeta, zaetae, f. ... *room, apartment*

Zephyrus, Zephyri, m. ... a *Zephyr* (= a west wind)

INDEX

Note that in this index, reference is made to page numbers, not sections.

Abbreviations, xv.

Ablative, of comparison, 14; of cause, 153; summary of uses, *ARA,* App. E, pp. 424–26.

Accusative, of respect, 262; of exclamation, 267; summary of uses, *ARA,* App. E, p. 424.

Adverbs, superlative degree of, 5; summary of comparison, *ARA,* App. D, pp. 420–21.

Agreement, exception to rule of, 61, 129.

Apodosis, 109, 114.

Apollonius of Tyre, 1, and readings in Lessons 1–12.

Bulwer-Lytton, Edward, 124.

Catullus, 187, and readings in Lessons 37–48.

Causal clauses, 55.

Choliambics, 202.

Clauses of characteristic, 67.

Concentric word order, 257.

Conditional sentences, with ind., 109; with subj., 114–15; in indirect statement, 119; summary, *ARA,* App. K, pp. 476–77 and 479.

Cumulative vocabulary, 386–509.

Dactylic hexameters, 233.

Dative, of reference, 139; of agent, 195; summary of uses, *ARA,* App. E, p. 423.

Deliberative subjunctive, 231.

Deponent verbs, pres. imperative second pers. sing. of, 41; fut. ind. second pers. sing. of, 164.

Elegiac couplets, 218.

Ellsworth, J. D., xi, xii.

Eo, ind., 171; subj., 176; imperative, 181; inf., 181; part., 181; summary of forms, *ARA,* App. J, pp. 463–65.

Fero, ind., 156; subj., 161; imperative, 166; inf., 166; part., 166; summary of forms, *ARA,* App. J, pp. 459–62.

Future, act. ind., 63, 68; pass. ind., 94, 99; summary of forms, *ARA,* App. H, pp. 441–44.

Future perfect, act. ind., 73; pass. ind., 104; summary of forms, *ARA,* App. H, pp. 445–46.

Genitive, partitive, 129; objective, 153; summary of uses, *ARA,* App. E, pp. 422–23.

Gerundive, instead of gerund, 123; in pass. periphrastic conjugation, 195; summary, *ARA,* App. K, p. 471.

Hendecasyllabics, 187–88.

Imperative, 26–27; in prohibitions, 226; summary of forms, *ARA,* App. I, pp. 447–49.

Impersonal verbs, 5, and *ARA,* App. K, p. 470, note 1; impersonal use of regular verbs, 143, 195.

Indirect statement, subordinate clauses in, 88; conditional sentences in, 119; summary, *ARA,* App. K, pp. 478–79.

Infinitive, historical, 108, and *ARA,* App. K, p. 470.

Interlocking word order, 252.

Irregular verb forms, summary, 376–77; other verbs conjugated like, 378.

Livy, 125, and readings in Lessons 25–36.

Locative case, 67, and *ARA,* App. E, p. 426, note 1.

Malo, ind., 140; subj., 145; imperative, 150; inf., 150; part., 150; summary of forms, *ARA,* App. J, pp. 455–58.

Marlowe, Christopher, 371–72.

Meter, hendecasyllabics, 187–88; choliambics, 202; elegiac couplets, 218; dactylic hexameters, 233.

Models, summary, 373–74; guide to application of, 375.

Nolo, ind., 140; subj., 145; imperative, 150; inf., 150, part., 150; summary of forms, *ARA,* App. J, pp. 455–58.

Optative subjunctive, 200.

Ovid, 249, and readings in Lessons 49–60.

Periphrastic conjugation, act., 148; pass., 195; summary, *ARA,* App. K, p. 471.

Pliny, 64, and readings in Lessons 13–17 and 19–23.

Possum, ind., 125; subj., 130; imperative, 135; inf., 135; part., 135; summary of forms, *ARA,* App. J, pp. 451–54.

Potential subjunctive, 113.

Pronouns, indefinite as adj., 231; interrogative as adj., 240.

Protasis, 109, 114.

Semi-deponent verbs, 14.

Sequence of tenses, primary, 78; secondary, 83; summary, *ARA,* App. K, p. 473.

Shakespeare, William, 61–62, 185–86, and 309–10.

Simile, 246.

Subjunctive, in causal clauses, 55; in clauses of characteristic, 67; in indirect statement, 88; potential, 113; in conditional sentences, 114–15; optative, 200; deliberative, 231; summary of uses, *ARA,* App. K, pp. 472–79.

Subordinate clauses in indirect statement, 88, and *ARA,* App. K, p. 478.

Suetonius, readings in Lessons 18 and 24.

Sum, ind., 125; subj., 130; imperative, 135; inf., 135; part., 135; summary of forms, *ARA,* App. J, pp. 451–54.

Superlative degree of adverbs, 5; summary, *ARA,* App. D, pp. 420–21.

Tennyson, Alfred, 247–48.

Verbs, impersonal, 5; semi-deponent, 14; exception to rule of agreement, 61, 129.

Vergil, 311, and readings in Lessons 61–72.

Vocabulary, assigned for memorization, summary, 379–85; cumulative, 386–509.

Vocative case, 21–22; summary of forms, *ARA,* App. F, pp. 427–28.

Volo, ind., 140; subj., 145; imperative, 150; inf., 150; part., 150; summary of forms, *ARA,* App. J, pp. 455–58.

Word order, interlocking, 252; concentric, 257.